THE
ENVIRONMENT OF
HUMAN SETTLEMENTS
Human Well-being in Cities

Volume 2

Supplement to the International Journal HABITAT

The present book is dedicated to Mr. J. DE SAEGER, Minister of Public Health and Family of Belgium, who has consistently expressed his concern about a practical approach of the problems of Environment and Health. We thank the Committee which has supported the activity of W.E.R.C. and in particular its President, Mr. N. HILGERS, Deputy Cabinet Chief.

THE ENVIRONMENT OF HUMAN SETTLEMENTS

Human Well-being in Cities

Proceedings of the Conference held in
Brussels, Belgium, April 1976

Volume 2

Editor in Chief

P. LACONTE
University of Louvain, Belgium

Editors

G.EPSTEIN
Shepheard,Epstein and Hunter, London

J.E.GIBSON
School of Engineering and Applied Sciences,
University of Virginia

P.H.JONES
Institute of Environmental Sciences,
University of Toronto

U.LUOTO
Ekono Consulting Engineers, Helsinki

PERGAMON PRESS

OXFORD · NEW YORK · TORONTO · SYDNEY · PARIS · FRANKFURT

U.K.	Pergamon Press Ltd., Headington Hill Hall, Oxford OX3 0BW, England
U.S.A.	Pergamon Press Inc., Maxwell House, Fairview Park, Elmsford, New York 10523, U.S.A.
CANADA	Pergamon of Canada Ltd., P.O. Box 9600, Don Mills M3C 2T9, Ontario, Canada
AUSTRALIA	Pergamon Press (Aust.) Pty. Ltd., 19a Boundary Street, Rushcutters Bay, N.S.W. 2011, Australia
FRANCE	Pergamon Press SARL, 24 rue des Ecoles, 75240 Paris, Cedex 05, France
WEST GERMANY	Pergamon Press GmbH, 6242 Kronberg-Taunus, Pferdstrasse 1, Frankfurt-am-Main, West Germany

First edition 1976

Library of Congress Catalog Card No. 76-5192

In order to make this volume available as economically and rapidly as possible the author's typescript has been reproduced in its original form. This method unfortunately has its typographical limitations but it is hoped that they in no way distract the reader.

Printed in Great Britain by Express Litho Service, Oxford
ISBN 0 08 021177 1

CONTENTS

IV - DECISION-MAKING FOR HUMAN WELL-BEING IN CITIES

V - URBAN AND LAND USE PLANNING AND CITIZEN PARTICIPATION

VI - DESIGN AS AN AID TO SOLVING URBAN PROBLEMS

VII - REPORTS ON DISCUSSIONS FROM THE FLOOR DURING SESSIONS

INTRODUCTION

The Belgian Ministry of Public Health and Family commisioned the Conference "Human Well-being in Cities" and asked W.E.R.C. to prepare a
synthesis of it for inclusion in the National Report of Belgium to the U.N.
HABITAT Conference in Vancouver. Moreover, it authorized the publication of the proceedings.

This second volume contains 33 papers grouped under the same headings
as in Vol. I which arrived too late to be printed and distributed for the
Conference. It also contains the opening addresses of the first day which
provides background information on the Conference.

The editors decided to assemble the discussions of the participants and
their summaries as quickly as possible in order to produce Vol. II in time
for the U.N. HABITAT Conference at Vancouver.

At the end of the Conference a text of declaration was drafted by G. EPSTEIN,
taking into account the thoughts of the members of the programme committee
present in Brussels: P. H. JONES, H. GIBSON, P. LACONTE, H. CHEST-
NUT, E. A. WOLFF. This declaration will be submitted to the HABITAT
Conference. Moreover, individual participants submitted statements for
inclusion in the proceedings. They are included at the end of the volume.

The editors reviewed the main 20th century planning manifestos, inter alia
the Charter of Athens and considered there was need for a set of new
principles sufficiently general to apply to developing as well as to developed
countries and sufficiently precise to be of use to planners and decision-
makers.

It is hoped that the Brussels declaration on human well-being in cities will
arouse discussions at the HABITAT Conference and Forum, and possibly
influence some participants in their future work.

It is our personal pleasure to thank the organizations which, by their help,
made the Conference possible: the Belgian Minister of Public Health and
Family, who commissioned the Conference and appointed a special committee for this purpose   (The members of this committee were: N. HILGERS,
J. BOUCQIAU, K. DE BRABANDER, A. LAFONTAINE and M. RENSON);
Interenvironment - Bond Beter Leefmilieu, which is the Belgian member
organization of WERC and has brought its valuable help within the framework of its programme of activities for the Ministry of French Culture;
the City of Bruges, which took charge of the organization of the special
session on design, with the aid of the Ministry of Flemish Culture; the
University of Louvain which hosted the last session; the British and Canadian
Embassies; the Associations for Gas and Electricity; the historical heritage
programme of Stella Artois.

As a concluding remark we wish to emphasize the role of the speakers and participants themselves. The group identity of the Conference grew remarkably fast and generated lively discussions between people of various disciplines coming from 21 countries. The ideas and personal contacts gathered on this occasion might be the most lasting result of this Conference.

DECLARATION OF BRUSSELS ON HUMAN WELL-BEING IN CITIES

World Environment and Resources Council

<u>Most of the large cities of the world are in trouble</u>, and yet in the decades to come a vast additional number of people will live in cities. Enormous population increase produces the steep graphs we are familiar with, yet the graphs showing urbanization are even steeper due to the migration from country to city.

<u>People in existing cities</u> see them becoming more inefficient, costly to run and unpleasant as well as unhealthy to live in and are becoming impatient to correct past mistakes so as to make them livable and workable again. Those concerned with the growing cities of the future must be warned not to repeat past mistakes.

<u>What has gone wrong with the existing cities</u>? The older cities used to be fine-grain organisms that had slowly developed over centuries. When their growth accelerated they continued to expand concentrically, thus choking the old centres. The pattern is similar all over the world: In the last thirty years many cities of the third world have grown so much that the original town is by now just a small nucleus in the middle of a vast city area; it is a pattern which industrialized countries have seen develop over two centuries, with the familiar pattern of paralysed centres, long journeys, lack of contact with the countryside or the centre and expensive servicing. Also, and especially in the last twenty-five years, the old centres became invaded by elements so large and savage as to disrupt their fabric and their lives. One invasion was that of thousands of vehicles for which there was no room; they pollute, slow down movement and cause danger. The second one was that of super blocks of all kinds, mostly for vast organisations. They occupy the old centres, congest them with over-concentration, displace houses and push people out to the city's periphery. Thus concentric growth continues, further choking the centre.

<u>Both the vehicles and the super blocks are wasteful</u> of energy and other resources and neither of them can be assimilated. We may make room for the vehicles by building ever larger roads but while we destroy what generations have cherished, we do not even solve the problem; we make it worse by attracting more and more vehicles. Also, we may try to relieve the congestion of super blocks by leaving large open spaces around them; they tend to be too large and wind-swept for comfortable human use.

<u>It is time we defended life in the city</u>: The invasion of vehicles can be limited either by law or the imposition of its actual real cost, thus enabling transport to provide faster movement and make room to breathe and walk. Also, the city can limit the size of single-use complexes by insisting on mixed uses of housing, shops, offices, schools, etc. City life would be enriched and the community would gain long-term economic advantages. Insistence on

xi

mixed use is also a necessity for historic conservation and the creation and
preservation of green spaces because these are only possible in the framework
of balanced use and vitality.

The tools for this job of correction and improvement are being forged and
they have to be developed by way of direct involvement of the inhabitants,
neighbourhood government, tax relief for improvements, municipal ownership,
etc. It is no use looking for the villains who have been responsible; we
must begin now, before it is too late, to return to a more balanced, more
efficient and more pleasant life in the city.

There are no villains: it would be easy if we could explain that it is all
the fault of the social system, or the profit-seeking promoter, or the greedy
car industry. But in truth it would be too simple; cities in socialist
countries have been invaded with equal savagery by super blocks for vast
bureaucracies, have been carved up by huge roads, had their people pushed out
to the periphery and their centres become lifeless. It would be nice if we
could blame the rich for uncontrolled growth and for wasting resources; it
would be true but we know both rich and poor will waste that which is
available in abundance.

We are all responsible: looking at our cities we should have known that no
organism can keep growing while restricting the heart and blocking the
circulation. We never had a theory of the growth of social organisms, what
they can assimilate, what they will reject. The penury of centuries had only
given us knowledge about deficiencies: we know the results of a deficient
diet, of insanitary housing, of lack of education. What we have not yet
learned is how to cope with excessive possibilities; it is a new problem.

Just because you have plenty of food does not mean you should eat it all;
you get fat and congested. Just because you can make plenty of cars does not
mean you should drive them everywhere; you inflate and immobilize the city.
We shall only achieve balance once we know how to deal with both scarcity and
excess.

What we urgently need is a theory of possibilities and limitations which,
applied to social organisms such as cities, throws the responsibility for
mature choices on society. This has nothing to do with denying progress but
has everything to do with deciding "what? how much? for what? how fast?".
Both humans and social organisms can only assimilate that which fits both in
quantity and quality. If it does not, it will either transform you or be
rejected by you. A theory related to cities, of the possibilities of growth
and the limits of assimilation must be based on a knowledge of the city and
its aim is to enable an adult society in the city to make sensible choices.
The question of human well-being in cities is too important to be left either
to spontaneous growth or to technicians in separate fields. An integrated
view of human, technical and economic factors must guide development.

There will always be those who advise "no growth" but it is of no use to those
whose life depends on development. There are others who advise "catching up
quickly" but it makes no sense to unbalance life in order to improve it.
Naturally there are times when drastic action and change may be essential:
great ills call for great remedies. But for the remedies to be lasting, they
must not become the source of different ills in the future.

<u>In the meantime, life goes on and the cities grow</u>. We must give some guide-
lines based on the past experience of cities, foreshadowing the integrated
city, the city of a balanced society. There are obvious differences between
conditions in industrialized and developing countries, as well as differences
in climate, social systems, topography and tradition, but the basic functions
a city has to fulfil are similar everywhere.

<u>These questions and guidelines should have been applied to the older cities
many years ago</u>. They all point away from the concentric pattern of growth
to strip settlements which can integrate with nature, can follow major lines
of transport, and give the inhabitants easy access both to the <u>city centre</u>
and to the <u>country</u>, a city with the advantages of the large <u>and</u> the small
city. They could ensure a balance between city and country so necessary to
the mental and physical health of human beings.

14 Suggested Guidelines for plans of growing city

1. The city or its extension must be economical to build and to run.

2. At all stages of the city's growth there should be a proper balance be-
    tween the number of dwellings on the one hand and all other equipment
    and facilities such as schools, shopping, leisure, etc., on the other
    hand. This has been the case in any good town that ever grew. It means
    that the town must be a finished entity at all stages of its growth.

3. An essential characteristic of real cities is nearness. This is nearness
    or easy access as seen from the home and refers to nearness to the centre
    of the city, nearness to transport, to schools, work, shops, cinemas,
    libraries, offices, etc.

4. A city needs economical and convenient public transport which can expand
    simply as the city grows. The plan should also enable the use of cars
    and the possibility of parking near the home and at the centre.

5. The eventual size of a new city or city expansion cannot be written into
    a programme since it cannot be foreseen. Cities, like institutions, grow
    or fail to grow in unexpected ways. Therefore the plan or the system
    must be such as to allow for the possibility of appropriate growth.

6. At the various stages of development there should be virtually no need
    for advance investment which might prove abortive if the city fails to
    grow further.

7. The principles of planning should be clear and few in number so that
    architects and engineers can fit their work into the general context with
    a minimum of directives, and so that the inhabitants can understand
    what goes on and why.

8. Whether money and resources are available or not should not affect the
    city's layout. Buildings can be improved and renewed later; roads and
    utilities too. The city needs hope; it needs a future

9. Too low a density should be prevented in a city if possible, but this is
    not only a question of population per hectare. It is also a matter of
    town-feeling and shelter. A fair density of population is in any case
    required if central areas are to be within easy walking distance of homes
    and if people are to have a choice of different schools, shops and other
    facilities. Also, there are savings in utilities, transportation, road
    costs, etc.

10. As far as possible the central parts of the city and its social and other
    facilities should be so sized in relation to demand as to ensure their
    intensive use during the day and evening.

11. The city should not have to rely on an expansive infra-structure. All
    areas, including the centre, should be built on natural ground.

12. The centre of a city should be for people on foot, not for machines.
    Shops and other buildings in the centre or the local centres should have
    front access for pedestrians and rear access for vehicles and service.

13. Open space and large sports facilities should be on the edge of the city
    but within walking distance from homes. Larger industries should also
    be on the periphery, near main lines of transport and with ample expansion
    areas.

14. There should be reasonable separation of pedestrians and traffic.
    Pedestrian routes throughout the city should be at ground level and
    should generally be sheltered by arcades and shaded by trees.

... and Some Questions to be Asked About City Plans

15. Will the city be a satisfactory and balanced one, whether it stops growing
    at a population of fifty thousand or a million?

16. Is there a natural progression from the privacy of the home to the street
    or court, to the neighbourhood, and to the city as a whole?

17. Is the plan such that there will be freedom to choose, as the city grows,
    whether we build higher or lower, more apartments or more houses? Can
    layouts be varied as the city grows and as we learn from experience?

18. Are the central areas so planned as to leave flexible, i.e., for future
    decision as construction proceeds, what the intensity of the build-up is
    in the centre? Can buildings be planned without having to fit a precise
    grid or rigid framework? Can they be renewed or altered later?

19. Is there easy access to the surrounding country? Does the city integrate
    into the countryside without destroying it?

20. Has the city got a pattern and form which one can understand?

21. Is the neighbourhood or quarter a place one can see and feel, yet not
    isolated from the rest of the city?

22. Is it quiet where you sleep? Is it lively and animated where you gather

together? Will the city bring to life again the street and the square as places for people? Can you walk under trees?

Data answering these questions and many others about cities should be reviewed in a simple and worldwide information system, to enable people to benefit from experience of others to the extent there are elements of the experience that are comparable.

Government for cities as if people mattered.

All inhabitants, not only formal leaders of cities, must work together to establish proper objectives for the changing cities.

Various power groups may exist and compete for control.

All persons desiring to be a part of the city decision-making process should have a chance to express their opinions and to obtain a reasonable response. The approach used to infuse public opinion into the political process will differ among cities in different parts of the world.

Public participation should be infused in the planning process of the individual neighbourhoods of the city as well as in the integration of the various partial plans.

The most universal characteristic of man in cities is to be surrounded by other people with whom he relates and forms a decentralized community.

STATEMENT BY THE DIRECTOR-GENERAL

H. Mahler,
World Health Organization

Mr Chairman, Ladies and Gentlemen,

The quality of life, particularly as it is related to man's habitat, is one of the major issues of our times. A fundamental aspiration of most people is to realize an improvement in the quality of their lives, and this aspiration is often centred on having a clean, decent, safe home in which to live in harmony and raise a family. This implies the economic development necessary to provide the structures and services that are required. Although economic growth does, on balance, help towards the realization of this aspiration, the relationship of the one to the other is not directly proportionate. For one thing, gains in a material sense that are important to the quality of life may be off-set by disruptions of personal relationships caused by the social changes and geographical mobility associated with economic growth.

Many developing countries are currently experiencing a high rate of population growth that outpaces their ability to provide essential services to people. Many of these countries are also experiencing a high rate of migration from rural to urban areas, causing the rural population to be depleted of its young and more productive members and at the same time exceeding the capacity of urban settlements to assimilate the newcomers and provide them with minimum services. One overall result of this is a serious imbalance between population and resources in the rural as well as the urban areas. In both types of areas this can only exacerbate a situation in which hundreds of millions of people have no access to safe water, lack proper means for the disposal of their own wastes, suffer basic dietary deficiencies, and are un-protected from the elements and from insect or animal vectors of disease.

There is also today a keener awareness of the importance of the social

environment for man's full development. From his earliest days his personality and character, his intellectual and social growth, are moulded by his
contacts with others. While he benefits from grappling with the day-to-day
problems of life, over-exposure to stress such as that caused by excessive
noise, gross overcrowding, or the consequences of uncontrolled industrial
activity may affect his mental and social well-being.

The World Health Organization has, from its inception, promoted the
improvement of the physical and social environment as a means of attaining
health, and we are acutely aware of the present toll in human suffering and
misery caused by the disease and psychosocial problems that arise from
environmental deficiencies. The task of improving the quality of life through
enlightened approaches to the development of human settlements, although
challenging and difficult, was never more imperative. It is an effort that
demands that people work together and share their limited resources in a
perhaps unprecedented demonstration of goodwill.

The World Health Organization is happy to join, both as a sponsor and as a
participant, in this Conference which focuses attention on issues so important
for the future of mankind. It is our sincere hope that the Conference will
accomplish its aims and that each of you will bear away with you knowledge
that you will use to set other forces in motion for the advancement of the
quality of life in human settlements.

OPENING ADDRESS

K. Poma, Secretary of State for the Environment

Ladies and Gentlemen,

On behalf of the Belgian Government, I have the honor of expressing here
the interest of the Belgian Government for the Brussels Conference staged
by the World Environment and Resources Council.

First and foremost, I would like to situate this Conference on the Environment
in the more general context of International efforts now underway for the
improvement of living conditions.

Is today not the most appropriate moment to try and establish general guide
lines for an ecological policy aiming at human well-being at a time when
old values are being questioned and we are all searching for new paths to
follow? Should not the cyclical mishaps of our economies encourage us to
examine the mistakes of the past from which we could draw fruitful lessons
for the future? This is why I feel that the environment of human settlements
is more topical than ever.

The difficulties that we are facing, actually boil down to a choice of societies.
We are going to have to leave our affluent society behind, based on quantity,
and construct a society of well-being based on quality.

In a nutshell this means "A society for mankind and in the service of mankind".

The prerequisites for such a society are the following:
- efficient and optimal use of known energy sources and raw materials;
- research for new alternative sources of energy and raw materials;
- the re-establishment of the environment's natural balance by means of

fighting pollution of all types;

- the return to a harmony between human beings and their cities and their
rural environments.

Man came from a natural environment where he first found his means for
survival and began to multiply. Demanding more and more living space,
he expanded outwards, relentlessly using up more and more natural resources.
In doing so he forgot far too often that space is not an inexhaustible
commodity, nature's riches are not always replenishable and that their
regenerative capacity is limited.

For centuries towns were constructed according to specific needs: Initially
military and religious and subsequently economic, cultural and commercial.

For many years town and country planning was subject to an economy which
itself was subject to the specific geographic location of natural resources,
particularly energy sources, and the availability of a communication and
transportation network.

Settlements were subject to similar constraints. Housing in the immediate
vicinity of the places where people worked as well as disregard of nature
meant that one did not always take into consideration sanitary, well-being,
cultural and leisure requirements.

At the same time, industrialization where it occurred, and its ethnographic
and economic repercussions partially destroyed the natural environment
and brought it out of line with human needs.

Certain urban and economic agglomerations are no longer adequate, the
lack of parks and open spaces is often characteristic and the damage being
inflicted on the environment is increasingly wide-spread and irreversible.
This means we are going to be forced to conceive new town and country
planning projects which in many cases go beyond political boundaries.

If these projects are to be effective, they must not be isolated from their context. They must establish the joint needs for both urban and rural areas with regard to means of communication, social services, job volume and diversification, housing, regulation of second homes and isolated building, regulation of leisure time and regulation of the various forms of tourism.

Without wishing to anticipate on what the different "rapporteurs" will tell us, it would seem nonetheless important to mention the following;
- the desire to integrate ecological criteria into the decision making process on an equal footing with all other economic and social considerations;
- systematic evaluation of the ecological impact of public investments, including those taken in connection with private initiative ;
- a more reasonable choice. of leisure zones on the one hand and protected zones on the other in relation to the absorption capacity of natural space;
- integration of natural resource inventories into the town and country planning documents;
- the special attention paid to urban areas with a high social or cultural value;
- finally the present appeal for more active collaboration between government institutions and private organizations dealing with the environment of human settlements, efforts to humanize urban areas as well as the further development of services in the field of nature conservation.

The Belgian Government has given its full support to this international non governmental conference. It hopes that the results of the discussions among decision-makers and experts from various disciplines will provide a valuable input to the United Nations Conference and Habitat Forum.

A CITIZEN'S VIEW ON THE ENVIRONMENT BATTLE

Mr. M. Didisheim

University of Louvain, Brussels, Belgium

When our chairman gave me the floor he said that I was President of Inter-environment.

I am afraid that it is no longer true since I gave up this position a few weeks ago, for professional reasons.* But my heart is still with this con-federation that comprises over 120 citizens associations in Belgium and works with more than 400 local groups, and I feel that I can still speak in their name to welcome you, just as the minister did it a moment ago in the name of your government.

My intention today is to confine myself to three remarks, all three of them being the result of our groups' experiences in the field. Our member-associations have varied interests and are active in practically all branches of environmental protection (namely nature conservation, urban problems, protection of our architectural heritage, fighting pollution). Their ex-perience thus embraces a wide range of cases and problems.

The most important conclusion I draw, after nearly ten years work in this line, is that the environmental issue does not amount to a few technological adjust-ments, as some people would like to put it. This is my first remark.

You can of course improve the environment if you agree to more careful city or land-use planning, or if you try to complete the classical economic cycle at all stages: research and development, production, distribution, con-sumption. It can be done and it is being done, and you will certainly reach some results.

But the fundamental problem is not there. What we found out is that in practically all environmental problems there are interests in conflict. Somebody has to make choices, to decide, to arbitrate between these con-flicting interests. Who?

Public authorities. I therefore draw your attention on the political dimen-sion of what we are engaged in and I say that the environmental issue is fundamentally a political one. To illustrate this I could give you many examples, some of them chosen because enormous interests are at stake. I decided to give you only one, a very simple one. Many of our urban groups, a few years ago, organised a campaign to convince municipalities to plant more trees in the streets, assuming that everybody wants trees.

It is probably true that most people want more trees, but we discovered that many of them did not want them in front of their own house because they stop the sun. These people can no longer park their car in front of their house and . . . pigeons do not always behave.

Local authorities had to arbitrate. Now this is a simple, trivial example.

But it shows that arbitration is difficult for city counselors or aldermen who are elected.

Sometimes the conflicts are more acute because the interests are more impor-tant. How to choose between those who have enough of urban motorways and the car lobby or the cement industry who wants more work?

How to arbitrate between developers who want to build more profitable office blocks and local inhabitants who are slowly chased away from city centres?

This is politics.

And this is where our groups come in, because there is no real environmental policy if public opinion is not there to put the pressure on politicians to help them create a real political will.

The title of this talk is "A citizen's view on the environmental battle". Battle means fighting against an enemy.

Who is the enemy? Public authorities? Industrialists? Corrupt politicians or unimaginative civil servants? Real estate developers? Or ourselves? Are we not at the same time car drivers and pedestrians? Polluted but also the Polluters? Our groups in fact took some time to discover who was the enemy. The process of working together helped a great deal in finding out. Person-ally I often wondered what made a group whose main interest was the pro-tection of a rare species of wild orchids join hands with citizens committees engaged in local urban action.

In the beginning they had nothing in common. When we tried to federate them, they were even opposed to one another. Then they slowly found out:

-that divided they were losing battles;
-that they were all marginals towards the established ideas and values;
-and that they were all hoping for another type of society, where their own, individual aspirations would be seriously taken into account when it comes to taking decisions.

These three things acted as a cement between the bricks. The enemy was found, we were fighting against dominant ideas, a dominant culture in a society dominated by engineers, and obliging decision makers businessmen, where iso-lated citizens had little to say, especially if they were not on the "honour-able" side.

This is exactly what we don't want. A society where only technical feasi-bility and paying proposition count, where if you hold some share of the power you can without control build skyscrapers and fly-overs, and destroy people's lives because 30 years ago you have been fascinated by New-York. Every village in Belgium wanted its motorway, its industrial park and its tower-building.

This explains why people in this country are so outspoken against this type of society.

Anyway, we got united and we said that nature protection was not good enough, that fighting pollution alone was not to give the state a good conscience and that rehabilitating our cities was only part of the game. From there on we

demanded that the system (which means the state plus the economic and social
forces, which means in fact all the decision makers) should add new priorities
to the more classical ones and should produce a total, decent environment for
everyone.

This "total" concept means that it is not only material (i.e. physical or
chemical, built or unbuilt) but also immaterial ugliness or beauty, charm
and even irrational elements which are important for men's equilibrium are
parts of it (if you pull down a block of houses, you don't only destroy houses
but you disrupt a dense network of social relationship impossible to duplicate
elsewhere).

This, by the way, is why we attached so much importance to the rehabilitation
of city centres in Europe during last year's campaign.

Fighting dominant ideas in order that other criteria should be taken into
account was my second remark, the first one pertaining to the political
dimension of our action.

In a third comment I would like to argue that a real, comprehensive, total
environmental policy would have far reaching consequences.

I have just been trying to enlarge the definition of the word "environment"
(which is not technological adjustments, which is not to be confused with
pollution or nature conservation). I am now saying that through a policy of
environmental control and resources management (these things interact and
go together) you can change society.

I have no time to elaborate on this and I shall therefore only take a few
examples chosen in four fields of activities:

-the economic one
-the political one
-the legal one
-the ethical one.

A) The economic one:
it is all too easy to prove, I believe, that a real environmental control
policy would have effects on costs of production, on prices, on employment,
on regional policies and even on foreign trade.

If you are strict on norms of emission and if you impose filtering equip-
ments to your factories or if you go as far as imposing non-polluting processes, you will obviously put your country at a disadvantage by comparison
with a country or a region that does not.

Another example of the influence of environmentalism and the quest for a
better resources management is the debate on growth or no growth. Whether
you like or not, it already has had a profound influence on economic thinking.
Ideas like more recycling, less waste, more durable foods, change the standard measurement given by the GNP, the technique of the "environmental impact statement" would have been unthinkable fifteen years ago.

Believe that these examples speak for themselves and that they are sufficient
to prove my point in the economic field.

B)   The influence of environmentalism in the political field is also easy to
illustrate, both at national level and at international or even planetary
level.

At national level, political parties, trade-unions, governments have added
environmental chapters to their program, Ministries and Agencies have been
set up. Citizens fight political and legal battles.

At international level, countries and multilateral organizations sign agreements. Now I am not saying that these agreements which are not yet properly
enforced and sanctioned are the embryo of an international government. But
I am sure that what went on at Stockholm, what goes on within the EEC, at
OECD, in the UN and elsewhere is a sound basis for a code of good conduct
between nations in the field of environment, provided they accept to give up
part of their sovereignty.

C)   In the legal field I should only ask you to think of the way in which the
concept of private ownership of land has changed in order to allow for better
planning and for public amenities as well as in order to fight speculation.

D)   The last example I want to take to illustrate the far-reaching consequences of a real environmental control policy is the ethical field:
what we are aiming at is a set of other values to be taken into account, the
importance of which is not really measurable, like the charm of a city, simple
joys, more solidarity, less artificial needs, respect for other species as
well as for our own.

All of this has some moral aspects, all this demands sacrifices and more civic
sense; in other words it implicates deep mental changes as well as new
attitudes. This in fact amounts to one thing: a more adult society.

You see, we are far from technological adjustments or the protection of wild
orchids!

The time has now come for me to conclude:

I know that many politicians and many businessmen don't like citizens committees: "They are not in the constitution they say, they are not in our
laws, they represent nothing!"

I say that they are a sociological and a political fact (and everybody should
know by now that a fact is stronger than a Lord Mayor!)

I say that they are good for democracy because when faced with very complex
problems, when what Gallbraith calls "the technostructures" are so big and
impersonal, when a private person feels utterly helpless if confronted with
those technostructures, when economic pressure groups become too powerful,
when control or political sanction is no longer strong enough, well, if faced
with all these aspects of today's life that we all personally, physically feel,
we cannot react, then democracy no longer exists and it is hypocrisy to involve the constitution to fight those who want to revive it.

I therefore say that, in the environmental field as in others, citizens'
participation is a positive factor. But it must be spontaneous, it must be
free of political or other influences.

We are engaged, I said, in a political battle with far-reaching consequences. We are aiming at another type of society or even civilization. A more complete, more adult society I called it.

We are far from it, but that's why fighting for it is fun.

To illustrate this and to end my talk I'd like to recall what Konrad Lorenz, who got a Nobel Prize for his works on animal language wrote: he said:

"I just found the missing link between Ape and Man . . . and that is us".

*Mr. Didisheim is now the Secretary-General of the
King Baudouin for the Quality of Life

THE ECOLOGICAL BASIS OF THE URBAN SITUATION

A. G. Bourne

Consultant, Flitwick, Bedfordshire

In any discussion of current environmental problems there are bound to be sharp divisions of opinion as to their cause. Nothing is more likely to unleash a torrent of diametrically opposed beliefs than this one fashionable area of debate and genuine concern.

That this should be so in a world torn apart and confused by bitter political enmity is not surprising because deep down at the bottom of all our current crises there lies but a single cause. This paper is about that cause, its aetiology and the consequences of its persistence.

The crisis or crises in human affairs seem to be particularly acute in the larger connurbations and attempts to solve the problems usually fail because the would-be solutions are made in ignorance of the fundamental cause of the problems. The results, therefore, are usually patchy or at best cosmetic, achieving perhaps an erasure of the symptoms but little in the way of eliminating the cause. There are many symptoms - a general disenchantment with the urban way of life, inequality of living standards, unequal distribution of wealth and the material symbols of affluence, escalating costs of running large connurbations and the resulting breakdown of services and facilities and so on. These seem to be a long way from the province of the ecologist but, as I shall try to show, they are but the symptoms of a growing ecological disaster. I have described these symptoms in terms of population pressures elsewhere [1] and although that is, perhaps, an oversimplification it is nevertheless a crucial factor in our current problem.

However, the difficulties inherent in population policies tend to engender either an evasiveness on the part of those responsible for major decisions in the community when such topics come up for discussion, or, they divert attention from the underlying ecological causes because of their strong emotional content.

The problems of urban Man are thought to be the province of the sociologist, the psychologist, the economist and the planner. Opinion, generally, is that the ecologist has little to offer when it comes to understanding the complexity of the human situation. That there may be an ecological background to the problem is rarely considered seriously. Contrary to this generally accepted view I believe that most of the problems of urban Man* stem from an overstrained ecological base and that the situation has now become critical!

The problem arises because Homo sapiens, for all his ingenuity, is

* I am restricting my argument to the case of urban Man for the purpose of this paper, but the same problem besets the whole of mankind.

subject to those forces that dictate the behaviour of all organisms and set the limits to their numbers. In his Fawley Foundation Lecture, Lord Ashby [2] expresses the view of a biologist that there is no guaranteed tenure for man on Earth, a view with which I concur. In the same Lecture, developing his argument further, Lord Ashby continues "In the much shorter run there is even less reason why Western Technological Man should survive more than a millenium or so. It would be an historical anomaly if our present economic and social system were not to go the way of the cultures of Minoans and Aztecs!"

The evidence suggests that the demise of most, if not all, past civilisations was brought about through the same ecological causes that threaten our present industrial civilisation. The difference between the past and the present situation is that the enormous human population (ca 4000 million) has changed the nature of the problem to such a degree that we may be faced with something more serious than a crisis. Ashby came to a similar conclusion when he expressed the view that "we are approaching a climacteric" which means that if he is right, and I believe he is, "Our whole strategy for dealing with the dilemma has to be different." However to change our strategy we have first to recognise our dilemma and to do this we must understand the underlying ecological causes of the climacteric. To comprehend the ecological substrata of our civilisation it is useful to learn how Homo sapiens started on his particular evolutionary path.

The essential point to make here is that sometime in his remote past Homo or his immediate antecedents became specially adapted to an unstable ecosystem. Ecosystems fall roughly into two categories, mature (climactic) and immature (successional). The latter, as the term implies, are tending towards maturity, so in practice all grades of system exist from newly developing to established systems.

Whatever the ecosystem the energy base is provided by the Sun and the rate at which the solar energy is "fixed" by the photosynthesising plants sets the limits on the system's productivity. The energy fixing plants are the only way that solar energy can enter into an ecosystem**; they are as it were, the energy terminals linking the stellar power source and the consumers.

The productivity of the green plants is the vital factor in an ecosystem and it is one that is dependent on a number of very important environmental conditions - the length of daylight hours, temperature, length of growing season, the availability of water, and above all on the supply of solar energy. The rate at which this energy is "fixed" provides the gross productivity of an ecosystem. Not all the energy so fixed is available to the ecosystem as a whole for over half is utilised in the plants' own respiration. It is the energy remainder, or the net productivity, that drives the ecosystem and provides the energy for the plant eaters or herbivores. The quantity of this remainder decides the nature of the ecosystem. However it is not only the fixation of energy that is important - it is also vital that the energy is distributed through the system, and this is achieved by a complicated system of food chains or food webs. The more mature an ecosystem the greater the

** Here I am referring to natural ecosystems.

consumer population it can support and the more complex the food web.
If we take the association of the different parts of the food chain to form
an energy pyramid, with the producers (photosynthesising plants) at the
base and the various consumers (eg herbivores, carnivores etc) lying
in layers on top of each other, it is evident that the greater the
number of consumers the larger the energy base of the pyramid.

The net production of an ecosystem can be expressed by the equation:

$$GP - (R_1 + R_2) = NPE$$

where GP is the gross productivity of the photosynthesising plants, R_1
and R_2 represent the respiratory requirements of the plants and the
consumers respectively, and NPE is the net productivity of the
ecosystem. The NPE is the energy stored within the system and it is
the quantity of this energy that decides whether an ecosystem is
developing or mature. In the latter the NPE tends to zero, that is,
there is little or no energy remainder. Such systems take a long
time to develop and are self-sufficient and represent the most efficient,
complex and stable of all ecosystems. The complexity and rich
diversity (though small populations) of their constituent species ensure
that should an environmental crisis occur some part of the system will
survive. The diversity of species also provides a gene bank from which
new species may arise, particularly in times of changing environmental
conditions.

In contrast to these mature systems, the successional ecosystems are
relatively uncomplicated, and are, therefore, more sensitive to changes.
However, because successional ecosystems tend towards maturity, they
gradually achieve greater complexity and thereby lose their vulnerability
to alterations in environmental parameters.

These developing ecosystems have an abundant NPE, especially in their
earlier developmental stages and consequently they can support large
populations of a few species. As the system matures it increases in
complexity and attains a greater diversity of species with small
populations. Nature achieves stability by investing in diversity and
complexity.

All organisms - there are no outsiders - occupy a niche in one or other
of these ecosystems, and it seems that this is a rule that is as immutable
as the second law of thermodynamics.

Before we examine how Homo sapiens fits into this scheme of things, we
should look briefly at the behaviour and dynamics of the populations
of organisms within these systems. Obviously there must be
mechanisms that regulate the numbers of organisms. The most obvious
one is the supply of energy (the others are essential chemical elements
and living space). In an ideal environment with unrestricted resources
an organism's population growth would be exponential. However in the
real world exponential growth cannot go on forever, and as the organism
uses up its energy supply (or its oxygen or water), its growth curve
becomes S-shaped - the top of the S corresponds to the carrying capacity
of the environment. This latter may vary according to changes in the
environment (eg climatic changes).

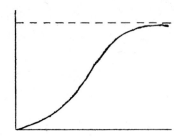

As it is also very pertinent to our thesis, we should recognise the sort of changes that may affect the carrying capacity of the environment. Any alteration in the environmental parameters that increases or decreases the biosphere, and I am using Vernadsky's [3] definition of it as that part of the planet in which life exists, affects the carrying capacity of the environment. As an example we could cite the onset of an Ice Age, wherein low temperatures, reduced land surface and water (in its liquid form) restrict the biosphere. Of course this is an extreme case, but even a very small drop in average annual temperature, rainfall or a reduction in the growing season can have an effect on plant growth over larger areas of the world's surface.

Where is Man's place in this planetary regime? His large population precludes him belonging to a mature ecosystem; indeed in those places where he has returned to a mature system, for example in a tropical rain forest, he has been forced to exist in small numbers. Homo sapiens with his vast overall population must occupy a niche in a protracted successional ecosystem (low species diversity/large population), and his early success must be attributed to his opting to occupy such a niche.

The question of when this happened is of interest. It probably occurred in different places at different times, but it seems likely that several man-like organisms achieved at least a facultative successional ecosystem role sometime prior to the Pleistocene. Certainly several forms of man-like organisms were living side by side prior to and during the Pleistocene period suggesting a certain diversity of species. This situation was gradually reduced through the Pleistocene until only the genus Homo remained and by the end of the period only one species, sapiens, was extant.

The original adoption of a successional ecosystem species role may have been forced on Homo's antecedents through alterations in climate, tectonic activity or other environmental changes. There is plenty of evidence to show that such changes were occurring during Man's early development in Africa [4] and Eurasia. Once established in this role the antecedents of Homo would seek out successional ecosystems, such as river valleys that were subject to annual or other periodic flooding, regions devastated by volcanic activity, and estuaries and coastal strips where the marine organisms would provide extra sustenance acting as supportive energy source to a land-based organism.

Then came the trauma of the Pleistocene with its obliterating ice-sheets in the Northern Hemisphere and torrential rain in the lower latitudes.

The advancing and retreating ice-sheets respectively decreased and
increased the biosphere, and each retreat provided vast new opportunities
for those organisms able to move into the exposed land and waters.
Homo was one such organism prepared to move into and dominate the new
ecosystems, and there is no doubt that by the end of the Pleistocene, ca
20,000-10,000 BP, he was becoming irretrievably a successional
ecosystem species. His ability to live off both animal and plant material
suited him admirably for the new life, it enabled him to move and live
almost anywhere and it did not matter too much whether he assumed a
herbivore, omnivore or carnivore role. By the use of fire and
domestication (the evidence of domestication is first found towards the
end of the Pleistocene) Homo ensured that the ecosystem on which he
depended would never develop to maturity. <u>To maintain a large
population Man cannot allow the ecosystem to mature.</u>

This ability to maintain an ecosystem that provided abundantly for his
needs, coupled with the post-Pleistocene extension of the biosphere
enabled Homo's population to begin its rise up the exponential curve,[5]
far beyond that which a mature system could sustain. Recent work
suggests that the energy available at the planet's surface has remained
fairly constant during the period since the retreat of the Pleistocene
ice-sheets*. If this is so, then the premise is that the biosphere and
its biomass must reflect that constancy. Therefore if one species
increases - on the scale experienced by the species Homo sapiens - then
it must be at the expense of the other species, and that is just what has
occurred and is still occurring today. The consequence of this
demise of species are a reduction in diversity and an increase in
ecological instability. Any further increase in human biomass will
necessitate additional readjustments in the ecosystem which will
exascerbate the inherent instability. To maintain a growing population
Homo sapiens has to resort to subsidising the energy available to the
producers at the base of the energy pyramid.

The importance of this to urban Man can best be seen in the light of his
history. The establishment of semi-permanent and permanent settlements
followed on the change from a hunter-gatherer way of life (the change was
probably forced by the reduction in numbers of suitable prey, brought on
by Homo sapiens inadvertently overstraining his energy base) to that of
pastoralist and agriculturalist. The possible exception to this general
rule is where a community came to rely on aquatic organisms in lakes,
rivers, estuaries and coastal waters.

Although community life, that is larger groups consisting of several
families, probably began during the hunter-gatherer period of Homo and
developed during the early pastoral times, it appears that it was in the
beginning of settled agriculture that more permanent communities and
therefore settlements were founded. What evidence we have of the
earliest permanent villages dates from the Neolithic. The Neolithic
village for all its simplicity is the antecedent of the modern city - as
Mumford [6] puts it, "Lacking the size and complexity of the city, the
village nevertheless exhibits its essential features."

* They have not yet completely disappeared - at least one continent
is still covered with ice.

The initial stimulus for settlement was the availability of good
agricultural land which at first provided a surplus of food. The
population grew to absorb the extra food but this meant that land which
had helped to supply the food had to be given over to human habitation.
Consequently when the carrying capacity of the land that was left could
no longer supply a community's needs, it had to extend the boundaries
of the settlement and bring more land under cultivation. Settlements
close to one another gradually merged and the supporting productive
region thus moved further and further away from the centre making
transport a necessity; thus the ingredients of the city were established.

The foundation of the city of Rome followed a similar pattern of
development. The original settlements on the seven hills overlooking
the flood.plain of the Tiber depended on the fertile soils of the plain.
As their populations grew, the settlements spread over the fertile plain
until they joined forming the larger settlement that became the city. To
feed the citizenry land further and further away from the centre had to
be brought under cultivation until eventually the Romans came into conflict
with their neighbours the Etruscans. The outcome was intra-specific
competition which started the series of conquests that led to the
acquisition of a vast empire which, to be maintained, had to rely on the
productivity of regions far from Rome itself, including the then fertile
soils of North Africa. Eventually Rome collapsed because its
ecological base was over-extended and its supply lines became vulnerable.
The inevitable consequences were high food costs and lack of maintenance
of roads, aqueducts and defences, with concomitant disenchantment,
breakdown in services and a way of life.

The example of Rome can be seen reflected in numerous other situations
throughout the history of settled communities, but none are on the scale
we are experiencing in this latter half of the twentieth century when an
increasing proportion of the world's population (60 to 80% in some
Western countries) are living in cities and their suburbs. This
phenomenal growth has only been possible by extending the energy base
of the human food pyramid, firstly, as mentioned previously, by bringing
more land under cultivation, and secondly, particularly in the last 100
years, by injecting supplementary energy into the base through the use
of fossil fuels. <u>Homo sapiens can only maintain his population growth if
he can increase his energy base.</u>

Current plans to extend the areas under cultivation would, even if
successful, only provide the opportunity to increase the population, for
as our experience has shown, the availability of food stimulates
population growth until the supply is utilised. However the success of
the present programmes is likely to be very limited because of the nature
of the remaining land surface. The northern lands are covered for the
most part by highly specialised ecosystems with low productivity levels
and to maintain them in a state of agriculture would be energy intensive.
Removal of the tropical rain forests would likewise be energy intensive,
because the soils in such regions are low in energy, as would the plans
to recover the desert lands. Indeed the reality is that more land is
being absorbed in the spread of urbanisation than can be brought into
cultivation-thus evoking the Law of Diminishing Returns. In the two
decades preceding the United Nations Conference on the Human
Environment in 1972, 750,000 acres of farmland in England and Wales
were used up for urban development.

To maintain even the present production of the agricultural base, additional fossil fuel energy inputs in the form of fertilisers, pesticides and irrigation are required - the cost in energy and economic terms of modern agriculture has been eloquently put by Leach [7]. As it is, the present demand, for all purposes, for fossil fuel energy is such that the resources will be exhausted within a few generations. To increase the demand further can only accelerate the rate of exhaustion. Once exhausted, or reduced to such levels that the cost of winning them becomes prohibitive, the carrying capacity of the planet will rapidly decrease.

The effects of this situation on urban Man are obvious. The competition for the energy resources between industry, commerce, the military and agriculture promotes problems of a magnitude undreamt of by preceding generations. The guaranteed supply of food was the essential feature in Homo sapiens success and paradoxically provided the cause of his present dilemma.

The overall situation then is that the species Homo sapiens has overstretched his ecological base, for without the already considerable supplementary energy his food, production and, incidentally, his supplies of water and other materials would diminish. In other words without these supplementary supplies the carrying capacity of the planet would be reduced as effectively as through drought or glacial advance. It is this that presents us with our climacteric.

The climacteric that I foresee and the one Ashby detected is the result of Homo sapiens' exhaustion of his ecosystem. If this cannot be maintained or if reductions occur in the biosphere either through his own actions or natural changes, Homo must find alternative ways of providing energy. The hunter/gatherer overcame their climacteric by adopting pastoralism and agriculture - a system that has been maintained, albeit unevenly, for the past twelve millenia.

In the long term it seems certain that the human population will be either voluntarily or involuntarily reduced, and there does not appear to be anyway round this probability. In the short term the pressures of population will increase the disruption of the urban way of life - its very vulnerability makes this certain unless swift remedial action is taken.

History and ecology suggest that the answer is the establishment of much smaller settlements sited close to their food-producing land, water and energy supplies with less dependence on supplementary energy. Concomitant with this are population policies that ensure that the settlements are not living beyond their means. In the less crowded developing countries, particularly in Africa, there are greater opportunities not least because the life and structure of small settlements has not been entirely lost, and there is a close relationship with the food producers. With an awareness of the inherent dangers of size, the new communities could be based on the structure of the existing village. A limit on the size of the village, geared to the carrying capacity of the land could, and should, be achieved.

Homo sapiens, as we have seen, responds to and demands from the

environment the energy, water and the life-producing elements in the
same way as all other organisms. However, he is unique in that he
has been able to create an artificial ecosystem upon which he can
maintain an enormous population. He has created a technology that has
provided him with the means to accelerate ecological processes.
Unfortunately, this uniqueness does not liberate him from the ecological
realities of the planet Earth. His future, if he is to have one, now lies
in his ability to design a way of life within the constraints that the plant
imposes. If he does, his future is assured; if he does not, the prognosis
is simple, growing disenchantment, higher costs of maintaining our urban
civilisation and lastly escalating intra-specific competition with its
accompanying violence and destruction. We have had some sharp
reminders recently of how nationalism, a disease that has bedevilled
civilisation for centuries, can very quickly and very easily be generated
in a resource hungry world [8].

We have traced the cause and the aetiology of the problems that beset
modern Man - the conquerors of its persistence are obvious. If we
recognise our dilemma we change our strategy just as our hunter/
gatherer forefathers did. It is unlikely that we shall solve our problems
in this generation or even the next, but we have to change our strategy
now so that those that follow us will have a chance to achieve what we
cannot hope to achieve. I believe that a solution is not beyond the
capabilities of the species Homo sapiens.

(1)   BOURNE, A.G. (1972) "Pollute and be Damned". Dent, London.

(2)   ASHEY, E. (1975) In The Times Higher Education Supplement,
       No. 217, p.13.

(3)   VERNADSKY, W. (1929) "La Biosphere", Libraire Felix Alcan,
       Paris

(4)   BISHOP, W.W. (1971) "The Late Genozoic Glacial Age". Yale,
       Yale.

(5)   BOURNE, A.G. (1975) in "The Man/Food Equation" pp. 127-137,
       Academic, London

(6)   MUMFORD, L. (1956) in "Man's Role in Changing the Face of the
       Earth". Chicago, Chicago.

(7)   LEACH, G. (1975) in "The Man/Food Equation" pp 139-163,
       Academic, London.

(8)   BOURNE, A.G. (1974) in "Proceedings of the Caracas Seminar"
       pp 1-7. Sierra Club, San Francisco.

ADDRESS BY THE RECTOR OF THE LOUVAIN UNIVERSITY

MGR. E. Massaux

Ladies and Gentlemen,

On behalf of the University of Louvain, I have the pleasure of welcoming you to Louvain-la-Neuve and welcome this opportunity of expressing our interest in the Conference staged by the WORLD ENVIRONMENT AND RESOURCES COUNCIL on the theme "Human well-being in cities".

First and foremost, I would like to put the conference on the environment in the more general context of international efforts now underway for the improvement of living conditions.

Is not today, when old values are being questioned and we are all searching for new paths to follow, the most appropriate moment to try and establish general guide lines for an ecological policy aimed at human well-being?

As State Secretary POMA said on the opening day : "The difficulties the industrial world is facing does raise the question of a choice of societies. Are we going to have to leave our affluent society behind, based on quantity, and construct a society of well-being based on quality? This means "A society for mankind and the service of mankind".

Man came from a natural environment in which he first found his means for survival and began to multiply. Demanding more and more living space, he expanded outwards, relentlessly using up more and more natural sources. In doing so he far too often forgot that space is not an inexhaustible commodity, nature's riches are not always replenishable and that their regenerative capacity is limited.

For centuries, towns were constructed according to specific needs : initially religious and military, and subsequently economic, cultural and commercial.

For many years, town and country planning was subject to an economy which was itself constrained by the specific geographic location of natural resources, particularly energy sources, and the available means for communication and transportation.

Smaller settlements were subject to similar constraints. Housing in the immediate vicinity of the places where people worked often grew up with an almost complete disregard of sanitary, social, educational, leisure and other human needs.

At the same time, industrialization where it occurred, with its ethnographic and economic repercussions partially destroyed the natural environment and developed it in a way contrary to human needs.

Many conurbations resulting from Man's Economic development are no longer adequate, the lack of parks and open spaces is often characteristic and the damage inflicted on the environment is increasingly wide-spread and irreversible. This means, we are being forced to conceive new town and country planning projects which in many cases must transcend political boundaries.

The University of Louvain has made its contribution to this progressive planning attitude by taking the opportunity of a move, imposed by political circumstances, to create 'ab initio' a human settlement, where university functions and city functions can live together in harmony.

Later this morning, you will be able to see it yourselves and evaluate the results at this stage. It is too early to form a considered judgment on Louvain-la-Neuve, but as an experiment, it has attracted worldwide attention and will be presented by the Belgian Government as a "demonstration project" at the United Nations conference on HABITAT, in Vancouver.

LOUVAIN-LA-NEUVE: A PRACTICAL APPLICATION OF PLANNING TECHNIQUES

P. Laconte
Director, University of Louvain, Belgium

This paper describes the objectives and programmes set out by the University of Louvain (U.C.L.) for the successful implementation of its transfer to a new site located 18 miles from Brussels.

1. LONG-TERM UNIVERSITY PLANNING AND TOWN PLANNING.

In 1968 the academic authorities decided to transfer U.C.L. to the Plateau of Lauzelle. They chose a university integrated into a new town which included industry, rather than the construction of an autonomous university campus, in order to foster town and gown interaction and the service rôle of the university towards the government and industry.

The long-term planning objective was to have a balanced community of 50.000 people (with a maximum of 15.000 students). The shorter-term objective was to have by 1980 a resident population of some 13.500 people (including 8.000 students and 5.500 residents : U.C.L. staff, people occupied in business and trade, wishing to live in Louvain-la-Neuve).

This was the only basis for overall planning. Considerable flexibility was to be maintained for developing the entire new town around a strong linear backbone.

U.C.L. opted for a master plan using some 350 hectares (a little
less than 900 acres) out of the total area of 900 hectares which

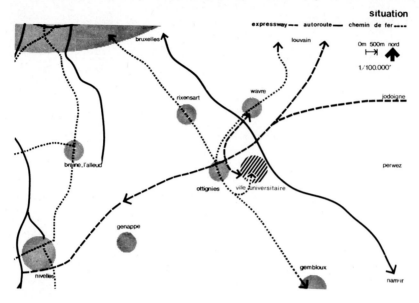

Key to the maps and photographs

The above map shows the location of Louvain-la-Neuve at some 18
miles to the south-east of Brussels. It is not a new town in the
political sense but a planned unit development within a rural a-
rea undergoing gradual urbanisation.

This site is served by a major motorway and a new railway linking
it to the Brussels-Luxemburg line.

The other map illustrates the linear development of the university
and town, which is centered along a main pedestrian street with
arcades and a succession of piazzas.

The photographs illustrate the general character of these streets
and piazzas. For example, the first and the last photograph show
a piazza with a wooden floor which has a cross road and parking
space underneath (photos H. Dave, Ottignies).

had been acquired for the university and urban development. Within

these 350 hectares, high density-low rise construction would enable

a maximum of 50.000 people to be housed in an area with an average

diameter of some 2000 meters.

The general lay-out is based on a linear design cut by a transversal axis along which the community facilities are located. The town centre is located at the intersection of the two axes.

The design of the residential areas excludes detached single family houses. Development is based on the following proportions : 10 % attached single family houses (terraced houses), 55 % flats in one or two storey buildings and 35 % flats in 4 to 7 storey buildings.

The university's open spaces are meeting places for the whole population. They are located in squares linked by pedestrian routes.

The master plan allows for the parallel growth of urban services and population.

Access to Louvain-la-Neuve is by a network of motorways, roads and railways with a new station in the centre. This puts Louvain-la-Neuve at 25 minutes from the centre of Brussels. The lay-out intends to dissuade the use of the motor car for internal traffic.

2. METHODS OF ACQUIRING AND SELLING LAND.

U.C.L. was able to acquire the 900 hectares through a State loan at low interest rate. From the very beginning, the university had to play the part of leader in the development of the new town and it decided on a policy of retaining ownership of the land and giving long-term (from 50 to 99 years) leases to potential builders.

The financing of land purchases, followed by long lease and not

by resale, raises a problem for private and public authorities.
The cost of land acquisition is written off by the owner over a
period of 30 years whereas income is spread over 50 to 99 years ;
this obvious difference between expenditure and income brings about
a cash-flow problem.

In Louvain-la-Neuve this problem has been solved by the low
interest rate paid by the U.C.L. to the State for the loan which
enabled the land to be purchased. Furthermore, the "Crédit Communal
de Belgique", the local authorities' main banker, gives specific
aid to long leases, in order to subsidise that form of land policy.

3. INDUSTRIAL RESEARCH AND DEVELOPMENT.

The basic objectives of this aspect of Louvain-la-Neuve are :

1° to encourage scientific interchange between the university
   and industrial research, while maintaining a total
   independence of the university from industry.

2° to contribute to the economic progress of the area by attracting
   firms using advanced technology.

3° to diversify the social mix of the Louvain-la-Neuve population.

The implementation of these objectives led the university
to approach potential investors. Academics who had regular
contacts with industry have played an outstanding rôle in this
approach. As a result, more than fifteen firms (research and
development and advanced technology production) have chosen the
Louvain-la-Neuve location, six of them during the last 12 months.

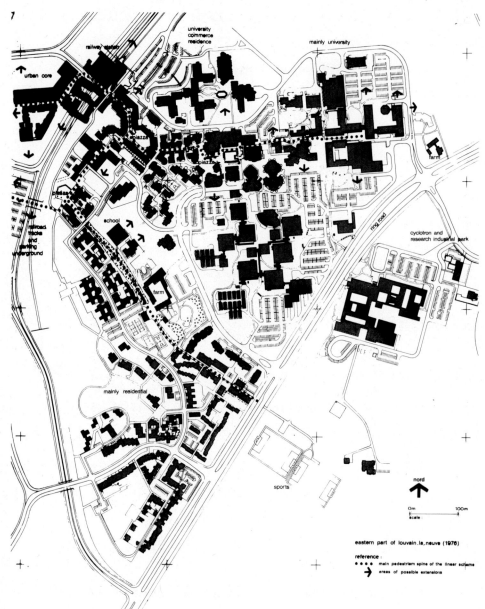

eastern part of louvain.la.neuve (1976)

reference :

● ● ● ● main pedestrian spine of the linear scheme

➜ areas of possible extensions

To ensure a specialisation interaction between academic research
and industry, the experience of Louvain-la-Neuve suggests that a
policy of strict selection be applied. This means refusing plain
manufacturing or warehousing and accepting research location
requests, even with some risk.

The park which covers in all 150 hectares (about 350 acres) is divided into two parts ; to the north, a smaller area assigned particularly to education centres, management centres, software, etc., and to the south a larger area more specifically assigned to laboratories and industrial research or services connected to research.

The management is supervised by the Regional Development Council in association with the University. Land is leased to industry ; the buildings are built either by the firms or by the Development Board (long-term lease). Industrial research 'flats' are available for short-term occupancy (1 year lease).

Results of our action tended to come slowly (three or four years of contacts, before reaching a decision).

The development of the R & D industrial park has brought about
a network of personal contacts with academics keen on applied research,
with research managers of industry and with civil servants in charge
of State activities related to research. It has helped personal
contacts between the people of these three groups.

In some cases this has brought interesting cross-fertilization
effects. It should be noted that the research assignements have not
necessarily been implemented in new buildings or in research 'flats'
but sometimes in existing laboratories of the university.

The close proximity (less than 1 Km) between most of the firms
and the social facilities and restaurants of Louvain-la-Neuve which
are used by their personnel, encourage contacts more effectively

than any organized procedure.

4. INTERACTION BETWEEN ENVIRONMENTAL RESEARCH AND APPLIED

ENVIRONMENTAL CARE.

There are several practical examples which illustrate the environmental approach of the university at Louvain-la-Neuve.

Firstly, the general conception of the project is based on
the creation of a town at a human scale without all the environmental difficulties usually associated with town life.

Secondly, in order to minimize air pollution, the university
has made strict provision for the control of the production of
energy by non polluting means (for example natural gas; a long-
term contract was drawn up with the supplier).

Finally and most importantly, a policy for the conservation
of the natural water reserves has been established. There is a
dual rain and sewage water collection system. The run-off water
is channeled to an artificial reservoir at the lower part of the
site, which is also used as a social amenity. The sewage water is
taken to a pilot sewage farm, and from there to the same reservoir.

MESSAGE FROM MAYOR OF MILAN

Aldo Aniasi

Chairman of the World's Cities Cooperation Centre and
of the Conference of Mayors of the World's Major Cities.

As Chairman of the World's Cities Cooperation Centre, I take great pleasure
in expressing my deepest consideration and appreciation to you, Mr. President
and to all participants of the World Environment and Resources Council.

Your conference and the meeting of Mayors of the World's Major Cities which
has been held every April since 1972 in Milan in collaboration with the
World's Cities Cooperation Centre, have in common not only the interest of the
problems concerning the quality of life and a better well-being for the citizens, but particularly this year due to the fact that both these meetings are
in preparation for Habitat, the World Conference on Human Settlements that the
United Nations will hold in Vancouver.

The WERC Conference is directed to such a vast group of people: from scientists to administrative authorities, from technicians to professionalists,
and from consultants to economists. The meetings in Milan, although open to
collaboration from all scientific and cultural forces both associative and
professional, have wanted to represent a first approach to these problems
allowing however for a direct intervention from authorities of the local and
city governments, keeping in mind that the municipalities represent the
decision-making centers which most involve and influence the life of all
citizens.

From the lively and stimulating discussions that without a doubt will develop
from both these conferences, as well as from Habitat, it is hoped that a new
and global awareness will be aroused concerning the problem of an efficient
system of direct relations between cities.

The stimulus deriving from this new strategy and organization of the cities at
the level of cooperation and development as a means of overcoming the traditional and inevitable forms of assistance and support, will in the meanwhile
favor the coming about of a new equilibrity based on citizen participation and
new criterias for city government and planning.

The exchange of information and people working within the municipal administration, committed to resolving the problems of all, will be the ground for relations which will prove to be more democratic and extended to all levels.

The problem for everyone, and in equal measure for the local authorities and
specialists, is one of overcoming schemes which are much too rigid that have
been adopted by national and state organizations.

The dramatic problems of human society within urban areas are common to all
people and to all cities whatever their level of economic development be and
the political system within which they operate.

The problem remains that of finding not only internally within each country,

but also in an international context, a way of organizing the voice of the
cities so as to attribute to the same the importance it deserves.

The cities, as we intend them today, are a relatively new experience, however,
they can also be a developing economic factor of civil and social progress if
a desirable ground for their survival can be found and if they are not forced
to put up with the negative effects of wrong economic choices which would determine an absurb overcrowding and a lowering of the quality of life, only
emphasizing in dramatic terms and false contrast, the urban-rural relationship.

These are the urgent themes to be faced both by specialists and local authorities alike. They must be put forward with courage and determination at Habitat
if we want the United Nations conference to attain its objective of international collaboration and the development of human settlements as an opportunity for
civil progress rather than presenting an occasion for comparison between what
each country can boast of having contributed.

I firmly believe that for this to be possible an active involvement and commitment is needed, as has been shown by the Secretariat of Habitat. I am confident that collectively working together, in particular at such initiatives as
the WERC Conference in Brussels and the Conference of Mayors of the World's
Major Cities in Milan, is not only a positive fact, but both fruitful and indispensable.

The cities must be capable of directly collaborating one with the other and
specialists must be available to provide what assistance is required of them
in this great cooperative venture, undertaken for peace and progress, in the
name of mankind.

RESULTS AND PROSPECTS OF URBAN ACTION IN BRUSSELS BETWEEN 1968 AND 1975

by Mr. Rene Schoonbrodt
President Internvironnement Bruxelles
President Atelier de Recherche et d'Action
Urbaines

1. <u>NATURE OF THE PROBLEMS FACING INHABITANTS OF THE BRUSSELS CONURBATION.</u>

a) Change in urban activities : in Brussels, urbanisation follows the pattern of : a high demand for the creation of offices, from the public and private sectors; hence :

- residential districts are "eaten away" by offices (Quartier Nord, Center, all the 'Pentagon', etc...);

- single function areas of offices : dead, ugly, lifeless (rue de la Loi,...)

- extension of luxury shopping areas (increasing number of commercial galleries);

- demand for expensive dwellings;

- inhabitants driven towards the outskirts (and peripheral towns);

- disappearance of craft and manufacturing industries.

This process is classic in all towns of capitalist societies. The case of Brussels is typical :

- it is a small city : one million inhabitants, old population (inter alia, it is residual, as young people emigrate)

- the office assault is remarkable : influence of the E.E.C., influence of NATO, influence of the increased number of national institutions and their repercussions in the increase of private offices.

b) This type of urbanisation favours communications by private car. Hence : the construction of roads and urban motorways driving out inhabitants with successive expropriations, the felling of trees, the narrowing of side-walks, ... reducing the quality of life in the town (consequently : emigration, which is also made easier by the quality of rail links).

c) The processes of urbanisation are made possible :

- by the active and passive complicity of Public Authorities : State, Communes;

- by the mechanics of the ground, by the decrepitude of certain districts, etc...;

- and, in the early stages, by the absence of a reaction from the inhabitants, ...

li

2. REACTIONS.

a) In the past, there existed, among the inhabitants, volountary associations mainly concerned with aesthetic questions : the A.S.B.L. Quartier des Arts, the 'Ligue Esthétique Belge' (Belgian League for Aesthetics), and many others.
Trade union and family organisations are primarily concerned with housing and the immediate environment (green spaces, playgrounds, minimum municipal equipment, ...) : but, on the whole, urban problems escape consideration.

b) In reply to the urban agressions experienced in the Brussels conurbation, various spontaneous reactions have been born :

- The 'Comités de quartier' (local action committees) : these react to projects which affect the life of their neighbourhood, directly : threats of expropriation, housing difficulties, the re-housing of persons expropriated, road works, etc...
In this group, a distinction can be made between two types : committees working in popular districts and those which are active in so-called residential areas.
Both types of area are subject to the same threats (same projects and same authorities involved); but their sociological composition differs : hence, the difference in their analyses of the situation and in their choice of action leaders and the means of acting.

- The 'urban action groups' are not directly involved with the problems of districts, but with specific problems : such as, the necessity to develop alternative projects to official projects (role of the 'Atelier de Recherche et d'Action Urbaines' - Workshop for Urban Research and Action, ...); or with promoting certain aspects, for instance public transport (mission of the 'Comité d'Action pour les Transports Urbains' - Action Committee for Urban Transport), popular housing and

persons on the fringe of society (by "Habitat Humain", ...) or green spaces (role of the 'Entente Nationale pour la Protection de la Nature' - National Union for the Protection of Nature, ...). Their sociological composition (members and leaders), their analyses, and methods differ greatly and cover the whole political spectrum, from left to right.

c) The extensive nature of the threats and the awareness that solidarity, even partial, is necessary between action groups and neighbourhood committees has led to the creation of a confederation called : "Inter Environnement-Bruxelles". This confederation includes more than 40 associations; it is a member of the national confederation, "Inter Environnement-National".

3. TWO EXAMPLES AMONG OTHERS.

a) The Workshop for Urban Research and Action. (ARAU)

This has fixed itself two objectives :

- democratize the decision-making process in respect of urban development;

- propose another image of the town : the '<u>lived-in</u>' town.

    At the present time, the pursuance of these objectives is carried out with :

- the organisation of press conferences : at which, on each occasion, there is the critical examination of a given project (drawn up by the Town of Brussels) and the presentation of an alternative. The credibility of the ARAU with both the mass media and Public Authorities depends, above all, on its ability to put forward well founded alternatives (which presupposes the technical ability to study them, present them and defend them);

- the organisation of informational conferences (these are followed by a debate);

- the setting up of Urban Schools (that is : every evening of one week, once a year, is given over to studying one or several topics);

- the creation of an "Urban Action School" to train urban militants, systematically.

    It can be said that the ARAU is very much present on the Brussels scene. A few figures will serve to illustrate this fact : between July 1974 and June 1975: ARAU held 10 press conferences, one Urban School over 6 evenings, six conferences (to that, must be added : 24 Board meetings, 4 general assemblies and many working and representation meetings).

    What are the criticisms generally made about the ARAU ?

- from administrative bodies : dangerous protesters;

- from more left-wing groups : efficient but bureaucratic.

b) Inter Environnement-Bruxelles.

After having established a precarious balance between the various groups involved, Inter Environnement-Bruxelles has exerted maximum pressure in two areas :

- to obtain a development plan covering the whole of the Brussels conurbation by :

. setting up a 'grid-plan';

. reacting against the preliminary draft sectorial plan prepared by the Minister for Brussels Affairs;

. blocking the construction of motorway extension into the urban area, etc...

- the renovation of the former habitat through the improvement of old houses (and not their demolition).

4. <u>PARTICIPATION = INTEGRATION OR CONFLICT ?</u>

a) How is the balance-sheet ?

Action in Brussels has been remarkably efficient. Several factors have combined to explain this efficiency :

- the politico-community encirclement of the Brussels conurbation;

- the process of political regionalisation within the country;

- multiplication of case of abuse : urban redevelopment synonymous with deportation of inhabitants (10,000 in the Quartier du Nord);

- compromises by Public Authorities have a mobilising effect : on certain levels of authority, certain administrations, public opinion, the press,..

- the organisational ability and the courage of groups, ...

But what is the balance-sheet ? First of all, conservation; reconstruction will follow.

b) The participation of inhabitants is the necessary condition for improvement of the quality of life. In which way ? In the capitalist system : the participation of inhabitants must take the form of a struggle : against moneyed interests and the structures (State, ...) controlled by these interests.

There is no doubt that the inhabitants committees which make the most exact analyses and which practice the most attacking policies of action will develop closer contacts with the political and trade union groups which have the same analyses and the same practices to the same ends.

TELECOMMUNICATIONS AND HUMAN DEVELOPMENT: AN EMERGING STRATEGY

Kas Kalba

Harvard University, Cambridge, Mass., U. S. A.

ABSTRACT

Human settlements are rarely considered in relation to the emerging information economies and associated telecommunications developments of advanced industrial societies. Yet information activities and telecommunications innovations are already beginning to shape the structure of urban and rural communities as much as physical or transportation developments. Moreover, new
communications systems (e.g., video conferencing, cable television, data communications, etc.) can be used to improve the delivery of social and commercial services, increase citizen accessibility to information, and facilitate
administrative coordination.

The following paper examines these trends and developments and evaluates
their implications for human settlements. It summarizes a number of relevant
telecommunications demonstration projects and poses some of the policy issues
raised by application of telecommunications to human development.

INTRODUCTION

Although I will be examining some specific examples of how telecommunications
are being used for urban service delivery, my main purpose in the following
paper is to place a number of telecommunications developments on the agenda
of those who are concerned with the preservation of the urban environment.
For this reason I have chosen to outline some of the principal dimensions of
the relationship between telecommunications and the urban environment rather
than to probe the details of a particular technological application.

Cities, after all, are expressions of our basic need for social, economic,
and cultural agglomeration. Their density reflects the compact nature of our
social, economic, and cultural relationships. And the physical durability
of our major urban institutuions, whether banks, libraries, or government
buildings indicate the long-term stability of our traditional communications
patterns, so dominated by territorial proximity and centrality.

But our communications needs and patterns are changing. The radio and television program has intervened into the tightly-knit circle of word-of-mouth
communication. The telephone has extended word-of-mouth diffusion to regional, national, and even global proportions. The computerized information system has reduced our need to remember certain facts and at the same time increased our dependence on stored knowledge. The facsimile-supported memo has
turned many of us into mini-publishers. In short, our information environment, in this information age, with which urban decision makers reckon so in-
frequently, has exploded.

And it continues to explode with the advent of each new communications technology, whether pocket calculator, cable television, satellite communications,
video discs, or electronic funds transfer systems, in our everyday environment. To be sure, to the traditional analyst of cities, so used to observing
monumental physical structures, these "gadgets" appear hardly tangible.

And yet, it is these communications technologies and the underlying industries
from which they stem or to which they will soon be applied that reflect the
new environment in which we live as much as eight-lane highways, skyscraping
office centers, or space capsules. In fact, more so, because they reflect
more accurately the transition that advanced industrial societies are undergoing from an economic, social, and urban life organized around manufacturing
activities to a post-industrial "information society" where telecommunications developments are likely to have an increasing impact on our status as
citizens, residents, workers, and consumers.

THE INFORMATION SOCIETY

Let me take a moment to discuss this "information society."

I could do so, of course, by referring to the works of scholars on both sides
of the Atlantic, such as Machlup (1), Parker and Porat (2), Voge (3), Attali
(4), and others, who have been analyzing our transformation into a society
that is increasingly oriented around information-related activities. But
perhaps some numbers will convey more effectively the magnitude of what is
occurring. As the accompanying table compiled at the Program on Information
Technologies and Public Policy at Harvard University indicates, information
industries in the United States accounted for some 307.9 billion dollars of
gross revenues in 1973.*

Table 1   The Information Industries-- Approximate Gross Revenues

Estimates gathered from U.S. govern-ment, trade associations and other sources; all figures in current dollars; double counting not eliminated.	(in billions of dollars)			
	1970	1971	1972	1973
Broadcast television	2.8	2.8	3.2	3.5
Cable television	0.3	0.3	0.4	0.5
Broadcast radio	1.1	1.3	1.4	1.5
Telephone	18.2	20.0	22.4	25.5
Telegraph	0.4	0.4	0.4	0.5
Specialized common **carriers**	0.0	0.0	0.0	0.0
Satellite carriers	0.1	0.1	0.1	0.1
Mobile radio systems	2.0	2.2	2.4	2.6
Motion pictures	3.8	3.8	NA	NA
Organized sports, theaters, etc.	4.4	NA	NA	NA
Computer software suppliers Computer service suppliers	1.9+	2.4+	3.0+	3.7+
U.S. Postal Service	6.3	6.7	7.9	8.3
Private information delivery services	0.7+	0.8+	1.0+	1.2+

*I am employing the American usage of the term "billion," meaning a thousand
million.

Table 1 (cont.)

Newspapers; wire services	7.0	7.4	7.8	8.3
Periodicals (including newsletters)	3.2	3.4	3.5	3.7
Business consulting services	0.9	1.1	NA	NA
Advertising	7.9	7.6	NA	NA
Marketing	32.4	37.7	41.3	43.4
Brokerage industries	40.6	47.4	54.4	NA
Book Publishing and printing	3.4	3.7	3.9	4.1
Libraries	2.1	NA	3.6	NA
Schooling	70.0	76.3	83.2	89.5
Research and development	26.5	27.3	29.2	30.6
Federal information institutions				
Census Bureau	0.1	0.1	0.1	0.1
National intelligence community	4.0+	NA	NA	NA
National Technical Information Service	0.0	0.0	0.0	0.0
Social Security Administation	1.0	1.2	1.3	1.4
County agents	0.3	0.4	0.4	0.5
Banking and credit	61.1	68.9	76.9	NA
Insurance	92.6	103.5	121.4	NA
Legal services	8.5	9.6	NA	NA
U.S. Gross National Product	977.1	1055.5	1155.2	1294.9

Source: Program on Information Technologies and Public Policy, Harvard University, **A Perspective on Information Resources: Program Scope, Aims and Practices**, Annual Report, 1974-1975, Volume One.

When banking, credit, insurance and legal services are added to this amount-- and whether it is legitimate to lump these financial and professional services together with information industries is part of an ongoing debate; but in any event these are non-manufacturing industries-- the combined annual revenue total for 1973 amounts to 515.8 billion dollars, as compared to that year's GNP of 1,294.9 billion dollars. This represents not only a sizeable proportion of economic activity but also a rapidly growing one, experiencing growth rates over twice as high as GNP. The emergence of the information sector is similarly refelcted in studies of the labor force, which project these activities involving some 55% of the labor force by 1980 (Ref 2).

While measuring the exact magnitude of these shifts in economic activity remains a difficult task, assessing their societal significance is even more challenging. Some analysts, such as Japan's Yoneji Masuda (5), have suggested that we are on the verge of a utopian age, where voluntary information-based communities will constitute the core of a new global social system. Others, such as Jean Voge (3) of France, contend that we may be reaching a point of economic and social stalemate, where economic productivity in advanced industrial societies can only decline as the manufacturing sector begins to disappear. What these extreme visions share in common, however, is a sense of dramatic transition in the course of industrial development, as the pursuit of economic opportunity shifts to a search for quality of life, and where the blessings of industrial abundance may be replaced by the new mental hardships of ubiquitous information overload. What they also share is the recognition that telecommunications-- that is, media innovations as well as our ability to program and regulate these media-- pay a key role in the transition that advanced industrial societies are experiencing.

THE TECHNOLOGICAL OPPORTUNITY

What are some of these emerging telecommunications systems and how are they likely to affect urban development specifically? Let me address these questions by focusing on how an existing medium of communications, the effects of which we are only beginning to understand, namely, television, is likely to change in the next ten to fifteen years. These changes can be summarized as follows (and here I am synthesizing, in effect, what has been projected by numerous technological studies as well as what is already available, in most cases, on an experimental or prototypical basis).

First, the channel capacity of television will change. By means of cable television, broadband compression techniques, and ultimately, waveguides, laser communications, or fibre optics the capability of delivering many more television channels to the home will become possible. Today's cable television systems in the United States are mandated by the Federal Communications Commission to carry 20 television channels and some systems are already providing 30 or more. As a result, cable TV subscribers will increasingly have more choice as to what they watch on television.

Second, those who provide television programs will be able to be more selective about who they reach. Through local distribution technology, scramblers and converters, and eventually through computer addressing by cable television, programmers will be able to pinpoint the specific audiences (e.g., by neighborhood, ethnicity, or special interest) that they are most interested in reaching. Early forms of this capability are the pay television services, local origination programs, and medical programming for physicians that are provided on cable television in the United States.

Third, programmers will not be limited to transmitting only video programs, but also data, facsimile special audio services, and stop-frame programming. Various hybrid communication forms will undoubtedly emerge from these developments, combining still pictures, moving images, captions, textual printouts, and/or supplementary sound tracks. For example, in both Japan and the United States there now exist educational television systems with dual sound channels, which are used for teaching foreign languages and other instructional purposes.

Fourth, viewer feedback through the TV set will become possible. The subscriber will be able to send messages back to the programming source, requesting specific programs, registering opinions, responding to questions, executing financial transactions, purchasing products, or voting for candidates.

And fifth, both programmers and viewers will have access to increased storage capability. Data banks will monitor various transactions between the viewer and the programmer, storing these for future reference. The viewer will also be able to record television programs on video discs or cassettes (or to acquire them directly in that form) for playback at a convenient time. Television, as a consequence, will become more like a book, a record, a computer, a telephone, than a mass broadcasting medium; it may become everything but television, as we know it today.

This brings up, in fact, a much more general point. Not only television, but also other communications technologies, computers, telephones, and teleprocessing, for example, are undergoing rapid technological transformation and are in the process of converging with each other. Computers are merging with telephone and television. Mass media are behaving as if they are specialized information services. And communications systems that we are accustomed to using at the office are becoming available in the home (e.g. electric calculators).

THE URBAN DEMONSTRATIONS

But having listed how technology is developing very rapidly in the telecommunications field, it is time to ask some serious questions. Will this technological cornucopia serve a useful social purpose? Can it help to enrich our cities and communities? Can it help maintain family life and cultural traditions? Or will it simply subject our lives to greater technological dominance? After all, as one cartoonist has already suggested, the new communications technology may simply enlarge our anatomies and not our social resources. The eyes and ears will become larger in reaction to all the new communications channels. The hands will grow more fingers to be able to push all the buttons; the legs will shrink, since there will be little time or need for walking; and the human rump will quadruple in size. (This is certainly one interpretation of the relationship between telecommunications and human development, but hopefully not the only one.)

More specifically, it is precisely these questions of the social and urban impact of telecommunications that those who are working on the technological and conceptual frontiers of urban telecommunications are trying to answer. Let me provide some examples of the work that is going on, and then add some critical observations.

One major area of experimentation is telemedicine; that is, the performance of medical and health-related tasks with the assistance of remote, electronic communications. Experiments in telemedicine have been conduced in the United States for over a decade now, under the sponsorship of the Department of Health, Education, and Welfare, the Veterans Administration, the National Science Foundation, and other government and private agencies. Since 25 or more separate demonstrations have occurred in this field, the results are too numerous for me to report here (Ref 6). But, what might be useful is to discuss at least one of these experiments, which reflects how telecommunications could transform the urban delivery of health care.

In New York City, Mount Sinai hospital has instituted a 2.5 km. link, using two-way television, between its medical center and a health clinic for child health care that is located in a low-income neighborhood in East Harlem. Before this link was made available, a physician would make periodic visits to the neighborhood clinic to take care of patients and perform examinations. But still, parents whose children had emergency health problems or whose children had more complex problems than could be handled by the visiting physician still had to travel to the main medical center facility. Yet in many cases they were unwilling to do so because of unfamiliarity with this huge hospital complex or because of transportation difficulties of one sort or another. The telemedicine systems has resolved a good many of these problems, since medical care by telecommunications is now available to the neighborhood more of the time than when the clinic depended on the visiting physician and because specialists from the medical center (e.g. orthopedists, psychiatrists, as well as pediatricians) can now examine a sick child over television before determining whether a visit to the medical center is really necessary. Finally, when a visit is recommended, parents are now more willing to keep

their appointments because of the previous contact with the physician over
the two-way television.

Now, the results of this single experiment when joined with the results of
the numerous other telemedicine demonstration projects that have already been
conducted, lead to a number of basic conclusions. First, both patients and
medical staff have been willing to use telecommunications-mediated health
care service delivery and have found this delivery mode convivial and useful.
Second, a great variety of diagnostic, consultative, and therapeutic medical
procedures have been successfully performed utilizing telemedicine, including the remote analysis of x-rays, the transmission of electrocardiograms,
televised dermatological examinations, the accessing of specialists for consultative purposes, group psychiatric counselling, and numerous others.
Third, telemedicine systems have supported the administrative and educational functions of medical organizations by providing new channels for training and supervising medical staff, for transmitting medical records, for
simplifying the rapid procurement of drugs and other medical supplies, and
for transmitting continuing medical education to physicians and nurses. And,
finally, fourth, it has become evident that the key problems which limit the
broader application of telemedicine are not technological, or even in many
cases economic, but rather institutional and regulatory. A telemicroscope
makes it possible to analyze a blood sample at a distance of a hundred kilometers from the patient; but it does not necessarily help two independent
medical institutions recognize that by sharing a telemedicine link they can
reduce their operating expenses considerably.

The accomplishments of these early telemedicine demonstration projects are
being replicated in other areas of urban service delivery and administration,
most notably education, but also social service delivery, police and fire
services, government communications, and other areas. For example, in the
New York City region, the Metropolitan Regional Council, an association of
local government officials has been operating a two-way video conference system that facilitates the interchange of specialized expertise, and training
skills among 10 local governments, as well as provides a new channel for the
resolution of problems that involve more than one local jurisdiction (Ref 7).
Similarly, about a year ago the National Science Foundation awarded three
demonstration grants to test the application of two-way cable television systems for a variety of municipal functions, including the training of fire
safety and daycare personnel, the provision of information services to the
elderly, the coordination of social welfare services, and the support of
adult education programs.

The recognition that various specific urban and social services can be delivered via telecommunications has also generated experiments that are directed
at a whole range of communications functions. In Japan, for example, the
Ministry of Posts and Telecommunications and the Ministry of International
Trade and Industry, in conjunction with a consortium of some 50 private corporations, have organized two experimental programs that are aimed at testing
a variety of broadband communications technologies and applications for the
home including pay television, facsimile news services, interactive consumer
information, shopping from the home, health counselling, computer-assisted
instruction, etc. (Ref 8). In both cases the experiments are being carried
out in new towns (Tama New Town and Higashi-Ikoma), since it is presumably
easier to implement these wired city testbeds in new town settings than to
rebuild the telecommunications networks of an existing city and because new
town residents may be more responsive to innovative communications services

than residents of older communities. Similar multi-purpose demonstration programs in the United States have also been conducted in new communities; for example in Jonathan, Minnesota, and Reston, Virginia.

Other experimental projects have been aimed at the scientific and business communities. In Canada, a wired city laboratory has been established at Carleton University in Ottawa with the support of the Canadian Department of Communications (Ref 9). This communications facility has been used for technical research as well as for a number of social psychology experiments, which have attempted to compare the effectiveness of various communications modes (e.g. face to face vs. two-way television vs. audio conferencing) for small group decision-making, negotiations, informal meetings, and university seminars. In Los Angeles, a group of researchers at the University of Southern California have been working with an insurance company to assess how telecommunications could facilitate the decentralization of the firm from a single centralized location to several satellite facilities that might be closer to its labor force and thereby could reduce the travel costs of the firm and the employees. Similarly, the uses of telecommunications in supporting economic development in rural areas has been investigated over the past five years, by the New Rural Society Project at the University of Fairfield in Connecticut (Ref 10).

THE DEVELOPMENT IMPACT

Having described some of the recent demonstration projects, I would like now to consider some of the implications of these various communications services for urban development. Will their utilization shape urban growth? Will the character of the urban social environment be altered and will these services help the urban decision maker cope with some of the problems of urban decay, accessibility and inefficiency that continue to confront us?

My answer to these questions is three-fold. First, I do not believe that the demonstration projects in themselves are the best clues to what long-term impact telecommunications will have on the urban environment. They provide us with information on what is possible rather than on what is probable. Paradoxically, to understand how new telecommunications will affect cities we may be better off by pursuing historical analysis rather than laboratory experiments, that is, we need to know how telecommunications have already affected urban development (and I will be more specific on this point below). Second, I am convinced that specific urban problems can be approached in terms of the new communications tools at our disposal, as long as we do not overlook the fact that institutional changes are likely to be necessary compliments of any technological innovations that are introduced. And third, I will argue that as new communications technologies are introduced on a widespread basis they may generate new social consequences, not all of them positive, at the same time as they help to resolve some of today's urban problems.

Let me discuss each of these points more specifically. Take first the point concerning the impact that telecommunications have already had on the urban environment. Using television as my main example, I would contend that this communications mode has already contributed (not necessarily caused, but nonetheless contributed) to the decline of the extended family; the gradual disappearance of the neighborhood as a basic social unit; and, more generally the dispersal and suburbanization of cities (at least in the United States). In the United States, we now as a society spend more hours watching televi-

sion each year than we do in formal employment; only sleep consumes more of
the nation's time. And so, as the child spends more time watching television, there is less need, for example, for grandmother; her role as babysit-
ter has been displaced. There is less need for extended families. And as
adults spend more time on television, they spend less time in social contact
at neighborhood stores, bars, movie theaters, parks, or simply talking on
the street to neighbors; the neighborhood's social role is diminished, the
streets become unsafe and shopping becomes a more functional and less social
activity.

But in the case you may mistake these comments as condemnations of television, let me pursue them a little further. Television, I would argue, has
also widened the child's horizon of possible career opportunities; he or she
no longer aspires only to what a parent or an uncle or aunt do for work. It
has brought the father back to the home more than at any previous period of
industrialization. And it has enabled families to live somewhat further
from the central city, enjoying more space and natural amenities, while not
being entirely isolated from urban society's social and cultural benefits
(Ref 11). In short, the impact of television has been mixed; but nonetheless
profound.

What the experimental projects that I have described do not tell us is how
the new communications technologies will affect urban physical and social
development on a broad scale; by concentrating on immediate uses they disregard ultimate impacts. Nor do they necessarily inform us about which of
the many new communications services will actually be introduced on a wide-
spread basis. To show that video conferencing is convivial, or that shopping
from the home is feasible, does not mean that those services will actually
be adoped. Numerous other factors contribute to the innovation process, including the presence or absence of competing services; the effects of government policies; the choice of marketing strategies; and the availability of
investment capital, disposable consumer income (or credit financing), and/or
public subsidies.

Take the case of television again. In the years immediately following World
War II consumer surveys indicated that demand for television in the United
States was virtually non-existant. By contrast, futurologists were predicting that within 25 years helicopters would be used to commute to work. As
it turned out, helicopters have not yet succeeded in the consumer market,
while television has boomed. (Perhaps a key factor was that credit financing
was made available for the purchase of TV sets but not for helicopters.) My
first point, in sum, is to emphasize our need to understand the various factors that determine how innovation occurs and how social impacts result from
innovation, which we can achieve through retrospective analysis as much as
through projective surveys and experiments.

My second point is that certainly some of the new communications services
that are becoming available will prove to be useful tools in expanding access to urban services, increasing administrative efficiencies, and improving service quality. Wider application of telemedicine, for instance, could
increase access to specialized medical and social services for the poor,
elderly and handicapped as well as enable a greater degree of resource sharing among medical and social service organizations. In the long run, it
could also reduce the need for hospital beds per capita, since it would become easier for those patients who are not critically ill to have access
to medical supervision either at a neighborhood clinic or directly in the

home.

Taking a quite different example, namely, banking, new developments in electronic funds transfer systems, which have made it possible to install "automated bank tellers" on the street corner or in a clothing store, will increase consumer access to urban financial services; while teleconferencing
systems in the office sector may make it easier for employees to live closer
to work, thereby reducing travel congestion, energy consumption, and air
pollution (Ref 12). However, to implement these various services will require changes, in many cases, in existing laws, institutional structures,
and economic relationships, not to mention psychological adjustments. For
example, in the United States telemedicine visits still do not qualify for
medical insurance payments and state banking laws present servere constraints
to the expansion of electronic banking services. (As for psychological adjustments, I can personally attest that working from the home through telecommunications is not as easy as it sounds, especialy when one has to cope
simultaneously with two incoming long distance phone calls and a screaming
three-year old daughter who has just broken her favorite toy and needs your
help.)

My third point, finally,. is that as we begin to use telecommunications for
improving the delivery of urban serives, or in facilitating the coordination
of government and business organizations, we may incur new problems that are
basic to the information society toward which we are moving. For instance,
as telecommunications facilitate decentralized access to urban services this
may further encourage the urban sprawl that we are already experiencing, and
thus increase rather than reduce our needs for travel and energy. (Although,
it is also conceiveable that decentralization could occur on a multi-nodal
basis, which could be favorable for countries such as France, Italy, or Sweden that have been grappling with the problems of regional economic development for a number of years.)

Moreover, as more and more channels of information become available, information overload may become the new social crisis. At the very least, as we
become more dependent on telecommunications, we will spend less time on more
traditional past-times. Will we spend less time on social activity and re-
creations outside the home; less time in reading books; less time for sleep
or child care? Whatever the specific consequences that occur they will affect not only the individual but also the shape of our social and urban environment, not to mention those economic institutions which support the
activities that will be displaced (e.g. book publishing, restaurants and
movie theaters, or transportation systems).

THE POLICY CHALLENGE

These lingering questions about the long-term impact of telecommunications,
along with the positive uses of new communications technology, pose a challenge to urban decision-makers and planners as they try to integrate telecommunications developments with other factors affecting urban growth. And
it is to this point, the policy challenge of urban telecommunications, that
my remaining comments are addressed.

Clearly, this policy challenge can not be answered by a simple static solution, since the developments in question are highly dynamic. A quick decision to invest in a particular technology can be rendered obsolete as soon
as some new technological development, some new political and regulatory con-

text, or some new urban need is identified. In short, policy making in urban telecommunications must remain above all flexible.

But given this essential premise of flexibility, there are several decision-
making conflicts which must be resolved in the course of formulating urban
telecommunications policy. First, there is the conceptual conflict between
technical, social, and economic perspectives on communications technology.
Should our policy process be influenced by what is technologically possible,
what is socially desirable, or what is economically viable? To me, at
least, the answer is quite obvious. We need to take all three factors into
consideration. But what this means is that policy making and educational
institutions must assume the responsibility of integrating these various perspectives, a highly challenging task in itself.

A second policy conflict that arises at the urban level is more operational.
Assuming that an urban government accepts the need for telecommunications
assessment and planning, the problem of how to integrate this new orientation
with traditional government responsibilities in health care, education,
transportation or public safety is of no small order. A local transportation
agency may not be interested in exploring how telecommunications can be substituted for travel, when it feels that transportation itself does not have
an adequate budget. Or an agency that has a very specific view of telecommunications (e.g. limited to police radio communications, or emergency medical communications) may not be interested in evaluating how telecommunications could be used to restructure the facility requirements and locations
of police stations or medical clinics. In short, some organizational
changes, always difficult to implement, will be required.

The third potential conflict, which needs very little introduction, is between national and local government authorities. In many countries, telecommunications, for social, economic, or military reasons, have been treated
as distinctly national systems. It is at the national level that the laws
governing telecommunications are made, that system integrity and technical
development is managed, and that expert knowledge is located. As urban and
provincial authorities become more aware of the social applications and impact of telecommunications, the question of division of authority and expertise among several levels of government will become increasingly critical
and complex. (The ongoing debate between national and provincial governments
in Canada over broadcasting policy and among federal, state, and municipal
cable television authorities in the United States are only two examples of
this emerging conflict area.) The question of expertise is particularly
acute, since local authorities in most countries have traditionally had little interest in broad telecommunications policy. However, as I have recently found in a study of municipal cable television decision making in
the United States, local government can gain expertise, in a highly complex
technological area such as cable television, quite rapidly (Ref 13).

A fourth policy conflict, and perhaps the underlying one in many advanced
industrial societies, is between public and private responsibilities in
telecommunications. How many aspects of the telecommunications system
should be controlled, directly or indirectly, by government and how many
should be left in the hands of private enterprise? Even in many European
countries, where the government role in telecommunications is quite extensive, private enterprise is often responsible for manufacturing equipment
and for producing programs. Should a similar relationship be maintained
with respect to the new technologies or must a new allocation of responsi-

bility be considered if technical innovation and social effectiveness are
to be ensured?

Finally, there is the question of how the urban citizen, resident and consumer will be integrated into the telecommunications policy process. Will
his role be merely one of subservience to high-level policy making or will
it be a more active one. We must remember, in this regard, that the new
information society, supported by a broadband communications infrastructure,
can be as disruptive of the lives of its citizens as the much more visible
urban demolition programs and super-highways that have already, in some
cases, undermined community life. The new information society will shape
living patterns, both physical and social; it will affect occupational
choices and the environment of the workplace; and it will determine our mental images of society, our information processing capabilities, our privacy, and our other day to day activities.

As a result, of all the new policy challenges raised by the new urban communications technologies, it is this one-- how policy will shape, and be
shaped by, citizens-- that is the most important. Some, of course, argue
that the communications system itself will provide the solution to this
policy dilemna. Two-way mass communications to the home will allow for
citizen feedback to government and industry on a continuing basis. But
there are others who are more skeptical about the political promise of this
"digital democracy " of the future. How we, as citizens and decision makers,
reconcile this optimism and this skepticism will determine how resource-
ful or repressive the emerging communications environment turns out to be.

REFERENCES

(1)   Machlup, F. (1962) The Production and Distribution of Knowledge in the
         United States, Princeton University Press, Princeton, NJ.

(2)   Parker, E.B. and Porat, M. (1975) Social Implications of Computer/Tele-
         communications Systems, Report No. 16, Program in Information Tech-
         nology and Telecommunications, Center for Interdisciplinary Research,
         Stanford University.

(3)   Voge, J. (1973) De L'Education, de La Recherche, de L'Information et
         des Communications dans La Crossance Economique, Ecole Nationale
         Superieure des Telecommunications, Paris.

(4)   Attali, J. (1975) La Parole et l'Outil, Presses Universitaires de
         France, Paris.

(5)   Masuda, Y., "The Conceptual Framework of Information Economics," IEEE
         Transactions on Communications 23/10 (1975)

(6)   Park, B (1974) An Introduction to Telemedicine: Interactive Television
         for Delivery of Health Services, Alternate Media Center, New York
         University, New York.

(7)   Bretz, R. (1975) Two-Way TV Teleconferencing for Government: The MRC-TV
         System, Rand Corporation, Santa Monica, Ca..

(8)   Living-Visual Information System Development Association (1974) Tama
         CCIS: Experiment Project Plan for the Living Information System

Development, Living Information System Development Headquarters, Tokyo.

(9) Coll, D.C. et al., "Multidisciplinary Applications of Communication
        Systems in Teleconferencing and Education," <u>IEEE Transactions **on**
        Communications</u> 23/10 (1975)

(10) Kohl, K. et al., "Facilitating Organizational Decentralization Through
        Teleconferencing," <u>IEEE Transactions on Communications</u> 23/10 (1975).

(11) Kalba, K., "The Electronic Communicty," in Adler, R., editor (1975)
        <u>Television as a Social Force</u> Praeger, New York.

(12) Kalba, K., "Telecommunications for Future Human Settlements," <u>Ekistics</u>
        35/211 (1973).

(13) Kalba, K. (1975) <u>City Meets the Cable: Technological Innovation and
        Community Decision-Making</u>, Program on Information Technologies and
        Public Policy, Harvard University.

NEW TECHNOLOGIES OR NEW MENTALITY?

"Soft" Solutions for improving People's Mobility: Reserved Lanes and Streets for Trams and Buses in Brussels.

Françoise Duesberg
Service Environnement du Crédit Communal de Belgique, Brussels, Belgium.

TRAFFIC AND CITY PLANNING - OBJECTIVES

Our cities are sick.
This is a commonplace, which has inspired in the past years a prolific literature as well as people's common talk.
Whithout being too pessimistic and drifting into an over-simple anti-urban ideology (the big town synonimous of "hell" ans the countryside of "paradise"), we must admit the existence of a malaise.
The reasons of this malaise are numerous and can be explained only through a socioeconomic analysis of the urban space : such a thorough investigation is not our present purpose.

We will focus on one of the most violently accused in the dock : the automobile traffic. Not only does it affect the physical environment : air pollution (impairing human health, vegetation, historical buildings), noise, stress, accidents, space consumption, ugliness....., but these negative effects, in turn, lead to a devitalization of central cities, invaded by motor vehicles (and offices), and deserted by inhabitants and visitors.

Last but not least, and apart from these environmental consequences, the mobility itself is hampered by the predominance of the automobile in the city.
Pedestrians and cyclists, public transportation and paradoxically car drivers themselves, all of them suffer from the privileges granted to the car.

Such are the evils. What about the remedies ?

The usual temptation for local authorities has been up to now to try to solve each problem by acting upon its immediate and most obvious cause :

- fighting physical "nuisances" with technical means, such as : experiments on motors, anti-noise walls, green screens to hide highways or parking-lots and so on; these measures are usually expensive and not vere efficient because they don't reach at the deep cause, which is the automobile traffic itself.

- fighting social and human decline of central cities with measures that don't take into account the possible responsability of traffic conditions; this omission may jeopardize the success of the best initiatives.

13

- fighting <u>traffic congestion</u> by opening up more space for cars : more express roads, more parking places ..... without, again, questioning the primary factor : the amount of automobile traffic itself in the city - and, one step further, without reconsidering the entire organisation of the city.

We should admit the following basic principles.

1. Traffic problems in our cities - pollutions, congestion and so on - cannot be solved by using traffic techniques only. These techniques will be ineffectual and even harmful if they are not used in accordance with :

    a. a general traffic policy, aiming at reducing the amount of automobile flows in the whole city;
    b. a general planning policy defining objectives for the whole city (localization of activities, protected areas, nuclei and axes of development.....).

    "What future for our city , What kind of life in it ?
    And what place for the car ?" Only when such questions are answered, can traffic techniques and policies become a useful tool.

2. Inversely, the general objectives for the city (better housing, revitalization of centres, protection of green areas, visual quality, social integration ...) cannot be achieved if nothing is done simultaneously against unnecessary (°) automobile traffic and in favour of other ways of communication and transportation.

    In short, the important is not what technology is adopted, but with what mentality it is adopted. The efficiency of a traffic or transportation technique does not depend on how spectacular, costly or revolutionary it may be. The essential point is : "in what spirit do the authorities apply such a technique ?". And more precisely : whatever the method, is the ultimate purpose to achieve the following main objectives :

    . to increase the <u>accessibility</u> of each point of the city for all people and
    . to preserve and enhance the quality of the city <u>environment</u> - public health, scenery, social life and so on ?

    Accessibility and environmental quality are not incompatible, if it is admitted that automobile traffic does not have the priority. This again is a matter of mentality.

THE CASE FOR "SOFT" AND "CONVIVIAL" SOLUTIONS

All the value of traffic and transportation techniques rests in the purposes they serve. Having accepted this idea, how shall we choose between different techniques, all of them likely to provide good communications and to fit in with the general planning of the city ?
Following requirements should be considered with the utmost attention.

(°) This implies limitations in function of several criteria : time, place, purpose of the journey, category of users ....

Low costs
Increasing sums are invested for allowing people to move from one place to
another. Part of this voracious budget should be devoted to the improvement
of people's life and environment.

Low energy consumption

Short execution delays.

Although traffic policies need long-term views, it is urgent to find solutions rapidly applicable, since the situation is becoming worse everyday.

No harm to the city.

The benefit expected from important traffic or transportation projects
can be seriously affected by the nuisance created during the works
(excavations, mud, noise, diversion of users ...) and afterwards (noise,
air pollution, cut up neighbourhoods, space consumption etc...)

Flexibility.

An adjustment should be possible in case of change in the pattern of the
city, in mobility behaviours, in mentalities....

Attractiveness to users.

When deciding between several techniques, one should take into account
how pleasant they will compare for the public. This includes not only
the usual parameters : speed, frequency, comfort, fares ... but also
more subjective factors - feelings and impressions related to the quality
of the itinerary (underground or on the surface, followed thoroughfares...),
the design of the vehicles, the access from the sidewalk and the buildings.

There is a variety of existing or imaginable techniques that meet or could
meet such requirements. One of these methodes is immediately available.
It can be set up quickly, at low costs, without damaging the environment;
it can be modified when needed; it is psychologically attractive because
users, though not hidden in the ground, have the satisfaction of moving
faster (and cheaper) than the jammed motorists.

This is the system of reserved lanes and streets for trams ans buses (°).

It consists in separating public from private traffic, both remaining at the
level of the ground but using different roads or different parts of the road.

Reserved lanes and streets are not, of course, a miraculous solution...
One should never say there is ONE solution for one problem in such an
intricate field as city planning.

(°)   We notice (in the minds if not in the facts yet) a general come back
      of "soft", light methods - and not only in the field of transportation :
      there are for instance moves in favour of small neighbourhood gardens
      and adventure playgrounds, or in favour of the village school against
      the barrack-type concentration; in favour of the restoration of
      existing housing against its destruction and the construction of huge
      modern buildings ....

They can be a precious tool however - if two conditions are respected.
First, they must be integrated into a complete and diversified traffic
and transportation system.
Secondly, the authorities should create them with one resolute idea in the
back of their mind : to facilitate the movements of pedestrians, cyclists,
semi-public and public vehicles, whatever the sacrifices such a policy
imposes to automobilists.

AN INTEGRATED TRANSPORTATION SYSTEM BASED ON RESERVED LANES

AND STREETS

Tram and bus-lanes (or streets) are not a universal solution. In fact, each
kind of urban environment requires an appropriate network. The main parameters to consider are : the density of population in the served area, the
radius of the served area, the concentration of activities (importance of
the attraction poles), the fragility of the environment ....
The result for the whole urban area is a combination of various types of
networks.

1.   "Heavy" solutions (subway, railway...) are recommended only where high
     population densities, high levels of economic concentration and a
     large radius of action generate important traffic flows (more than
     10,000 passengers/hour).

2.   "Softer" solutions (reserved lanes or streets for trams and buses for
     example) apply to most European cities, whether they form the main
     network (cities having no usual flows above 10,000 passengers/hour) or
     they are the indispensable complement to the heavy network.

3.   Eventually, when the subway, the trams or the buses reach sensitive
     parts of the city (as the highly populated and frequented historical
     centers), they should be completed by very light and flexible systems
     of mobility, functioning in connection with the pedestrian and bicycle
     networks.

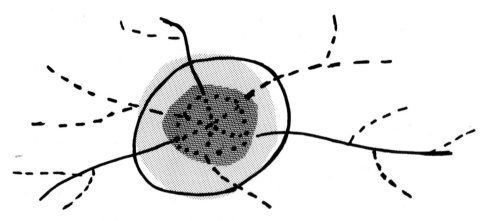

_____ "heavy" network (subway, railway)
----------- "light" network (bus-lanes, tram-lanes, ...)
.... extra-light network (para-transit, electric cars, etc....)

Present Tendencies

The idea of a diversified and integrated communication network has not
materialized yet in most Belgian cities. It is usually expected that one
single important operation (building an expressway or digging a few big
subway lines) will solve the town's traffic problems.

Actually, this is not quite the case in Brussels, where an original
method is being applied : rather than covering the entire city with a
complete subway system (which would have been extremely damaging, costly
and slow to carry out anyway), it has been decided to create what is
called either "pré-métro" or "semi-métro".

"Pré-métro" because at a first stage, some of the existing tramway lines
merely come down into the future subway tunnels, so that a part of the
trip is made underground. The next step will take place in September
1976, when the trams will be replaced by real subway vehicles.
This gradual formule has economical advantages (it is quickly operational
and so more profitable) and psychological advantages (a soft transition
from tramway to subway helps educating the people to the new system).

It is also a "semi-métro" because, even at its final stage, the subway
will serve only a few areas in the city and will keep working in
conjunction with the traditional transportation methods. In theory, the
principle of complementary of heavy and fine-spun networks is respected.
Its application however does not seem to have been thoroughly studied.

The creation of the subway offered an excellent opportunity of reviewing
the entire pattern of communications in the whole urban area. In
practice, one has simply superimposed the subway on the previous
structure without deeply modifying it and also without systematically
connecting it with the new one. The communications for people living and
working along a subway line will no doubt be improved, but large sectors
of the town and the suburbs will still depend either on the private car
or on buses and trams laboriously converging to a congested center.

All the efforts of the authorities are concentrated upon the subway,
while there is no radical attempt to a) improve public transportation
from all suburbs to the central city, and also between different suburbs
b) to relieve the center from the automobile pressure.

Reserved lanes and streets would preceisely be one of the most appropriate
ways to achieve both objectives : they would easily increase the speed of
buses and trams, make them attractive to people, who would be tempted
not to use their car to go to town every day, especially as drivers would
be excluded from many streets anyway.

As a matter of fact, reserved lanes exist in Brussels, in particular for
tramways. In september 1976, there will be 40 Km tram-lanes ("tram on
site propre"), plus 10 Km subway and 10 Km "pré-métro", in all 60 Km
separated against 70 Km mixed with the general traffic ("en site banal").
One should notice that in 1965 Brussels had already 54 Km tram-lanes :
the progress, in kilometers, is not spectacular.
A few kilometers bus-lanes have also been created, but their efficiency
is limited; it is not only a matter of low quantity, but also of design.
All depends in what spirit they have been conceived.

A CLEAR CHOICE : PRIORITY TO PUBLIC TRANSPORTATION OR TO THE CAR

Reserved lanes are an ambiguous tool. At first sight, they serve only
one purpose : to improve the traffic of trams and buses.
But the analysis of the existing lanes shows that the essential - and
unavowed - purpose is in many cases to increase the fluidity of the
automobile traffic.
We often hear authorities assert that "collective and individual transportation are complementary", that both have a part to play in the city and
must be equally promoted.
But what kind of complementarity ? Questioned on this subject, the
authorities confine themselves to theoretical generalities : the car should
be reserved to those "who really need it, the doctors for instance" and
"the others, the employees ...." should use public transportation. The
interlocuter seldom situates himself among "the others"...

Objective investigation indicates that automobile and public transportation
are complementary only up to a certain point. Without rallying to the
slogan "Mon auto, c'est ma liberté" stuck by some drivers on their vehicle,
we must admit that the car may be a valuable instrument. But in large
sectors of our cities, its real vocation is to be relegated to a subordinate
rank, because even its normal use is not compatible with proper conditions
for public transportation and pedestrian traffic. To promote these two
latter and to content the car drivers are - at least in city centers -
conflicting objectives.

What choice do Brussels bus and tram-lanes reflect ?

Priority to the car
None of the few bus-lanes created up to now in Brussels has imposed
the slightest restriction to the freedom of car drivers. In fact,
these would rather enjoy better driving conditions, since they
no longer have in their way slow, cumbersome vehicles.... Besides,
each creation of bus-lane has been the occasion of road works
intended to increase the speed of cars : more lanes, lanes for
left-turns, etc... usually to the prejudice of pedestrians whose
walking space was each time seriously cut down.
All this is clearly observable in the design of roads as the rue
Belliard, rue de la Loi and boulevard du Botanique.

Bottlenecks
Owing to a lack of coordination, bus-lanes and tram-lanes are the
cause of numerous bottlenecks : after a fast section, buses and trams
often come up against a jammed section where they have to clear their
way among the cars.
Such bottlenecks are not only the result of hazard or negligence :
reserved lanes are created only where the width of the street makes sure
that drivers would not suffer from the advantages conceded to public
transportation, or will even benefit themselves from the new road-
design. Where the street narrows, reserved lanes are out of question.
As to the idea of reserving the street itself to buses, the mere
thought of it has never been seriously considered in Brussels.

Problems at cross-roads
A large part of the speed gained on reserved lanes is lost at

cross-roads, because buses and trams have no right of way over the
other vehicles. There has been one attempt of "green waves" on a
section of the tramway-line nr "90", that had 68 traffic-lights on
its whole length. No other attempt has followed, when all buses and
trams in Brussels waste a lot of time waiting at cross-roads. This is
espacially frustrating for users when the tram or bus-stop is put
<u>before</u> the traffic-light.

The only solution considered up to now in Brussels, is to separate
the traffics at cross-roads by digging tunnels either for trams
(subway) or for cars - but such heavy techniques should be used
with moderation.... Systematical "green waves" would - at lower
costs - greatly improve the quality of public transportation. Of
course, one problem would still exist : the intersection of two or
more lines causing bus or tram-jams. It can be partly solved however
with the help of computers (in Holland, a computer system gives the
right of way to the tram wich is the most behind its schedule).
Unfortunately, Brussels has no central computer for public transportation.
Not much has been done either to reduce the time wasted at stoppings -
except for the subway, where passengers pay their fare in advance and
will have sixteen doors at their disposal in the new vehicles.

Lack of control

The efficiency of bus and tram-lanes rests on the way their prohibition
to the cars is enforced. To turn a blind eye to trespassing vehicles
indicates a broad tolerance towards the private automobile.
It is still too often considered as normal that trams and buses would
be restrained by cars in case of need and that they share the common
destiny of the whole city traffic....

There have been some recent attemps in opposition to this mentality.
For instance, buses leaving a stopping and resuming their road have
the priority over the coming traffic.

A wide gap nevertheless subsist between the words, the intentions
("Public transportation must be favored at any rate") and the facts
(it <u>may</u> be favored <u>if</u> this is not to the expense of car drivers and
it <u>must</u> be favored <u>if</u> this is to their good).

Why this gap ? How could it be reduced ?

THE CRUX OF THE MATTER : A REVOLUTION OF MENTALITIES

The reasons why reserved lanes and streets for buses and trams are so
scarce and defective are above all social and political.
One factor is peculiar to Brussels : the multiplicity of administrative
competences over the territory of the city (several Ministries, the
Province, the Town of Brussels an 18 other Communes, the recently
established "Agglomeration"...) impedes a coordinated policy of public
transportation.

For example, one of these autorithies, the Town of Brussels, has often
opposed technical arguments to the bus-lane system : it prevents the
delivery of goods and gasoil; many streets are too narrow; and buses

having a lower frequency than cars, it is abnormal, especially at
off-peak hours, to block a part of the streets to the latter in favour
of buses coming at long intervals.
Such arguments actually reflect - in technical and administrative terms -
the state of mind of the public opinion : people cannot imagine their life
without a car and they consider the use of that car as an imprescriptible
right.

As long as this mentality pervades, no real improvement of our city life
can be expected. Under the pressure of aggravating traffic conditions ans
nuisances, an evolution is possible - but it seems that the human being
is able to tolerate a lot (traffic jams, high expenses, air pollution,
etc...) before he accepts the slightest concession to his rights of driver.
So, on the one hand, the authorities must be courageous enough to act
against what is considered as the public opinion and take openly the
side of public transportation. On the other hand, all those who can
influence mentalities - the mass media, the educators...- should aim at
having people ask for themselves a priority to public transportation and
to pedestrian and bicycling facilities. The day children will refuse to be
carried to school by car because they don't like it, a great step forward
will be done.

Of course, one might hesitate before taking such measures : they don't reach
only the way people travel in the city but also, indirectly, the way they
behave relate with each other, etc... And maybe this idea, that deep
changes in our society could be brought by a modification of transportation
policies, has partly retained the authorities from getting involved, for
instance, in the systematical creation of efficient reserved lanes and
streets from trams ans buses.
Hence the question : can anything at all be done in the field of transportation if a revolution in social values and in social structures does not
occur before ?

MODERN TECHNOLOGY OF AIR POLLUTION CONTROL

Harald F. Funk, Consultant, Murray Hill N.J. USA

ABSTRACT

Air pollution control begins with gas purification. Hence a new approach in gas purification has been applied successfully. With such a cryogenic technique, gases can be purified from undesirable components especially sulfur. This system can been adjusted for purification of gases from waste gasification and can even be adopted for treatment of stackgas.

INTRODUCTION

The awareness of having to intensify the air pollution control has been growing steadily, during the last decade. Many articles and books have been published about pollution of all kind, may it be the problem with water, heat, noise or radiation, solid waste and so on. The most acute of all will be the purification of air. The emissions of impurities into the atmosphere during 1968 for instance were estimated at 200 million tons in USA alone. The total on emissions of carbonmonoxide (47 %), hydrocarbons (15 %), nitrogen oxides (10 %) and sulfurous gases (15 %) as well as particulates (13 %) is in the order of about 9600 million tons, worldwide but only 545 million tons are caused by the human element. In absolute figures those quantities are impressive. However considering the total mass of air which is in the order of 5 to 6 quadrillion tons the concentration of impurities would amount to about 2 ppm not counting carbon dioxide. On the other hand these impurities - many of them are quite toxic - are being concentrated in the most populated areas. Carbon dioxide as a rule is not being considered to be harmful. However the output of this component is enormous (20 billion tons per year); thus resulting in an increase of concentration by 0.2 % annually. This inturn creates a so called greenhous effect elevating the earth's temperature by 2° or 3° F and up-setting the thermal balance.

PROBLEMS WITH AIR POLLUTION

Therefore institutions like the Environmental Protection Agency (EPA) have established maximal allowable values, with the result that many a plant such as coke plants, paper mills, smelters, and incinerators were shut down and many others were fined for exceding the limits of emissions. These standards of emissions were extended to exhaust gases from internal combustion engines, since automobiles and trucks are contributing to a great deal (42 % in USA to 60 % in West Germany) of all air pollution. One will understand the situation better with reference to numbers. For instance 1000 gallons of fuel generate 1363 kg CO, 91 to 106 kg hydrocarbons, 23 to 30 kg NO_x and 2.3 to 4.5 kg sulfur dioxide as well as 136 g dust. Knowing that a Diesel engine in average is yielding only one tenth of CO and half of the NO_x emissions,

21

one wonders why the public and more so the Government offices do not draw
any conclusion!

Other offenders are steam and power plants contributing to 14 % in USA and
21 % in West Germany of total air pollution measured. Then chemical and
petrochemical plants as well as petroleum refineries, steel mills, cement
plants, paper mills, coke ovens, incinerators and others are having problems
as well. A considerable amount of air pollution is caused by coal burning and
heavy fuel oil with a relatively high concentration of sulfur. 1952 in London
during winter when heavy smog occurred, up to 1.3 ppm of SO_2 and a high
concentration of soot (4.5 mg/m^3) have been measured in air. During that
period 1600 cases of death have been reported on that account. Since then
drastic steps have been taken to avoid a repetition of such a condition.
Pretty grim pictures have been painted for the future with threatining
predictions and the engineers as well as the whole technology have been
accused for the deteriorating situation.

But one must emphasise that it is not the use of technology causing such a
dilemna but it's abuse.

ATTEMPTS FOR IMPROVEMENT

In closing down plants one does not help the economy. It is not only a loss
of investment cost but more so a loss of jobs and the Government does not give
a helping hand by sending out smoke inspectors, who write fines like tickets
for parking violations. The point is that the industry needs any assistance
it can get, it needs help rather than punishment. It means that equipment has
to be installed for extra cost usually carried by the private industry
burdening the economy and reducing profits.

In many cases new technology is available but the revisions to be made in the
plants structure would be too costly and are frequently linked with interrup-
tions of production.

In such a case it ought to be the responsibility of the Government to aid
the industry in giving assistance not only in form of loans but also in the
form of consultation to chose the type of facilities necessary to cope with
certain situations. One has to appreciate that EPA in Washington for instance
has helped to build pilot plants to demonstrate new processes,andwhile money
has been invested in projects which turned out te be a failure other projects
have not received the Governments support and turned out to be feasable after
the private industry made big efforts on it's own. Which tells us that quite
a part of the Governments aid was not rewarded by success.

NEW PROCESSES

Some of the new processes however not only solved the pollution problem but
also improved the earnings of a plant. Here I wand to refer to a case in
Clairton, Pennsylvania where coke oven gas had to be purified from H_2S while
benzene was to be recovered and hydrogen to be separated to be used as feed
for an ammonia plant. It was quite a task. The US-Steel Corporation had
invested many millions of Dollars for a pilot plant and it's operation.

Then the new process was applied and this plant is not only producing more than 1200 tons per day of ammonia and recovering the light oils at a high degree of purity but also yields some 100 tons per day of elemtal sulfur now, which used to go up into the air.

As it was pointed out before one of large contributor to air pollution (about 14 % to 21 %) is fuel combustion in stationary sources. Here the Government has taken drastic steps and would allow only fuel of low sulfur concentration to be burnt except in some cases where stack gas is being cleaned prior to the discharge into the atmosphere.

So far it has not occurred that stack gas also can be purified by physical means while applying cryogenic techniques, which would eliminate scrubbing or chemical treatment of all the gas. Besides it would entitle a company to consume fuel which is high in sulfur thus allowing the advantage of getting fuel at low cost. Some companies have decided to build higher stacks to warrant a better distribution of emissions and they even would dilute the stack gas with air if necessary. This of course would not make any changes in the total quantity of harmful components discharged.

Papermills also make an effort to improve the pollution control. Here again new processes are being developed, which might even improve the recorery rate of fibers, and by products would be yielded such as hexoses and pentoses, which in turn can be processed further to a variety of products. The papermills at times are under pressure because of tough competition, claim that purification costs add about 5 % to the total operating cost. New processes however might improve the profit picture.

Many incinerators have been shut down in the United States because of emission problems, but the capacity can not be replaced immediately thus causing a problem of solid waste desposal. To find improvements the Saarberg-Fernwärme (West Germany) has attacked a new approach and is determined to build a plant to gasify solid waste. This system is linked with a cryogenic gas purification system in which none of the impurities can escape to the atmosphere. The gas then can be utilized without reservation for heating or power generation or preferably as synthesis gas to produce methanol and it's derivatives.

Petroleum refineries are being accused for being one of the largest contributors to air pollution in regard to hydrocarbons and sulfur compounds emission. Here is a typical case for application of the regenerative type of cryogenic plant. A study on Montreal's Oil Refineries has shown that the refinery off gas which can be collected from 4 adjacent medium sized refineries would accumulate to about 11000 SCFM. This gas is discharged from various units mainly the cat cracker and catreformer.

The composition is as follows:

TABLE 1

	Mol %	MSCFH
H_2	40	260
N_2	10	65
CO	1.2	8
CO_2	0.5	3
H_2S	1.8	12
CH_4	34.8	227
C_2-	3.1	20
C_2+	4.0	26
C_3-	3.1	20
C_3+	1.5	10
	100.0	651

This gas normally would be charged to the boilers and in rare cases to the flare. However containing 1.8 % of H_2S it would require purification. Such a treatment can be linked with separation of various components and hydrogen could be returned to the refinery's treating units. A modern oil refinery is equipped with hydrogenation units, it always can use hydrogen and would welcome such a source, especially since hydrogen has a comparatively low heating value but it es expensive as a commodity. Such savings a refinery can make, would offset the cost of purification.

A comparison of a classic purification unit of coke oven gas with the new approach would even convince a layman of it's merrits. Coke oven gas has been know as a "dirty" gas and it's clean up always presented a problem. Here is a typical composition:

TABLE 2

Component	Vol %
H_2	51.1
N_2	6.5
CO	7.7
CO_2	2.3
CH_4	28.5
C_2H_2	0.17
C_2H_4	2.3
Illuminants	0.83
O_2	0.6
	100.0

plus traces of HCN, H_2S, organic sulphur and No

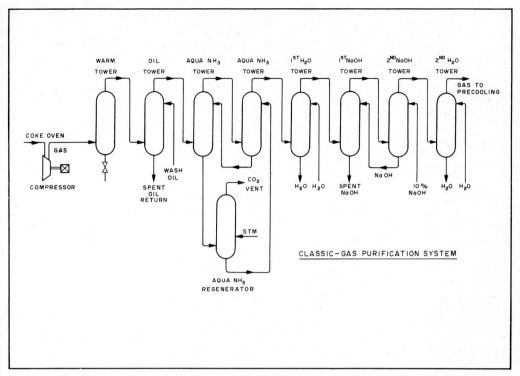

CLASSIC-GAS PURIFICATION SYSTEM

In this classic system (see figure 1), the first tower takes the duty to reduce the NO content by oxidizing NO to NO_2. The actual NO-concentration leaving this warm tower is in the order of 10 ppb. In the second tower, the BTX (benzene, toluene and xylene) besides naphthalene are removed. The BTX content is below 600 pm and the naphthalene below 0.2 grains per 100 CF. The No. 3 and 4 towers are there to remove CO_2, H_2S, and HCN from the gas as being passed through a 5 % aqueous ammonia solution. The CO_2 concentration is reduced to less than 200 ppm then the rich ammonia is sent to two regenerators where the CO_2 is stripped from ammonia with steam.
The 5th tower (the first water tower) is to remove ammonia carried over from the aqua NH_3 towers. The ammonia solution (about 1 %) is passed on for make up of the 5 % solution.

The No. 6 and 7 towers hold a 10 % sodium hydroxide solution to remove all the HCN, H_2S and to reduce the CO_2 level to less than 5 ppm. The No. 8, the final Water tower is retaining any caustic entrainment as well as ammonia which may have been carried over. This treatment is not complete since the gas is being passed on to an precooling unit prior to the gas separation plant.

In contrast to that, the application of regenerators is relatively simple (see figure 2).

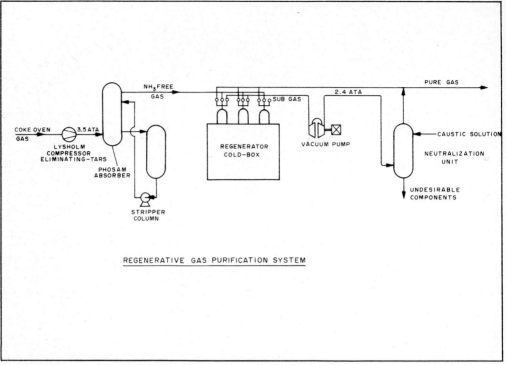

REGENERATIVE GAS PURIFICATION SYSTEM

The coke oven gas is being freed from ammonia and tars, then it is passed on to a regenerative type cryogenic plant. Here the less volatile components are being retained. These components possible C_2-fractions and heavier are frozen out and are collected in a separate phase. That stream of gas which in this case amounts to to less than 10 % in being treated chemically in a caustic tower to remove the harmful components, while the illuminants are being recovered and fed into the pure gas stream.

This way there is no loss of heating value there is no risk for explosions, since the NO has no time to react with dienes to form explosive gums and the product gas stream is freed from impurities in the same unit which can be equipped to yield either synthesis gas or single out components such as hydrogen or methane.

One can recognize the versatile application of such a "tool", since it combines gas purification with recovery of valuable components. In applying such a technique all kinds of gases can be purified effectively such as refinery off gas, gas from coal mines, from incinerators, gas from smelters and L-D-furnaces and even sewer gases if necessary.

Air purification actually begins with gas purification! Just as well as district heating is more efficient and causes less of harmful emissions than individual stoves, a general clean up system would he more effective if industrial areas can be integrated with a purification system, as illustrated above where several refineries could be linked for that purpose.

PRO'S AND CON'S ON THE FUTURE

In some instance the municipal Governments were aiding the industry in
granting relief from taxes for installations of district heating plants as
has been considered by some municipalities in the Saar district of West
Germany.

The energy crisis in 1973 resulted in a considerable jump of fuel costs.
Thus the economic evaluation on energy conservation had to be revised. But
here again in many cases the law would prohibit certain steps. For instance
power generation is monopolized to a degree that many sources of waste heat
can not be tapped. Since oil and natural gas are eventually nearing a
depletion, these utilities ought to be considered as resource for chemicals
rather than fuel. Therefore the trend toward power generation from nuclear
reactors is justified especially since one kg of uranium will render an
equivalent of energy to 5 tons of oil. However the fusion would yield more
energy yet considering that one gram of deuterium would give as much as
8 tons of oil. Lithium 6 would yield even more and it is said to be a greater
source of energy than all coal, oil, natural gas, and the Athabasca tar sands
as well. Further more the nuclear reactors oparating on the principle of
fusion would not have to cope with radiation linked with fission.

Considering the efforts being made and the possibilities available it is up
to our endeavor to improve the environmental conditions provided one puts the
technology to proper use.

REFERENCES

1.   Nigel Calder,   The environment game.
                          Fischer pocket book, Frankfurt/Main, 1973

2.   Philip Nobile and John Deedy,
                          The complete ecology fact book.
                          Doubleday, New York, 1972

3.   Dennis Meadows etal.
                          The limits to growth.
                          Universe books, New York, 1973

4.   S. David Freeman,   Energy the new era.
                          Vintage books, New York, 1974

5.   S. J. Viron,   Ammonia and Urea from steel making by Products.
                          Paper presented during the blast furnaces coke oven
                          and raw materials conference in 1961

6.   R. Becker,   Coke-oven gas separation in a regenerative system.
                          Kältetechnik 16, No. 8, 239 - 241 (1964)

THE RELATIONSHIP OF THE ENVIRONMENTS OF HUMAN SETTLE-MENTS TO HEALTH

Robert NOVICK - Sanitary Engineer
World Health Organization - GENEVA.

Although the importance of planning is being increasingly recognised in most countries, the improvement of settlements up to the present has been influenced mainly by economics, and other considerations have exercised little influence. This approach has not produced satisfactory results. It is now generally recognized that all the sectors concerned with development of human settlements - economic, physical, social and health - must be included in a comprehensive approach from the start and on an equal footing. From the viewpoint of health, the goal is. to ensure that health is accepted as an integral part of the planning and development of human settlements at the local, national and international levels. Achievement of this goal will require the clarification of health policies, based on clear understanding of the health effects resulting from the physical and social environments of settlements, and will necessitate identification of the relevant operational techniques, organizational patterns and manpower policies.

Health services throughout the world are now confronted with new challenges resulting from economic growth and technological advances and these are manifest in social disruption and pollution of the environment. Nevertheless in many developing countries the paramount need of the health services is still focussed on traditional problems such as communicable disease, nutrition, and maternal and child health. Rapid population growth frequently outpaces the capacity to provide even these minimum services to people, and a high rate of rural-urban migration exarcebates the situation by depleting the young and more productive members of the rural population, and simultaneously creating an overwhelming demand for the extension of urban services. The overall result is a crucial situation where hundreds of millions of people are lacking the basic needs of life, including adequate nutritious food, safe water and proper means of waste disposal, decent shelter and the opportunity for intellectual and moral growth.

I. ENVIRONMENTAL FACTORS ASSOCIATED WITH ILL HEALTH IN HUMAN SETTLEMENTS

Health problems associated with the physical environment can usually be identified comparatively easily. Improvements to the physical environment are at times carried out using sophisticated and costly techniques, but this is not always necessary. Significant benefits can be derived from the use

of simple technology which is in harmony with the economic
development and cultural patterns of the local area. The
following features of the physical environment have significance to health.

Housing and the Home Environment

It is estimated that more than 100 million people, mainly
living in developing countries, have inadequate housing. The
two most striking features of poor housing are overcrowding
and lack of basic sanitation, but extremes of temperature,
illumination and noise may also exert adverse physiological
effects. Although statistical evidence linking inadequate
housing with ill health is incomplete, overcrowding, lack of
facilities for cleanliness, and the presence of rats and
insects resulting from inadequate waste disposal all predis-
pose to disease. Home accidents rank high among the health
hazards.

Working Environment

Hazards to health in the working environment are caused by
chemical agents, physical factors, biological agents, accidents and psychosocial stress. Work satisfaction is being
increasingly recognized as important, particularly as mecha-
nization increases. Home industries in developing countries
are of special concern because of the potential exposure of
all family members to occupational hazards, and the difficulty of monitoring and of drafting health regulations capable of controlling the situation.

Water and Water Supply

Water is essential not only for drinking, but also for other
vital community functions including irrigation, industrial
processing and recreation. All of these uses have implications
for health but the problems of safe drinking water in developing countries are a particular concern. A survey of community water supply and sewage disposal conditions and needs
at the end of 1970 was conducted by WHO in 91 selected developing countries. The analysis shows that nearly half the
urban population of the developing countries use unsafe piped
water, and that about 80 per cent of the rural population or
over 1000 million people do not have water that can be considered comparatively "safe" (that is free from gross biological pollution).

Water is a primary medium for the transmission of disease.

The more important water-associated * diseases being typhoid,
cholera, dysentery, filariasis, malaria and schistosomiasis.

The task in developing countries is to provide access to safe
water for the millions of people not presently served. There
is a great need to develop appropriate technology, governmental infrastructure and to facilitate popular participation.

In developed countries the dependence upon surface water is
increasing and requiring attention to provide a high degree
of treatment for waters contaminated with both municipal wastes and thermal and chemical pollution from industrial sources.

The global incidence of water-associated diseases is such
that many health experts believe the provision of safe, ample
and convenient water supply is the most important single
activity that can be undertaken for the health of people
living in rural and urban areas.

Food

Aside from nutritional considerations food can serve as a
media for the intake of toxic chemicals and microbiological
agents. Infections resulting from the latter agents are the
most common food-borne diseases. Although everyone sometime
in his life has experienced foodborne disease, the reporting
of outbreaks is still far from adequate to give a reliable
picture of their frequency.

Another environmental aspect of food is the loss experienced
by spoilage. In some developing countries these losses can
be as much as 30-40 % of the perishable foods, and is particularly noted with foods such as fish which may at certain
times be available in large quantities. Losses occur because
of lack of transport facilities/or lack of a food preservation or of the facilities to undertake it.

Excreta, Sewage and Solid Wastes Disposal

Human excreta is one of the most dangerous substances with
which people can come into contact. It is the principle source
of the pathogenic organisms of many communicable diseases,
particularly infections of the intestinal tract (enteric
diseases). The spread of these diseases occurs when faecal
matter containing pathogenic organisms contaminates food,
water or the fingers and is subsequently ingested by a sus-
ceptible individual. The enteric diseases, including cholera,
typhoid, dysentery, and the diarrhoeal diseases, and virus
diseases such as infectious hepatitis, are among the leading
causes of death and disability in areas occupied by more
than two-thirds of the world's population.

----

* Water-associated diseases have been classified as follows :
(a) those related to poor sanitation (lack of water and/or
sewerage, inadequate personal hygiene) ; (b) waterborne
diseases (water is a passive vehicle of the infecting agent) ;
(c) water-based diseases (a part of the life cycle of the
infecting agent takes place in an aquatic animal) ; (d) water-
related diseases (infections transmitted by insects that breed
in water). Some belong to more than one group.

Ideally solid wastes should not contain any faecal matter,
but in practice this has been found difficult to prevent.
Where this occurs the handling and disposal of solid wastes
presents the same potential for disease transmission as the
collection and disposal of excreta and sewage. Inadequate
disposal of solid wastes creates additional hazards in terms
of production of malodours ; air pollution from open burning ;
and as a media for breeding of flies and rats. Rats may be a
reservoir of pathogenic organisms for plague, murine typhus
and leptospirosis.

A growing problem of all countries is the safe disposal of
liquid and solid wastes from industrial operations. Solid
wastes deposited in open dumps or landfills can contaminate
groundwater. Liquid wastes discharged to sewers and water
courses may contain dissolved chemicals, particularly poi-
sonous heavy metals. It has been demonstrated that some of
these may be concentrated in nature by organisms in man's
food chain.

Land

There are numerous health implications pertaining to the use
of land. The most obvious results from the indiscriminate
disposal of solid wastes, chemicals waste materials from
mining or ore processing, sewage and sewage sludge, whereby
the land is spoiled for further use. Other health implications pertain to land use policies such as the siting of
industries which may emit pollutants, or which may cause
traffic congestion, or the unsuitable location of residential
areas. In the squatter settlements of developing countries
poor drainage is a particularly common hazard to health
because of the lack of wastewater collection systems and the
characteristics of their siting. Good building land is usually
pre-empted by priority uses and shanty towns or squatter settlements are usually only found on sites that have been left
empty because of their unsuitability for development. Land
liable to flooding is commonly used and in addition to the
inconvenience due to this the water logged soil is the ideal
medium for transmission of parasitic diseases such as hook-
worm, pools of standing water may become contaminated and
conveny enteric disease or serve as ideal breeding loci for
mosquito pests and vectors contributing to the spread of
filariasis and other diseases ; and the difficulty and hence
the cost of providing underground water and waste collection
services is greatly increased on building sites which are
poorly drained and have a high water table.

Air

Air pollution can cause or contribute to human disease and
precipitate undesirable physiological effects. Three dramatic
episodes in this century, in the Meuse Valley (1930), Donora,
Pennsylvania (1948), and London (1952), have demonstrated

that, in extreme cases, air pollution can result in considerable loss of life and serious illness. However, the exact
nature and extent of the association between air pollution
and health have not been fully established, particularly with
with regard to trace elements and low concentrations of the
oxides of sulfur and nitrogen. In many cases the effects of
pollution of the ambient atmosphere, if present, are over-
shadowed by the ill effects of tobacco smoking. Odours may
interfere with general wellbeing ; polluted air may erode
buildings and metals and have a devastating effect on vegetation.

Airborne micro-organisms can be important in the spread of
some communicable diseases. Two examples, which have been
associated with poor housing and overcrowding, are influenza
and cerebrospiral meningitis.

Noise
In occupational medicine the harmful effect of loud noise,
particularly pure tonic noise over a limited range of frequency, has been recognized for many years.

In the community generally it is the psychophsiological and
psycho-social effects that are important. Noise frequently
leads to disturbance of sleep but, depending on a person's
psychological approach or state, a considerable degree of
adaptation can take place. The important aspect is the extent
to which irritation and annoyance are caused and the extent
to which these can result in increased stress. Stress is
important for it is a recognized factor influencing both
mental and physical health.

Energy
At present health problems resulting from energy production
are largely related to waste products from the combustion
of fossil fuels, particularly sulfur oxides and suspended
particulate matter. As energy requirements increase nuclear
power production is also likely to increase and with it the
potentail health hazards of ionizing radiation.

Vectors and Hosts of Disease
Insect and animal carriers of disease are of considerable
importance in human settlements where climate and inadequate
disposal of solid wastes and waste water enhance the propo-
gation of vectors. Dengue haemorrhagic fever and filariasis
spread by mosquitos are increasing in many urban areas.
Onchoceriasis, schistosomiasis and malaria are characteristic
diseases of rural agricultural populations exposed to vectors throughout the year.

II. HEALTH PROBLEMS
Historically communicable diseases have been among the most

important of the causes of sickness and premature death, and
so it still remains in the human settlements in most developing countries.

Recent work on the epidemiology of non-communicable diseases
has demonstrated the many associations with environmental
factors, often not as yet fully understood, but producing
variations which influence the quality of life in different
human setteements. Some of the associations are well known :
bronchitis with air pollution and smoking, lung cancer with
smoking, toxic chemicals with certain occupational diseases
and other diseases with factors including many environmental
pollutants and food contaminants and additives.

Among the health problems which must be mentioned are the
growing importance of accidents in the home, on the roadways,
in industry and in agriculture.

The effects of the environment and other related factors in
human settlements on man's mental health and his psychosocial
state of well-being are some of the most difficult to define
and quantify. The satisfaction a human being gets out of
life, his contacts with others, his exposure to stresses and
strains, worried and uncertainties whether these be caused
by economic (including employment) troubles, psychosocial
causes (including threats to his family's well-being), or
the effects of a poor environment (noise, persistent odours,
environmental pollution, uncontrolled industrial activities),
all have an influence on his mental, and hence indirectly,
on his physical, health.

Malnutrition has been shown to be the most important predisposing factor influencing a person's resistance to a disease,
its progress and the probabilities of a fatal termination,
and nutritional factors are plainly related to human settlements. The state of nutrition in a community is associated
with difficulties in food production, overpopulation and
inadequate health education.

The second over-riding predisposing factor is the efficiency
of health care. The scale of provision of medical facilities,
the numbers of doctors, nurses, auxiliary medical staffs,
the numbers of clinics and hospital beds, the efficiency of
local traditional medical practices, and the availability of
modern drugs vary from place to place. In some parts of the
world such facilities are virtually non-existent.

Socio-economic circumstances have a very important effect on
the health of human settlements and their investigation provides one of the most difficult of epidemiological problems.
The factors are numerous and include inter alia the basic
intelligence, the general education, health education, home

and parentcraft, and general levels of ability of the families concerned, their earning capacity, their dietary skills,
habits including alcohol and tobacco consumption, and recrea-
tions. Not only does each of them consitute an influence on
health, but the factors themselves are inter-related thus
making it difficult to assess the value of any one specific
influence.

III. REMEDIAL ACTION

Health promotion in human settlements is essentially dependent
upon provision of decent shelter, nutritious food, safe water,
hygienic disposal of wastes and access to health care. Health
therefore is a beneficiary of economic and social development,
and can be most effectively advanced when included as an integral part of the planning and development for human settlements.·

This approach of aligning health promotion with economic and
social development can be viewed as (a) helping people to
adapt to their environment and (b) helping to improve the
environment so as to facilitate adaptation. This approach
goes beyond the traditional approach of disease control and
involves a new orientation in the attitudes and training of
health workers and in the delivery of health services.

In broad overview, many of the deficiencies of the physical
and social environments of human settlements important to
health are the result of an imbalance between population and
resources. It is possible therefore to improve community
health by improving the state of balance by (a) interventions
which would improve the efficient use of existing resources/
or would find new resources (i.e. resource activities), and
(b) interventions which would influence population distribution (i.e. human resource activities).

Financial and Material Resource Activities

The general objective of these activities is to increase the
resources available to a country or settlement, thereby accelerating the rate of coping with deficiencies. There are many
ways that health can contribute to, and benefit from, these
activities. For example, improved community sanitation for the
control of rats and insect vectors could produce savings by
reducing the need for curative health services, and in some
countries make available significant quantities of food resources that would otherwise be spoiled.

The different types of activities to augment financial and
material resources can be grouped as follows :

1. improving utilization and maintenance of available resources ;

2. exploiting unutilized potential resources ; and
3. seeking new resources.

Human Resource Activities

The general objective of these activities is to moderate
excessive population movement which may exa erbate the balance
between population and resources in settlements. This is
possible through (a) providing people with necessary knowledge and skills to improve their income within their present
settlement (manpower development) ; (b) providing facilities
and amenities that improve the standards of living and reduce
the disparity between standards of living in various human
settlements (reducing disparity in living standards) ; and
(c) enhancing factors which help adaptation and adjustement
to the physical and social environments through popular participation in various activities of the settlement (popular
participation).

Although numerous examples of the symbiotic inter-dependence
of health and social and economic development of settlements
can be cited, it is a field that lacks precise definition.
In large measure the effective integration of health into the
planning and development of human settlements will be dependent upon elaboration of methods and justification of economic
and social costs related to the benefits to health, and contributions of health. For the effective operation of this
partnership role in development of settlements, health workers
will need to broaden their scope of interest to encompass the
general community, an operation which will involve some degree
of retraining and reorganization.

Priorities

The recognition of problems, the will to act, a framework
within which to act, and the capacity to apply the appropriate technology (i.e. manpower, finance, organization,
popular participation) are prequisites for action. Decisions
regarding these can only be made effectively by local and/or
national authorities with the presence of popular support.
Therefore, specific recommendations can be made only for
specific situations. However, the following health priorities
are a guide to action since they cover the four major factors influencing health in human settlements.

Malnutrition is a feature of many human settlements and the
evidence indicates that it plays a predominant role in influencing disease prevalence and mortality, particularly in
developing countries. A vicious circle exists in that diarrhoeal diseases, a prominent cause of infant and child death
in these countries, exacerbate the state of malnutrition.

Communicable diseases still have a profound negative influence
on health, even though there have been great advances in con-

trol. Many are related to poor environmental conditions, contaminated water supply, inadequate wastes disposal and failure to manage the environment to control animal and insect
vectors of disease.

Environmental health conditions have a major influence on
health. In addition to contaminated water supply and lack of
hygienic waste disposal, ill effects are created by overcrowding, the physical structure of dwellings, air pollution,
contamination of food, mismanagement of land and hazardous
exposures in the working environment.

Health care services in many parts of the world are gravely
inadequate. In some settlements there is a virtual absence
of health staffs, clinics and hospital beds. Community participation is one of the most valuable ways of extending the
provision of health care services.

REFERENCES :

The material in this paper has been drawn from the following
documents prepared by the World Health Organization for
Habitat : United Nations Conference on Human Settlements and
also for the Technical Discussions at the Twenty-ninth World
Health Assembly on the subject "The Health Aspects of Human
Settlements".

1. Martin, A.E. (1975) Health and environment in human set-
    tlements, United Nations (Unpublished restricted document
    A/CONF/70/B/2).

2. World Health Organization (1976) Human settlements and
    health (Unpublished WHO document CWS/HS/76.1).

3. Novick, R.E. (1976) Human settlements infrastructure.
    Basic sanitary services : water supply - excreta, sewage
    and solid wastes disposal - drainage (Unpublished WHO
    document CWS/HS/76.1).

4. World Health Organization (1976) Community development
    approaches for the improvement of health (Unpublished
    WHO document SHS/HS/76.1).

5. World Health Organization (1976) Human settlements infra-
    structure. Control of environmental pollution and other
    hazards (Unpublished WHO document CEP/HS/76.1).

6. World Health Organization (1975) Suggested outline for
    use by countries in discussing "The Health Aspects of
    Human Settlements" for the Technical Discussions at the

Twenty-ninth World Health Assembly 1976 (Unpublished WHO
document CWS/75.2).

7. World Health Organization (1976) Background document based
    on summary reports received from countries and other mate-
    rial for reference and use at the Technical Discussions
    on "The Health Aspects of Human Settlements" (Unpublished
    WHO document A29/Technical Discussions).

PLANNING FOR URBAN WASTES AS A VALUABLE RESOURCE

Geoffrey Stanford
Agro City Inc., Greenhills, Texas, U. S. A.

1. INTRODUCTION

In this era of explosive population growth and massive flight to the city it
is understandable that city planners should focus most of their attention
onto engineering issues: methods of housing the people, water supply,trans-
port & communication, for example. This focus on construction diverts their
attention from planning for people to planning for facilities, and the biological needs of the people are forgotten. This is particularly the case for
food supply. No matter how splendidly a city is designed, it cannot thrive
unless sufficient food is available for its people both now and into the for-
seeable future. So planning for city growth requires planning for increased
food supply; and any city plan which does not include provision for enough
fertile land for its agricultural base is incomplete. In this paper I will
offer the outlines of a regional plan for city growth which includes food
supply. It is a strategy which integrates the agricultural supply system
with the city consumption system and provides for detrital recycle. Thus
they can grow side-by-side in a balanced partnership with each other which is
based on the natural principles of the ecosystem energy flow. And, strangely
enough, as I unfold the outline, you will find that although it is founded on
wise wastes management, it also provides for water supply, for flood and erosion control, and for forestry and wildlife reserves. As a further bonus,
you will find that the basic regional energy budget is in surplus.

1.   BACKGROUND

I will start by giving a few working figures. Then I will give a summary
outline of some aspects of the soil-plant relationship, with special emphasis
on why the soil needs a continuing energy supply if it is to remain productive. And then I will show how a city can be planned to fit into this pattern, and so to secure its food supply.

1.1. Some Figures
Every person needs about 2,500 Calories of food per day (B3.28). Average
world production of grain is about 2 tonnes/ha (B3.28), so each person needs
about 0.125 ha. of agricultural land to provide their annual food in calories:
here I am talking of carbohydrate foods, whether grain or tubers - the
staples. In addition each person needs about 0.05 ha. of land to provide
their fresh vegetables and fruits - the varietals. Each city person produces
about 1 tonne of refuse per year, of which 800kg is of plant or animal origin
(see table 1.1.) and nearly all that material, in most large cities today, is
dumped into open pits or mounds and so is withdrawn from the ecosystem. This
material has an energy value, by dry weight, about half that of good quality
coal. Each city person uses 100-1000 liters of water per day (this large

range depends on the amount and type of industry in that city); and nearly
all that water, in most large cities today, is discharged (wasted) into
rivers or the sea. To grow 1 tonne of grain or timber requires about 1000
tonnes (1 million liters) of water. (B3.34). Each person needs about 2 ha.
of forest to provide a self-sustaining fuel supply for cooking and to feed an
electric generating plant (AA.25). These figures are not precise, but they
are correct to perhaps +50% for most societies, which is well within the var-
iances that already exist between peoples of different societies, and between
the extremes within any one society.

Table 1.1.

Composition of Municipal Refuse,%.

Paper & Packaging	60
Food	10
Garden Refuse	10
Inerts; glass, plastic etc:	10
Metals: (iron 6, aluminum 3, brass 1 copper 1)	10
	100%

1.2. Some Soil Theory

Green plants absorb sunlight energy and store it in their leaves and wood as
complex sugars; cellulose, for example. In technical terms, we can describe
this activity as a solar energy transduction and storage system .
In an undisturbed ecosystem the greatest part of this annual plant growth
falls at the end of the season to the soil as 'detrital rain'. A large variety
of insects ('comminuters') break it up into small fragments, most of which
they take underground(26.90).   These fragments are further biodegraded by a
myriad variety of fungi, bacteria, and other soil micro-organisms
('soilorgs'). Most of these soilorgs live in the water film that coats the
soil grains. They secrete their digestive enzymes into this water film; the
enzymes break down the celluloses and other insoluble large molecules of the
detritus into small soluble molecules. These diffuse into the water film;
the soilorgs absorb them in solution, and extract the stored energy component
to drive their own life cycles. At first sight this seems a haphazard program, but since all the soilorgs are working in this same way, it turns out
to be very efficient.
There are some interesting spinoff benefits from this seemingly crude program
which are of especial interest to us. Firstly, plant roots are working in
the same water film, and they can and do absorb some of the small soluble
molecules. This is one aspect of soil 'fertility'. Secondly, the fungal
threads are ramifying all over the surfaces of the soil grains in their search
for nutrients; this richly complex mesh of microfibrils ties the soil grains
together, and contributes to aggregation, crumb formation, and 'tilth'. This
is one aspect of soil conservation and reduction of soil erosion. Thirdly,
the same soilorgs, both alive and dead, make relatively large quantities of
slimes, mucigels and similar substances which have the capacity to absorb and
to hold water up to 1000 times their own dry weight (B3.34). This is one aspect of the water-holding capacity of the soil.
For these reasons a rich and continuous flow of detritus maintains soil fertility, resists soil erosion, and increases water holding capacity (80.44).
But when, through overgrazing, over-harvesting, and over-felling, the detrital
flow is reduced below a critical minimum, then these soil characters are impaired, with the results that we all know (B3.09). Excessive tilling of bare
soil will further aggravate these abuses, partly because bare soil is hotter

than is soil under a plant canopy, and so the available detritus is more
quickly biodegraded; and partly because the bare soil is subjected to the
full fury of wind blow and of raindrop assault (B3.37). As a result a
farmed-out soil, its ability to resist erosion already impaired, is subjected
to greatly increased erosional forces, and so the valuable once-fertile topsoil is easily carried away in the floodwaters to become objectionable riv-
erine and estuarine silt.
But these damages,even when well advanced, can be stopped and reversed: soil
fertility can be restored and erosion checked by re-using urban wastes in
accord with environmental principles. Paper, after all,is only timber which
has been finely comminuted. There is no fault in borrowing that timber from
the ecosystem and in using it to write and to print on, providing we return
it to the detrtal stream after we have finished using it. And equally there
is no fault in borrowing surface or deep aquifer waters if we return them
to the head-waters or the recharge basins of origin after we have used them.
With these principles established, I will now outline a resource and energy-
conserving strategy which can be adopted by urbanised societies now to secure
their food supply and to enhance their enviromental circumstances. With
evident modifications ,this strategy can be adapted for the development of
new cities anywhere.

2.   A PLANNING STRATEGY

2.1. Wastes Management

2.1.1.Solid waste. A city of 100,000 people generates about 400 tonnes of
refuse each working day. This refuse is collected in the normal way and is
passed through a shredder, and the fist-sized pieces are dumped in a pond
(see Figure 2.1.). Wood, some plastics, and the oils and fats will come to
the surface. They are skimmed off, and the oils are extracted and re-used;
the residues are put back into the shredder for further size reduction. The
paper and other plant residues, together with the now finely minced wood and
plastics, stay in suspension in the water. This slurry is pumped continuously
into the sewage treatment plant, while treated sewage effluent is pumped in
to replace it and to maintain constant level in the pond. At the end of each
week the pond is pumped dry, and the metals, glass, and similar heavy materials which have sunk to the bottom are dredged out, washed, and passed under
a magnet to recover the iron. Copper, brass, and aluminum are recovered, and
the inert residues are used as hardcore for roadbeds and fill material. In
these ways the refuse is entirely recycled.

2.1.2 Sewage. The solids:water ratio of sewage is normally about 1:1000.
Adding the paper slurry will raise the solids content to about 1:100; this
mix is easily pumped, and it can be treated as if it were the normal,thinner,
sewage stream. The treated sewage is clarified in the usual way. Some of
the resulting green water (clarified effluent) is pumped to fishponds and
other aquaculture programs; some is pumped to the solids pond as described
above (2.1.1). The remainder is pumped out and used to irrigate agricultural
and forest lands. Some of this irrigation water is lost by evapo-transpira-
tion, some of it is filtered as it flows through the topsoil and into the
streams and rivers; and some percolates through the deep soil and recharges
the underground aquifers. In these ways the green water is cleansed and restored to the same pure quality it had when it was taken by the city.
The sludge that is settled out of the treated sewage stream is an interesting
material; it contains much more carbohydrate than ordinary municipal sludge

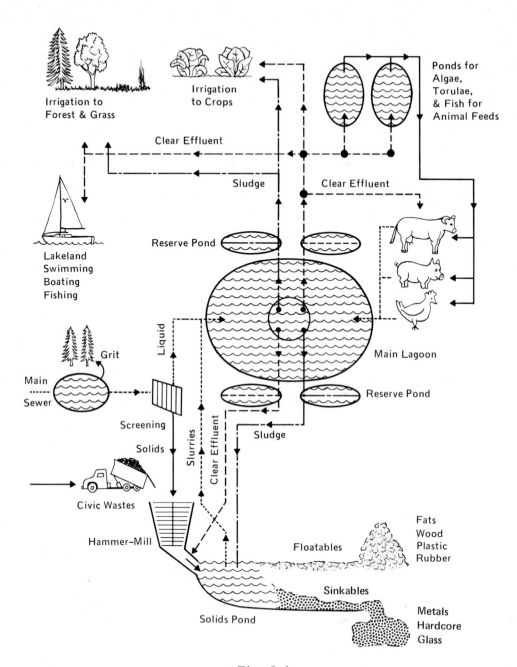

Fig. 2.1

(because of all the paper that was contributed from the solid waste) and so
has the characteristics of a good compost: it provides immediate fertility to
the soil. The high energy content of this excess carbohydrate provides a
more thorough destruction of pathogens in the sewage, and it also prevents de-
nitrification (destruction) of the nitrate in the raw sewage. So although the
C:N ratio (carbohydrate: nitrate ratio) in this mixed sludge is much higher
than in normal sewage sludge, the actual daily output of nitrate fertiliser
from this combined sewage/solids treatment plant is also much greater: it is a
resource-conserving strategy.
In these several ways wastes are seen as a resource for continued re-use, not
as a problem for disposal. The normal water and detrital cycles of the regional eco-system are re-established. The peoples who live in this system only
borrow these materials; they insert themselves into the cycle but do not disrupt it. They live symbiotically, because they perturb it and actively maintain the perturbation, but they no longer are parasitic on it.
With these background concepts extablished, I will next describe how the
regional food supply and economy can be developed to take advantage of these
management strategies.   And then I will show how any city that adopts this
strategy can be planned to grow quickly yet flexibly, while always maintaining
the prime detritus-based energy cycle.

2.2.   The Agro-Industrial Park

The greater part of the products of this combined sewage and refuse resource
recovery complex is spread over the agricultural land. It is most economical
therefore to put this complex in open country, perhaps 20-50km from the city
of supply; this new complex is preferably built near to an existing village
so that manpower is available at once to work in it. Since the program
quickly raises the soil fertility, a region which has poor original or present
fertility is acceptable. The metals recovered from the refuse provide high-
grade scrap, so smithies, and similar metal working industries establish nearby. Metal-working is an ancient craft easily learned, and it lends itself
well to being established at a family scale - 'intermediate technology'
(B3.23). Many of these products are used to build the ever-growing complex
and to provide the farm equipment for the evergrowing agriculture. Production
of soft fruits and fresh vegetables soon increases beyond the daily needs of
the city: canneries, jam-making, and other processing factories develop. As
ever more land becomes ever more fertile from the ever-increasing flow of detritus, so staple crops - beans, corn, manioc, are grown; and pasture and forestry is established to accept and cleanse the fast increasing supply of green
water. At this stage the system starts to support dairy herds, poultry farms,
and swine; egg- packing stations, milk, cheese and butter factories, and
slaughter-houses are now needed to process these products, to sell them to the
city, and to export the surplus wider afield. These factories produce large
quantities of biodegradable wastes, which in turn are processed into feed and
fertiliser. Unusable residues are discharged into the sewage or the solid
waste stream, and again recycled. Obviously therefore the most economical
place to put these factories is as close to the resources recovery complex as
possible, so as to minimize transport time and costs. By now that original
complex has become just one of many units, albeit the key component, in a
fully-established and thriving agro-industrial park. The many factories in
this park on the one hand support, and on the other hand are supported by, the
richly fertile agricultural soil around them. And together they supply the
city food and consume the city wastes.
In these ways the high costs to a city of waste diposal have been converted

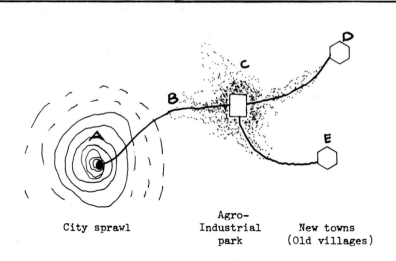

City sprawl   Agro-   New towns
                     Industrial   (Old villages)
                     park

Fig. 2.3.1. First stages of development of an
agro-industrial complex for an existing metropolis.

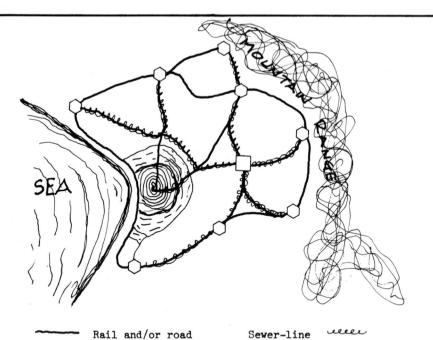

——————— Rail and/or road   Sewer-line ιιιιιι

Fig. 2.3.2. Completed development of the
satellite towns and included agriculture.

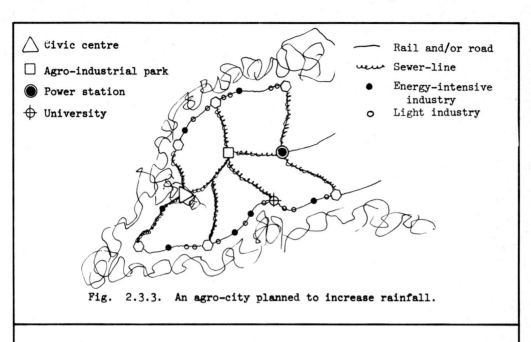

Fig. 2.3.3. An agro-city planned to increase rainfall.

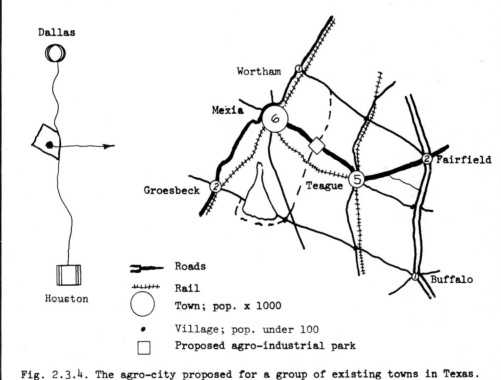

Fig. 2.3.4. The agro-city proposed for a group of existing towns in Texas.

into financial benefits both to that city and to many members of the community; this represents an increased tax base, and hence an increased income to the city; other things being equal, taxes can be lowered. Furthermore the social assets in terms of job-opportunity, growth of the technical skills pool, locally grown food, and improvement of the environment, benefit all the people.

2.3. The City Plan

At some intermediate stage of the development of this agro-industrial park a simple model of the system can be described as follows:-
The already over-large, and still fast-growing, city (see Fig. 2.3.1,a) has developed a transport corridor (rail, road, and pipe-lines) 50km or more out into the country (2.3.1,b). The first 15-25km pass through the densely built city and suburbs, the last 10-20 km are through fertile farmland, which is kept free of buildings under the plan.
The agro-industrial park makes a node at the end of the corridor (c.). The active day and night transfer of food from farm and factory to rail freight-car makes that area unsuitable for homes; these are built in the existing village, some 25-35km away, which provided much of the original work-force (d). When that village has become a town of some 10,000 people, most of whom are working in the agro-industrial park, building is stopped in accordance with the plan, and another town is started some 25-35km away (e). This new town is built either by expanding another existing village or by breaking new ground. In either case all prime flat land is reserved for agriculture and only the second-rate land on the montaine slope is used for building.
Large areas on the high ground above the towns are planted and preserved as forests; the purpose of this is to maintain rainfall, to prevent flooding, erosion and siltation from the higher ground and to provide recreation areas and wild-life preserves (39.81); it also provides an area where the green waters can be absorbed and filtered when the flat agricultural land is frozen or is otherwise unsuited to irrigation(40.47). Ultimately it provides a renewable fuel and building timber resource.(AA.25). In predominantly flat lands the forests are planted as shelter-belts (34.10) to a pattern which will also enhance rainfall (see section 2.4, following).
This pattern of building the villages, one by one, into towns to a limit of 10,000 people each, and then starting another, is continued steadily in a ring round the agro-industrial park. The final number and their distances apart are governed by the productivity of the land; this will be determined by its ultimate fertility and the rainfall. In dry regions, the available flow of sewage waters will be an important factor, and the installation of an efficient water supply and sewer collection system will be an essential factor in providing the integrity of the cycle.
Figure 2.3.2 shows a fully developed agro-city planned as a satellite town system around an established sea-port metropolis. Figure 2.3.3 shows an agro-city planned for a land-locked valley basin which presently has only small subsistence farming villages, is remote from a metropolis, and is to be developed as a planned new town. Figure 2.3.4 shows an agro-city planned for a decayed agricultural region which has lost its fertility, and most of its population, but which still has a good communications network; it is to be redeveloped to supply food to the two metropoli.

2.4. The Regional Plan- Weather Modification

It is evident that strong planning powers, effectively enforced, are required to develop and maintain this strategy. But it is important to keep it intact

so that a further benefit can be effectively developed for the region; increased rainfall, as I will now explain.

2.4.1. <u>The Ring City construct. Physical analysis</u>. The municipality, when
fully developed, consists of some 10 towns; those are spaced some 20km apart
in a ring whose diameter is some 75km. Each town generates so much heat that
it is several degrees warmer than the open country. Its factories, power
stations, and other sources of intense heat production (B3.22) are sited so
as to form, with those towns, a more or less complete ring around the municipality (Fig. 2.3.3). The region now can be seen as having a ring of raised
temperature which surrounds a core of lowered temperature. This lower temperature is due in part to evapotranspiration from the plant growth, and in
part to the lowered albedo (absorbtion of sunlight) of the vegetation. Water
laden winds that blow across this region will be raised by the combined
effects of (i) the turbidity arising from the eddy-currents caused by the
town buildings (ii) the heat islands effect of the towns (38.21), and (iii)
the air currents rising from the heat foci already described (37.01). If on
any given day those winds are raised by these forces sufficiently to cause
condensation and then precipitation of their contained water vapour,(AA.01)
this will fall as rain on the green agricultural core   (AA. 51). Clearly
this effect cannot operate every day of the year; but even if it operates on
only a few days in each year it improves the general water-balance of the
region; this improves the crop cover slightly, and so reinforces the phenomenon on the next occasion; a beneficial cycle is established because the increased vegetation protects the raindrops from immediate evaporation, and the
rainfall is retained in the plant root zone. This effect can be important;
consider for example a semi-arid zone with a mean annual rainfall of only
35 cm, of which 20 cm presently evaporates immediately before or as it strikes
the ground; this leaves only 15 cm for plant growth. Since 10 cm is needed for
basal growth, only 5 cm is available for crop yield. It is calculated that by
establishing year-round plant cover, at least 20 cm would be retained; this
could provide a doubling of the crop (63.30).

There is one feature of this program which needs to be emphasised; enhancing
the rainfall by this strategy does not 'steal' the rain from the people and
the region further downwind; this water is soon returned to the wind by evapotranspiration, and so can fall again: it has only been 'borrowed', as it were,
in transit. But, during the borrowing, an additional quantity of sunlight
energy has been fixed, to benefit of the municipality and of its peoples.

3.   <u>DISCUSSION</u>

Is this strategy practical: can it be done? And if so, why has it not been
done already? In technical terms, it certainly can be done. Indeed, until
the motor-car changed everything, it was normal for city wastes (domestic
refuse, some sewage, and a vast amount of stable-manures) to be taken at night
by horse and cart and by barge back to the farms in the same wagons that had
brought in food, hay and straw earlier that morning. The resulting fertility
of the soil surrounding the cities was astounding, and supported a flourishing
market-garden industry; for example the soil at Hampton, outside London, is
still unusually fertile fifty years after the last load was taken out there.
Of course, the example stops there, because the fertile ring was all round
the homes (which later were built on it) whereas I am describing a city built
round the fertile land.

The roadblocks today are emotional, political, and economic. If it hasn't
been done already, would it not be risky to be the first city to do it? When

land is divided into hundreds of different plots of all sizes in private ownership, how can you assemble into a single plan the large area needed? It
sounds sensible, but how can we know that it will pay off? and who will get
the profit?
But starts have been made. At Odessa, in West Texas, which is a semi-arid
region, we have a city of 80,000 people which is using all their urban resources to this strategy, and starting to restore the overgrazed prairie
around them. In Central Texas, between Dallas (2 million people) and Houston
(3 million) are ten cities which already exist in a ring around land which
was once fertile but which is now 'farmed-out' (Fig. 2.3.4) They are discussing with 3 counties and several federal agencies the possibility of
setting up this type of program together, to accept the wastes from Dallas,
and to export food to Dallas and to Houston. This plan calls for the orderly
growth of each city, one after the other, from their present shrunken size
(some which had 1,000 people when the land was fertile now have less than
100) to 10,000 each; they will then make a self-sustaining prosperous municipality of 100,000 people. And outline surveys have already been made to
adapt this strategy to, for example, Manila and Jakarta, and for new large
cities that are still in the early planning stages.

3.1. A Case Example

Greater Manila (Republic of the Philippines) provides a good example for the
application of this strategy, because it illustrates so many of the problems
that are facing other rapidly-growing cities in LDCs. The flight of the
people from the land is occuring quicker than their labour-productivity at
the farms is being replaced by mechanisation. Food supply per person is
dwindling partly from this lessened production, partly from the loss of soil
fertility, and partly from the increasing population. That all these factors
are not at work in every instance, and that some of them are conceealed by
fertilisation and green revolution programs, by lack of statistical surveys,
or by political considerations, further complicates the more obvious socio-
economic problems, such as the escalating costs of land under speculator
pressure, and the emphasis on industrialisation regardless of unemployment,
which are also at work in jeopardising the food supply. Around the central
city area are large slums alongside fine new office and shopping complexes,
the sewage management program cannot keep up with the rate of increase in the
population, and solid waste management is embarassed. Manila however has a
special point of excellence; under the personal attention of the President,
the people in one of the largest slums, the Tondo, are being rehoused on a
filled in marsh a few kilometres away, the Dagatdagatan.
A large centralised waste management complex can be developed in the new
Tondo area, and the small family industries which center on metals recovery
and refabrification can also be concentrated there. The bio-degradeable
residues can be taken out to say, the Araneta Ranch (100km. away) where the
land has lost its fertility. As the productivity rises again under this
program the children of the existing farmers, who are thinking of migrating
into Manila, will find that there is plenty of work for them at home; and
later the food-processing factories will need to import labour - where better
than from the Tondo? In this way the normal economics of job-opportunity
will stop the flight from the land and then reverse the flow: people will
move from Manila back to the country. On the other hand the fast-increasing
flow of perishable fresh foods from Araneta must be distributed in the metropolis; where better to develop a dairy and vegetable produce wholesaling
market, comparable to Covent Garden (London) or Les Halles(Paris) than at
Dagatdagatan?

3.2. Difficulties

In this short outline I have been able to give only the main features of an idealised flow-chart of the total strategy. Clearly these details will differ for each region in which it is applied. And I have not been able even to touch on some of the problems which it may entail: for example, will the people accept such large-scale long-range planning? Are there any health risks to man or the environment? Will the program cause excessive salt build-build-up in the soil, and so be self-destructive? But there is another, over-over-riding,question which must also be faced: are those risks any greater than the ones we already know we will have if we continue the present uncontrolled urban sprawl? Is it not therefore worth trying? And if we suspect that it cannot be carried through all its growth stages under a free economy as we presently understand that, then it can be done in a closed ecosystem: for example, an island, financed by a consortium of world monies - World Bank, US/AID, OPEC? Malta, Cyprus, or Majorca in the Mediterranean? Possibly not: the problems of land ownership may be too great. But the peoples of one of the islands of Indonesia, Micronesia, the Philippines, or the Malabar coast who are still engaged in subsistence farming, may welcome the opportunities inherent in this strategy for an orderly growth of homes, food, technology and industrialisation, based on the principles of closed-cycle planning. In those countries the ideas and experiences of Chang and of Weitz (B3.21;63.80) could be instrumental in gaining the farmer's attention, his participation, and his enthusiasm.

4.   SUMMARY

An urban planning strategy is offered which achieves a symbiotic relationship for a municipality in synthesis with its rural and agricultural hinterland. Taking the managment of municipal wastes as its apparent starting point,it is seen to provide a balanced energy-flow eco-system, soil stabilisation and flood control, a secure food supply for its people, and a favorable economic base for growth of industrialisation and technology. As an end-result it offers opportunity for regional weather modification and increased rainfall. This strategy is applicable to existing metropoli or to open land, to continental regions or to islands, and to almost any climate.

GLOSSARY

Such key words as 'city' and 'town' mean different things to different people: I describe below the meaning of some of the words in the sense that I have used them:

village:	about 100 families, or 500 people; a clan or tribe.
town:	about 10,000 people; most of them know each other.
city:	about 100,000 people; they can feel a common bond between each other, of 'belonging'.
metropolis:	over 1,000,000 people. The sense of communal responsibility is largely lost.
municipality:	a region which includes open land, villages and towns supporting about 100,000 people. A dispersed city.
agro-city:	a self-dependent municipality planned and operated through the energy cycle described in this paper. The region supports and is supported by the people under conditions which provide continuous opportunity for strong feelings of interpersonal responsibility.

REFERENCES

26.90   Kuhnelt, W. (1961) <u>Soil Biology</u>, Faber and Faber, London, England.
34.10   Caborn, J.M. (1965) <u>Shelterbelts and Windbreaks</u>,
        Faber and Faber, London, England.
37.01   Peterson, J.T. (1972) <u>The Climate of Cities</u>,
        U.S.E.P.A. North Carolina.
38.21   Geiger, R. (1971) <u>The Climate near the Ground</u>,
        Harvard University Press, Cambridge, Mass.
39.81   Kolata, G.B. (1974) <u>Theoretical Ecology, Beginnings of a Predictive
        Science,</u> Science,183,4123.
40.47   Sopper, W.E. and Kardos, L.T. (1973) <u>Recycling Treated Municipal
        Wastewater and Sludge through Forest and Cropland</u>,
        The Pennsylvania State Press.
63.30   Stanford, G.B. (1974) <u>The Odessa Project</u>,
        Environic Foundation International, Indiana, U.S.A.
63.80   Weitz, R. (1971) <u>From Peasant to Farmer</u>,
        Columbia University Press, New York.
80.44   Stanford, G.B. (1975) <u>The Utilization of Municipal Wastes in Soil</u>,
        Report for U.S.E.P.A., unpublished.
AA.01   Stanford, G.B. (1974) <u>Advertent Regional Weather Modification by
        Planned Energy Distribution in New City Design</u>,
        grant application, unpublished.
AA.25   Stanford, G.B. (1974) <u>Short-Rotation Forestry as a Solar Energy
        Transducer and Storage System,</u> in preparation.
AA.51   Stanford, G.B. (1973) <u>On Making Rain</u>,
        Institute for Storm Research, Houston, mimeo.
B3.09   Carter, V.G. and Dale, T. (1974) <u>Topsoil and Civilization</u>,
        University of Oklahoma Press.
B3.21   Chang, C-W. (1974) <u>A Strategy for Agricultural and Rural Development
        in Asian Countries,</u> Southeast Asian Regional Center for Graduate
        Study and Research in Agriculture College, Laguna, Philippines.
B3.22   Hanna, S.R. and Gifford, F.A. (1975) <u>Meteorological Effects of Energy
        Dissipation at Large Power Parks</u>,Bulletin American Meteorological
        Society; 56,10, 1069-76.
B3.23   Schumacher, E.F. (1973) <u>Small is Beautiful</u>,Harper and Row, New York.
B3.28   Brown, L.R. (1975) <u>The World Food Prospect</u>,Science,190, p 1053-59.
B3.34   Ehrlich, P.R; Holm, R.W. and Soule, M.E. (1973) <u>Introductory Biology</u>
        McGraw-Hill, New York.

WASTE RECYCLING

Henry P. NAVEAU and Jean-Paul NASSAUX

Groupe de Physico-Chimie Minérale et de Catalyse,
Université Catholique de Louvain, B-1348 Louvain-la-Neuve, Belgique.

Service Propreté Publique de l'Agglomération de Bruxelles,
rue de France, 71, B-1060 Bruxelles, Belgique.

SUMMARY

Waste recycling through separate collections of paper and glass is
examined in the city of Brussels for 1974 and 1975. Results are
encouraging and financial balance is positive. Potential for extension
of collects, both by shifting to weekly collection and by covering
the whole city would allow to recycle 31.000 tons of old papers and
16.000 tons of glass per year for a population of 1.050.000 people.
These amounts represent respectively 30 and 15 kg per inhabitant and
per year, and 12 % of urban solid wastes. Total revenue for the city
is estimated, taking into account installation of an incineration plant.
It is also shown that this method of recycling paper and glass is fully
compatible with incineration of urban solid wastes.

INTRODUCTION

Separate collections, particularly of glass and paper, have been much
developped these las years as a way of recovering and recycling
materials without applying to important technical means, while
alleviating the problem of disposal of urban solid wastes. First
separate collections in Brussels have been organized by the Borough
of Uccle in 1972, then progressively extended by the "Agglomération de
Bruxelles", an organization grouping the 19 boroughs of the city of
Brussels. The separate collections cover presently over two thirds
of the population of Brussels.

Amounts collected and cost price are examined for 1974 and 1975, as well as prospects for the future, taking into account foreseen installation of an incineration plant and possible increase in collection frequency.

ORGANIZATION OF COLLECTIONS

Separate collections are organized, since November 1973, by the "Agglomération de Bruxelles" in five boroughs of the city, with a total of 248.000 people. Other "communes" joined this group in the year 1974 (100.000 inhabitants in March, 105.000 in September and 107.000 in November). Finally, in September 1975, three more communes came into this group, bringing the concerned population to 727.000 people.

Separate collections take place once a month. They are announced from one to five months in advance by a prospectus indicating the streets for each day of collect. People are asked to prepare bundles of approximately 5 kg paper and to place glass vessels into normal refuse bins or in cardboard boxes to be picked up. These two separate collections are simultaneous, but they take place on a day different to usual collects. Collections on request are done in other communes ; they are not considered here.

Papers are stored at Neder-Over-Hembeek (10 km from center) and glass at Anderlecht (7 km from center). Papers are carried away by the buyer while glass is transported at the expense of the Agglomération but by a private transporter, to a bottle-plant.

Normal collects of solid wastes take place three times a week ; most of wastes is brought in two transfer stations, from where it is evacuated toward two landfills by a private firm. As to the rest, it is directly transported to a small incineration plant.

QUANTITIES COLLECTED

        Following data are reproduced in table I :
Population of the concerned communes on December 31, 1974 ; total quantities of refuse collected by the "Agglomération de Bruxelles" (including voluminous wastes) and quantities of paper and glass separately collected.

The annual amount of refuse generated in the different communes is calculated from those elements, as a proportion, based on population, of the total of the city refuse (368,5 kg/inhabitant in 1974 and 368,8 kg/inhabitant in 1975, or 1 kg per inhabitant per day). The result per person has not changed in one year. Population is considered on December 31, 1974, the middle of the observation period. The fall of population number in the 16 concerned communes has been equal to 2.14 % in three years ; the error on mean yearly results is thus below 1 % and is neglected.

Amounts of paper and glass collected by inhabitant in each commune
as well as their ratio to total urban solid wastes are also calculated
(table II). Examination of these tables immediately shows the quite
important increase in the yield of separate collections from 1974 to
1975. One can see that, especially for paper, the yield per inhabitant almost doubles in many cases, whatever the results in 1974.
Collected quantities are very similar for paper and glass in any
commune but vary widely from commune to commune, oscillating between
3 and 15 kg/hab./year in 1975 with an average of 6.06 and 5.74 kg
respectively for paper and glass. In the five communes concerned
during the whole year 1974, total amounts of paper have increased
by 93 % from 1974 to 1975, those of glass by 71 %. Glass collection
is, from the beginning, more efficient than that of paper but it is
more difficult to increase its yield. If, on another way, it is
assumed in first approximation that glass represents 7 % and paper
40 % of urban solid wastes, it appears that, in 1975, 22 % of glass
and 4.1 % of paper theoretically present have been collected by
separate collections.

Increase of yield within those two years is certainly due to
sensibilization of the population. It is likely that more households
participate at the collects and that each household keeps more of its
papers and glass for the monthly collection. The following fact is
significant from this point of view : in 1974, September collection
gave 40 % more paper and 45 % more glass than the average of April-
May-June, while, in 1975, this increase was 85 % for paper and 94 %
for glass. This shows that the population saved more paper and glass
during the 1975 holidays than during 1974's.

Discrepancies between collection rates in various communes could be
explained by different social conditions, particularly in housing and
by more or less advanced sensibilisation of population. It should
however be remarked that total amount of residue per commune is
theoretical because based on an average. Real amounts could be
somewhat higher or lower.

COST OF SEPARATE COLLECTIONS

Sale of Products

The sale price of old papers by the Agglomération has known important
ups and downs these last two years. Until March 1975, the price
included delivery at the paper mill, transport being done by the
Agglomeration's own trucks. Since April, 1975, price is fixed with
removal from Brussels by the mill. After deducing the estimated
transport price (until March, 1975), the average net price for sale
of paper is 1.300 FB/ton in 1974 and 100 FB/ton in 1975.

Unsorted glass is sold, in 1974, delivered at the mill ; the estimated
cost of transport by the agglomeration is equal to the selling price.
In 1975, glass is sold at 400 FB/ton delivered, from which the trans-

TABLE I. Population of the communes on 31-12-1974 and amounts of urban solid wastes collected, on the total and by separate collections

	Population (31-12-74)	Annual amount of urban solid wastes (1) in tons 1975	Annual amount of paper collected, in tons		Annual amount of glass collected, in tons	
			1974	1975	1974	1975
Auderghem	33,722	12,437	152.6	290.5	158.3	292.8
Etterbeek	48,665	17,948	141.4	302.0	189.3	270.3
Woluwe St.Lambert	46,854	17,280	142.7	350.2	163.5	342.1
Woluwe St.Pierre	40,439	14,915	203.1	414.9	211.5	398.7
Uccle	78,512	28,956	467.8	785.4	477.9	754.0
Berchem, Jette, Koekelberg, Ganshoren	100,393	37,026	176.8 (2)	525.7	221.6 (2)	529.0
Watermael-Boitsfort	23,719	8,748	66.8 (3)	364.7	56.1 (3)	233.6
Ixelles	81,515	30,064	141.8 (3)	703.1	165.8 (3)	675.6
Forest	54,017	19,922	27.8 (4)	270.0	33.8 (4)	323.7
St.Gilles	52,981	19,540	19.0 (4)	159.6	24.5 (4)	167.0
Schaerbeek, St.Josse, Evere	166,294	61,332	-	243.3(5)	-	184.4 (5)
Total	727,111	268,168	1539.2	4409.4	1702.3	4171.1
Agglomération	1,052,750	388,270	1539.2	4507.8	1702,3	4174.4

(1) Calculated on base of the total amount collected for the agglomeration, proportionately to the population of each commune.

(2) Organized from March 1974
(3) "   "   "   September 1974
(4) "   "   "   November 1974
(5) "   "   "   September 1975.

TABLE II. Amounts of papers and glass collected by resident and their proportion of total urban solid wastes, by commune.

	Papers collected by resident (kg)		Glass collected by resident (kg)		Proportion of the urban solid wastes in 1975 (%)	
	1974	1975	1974	1975	Paper	Glass
Auderghem	4.53	8.61	4.69	8.68	2.34	2.35
Etterbeek	2.91	6.21	3.89	5.55	1.68	1.51
Woluwe St.Lambert	3.05	7.47	3.49	7.30	2.03	1.98
Woluwe St.Pierre	5.02	10.26	5.23	9.86	2.78	2.67
Uccle	5.96	10.00	6.09	9.50	2.71	2.60
Berchem, Ganshoren, Jette, Koekelberg	2.15 (6)	5.24	2.70 (6)	5.27	1.42	1.43
Watermael-Boitsfort	7.74 (6)	15.38	6.50 (6)	9.85	4.17	2.67
Ixelles	4.78 (6)	8.63	5.59 (6)	8.29	2.34	2.25
Forest	2.77 (6)	5.00	3.44 (6)	5.99	1.36	1.62
St.Gilles	1.97 (6)	3.01	2.54 (6)	3.15	0.82	0.85
Schaerbeek, St.Josse, Evere	-	4.02 (6)	-	3.05 (6)	1.09 (6)	0.83 (6)
Average	-	6.06 (7)	-	5.74 (7)	1.64 (7)	1.56 (7)
Agglomération	1.46	4.28	1.62	3.97	1.16	1.08

(6) By extrapolating to amount which would have been obtained for collection during 11 months (no separate collection during holidays)

(7) Without taking collections in Schaerbeek, Evere and St. Josse into account.

portation cost by a private contractor (223 FB/T) must be deduced ;
this leaves a net price of 177 FB/ton.

Saving on Disposal

The price of removal and landfilling of urban wastes by a private
contractor has increased from 380 FB/ton in 1974 to 597 FB/ton in 1975.
Saving realized on residues which have not to be disposed of
is considered as a revenue.

Cost of Collects

Calculations based on several days shows that an average day of
separate collection allows to collect 8,5 tons of paper and glass.
Considering that the average cost price of one manpower-day is
1,226 FB, that 7 or 8 men are necessary for separate collection and
that working and material charges amount to 580 FB/ton, the price
of collection is as follows :

- Personnel : 7.5 x 1,226 FB =   9,185 FB
- Working and material charges : 8.5 x 580 FB =   4,930 FB
                                                                 ─────────
     Total :   14,175 FB

that is 1,660 FB/ton. The price for a normal collect is 1,550 FB/ton.
Separate collection thus costs 110 FB/ton more than normal collection
as regards collect costs only. It should however be pointed out that
material charges are an average and include for instance maintenance
and amortizing of packing-truck, more expansive than normal trucks
used for separate collections. Finally, if personnel charges were
not included since the "Agglomération de Bruxelles" did not engage
any supplementary worker to realize these collections, the balance
would be favourable.

TOTAL REVENUE

Final cost price, which in fact is a revenue for the agglomeration,
may be calculated as follows :

1974

Sale of paper	: 1,539.2 T x 1300 FB/T	=	2,200,960
Sale of glass	: 1,702.3 T –		–
Higher price of collects	: 3,241.5 T x -110 FB/T	=	- 356,565
Saving on disposal	: 3,241.5 T x 380 FB/T	=	1,231,770
			─────────
Total			3,076,105

1975

Sale of paper	:	4,409.4 T x 100 FB/T	=	440,940
Sale of glass	:	4,171.1 T x 177 FB/T	=	738,284
Higher price of collects	:	8,580.5 T x -110 FB/T	=	- 943,855
Saving on disposal	:	8,580.5 T x 507 FB/T	=	4,350,313

Total   4,585,682

which amounts to 4.36 FB per habitant for all concerned communes.

INCREASE OF FREQUENCY OF SEPARATE COLLECTIONS

The "Agglomération de Bruxelles" studies the possibility of modifying
the frequency of collections. Normal collections would take place
only twice a week whilst separate collections would be once a week.
It is important to try to predict the influence of this modification
on the material and financial balance of the separate collections.

Evaluation of collected amounts is difficult since it depends on the
motivation of the population, hence of its sensibilization. A vigorous
information campaign will be necessary. The regularity of the separate
collection certainly induces a positive habit and a carrying effect.
Besides, the obstacle of lack of space to keep papers and glass is
markedly reduced: they have to be retained only a few days. It seems
reasonable, on base of other experiences, (Ref. 1) to believe that
20 % of papers and 60 % of glass present could be collected. This
would be equivalent to 4.2 % of refuse for glass (15,5 kg/hab./year
or 16,300 ton/year) and to 8 % of refuse for paper (29.5 kg/hab./year
or 31,000 ton/year).

These results imply, in addition to extension of separate collections
to the whole area of the City of Brussels, the necessity to multiply
by 5 the amount of paper actually collected by habitant and by 2.7
the collection of glass. This goal seems realisable over a period
of years, the population acquiring quickly favorable habits as shown
by results of 1975. The weekly separate collections would gather
12 % of urban solid wastes, leaving 88 % by weight to normal collects.

In view of facilitating separate collections, placement of bins
reserved for papers and glass in apartment-buildings could be
an interesting opportunity. An information action would also be
carried among building-keepers as well as public and private administrations, big producers of old papers.

INSTALLATION OF AN INCINERATION PLANT

The "Agglomération de Bruxelles" has decided the construction of
an incineration plant for urban solid wastes, to be located at
approximately 10 km from the center of the City. Its start-up is

foreseen for the beginning of 1979. Extension of separate collection
could modify the heating valve (H.V.) of urban solid wastes (Ref. 2)
and it will decrease their amount. On another way, the saving
realized by non disposal of the products of separate collections
will also be modified.

Influence of Separate Collections on Incinerator Working

The H.V. of urban solid wastes is often estimated at 7,530 KJ/kg (Ref.
3). If, by kilo, 80 g of paper at 13,800 KJ/kg (Ref. 3) and 42 g
glass are withdraws, the H.V. of remaining wastes will be

$$H.V. = \frac{7,530 - (0,080 \times 13,800)}{1 - (0,080 + 0,042)} = 7,320 \text{ KJ/kg.}$$

Analyses have been performed in Brussels on 7 samples of 100 kg taken
on 3 days (April and November 1974, May 1975). These samples,
differing widely for the 3 days by their poisture and non-combustible
content had H.V. of 4, 980 to 7,865 KJ/kg with an average of
6,465 KJ/kg. The mean H.V. of the "cellulose" component was
8,745 KJ/kg. After a separate collection as foreseen here above,
H.V. of remaining wastes would be 6,570 KJ/kg as compared to 6,545
before ! This increase results from the high moisture content of
the withdrawn cellulosic fraction.

Anyway, it is clear that simultaneous separate collection of papers
and glass does not sensibly modify the heating value of remaining
wastes.

The amounts to be burned would decrease by 10 - 15 %.

Saving on treatment

Preliminary studies show that incineration cost for the "Agglomération
de Bruxelles" would be between 350 and 550 FB/Ton, depending upon the
characteristics of the installation (with or without heat and electricity recuperation or materials recycling). If one allows for a
collect of 31,000 tons of paper and 16,300 tons of glass, saving on
treatment would be somewhere between 16,5 and 26 millions FB/year,
in place of the 24 millions at current price of disposal by landfilling.

PROJECTION AT MIDDLE TERM OF THE FINANCIAL PROFIT OF SEPARATE COLLECTIONS

Financial profit of separate collections is based on sale of products,
saving on treatment considered and increase in collection costs.

Income by Sale of Products

Income by sale of products is function of sale price. The price of
100 FB/ton for old papers seems abnormally low ; it is a consequence
of the present economical crisis. A minimum price of 600 FB/ton,
departure Brussels, could reasonably be obtained in normal time.
It is not expected that price of glass will have important modifications.

Cost of Separate Collection

One could believe that the surplus of cost of separate collections
as shown here above will in fact decrease. Indeed, real charges are
lower than estimated ones due to the use of normal trucks, working
charges of which are below those of packing trucks. Then, yield of
collects should increase parallel to amounts collected. However, it
should be pointed out that, with weekly separate collections, amount
of refuse collected by normal collects will remain largely higher
than weight collected by separate collection : the yield of such
collects will, on a simple weight basis, be significantly lower.
Given these remarks, it seems careful to keep in our projection
a surplus of cost of 110 FB/ton.

Transport structure of urban solid wastes will perhaps be modified,
when starting the incineration plant, by installation of transfer
stations. This point having not been studied and playing a part
for paper and glass as well as for other wastes, it is not considered
here.

Total Revenue

On base of elements which have been defined, likely maximum and
minimum revenue have been established. They would be composed
as follows :

```
Maximum revenue
Sale of paper            :  31,000 T x   600 FB/T  =   18,600,000 FB
Sale of glass            :  16,300 T x   180 FB/T  =    2,934,000 FB
Higher price of collects :  47,300 T x  -110 FB/T  =  - 5,203,000 FB
Saving on treatment      :  47,300 T x   550 FB/T  =   26,015,000 FB
                                                      ----------------
Total                                                  42,346,000 FB


Minimum revenue
Sale of paper            :  31,000 T x   100 FB/T  =    3,100,000 FB
Sale of glass            :  16,300 T x   180 FB/T  =    2,934,000 FB
Higher price of collects :  47,300 T x  -110 FB/T  =  - 5,203,000 FB
Saving on treatment      :  47,300 T x   350 FB/T  =   16,555,000 FB
                                                      ----------------
Total                                                  17,386,000 FB
```

If amount of collected paper was halved, revenues would respectively
be 26,226,000 FB and 12,116,000 FB.

CONCLUSIONS

Amounts of paper and glass recycled per resident, since the beginning
of separate collections in Brussels have steadily increases.
Collections have received a very favourable welcome from population
and there are considerable possibilities for further increasing the
yield. From now, financial balance shows a profit, even if it looks
small by comparison with important expenses necessary to dispose of
urban solid wastes. This bal_nce has been unfavourably influenced by
the very low price presently given for old papers. It seems that
recycling of old papers by mechanical sorting is very expensive.
For comparison purpose, it can be said that a sorting process by air
classification proposed as part of the preliminary studies for the
incineration plant foresaw a net cost of 100 FB per ton of treated
wastes.

Projections made while considering extension of separate collection
to the whole city, increase of their frequency and installation of
an incineration plant point out to several conclusions.

First, separate collection are fully compatible with incineration :
heating value of urban wastes is practically not modified. Next,
these collections will produce an important profit for the "Agglomération de Bruxelles", up to 40 millions FB per year. This benefit
moreover extend to the whole country for which this recycling means
an economy on pulpwood and glass collets import. Finally, at the
environment level, it must be emphasized that recycling of one ton
of old papers in place of chemical pulp saves the annual production
of 0.25 to 0.30 ha of spruce forest or 0.5 to 0.6 ha of Belgian
hardwood forest. Separate collection of old papers in Brussels
in 1975 thus corresponds, when converted to equivalent of chemical
pulp, to the annual production of approximately 1,250 ha of softwood
forest while recycling anticipated within several years - 31,000 tons -
would correspond to the annual production of around 8,700 ha spruce
forest. This production will then be available for other purposes.
To this aspect must be added the energy economy and the lower pollution
coming from use of a material which does not need the "cooking"
necessary to transform wood into pulp.

It comes out of these elements that separate collection is an easy and
efficient method of recycling paper and glass while alleviating the
charge that disposal of urban solid wastes imposes on our cities.

BIBLIOGRAPHY

(1) Ch. Rocmans, M. Robyn, M. Henry, M. Van Marsenille et M. Van
    Leemput, Rapport de la commision BESWA pour l'étude du recyclage
    des ordures ménagères.
    Reiniging-Nettoiement, 5(2), 7 (1974).

    G.A. Thomas and J.R. Holmes, The choice between reclamation and
    the recovery of energy from refuse, Conf. Papers, 1rst Intern.
    Conf. on Conversion of Refuse to Energy, Montreux 3-5, 1975,
    164-172 (1975).

    J.J. Sauer et J.P. Schnydrig, La collecte séparée des déchets de
    plastiques et leur recyclage.
    ISWA Inform. Bull. 14-15, 17 (1974).

(2) J.P. Naveau, Influence of separate collection on calorific power
    of urban solid wastes.
    First Intern. Conf. "Conversion of Refuse to Energy", Montreux
    3-5 Nov. 1975. Conf. Papers 56-60 (1975).

(3) N.Y. Kirov, ed., Solid waste treatment and disposal, 1971
    Australian Waste Disposal Conf., Ann. Arbor Science. (1972).

PRODUCTION OF SINGLE CELL PROTEIN BY RECYCLING OF WASTE

Jens Hedegaard
Department of Microbiology
Polytechnical University of Denmark
2800 Lyngby - Copenhagen, Denmark

INTRODUCTION

Since the World Food Conference in Rome, 1975 (ref. 1), it became clear that the world population explosion, estimating the number of human individuals on earth to be by six billion at the year of 2000, would render traditional food production methods insufficient to supply an adequate diet for the overall world population.

New methods, new technology, new scientific research appeared to be of vital importance for the further supply of food and essential nutritional elements to maintain the food balance in the world and foremost in the countries under development. One of the possibilities for such an improvement of the world food situation could be the production of Single Cell Protein, i.e. production of a new protein resource. Such a production, when combined with the utilization/recycling of domestic, urban waste as a substrate for the Single Cell organisms might provide new perspectives for the overall food situation in the world of tomorrow, and thus to improve the human habitat.

Already in the early 1960's the first academic research on Single Cell production from various types of waste was undertaken to explore the possibilities of recycling certain types of waste with the consecutive production of microbial protein, but it is only during the last years that the true perspectives of using Single Cell Protein as an additional or additive food supply have been recognized.

In this paper certain aspects of Single Cell Protein production through recycling of the enormous and environmentally dangerous, urban wastes have been recognized not only by the governmental authorities but also by the world population.

Many aspects of Single Cell Protein production have been thoroughly examined at different symposia and in separate publications by different authors (ref. 1, 2, 3, 4).

It is the intention, by this review, to give a series of typical examples of possibilities for
1. Production of Single Cell Protein from urban waste as carried out actually, and to give

63

2. New perspectives for recycling of domestic, urban waste by the activity
   and consecutive protein production by different types of microorganisms.

SINGLE CELL PROTEIN PRODUCTION FROM HYDROCARBONS

Initially it is important to refer to four major publications in this field (ref.
1, 2, 3, 4). However, since these reviews were published, important new
research has been undertaken in this field. Although it has been difficult to
collect especially technological and economical data from the involved industries and manufacturers it is quite clear that the economical perspectives
for a profitable production of Single Cell Protein from hydrocarbons are today
far better than those indicated previously (ref. 5, 6). Also it must be emphasized that many more countries/companies are now involved not only in
pilot experiments but also in actual Single Cell production with hydrocarbons
as substrate on a larger scale. The problem of recycling of not directly
utilizable hydrocarbon products for the production not only of fertilizers but
also of Single Cell Protein is now being studied and positively looked upon in
all major industrialized countries as well as in the OPEC world (ref. 7). It
is quite clear that the amount of publications, now emanating in this partic -
ular field, indicates that an important problem for Single Cell Protein production is very much dependent on two major factors i. e. the hydrocarbon
source (substrate), and the type of microorganism used (ref. 8, 9). Certain
species of yeasts are used with extremely good results not only when it comes
to the overall production of Single Cell Protein, but also to the nutritional
value of this protein when it is considered for its value of rare amino acids.
In certain countries (ref. 8, 9) also bacteria of especially adaptable types
are at the present being used for the degradation of certain hydrocarbon by-
products with success (ref. 6). With respect to this last point it can be mentioned that with a Pseudomonas sp., a 50% conversion of methanol to Single
Cell Protein can be obtained, while a specie of Candida   showed the highest
promises in the degradation of ethanol   (ref. 7).

Fermentation processes of highly purified n-paraffins in a more complex
nutritional medium have shown extremely promising through intensive
research by both industrial companies and academic laboratories.

As earlier mentioned it is, at the present time, extremely difficult to obtain
an exact economical estimation of the financial aspects of the production of
Single Cell Protein from the various hydrocarbon sources i. e. alcohols
or paraffins   (ref. 1, 4, 5). Mention should also be made to the possibility
of certain species of yeast grown on alkanes. This emphasizes the importance
of the structure (chain-length) of the hydrocarbon substrate for the microorganism (yeast or bacteria). It is equally important, already now, to
emphasize that the selection of the suitable, adaptable microorganisms is of
vital importance. A careful selection of the suitable microorganism - often
among hundreds of the same species - has required an important effort from
the involved laboratories/companies. In most cases these particular strains
of bacteria/yeasts are still often professional secrets of the companies
involved, but it must be stressed that research in this field in the future will

conduct to a general knowledge of the microbiological aspect of the degradation of hydrocarbons and their consecutive conversion into Single Cell Protein.

It is quite clear from all major contributors to the studies of microbial degradation of the different types of hydrocarbons that two major aspects of the use of the produced Single Cell Protein are present. Primarily the composition of the produced Single Cell Protein is not readily adaptable for man because of the high concentration of nucleics acids with respect to the protein content. Secondly it is still questionable if some of the used micro - organisms, through their substrates (hydrocarbons), do not present or rather contain or produce toxic substances which might be detrimental to/dangerous for man. Generally speaking, one may therefore conclude, for the time being, that Single Cell production from hydrocarbons is possible but not yet conclusive when it is considered as a direct food resource for man.

It is generally agreed upon, however, by all major authors in this field that Single Cell Protein, produced from hydrocarbon residues is and will be in the future consist in a most valuable supply of food for domestic animals (rumens, poultry) and thus become an important indirect supplement to the human food situation in the world.

The production of Single Cell Protein from hydrocarbons represents, from a technological viewpoint, the great advantage that it can be carried out in continuous culture and that such a production also will be independent of climatic conditions and without costly temperature installations. These last points, further discussed in the chapter of Discussion, are of importance for the overall evaluation of the production of Single Cell Protein from hydrocarbons of different structure.

SINGLE CELL PRODUCTION FROM SEWAGE

Domestic sewage from both greater and smaller communities is a major problem in all countries today, both industrialized and in countries under development. The disposal of the urban sewage is posing problems not only because of its polluting effect on the environment, but also of the possibilities of its containing toxic and pathogenic elements. In most countries purification plants are now being imposed by law but require heavy investments which can or are not often being fulfilled.

Sewage from major industrial areas and from smaller communities have to be divided since their treatment and further, eventual, utilization as substrate for Single Cell Protein production is of quite different nature.

Domestic sewage from major industrial cities will most often contain compounds which are of a detrimental/dangerous nature for the production of Single Cell Protein from toxic materials contained in the sewage. This might not always be the case for sewage, emanating from smaller semi-urban cities with no major industries.

Sewage plants and their structure (filtration, biological purification) are too well-known to be explained in detail in this paper. It is, however, clear that this sewage from industrial areas cannot directly and should not directly be used for the production of Single Cell Protein, since the microorganisms and therefore also their content of valuable protein would be contaminated with compounds such as heavy metals and chlorinated compounds. Pilot experiments are actually being carried out at several places in the world and the following illustration indicates a possibility of cleaning up such major, industrial sewage to make it a possible substrate for production of microbial protein (fig. 1) (ref. 10).

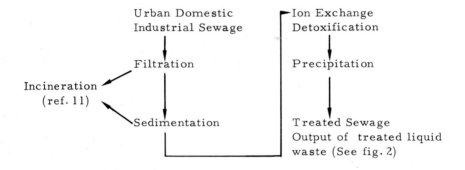

<u>Fig. 1</u>

A most interesting aspect of the possibility of recycling domestic, urban sewage is actually carried out in several subtropical and, could be, in tropical areas and is illustrated by the utilization of the photosynthetic capacity of an ecological system composed by a complex ecological variety of micro-organisms. After a first purification/detoxification/filtration/sediment-ation (fig. 1) it appears possible to feed larger reservoirs from the bottom with such treated sewage and let the complex microbiological eco-system overtake the further degradation of the remaining organic material contained in the sewage. Such a system would function in geographical areas where the photosynthetic activity is particularly high. The outflow from such a system would consist of a Single Cell mass which can be collected and, after centrifugation and drying, could be a valuable supplement for the feeding of domestic animals (cattle, poultry etc.), thus economizing other important food resources, otherwise readily available as food for man (fig. 2).

It is important to mention that recycling of domestic waste is actually being carried out in the People's Republic of China, both in and around the major cities but also in rural communities. It appears that the recycling of urban domestic waste in China has met with a considerable success although precise informations, technologically and economically are not yet available. This Chinese experiment and initiatives represent however an important new per-spective to what has so far been considered the classical solution to the world food problem i.d. the so called "Green revolution" (ref. personal commun-ications).

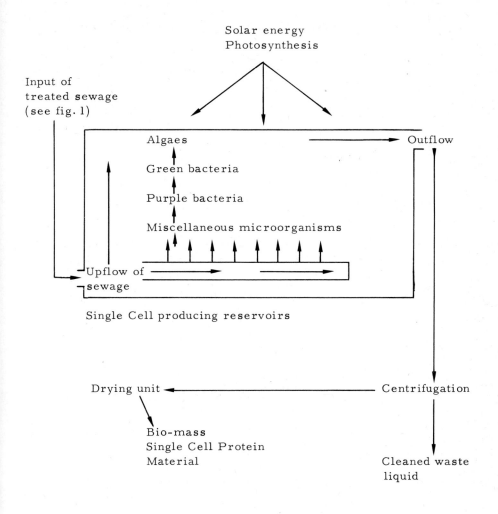

fig. 2

Another interesting aspect of using domestic sewage is the production of
edible fish (carps). It has been shown (ref. 12) that carps grown in treated
sewage increase considerably and rapidly in growth and the perspectives
of raising fish, directly for human consumption, from products of Single Cell
nature must be considered in the future.

Experiments carried out in Japan seem to prove that also the production of
algae can be considerably increased by the addition of treated sewage to
reservoirs where these algae, for both human and animal consumption, are
being fed with previously treated urban and treated sewage.

It is appropriate to note that an important project is actually being carried
out on the recycling of the wastewater of the river Thames with a consecutive augmentation of the protein production (poultry) (ref. 13).

The degradation of many of the compounds known under the name of nylon
etc. seems now to be possible by certain species of bacteria. This will
consist in an important progress in the cleaning up of sewage (fig. 1, 2) before
the use of the latter as a possible substrate for Single Cell Protein production.
New technics for the recycling of liquid waste from meat factories, fishmeal
factories, dairies etc. are now being developed in several countries and seem
promising as sources for the production of Single Cell Protein and nutrition
of different species, also of higher organisms (ref. 14).

RECYCLING OF SOLID WASTE - INDIRECT PRODUCTION OF
SINGLE CELL PROTEIN

The production of Single Cell Protein from solid waste has been the object
of intensive research during the last years. Attention should be drawn to the
fact that combined microbiological systems are capable to convert compounds
of cellulose nature into microbial protein. It is of particular interest, in
this respect, to mention the possibilities which remain in the recycling of
cellulose not only from paper-mills but also from residues from agricultural
production (straw) (ref. 15, 16) and from solid waste from typical urban areas
(ref. 17). It is of interest to mention that several projects are actually under
consideration for such recycling of solid waste particularly in countries
under development. The Danish government, DANIDA, are considering the
undertaking such or similar projects in certain countries under development.

In many major industrialized cities the disposal of solid waste still, however,
poses considerable problems and especially metallic wastes. Treatment of
these is yet a major problem in many communities in the industrial world.

The production of protein from solid waste may not be of direct nature, but
the material obtained by the disintegration of solid waste may lead to the
production of materials which, after microbiological degradation by soil
bacteria indirectly can increase the classical food production by increasing
of traditional crops.

The problem with this last type of solid waste must, however, be considered
in the view of the possibilities that such solid waste, degraded by microbial
ecosystems may often contain injurious compounds and especially heavy metals
and chlorinated compounds which then could enter into food chains and thus
become a questionable factor in the products, directly usable for man (ref. 11).

It is quite clear that while degradation of hydrocarbons may be and can be
carried out in pure microbial culture, the conversion of both liquid sewage
and solid waste requires much more complex microbiological systems.
Intensive research is, however, actually being carried out to isolate organisms,

both bacteria and yeast which are capable to complete the degradation of organic materials to such an extent that the result i.e. the obtained comp- ounds can be used, after purification, as an indirect resource for Single Cell Protein.

Although it is difficult to dissociate solid waste of the cellulose type, i.e. agricultural by-product (straw), from residues from paper mass production, it is quite clear that much research and new technology is required. Geo- graphical problems are here playing a major role since, in particular, paper mass production is primarily located in or close to urban areas in the nor- thern hemisphere (North America, Canada, Scandinavia and U.S.S.R.).

The possibilities of continuous recycling of solid waste are therefore intim- ately linked to favourable temperature conditions which obviously increase the cost and benefit of production of Single Cell Protein from these last mentioned types of solid waste.

A very particular aspect of production of Single Cell Protein is emanating from certain types of industries such as breweries and pharmaceutical industries. It is unnecessary to underline that the production of beer requires large amounts of certain species of yeasts. After the fermentation process is completed large amounts of yeast are too often discharged, although this material represents an important resource for Single Cell Protein utilizat- ion. In many countries this problem is now being looked seriously upon and in many cases the yeast residues from the beer fermentation process are now being collected and used as an additive to the protein supply in the feeding of domestic animals (cattle, poultry etc.). Considering the increas- ing production of beer all over the world we may stress the importance of the recovery of yeast from fermentation processes. The use of this yeast/ Single Cell Protein as a food supply in the raising of domestic animals and thereby indirectly as food for man must not be underestimated.

Another type of urban industries has developed particularly during recent years i.e. industries which are specialized in the production of highly specialized biologically active compounds such as vitamins, antibiotics, enzymes, etc. In all cases great amounts of microbial protein are being produced since these compounds today primarily originate from continuous culture of different types of microorganisms (bacteria, yeast, moulds). In too many cases the researched products (vitamins, rare amino acids, anti- biotics, enzymes, etc.) are of extra cellular nature while the microorganisms themselves, only producers, are too often discharged. They represent, however, as in the case with yeast from breweries an important resource of Single Cell Protein which ought to be considered as a possible food resource in the feeding of domestic animals.

SINGLE CELL PROTEIN FROM THE SEA

It is well-known that both fresh water and sea water are very efficient media
for the production of a complex system of microorganisms of different types.
The production of these microorganisms is very obviously much dependent
on two major factors i.e. the nutritional value of the water, temperature of
the latter, and the solar energy input (photosynthetic activity of microorganisms). Obviously most of these organisms are of photosynthetic nature
and the highest concentration of these organisms may therefore be found
outside or nearby estuaries of rivers or lakes in tropical or subtropical
areas. The heavy production of algae in the Sargasso Sea is well-known
but it is equally accepted today that an eutrofication is taking place in most
lakes and where the major rivers in the world are having their effluent into
the oceans. Recent information indicates that intensive marine research is
actually carried out as projects to investigate the possibilities to harvest
these microorganisms and algae and to bring them into use as a Single Cell
Protein supply not only for the feeding of domestic animals, but also for their
value as a resource of rare amino acids, vitamins and antibiotics. However,
much research and new technology will be necessary to make a success out of
such projects, but it is quite obvious that the Single Cell Protein production
in both fresh water and sea water represents perspectives which may not be
underestimated in the future.

SUMMARY AND DISCUSSION

In this review an attempt has been made to point out certain - but certainly
not all - possibilities for the production of Single Cell Protein by the recycling of domestic, urban waste and the use of the latter as a substrate for
growth of either pure microbial cultures or more complex microbiological
ecosystems (fig. 2).

It has been stressed several times that for the time being the microorganisms are mainly directly used in the production of essential growth and / or
health factors for man i.e. vitamins, antibiotics, rare essential amino acids,
enzymes, etc. It is, however, quite clear from the efforts undertaken by
the still increasing number of research institutes and private companies
that the perspectives of using microorganisms of different species do represent an important protein reserve and thus may become a vital protein
supply for the world population at a time where the world food crisis is becoming increasingly serious, and where the problems of the human habitat
both in the big cities and in the suburban areas are becoming a major problem
for both governments and the individuals concerned.

Much work and research has still to be carried out and especially when it comes
to the selection of new, better adaptable microorganisms capable of degrad-
ing the different types of waste, both hydrocarbons, sewage, solid waste
etc. Great efforts are already and must be undertaken in the nearest future
to accomplish such research and also to induce, eventually by mutations and/

or genetic changes of the microorganisms, the production and isolation of new strains of microorganisms which could be specially useful in the degradation of the various types of domestic urban waste and the recycling of this with the consecutive production of valuable Single Cell Protein. This will be of the greatest importance for the improvement of the human habitat in the future.

It is quite clear from all major work in the field of Single Cell Protein production available today that the financial aspects of this production are still subject to much discussion, especially when it comes to the use of hydro-carbons as substrates for this Single Cell Protein production. The increasing prices during the last years of hydrocarbon products may interfere with the cal - culations which were made in the early 1972's (ref. 5 and later ref. 6). For this review it has been extremely difficult to obtain new information about these economical perspectives for a thorough evaluation of the economical possibilities, but considering the amount of efforts, both in number and tech-nologically, it may reasonably be assumed that the production of Single Cell Protein by recycling of waste is now also being considered economically profitable.
One may not underestimate neither the pressure from the public opinion upon "waste producers" and governments to make a major effort and to take efficient legal measures to improve the well-being of man, both in his habitat in the cities and in the rural communities.
It is obvious from what has been mentioned in this review that Single Cell Protein is not directly a food resource for man. In certain cases, however, Single Cell Protein as produced from the above-mentioned sources (different types of waste) may be and is already used as a nutritional additive of great value to the food supply   in certain countries and under certain conditions.

For the time being it is therefore clear that Single Cell Protein is actually usable primarily for domestic animals capable of converting this Single Cell Protein resource indirectly into food which is tolerable to man.

The production of Single Cell Protein by recycling of waste represents still two major problems which have to be solved by intense research. Primarily, it is of vital importance to assure that the Single Cell Protein, produced under some of the above-mentioned conditions, has no toxic effect neither on the domestic animals nor, later on man. This problem may be solved by the continued selection of new microorganisms. Secondly it is quite clear that the balance between nucleic acids and protein in the Single Cell mass produced has to be, by new technology/purifications, adapted so that Single Cell Protein can become not only an additive but a true new food resource also directly for man and this to improve his possibilities to establish his better future in the habitat (ref. 18).

ACKNOWLEDGEMENT

This report has been made possible by generous contributions from DANIDA
(Danish Foreign Ministry) and from the Danish Ministry of Education. The
author wants to thank the different national and international agencies and
companies for valuable information.

REFERENCES

1. Sartaj Aziz and Barbara Ward, Hunger, Politics and Markets
        New York University Press, 75-34674, p. 88,
        New York,1975.

2. P. Davis, edt., Single Cell Protein
        Academic Press, 1974.

3. J.W.G. Porter and B.A. Rolls, Proteins in Human Nutrition
        Academic Press, 1973.

4. H. Gounelle de Pontanel, Proteins from Hydrocarbons
        The Proceedings of the 1972 Symposium.
        Academic Press, 1972.

5. Kihlberg, Reinhold, "The Microbe as a Source of Food"
        Annual Review of Microbiology, vol. 26 (1972)
        p. 427-467.

6. Micholt, C., Kannaerts, J., and Nyns, E.J.
        Evaluation of the Chances of Hydrocarbon-grown Single Cell Protein
        to gain a Share of the World Gross Potential Protein Market, Revue
        des Fermentations et des Industries Alimentaires - Bruxelles - T.30
        - no. 1, p.3-16.

7. Dr. Badakhshan, A., Iranian Committee on Protein (Personal Comm-
        unications).

8. Shacklady, C.A., Alkane-Grown Yeasts: A New Source of Protein.
        Nutrition Vol. 3 (pp. 76-84), 1975.

9. Bennett, I.C., Hondermarck, J.C., Todd, J.R.,
        Hydrocarbon Processing, March 1969 (Personal Communications
        from British Petroleum and Gas Oil of France, Marseilles).

10. S.E. Jørgensen, Ph.D. Thesis submitted at the Karlsruhe University,
        1976.

11. Willerup, O. H., Experiences with a Pyrolysis Plant for Municipal and Industrial Refuse, CRE, Conference Papers, Conversion of Refuse to Energy, IEEE Catalog 75CH1008-2 CRE Montreux, Switzerland, 1975.

12. Noble, Reg, Growing Fish in Sewage, New Scientist, p. 259, July 1975.

13. Smith, Sam, Thames Water, Livestock feed from sewage sludge, IIED Publication, 27 Mortimer Street, London, 1975 (Personal Comm-unication).

14. Aminodan A/S, Vestmolen, Skagen, Denmark (Personal Communication).

15. Peitersen, Nicolai, Production of Cellulase and Protein from Barley Straw by Trichoderma viride, Biotechnology and Bioengineering, vol. XVII, p. 361-374, 1975.

16. Peitersen, Nicolai, Single Cell Protein from Straw, Symposium on Enzymatic Hydrolysis of Cellulose, Aulanko, Finland, March 1975, p. 407.

17. Milbury, W. F., Riedel, T. W., and Jones, P. H.,
    Yeast Production Using Conventional Activated Sludge Methods for Treatment of Corn Processing Industrial Wastes.
    Department of Civil Engineering, University of Toronto, Toronto, Ontario, Canada, 1975.
    (Personal Communication).

18. Dasilva, E. J., Life Sciences Programme, Microbiology, Cell and Molecular Biology and Interdisciplinary Brain Research. Unesco, SC. 74/WS/70, Paris, 1975.

REPORT ON THE INTERNATIONAL CONGRESS OF SCIENTISTS ON THE HUMAN ENVIRONMENT (HESC)

Toward a Better Human Environment

Yoichi FUKUSHIMA
Secretary General of the Organizing Committee of the International Congress of
Scientists on the Human Environment in the Science Council of Japan (JSC)

22-34, Roppongi 7-chome, Minato-ku 106 Tokyo, Japan

PROCEDURE OF PREPARATION

As we all know, the problem of environmental disruption has steadily grown more serious, especially since the mid-1960's. To face up to this challenge, it was considered necessary in the Science Council of Japan to take up the related problems with closer attention, and various ad hoc committees were set up to deliberate the issue.

In 1969, these committees were reconstituted into one committee, the Special Committee on Problems of the Environment, so that a unified approach could be made to the whole question. (A short explanation of the JSC is in the Appendix.) After the United Nations Conference on the Human Environment held in Stockholm in June, 1972, the Special Committee in JSC expressed the opinion that JSC should sponsor an international congress of scientists on problems of the environment on the basis of scientific studies and researches done by scientists. Consequently at its 62nd general meeting in October, 1972, they resolved on setting about preparations for such a congress.

Since then, on the various occasions of related international conferences scientists were asked for their comments and opinions on the holding of HESC, and with this active backing, it was possible to exchange ideas on the nature and agenda of HESC. In September, 1973, a letter outlining guiding principles on the nature of the proposed congress, along with objectives and suggested topics for discussion, was sent out to a wide range of scientists throughout the world.

We decided the following guide lines from the start of preparation:
1. The congress will discuss all subjects strictly as scientists.
2. The desire is for subjects to be discussed on an interdisciplinary basis, covering all fields of natural and social sciences and technology. Some special problems also may be discussed by a specialist group.
3. The congress is open to scientists of all countries.
4. Japan will be able to make some special contributions based on the severe environmental problems experienced in this country.
5. The plan is not to adopt definite resolutions, and political controversy will be avoided.

NATIONAL LEVEL SYMPOSIA

Plans were then made and carried into effect to hold a national symposium to ensure the success of this international congress.

The first national symposium was held for three days, November 8 to 10, 1973. The subjects discussed included:
1. Human right to the environment.
2. PPP or Polluter pays principle.
3. Closed system of pollutants in industrial processes.
4. Emission control by total volume, with particular reference to air pollution.
5. Organic chloride chemicals with particular reference to PCB.

The second symposium was held for three days, June 13 to 15, 1974. Discussed were:
1. Human right to the environment (2nd round).
2. Organic mercury.
3. Comprehensive pollution of regions.
4. Man's impact on terrestrial ecosystems.
5. Development of pollution-free areas and pollution control.

75

The third was held in the Kyoto International Hall where the HESC was held in the next year, for two days, November 11 to 12, 1974. The subjects discussed included:
1. Development and protection of the environment.
2. Recycling - closed system in industrial processes.
3. Emission control by total volume and assessment of unpolluted areas.
4. Environment of Lake Biwa.
5. Pollution of Seto Inland Sea.

Special mention should be made, and gratitude expressed for the participation in the second symposium in June, 1974, of Dr. T. F. Malone, Secretary General of the Scientific Committee on Problems of the Environment (SCOPE) in the International Council of Scientific Unions (ICSU), and Professor K. William Kapp, representing the Standing Committee on the Environment (SCE) in the International Social Science Council (ISSC).

Mention should be made of the support for the convocation of HESC given by the United Nations Environment Programme, which in August, 1974, delegated to Tokyo Dr. R. Frosch, then director of UNEP Programme Bureau.

DECIDED PROGRAMME

Based on the above stated preparatory work we decided the programme of HESC as follows, and the congress was carried out according to the schedule.

Nov. 17 Monday, A. M. Opening Ceremony;
 Address by the President of JSC. Yuichi OCHI
 Progress report by Yoichi FUKUSHIMA
 Greetings by M. K. TOLBA, Deputy Executive Director, United Nations Environment
 Programme (UNEP)
 Read by C. Sryakumaran, Deputy Director of the Asia and Pacific Area
 Center of UNEP.

Nov. 17 Monday, P. M. Special Lectures;
 Tauo KIRA, Professor of Osaka City University
 "Man's place in Nature"
 K. W. Kapp, Professor Institut fur Sozialwiss. University Basel.
 "Environmental Disruption and Role of Science"

Nov. 18 Tuesday, A. M.
 Current Environmental Problems in Japan (S. TSURU et al)

Nov. 18 Tuesday, P. M.
 The Role of Scientists in the Task for a Better Environment
 A. K. BISWAS, Senior consultant, UNEP
 T. F. Malone, Secretary General, SCOPE, ICSU.

From November 19 to 21, we had discussion meetings of four Working Groups in parallel, which were as follows:

Working Group A

Interdisciplinary Discussion on Man's Impact on Terrestrial Ecosystems

A - 1: Agro-ecosystems
A - 2: Urban ecosystems
A - 3: Ecological cycle in regional scale
A - 4: Problems relating to regions
        Part 1: Environmental problems of Lake Biwa
        Part 2: Seto Inland Sea and its coastal region

Working Group B

Problems mainly within the Purview of Natural Sciences

B - 1: Environmental toxicology - Scientific basis for toxicological evaluation of industrial chemicals
B - 2: Alternative technologies - Recycling of domestic and industrial refuse
B - 3: Environmental problems of a global scale
B - 4: Methodology of environmental monitoring and assessment

Working Group C

Problems mainly within the Purview of Social Sciences

C - 1: Human right to the environment
C - 2: Legislative techniques for environmental protection
C - 3: Environment and market mechanism

C - 4:   Development and environment
Sub-section (A) Development, researches and assessment
Sub-section (B) Human settlements and environment mercury poisoning
Working Group D
                  Problems mainly in the field of Cultural Studies
        D - 1:   Problems of the cultural environment
        D - 2:   Information and education on the environment
Nov. 22 Saturday
                  Scientific tours in four groups:
                  Osaka Bay
                  Yokkaichi City in Miye Prefecture
                  Osadano Town Planning in Kyoto Prefecture
                  Lake Biwa in Shiga Prefecture
Nov. 23 Sunday
                  Recess
Nov. 24 Monday, A. M.
                  Plenary Session II
                  Summary Reports of the Working Groups
Nov. 24 Monday, P. M. to Nov. 25 Tuesday, A. M.
                  Plenary Session III
                  Analytical Tools and Policy Instruments for Conservation and Improvement of the Environment
                  —Toward a Better Human Environment
Nov. 25 Tuesday, P. M.
                  Plenary Session IV
                  Priorities in the Agenda for Scientific Research in the Field of Environmental Studies
Nov. 25 Tuesday, P. M.
                  Closing Plenary Session
   The Congress was scheduled to continue to Nov. 26, but because of the general strike of National Railways and main private traffics, we decided to cut the last day.
   Now I will explain Fig. 1 in comparison of the programme. I have already written this matrix, in September, 1974.

HOW THE CONGRESS WAS CARRIED ON

   As I have already explained, most of the important themes discussed in the HESC were derived from the discussions of the national level symposia or other conferences held abroad prior to the HESC. There are, needless to say, many important themes which were not discussed in the national level symposia; but, the most successful results were obtained in the sessions of the themes surveyed or discussed in some groups in the long preparatory stage.
   Environmental rights, total volume regulation and other themes in Working Group C, were discussed for long periods among the lawyers' group in our country. C - 1 and C - 2 sessions were approved by the participants most fruitful. Group studies on Seto Inland Sea and Biwa Lake: both themes were also surveyed and discussed for a long time. (A - 1, parts 1 and 2)
   On the other hand, in the session of Recycling (B -2), N. Y. Kirov, who undertook the chairmanship of the First International Conference on Conservation of Refuse to Energy, (CRE) held in Montreux, Switzerland from Nov. 3 - 5, 1975, just before the HESC, participated in the HESC, introducing the results and discussions of the Conference. (On this Conference, W. MacAdam reports in this WERC meeting. His report was read by E. N. Westerberg.)
   In Group D, the education on the environmental studies, many Japanese high school teachers reported their own experiences which were highly evaluated among the participants. This theme was not discussed in the national level symposia organized by the JSC, but they have their own association of teachers on the environmental education, and organized by themselves several symposia in the last few years.
   These experiences that the success in the congress is obtained mainly based on such group studies are, I believe, the most instructive to our future work.
   I think it is necessary to make some explanation on the Plenary Session II, in the morning of Monday, November 24, and on the Plenary Session III, which began on the afternoon of the same day. But before I touch on this matter, I must explain the programmes of Saturday and Sunday.
   On Saturday, November 22, most of the participants took part in each group of the scientific tours above mentioned. They inspected in each place, the serious situation of environmental problems in Japan with their own

Time order	Relevant Sciences	Causes of damage	Themes	Damage caused	direction of development of cooperation in sciences
Historical research →	Natural Sciences	Ecosystems (global); Recycling (industrial waste); P.P.P.	Noise; SOx; NOx; CO; CH; PCB; Org.Hg; Radiation; Toxicology; Pesticides	Direct damage (Remedy and relief); Indirect damage (Chronic)(Biocycle)(Genetic problem)	Discussions among experts; Common themes; Social scientists participating in discussions of natural scientists
	Economics	Costs and Benefits	Sunshine		
	Jurisprudence	Environmental rights; Total volume regulation			Natural scientists participating in discussion of social scientists
Present situation →	Coordination of sciences (Synthesis)	Total volume regulation in areas under development; Environment and development	SETO inland sea; BIWA lake	Surveillance system; Citizens' role (Local governments); Prosecution Movements	
		Alternative technologies; Research and studies; Education	Air pollution; Ocean pollution (Water pollution); Monitoring; Information; Simulation modelling	Cooperation and Responsibility of scientists	
	Methodological themes	Organization of Scientists; Responsibility of Scientists; Priority areas of themes	Assessment	Development of cooperation of scientists	
Perspective →	Preventive measures		Recommendations for preventive measures		Interdisciplinary discussions

☐ Items discussed in national level symposia

Fig.1 A Matrix of the Environmental Studies

eyes. They had discussion with citizens on the spot and almost all participants from abroad expressed their strong impression of the lesson gained from the bitter experiences of Japan.

On the other hand, chairmen or convenors of each session undertook to summarize the three days' discussions, (some sessions were one day or two) during those on Saturday and Sunday. Those summary reports were printed on Sunday night, and distributed among all the participants on Monday morning. The total printed pages amounted to about 100 pages.

On the Monday morning, the several representative members of the sessions expressed their own impressions briefly.

In Plenary Session III we discussed mainly the Assessment. (To discriminate from the other Session, we used rather sophisticated expression.)

Here I hope you may refer once more to Fig. 1, and understand the stream of the idea, why we discussed mainly Assessment in the PlenaryIII.

In Plenary Session III, which lasted from the afternoon of Monday November 24 to the morning of Tuesday, November 25, we heard the reports of R. E. Munn, Y. Y. Haimes and H. Chetnut, from the standpoint of natural scientists, and of F. R. Anderson and other Japanese speakers from the standpoint of social scientists.

In the final Plenary Session, in the afternoon of Tuesday, November 25 proposals of priorities in each field of scientific organizations were presented by T. F. Malone, the General Secretary of SCOPE, S. Tsuru, the chairman of SCE and K. Kaneko, Senior Officer of UNEP.

Malone pointed out the importance of the Data Bank, Systematic study of the methodology of assessment and Monitoring system, and especially the importance of the interdisciplinary collaboration of scientists. Tsuru proposed to organize an international research group of Seto Inland Sea and Kaneko proposed a United Nations Environmental Conference of Asia and Pacific regions.

CLOSING SESSION AND AFTER CARE

K. Husimi, chairman of the Organizing Committee in JSC, delivered the closing address, in which he pointed out the three main results obtained in the Congress.
1. The framework was established on how to analyze the problems of the environment.
2. We reached recognition on the importance of organizing systematic study on assessment methodology.
3. We also reached common understanding on the importance of the human activity in coming decades
   which would decide the fate of mankind, whether they might be able to survive or not.

A resolution to organize a Follow-up committee of HESC, which was proposed by K. Kaneko, and took in the speech of Husimi, was unanimously adopted by the participants. And we decided to entrust the follow-up work to the representatives of the following four organizations; i.e. SCOPE, SCE, UNEP, and JSC.

V. A. Kovda, President of SCOPE, representing the participants from abroad, expressed their thanks to the JSC.

Registered participants amounted to 516418 Japanese scientists and 114 from 30 countries abroad (26 accompanied)

APPENDIX

ON THE SCIENCE COUNCIL OF JAPAN

The Science Council of Japan was set up in 1949 following the Second World War in the course of the reorganization of various institutions for promotion of scientific studies, which had existed even in prewar days. As a comprehensive organization it covers all fields of science —the humanities, social sciences, the basic branches of natural science, technology, agriculture and medicine.

The council is made up of 210 members elected every three years by some 200,000 eligible voters. It is an official Governmental institution connected with the Prime Minister's Office. But, at the same time, in accordance with legal provisions under which it was established, the Science Council of Japan carries on its work independent of the Government, being responsible to deliberate and promote important matters related to the sciences.

In pursuance of these objectives, the Science Council of Japan is affiliated with international scientific organizations such as the International Council of Scientific Unions (ICSU). In this respect, it has a non-governmental organization (NGO).

From the time of its inception, the Science Council of Japan has taken up a wide range of subjects and made many recommendations on important questions. For the purpose of deliberation, many committees have been set up, which co-opt the services of experts who are not themselves members of the Science Council of Japan. The special Committee on Problems of the Environment has been organized as one of these committees, and had the initiative of the International Congress of Scientists on the Human Environment in 1972.

ENERGY FROM REFUSE
REPORT ON FIRST CRE CONFERENCE

Walter K. MacAdam, Senior Engineering Consultant
Wheelabrator-Frye Inc., Hampton, New Hampshire USA

The institutional aspects of conversion of urban refuse to energy,
including the problems of public acceptance, governmental support
and means of financing, far overshadow technological barriers to
implementation - This was the principal conclusion of the First
International Conference on Conversion of Refuse to Energy, held
in Montreux, Switzerland, November 3-5, 1975.

Sponsored by the World Environment and Resources Council, the US
Environment and Resource Council, the Institute of Electrical
and Electronics Engineers, American Society of Mechanical Engineers
and other major environmental and engineering societies, the
conference was adjudged to be an outstanding success, not only
in its attendance, but also in the quality of presented papers,
discussion by participants and extensive exhibit coverage.

A total of 99 papers and three panel discussions were selected
from almost 200 submitted manuscripts. Individual sessions were
devoted to such topics as refuse derived fuel, impact in recycling on energy content of refuse, institutional aspects,
experience in cost and performance, government involvement,
financing, pollution control, city projects, combined sewage
sludge and refuse disposal and comparative economics. Registration exceeded 750, with attendance from 27 countries.

Universally the interest of the governmental attendees, both local
and national seemed to center on three questions - how does one
select a reliable system - how can one be financed, designed and
constructed at minimum risk to the community - and how can such
a complex system be successfully operated over an extensive
period of time by a typical municipality without danger of malfunction or system damage?

It was evident that most of the systems deriving energy and
resources from municipal refuse were capital cost intensive.
A few, particularly those performing extensive preprocessing
and front end separation of materials or refuse derived fuel,
tended to be operating cost intensive.

81

It was pointed out that some city officials have been reluctant
to invest in large amounts of capital in plants involving un-
proven technology or uncertain reliability. Demonstrated
reliability seemed to be the most important consideration. How
then can new processes be developed on a full scale basis to
develop a history of reliability? This seems to be the dilemma
of many local and national government groups pressing for modern
and clean solutions to the dual problems of refuse disposal and
energy shortage. One approach reported by the United States
was national government funding of so-called "demonstration
projects". Unfortunately, some widely publicized initial difficulties with a number of such projects have at times tended to
undermine public confidence in new experimental systems.

Considering the interests of the WERC Brussels Conference on
the Environment of Human Settlements, this report of the Montreux
Refuse-Energy Conference will confine itself to the community
related aspects and institutional factors rather than description
of the numerous technical processes reviewed at CRE and included
in the published Conference Record. The highlights of various
institutional topics are reported separately in the following
subdivisions.

<u>Urban Priorities - Disposal versus Energy</u>

While there appears to be widespread public enthusiasm for the
concept of energy and materials extraction from refuse, the
impelling motivation from the local community standpoint centers
on refuse disposal through a process that maximizes <u>clean volume
reduction</u>. Energy extraction and materials recovery are considered
important primarily because of their ability to reduce the overall
net cost of the disposal process. It is noted that the importance
attached to disposal related to energy increased in proceeding
from the national to the local community level. (Papers C-1,
E-7, P-1)

<u>System Attractiveness related to Community Size</u>

It appeared that economically viable plants compared with alternatives such as landfilling were generally feasible for communities of more than 200,000 to 300,000 inhabitants within a radius
of approximately 15-25 km from a processing plant. However,
some unusual situations may permit application to smaller communities, particularly where refuse is used as a fuel supplement.
(Papers H-2, H-5, H-6, P-1)

Possibilities of Combined Sewage Sludge and Refuse Disposal

A number of communities have utilized or are planning systems
for combined sludge and sewage disposal. The net energy extraction possibilities from the sludge component is minimal however.
(Papers I-1 through I-6)

Air and Water Pollution Considerations

Effective control of air pollution to meet stringent requirement
has proved entirely practical in modern combustion systems. Pyrolysis and bioconversion offer the possibility of essentially
eliminating atmosphere emissions. Water pollution can be controlled in either case. (Papers F-1 through F-7)

Influence of Separate Collection on Energy and Materials Recovery from Refuse

Several studies assuming extremely high degrees of source reduction or separate paper or glass collection indicated a potential
reduction of about 20% in heat value of the remainder. This,
however, was considered to have no serious impact on the desira-
bility or long term viability of refuse-energy systems. In fact,
separate collection offered long-term beneficial possibilities in
reduced growth rate of refuse volume and increased tonnage capacity of processing plants. (Papers B-1 through B-5, E-7)

Role of National, State or Regional Governments

It was evident that many governments are taking an active role
in developing policies, carrying out research, assisting with
financing and providing technical support to communities desiring
to implement refuse-energy systems. This has also been helpful
in obtaining public acceptance of new systems. (Papers A-1, C-1,
E-1 through E-7, G-5)

Role of Private Industry

In addition to private industry capability for providing system
design and manufacturing, construction and operating services,
it was noted that private sources were able to provide a complete
system package including financing and may even pay local taxes.
In at least one case private industry owned and operated the plant,
relieving the community of the need to raise the capital from
general obligation bonds. (Papers C-1, M-4, P-1)

Case Study of a Multi-Community Project

A feature of the conference was the presentation of a case study
of a particular multi-community project. This included discussions
of this privately owned system by the mayor of one of the local
communities, the operating head of the industrial plant purchasing
the energy, the financing entity, the designer and builder and the
system operator. As stated in the presentation, "This case
illustrated a situation in which the establishment of a clean
refuse disposal system extracting valuable resources depends not
only on technology, but also upon the cooperative planning of
a combination of communities, energy users, private entrepreneurs,
financial institutions, and local and regional government agencies.
Waiting for government to do it alone is often as unproductive
as waiting for industry to step up singlehandedly to the task.
Given encouragement, however, a cooperative undertaking, with
community service as an objective, can become an economic, tax
paying solution to a social and environmental problem without
burdening municipal, regional or state bonding resources."
(Paper P-1)

Availability of Conference Papers

Complete copies of the presented papers are included in a bound
volume of the CRE Conference Record (IEEE Catalog Number 75CH1008-
2CRE) available in principal technical libraries or obtainable
on order from:

> CRE Conference 1975
> Box 97
> 1820 Montreux-Switzerland
> at SFr.95

In the USA, copies may be obtained from:

> IEEE
> 445 Hoes Lane
> Piscataway, New Jersey 08854
> at $36 - non members
> $27 - members of IEEE or sponsoring entity

DECISION-MAKING FOR HUMAN WELL-BEING IN CITIES

Robert Maxwell
Chairman, Pergamon Press, Oxford, England

There are other countries in the world whose clean air legislation and enforcement policies are even more advanced and perhaps even more effective than those in the United Kingdom. It may be of some value to hear a former legislator like myself who in 1968 introduced and obtained parliamentary and government approval to the Clean Air Act* of Great Britain. At the end of this introduction I provide a copy of the Act, so that those members of our conference who may be involved in thinking about or in assisting in the drafting of legislation, either at national, state or local level, may see how we in Britain have gone about it.

Those of you who have no experience of dealing with legislators or legislation direct can be assured that your local congressman or member of parliament or whatever his title is, is always very pleased to hear from either qualified individuals or groups who may be desirous of bringing about a change in a particular law or bringing new legislation that will improve the quality of life in their part of the world.

My experience of many years in Parliament is that professional individuals and many of their organizations do not know how to approach politicians and there is some shyness or coyness about doing so, and if I have passed on no other point to you than that you should not hesitate to come forward on either local or national level and make contact either with your local congressman or with the staff committee concerned with legislation in the area in which you have an interest - then I will have been of some service to you. I forecast that you will be very pleasantly surprised as to how well you will be received, with what care you will be listened to and, if you are lucky, how quickly your ideas could be brought about or put into a bill which will have the kind of consequences that we hope you desire.

All politicians and administrators concerned with human well-being in cities know that no matter what form of political society one lives in, the secret of success in this area depends not only on procuring and on making available the right amount of financial resources and the correct legislative and administrative framework with which we do it, but also and above all the need for close and early consultation with the people, whose lives will be affected by the implementation of proposed plans.

We tend to treat clean air - or used to in any case - as if it was an inexhaustible product. I can best illustrate the inaccuracy of that by quoting to you somebody whom some of you know, Professor Kell, of Cornell University, who said amongst other things - wherein he challenged the comfortable assumption that our world supply of oxygen is permanent and inexhaustible - he said oxygen will quickly disappear from the atmosphere if all the green plants should be killed and if you look at the sprawl and the amount of land that is being taken out annually on a world-wide basis, you

85

will readily see if humanity continues at that rate that is exactly what man
is in process of doing.

Grassland is being built on in the United States alone, at the rate of about
a million acres a year, thus removing oxygen from the air that would otherwise have been put into the atmosphere by the photosynthesizing of green plants.
The point will be reached where the rate of consumption exceeds the rate of
photosynthesis and the oxygen content of the atmosphere will then decrease.

Indeed, there is evidence that it may already be declining around such large
cities as New York, Philadelphia, Los Angeles, London, Paris, Tokyo, Moscow,
etc. This is why clean air legislation is of the highest importance.

Although everybody is agreed that air pollution is undesirable and that most
of its effects on health and damage to materials are well known, the pattern
of our industrialized civilization unfortunately makes it unavoidable.
Scientists and engineers who are concerned with studying this problem and
administering its effects over the past two decades are agreed that air
pollution procedure and its effects are very complicated.

The effects of air pollution and its remedies are costly and all that one can
say is that any advance in understanding of the mechanism that causes air
pollution will make the correction easier.

Special legislation has been necessary to protect workers in certain industries,
such as cement, asbestos - some of you have read in your local newspapers that
we have a scandal on our hands of an asbestos factory in the United Kingdom
which has been killing over 200 people twenty years after they stopped working
in that factory. That is entirely due to the fact that legislation introduced
in 1904 has not been enforced properly by the factory inspectorate in our
country and that the employers, although they were aware of the problem and the
danger to health, preferred to keep it to themselves.

I wont't go on to discuss with you the details of the Clean Air Act. As I
have said the Act will be available in the proceedings. It is not a very
long Act, but it is carefully drafted. Unfortunately, because of time overrun
I have not been able to give you as much background as I would have liked as
to how this bill came to be introduced as a private member's bill, in other
words by the will of one member of parliament persuading the rest of his
colleagues in the Government that this legislation was necessary. Clearly I
was lucky, clearly its timing was right and it was felt by the community as
being necessary.

* See Appendix 1 page 339

FROM THEORY TO PRACTICE: ROLE OF THE EUROPEAN COMMUNITIES

Myles McSwiney
Environment and Consumer Protection Service
Commission of the European Communities

The European Community now has nine Member States, Belgium, Denmark, Federal Republic of Germany, France, Ireland, Italy, Luxembourg, Netherlands and United Kingdom, with a total population of about 255 million. The degree of urbanisation (% of population living in towns with more than 20.000 people) ranges from 50 % in Ireland to over 80 % in Germany, Denmark and United Kingdom.

+

The Community has been immensely successful in removing barriers to trade between the Member States and in promoting the free movement of persons and capital within the Community. The citizens of the Member States have benefitted by receiving higher incomes and a wider choice of goods. But prosperity has not reached all areas or all social classes nor has it been achieved without damage to the environment. When they met in Paris in October 1972, the heads of state or government of the Member States declared that "economic expansion is not an end in itself : its first aim should be to enable disparities in living conditions to be reduced. It must take place with the participation of all the social partners. It should result in an improvement in the quality of life as well as in standards of living. As befits the genius of Europe, particular attention will be given to intangible values and to protecting the environment so that progress may really be put at the service of mankind".

Having accepted the need for remedial action, the Communities lost no time in taking appropriate measures. In 1973, the Commission proposed and the Council of Ministers approved a comprehensive Programme of Action on the Environment. This was followed by the Social Action Programme in 1974 and the creation of the Regional Fund and the Regional Policy Committee in 1975.

POLLUTION CONTROL

The Programme of Action on the Environment set out the objectives and principles of environmental policy and described the action to be taken to reduce pollution and nuisances and to improve the environment. This statement of intent has been given substance in a steady flow of proposals from the Commission to the Council of Ministers.

+ Strictly speaking, there are three Communities – the European Coal and Steel Community (1951) and the European Economic Community and the European Atomic Energy Community (1957) – but they share the same institutions.

The Commission urged that the Community, in addition to giving aid to the poorer regions, should seek agreement between the Member States on common policies to reduce concentration in the congested regions.

The institutional machinery to give effect to these intentions has now been forged. In 1975, the European Regional Development Fund and the Regional Policy Committee were established. 1300 million units of account will be available from the Fund, in the period 1975-1977, to assist Member States in their efforts to promote development in disadvantaged areas.

The Regional Policy Committee's principal task is to assist in the coordination of the regional policies of the Member States. It will also be expected to assist the Community institutions to ensure that other Community policies and the financial resources available to some of them make a better contribution to regional development.

FOUNDATION FOR THE IMPROVEMENT OF LIVING CONDITIONS

A profound understanding of the roots of social and environmental problems is the base on which effective policies may be built. The Community decided in 1975 to establish a European Foundation for the Improvement of Living and Working Conditions, to be located in Ireland. With the creation of this Foundation, which is now set up in Dublin, the community has a body which will gather and defuse knowledge about concrete experiences in several members states aimed at improving living and working conditions.

The aims of the Foundation are not yet fully understood throughout the Community. We received a letter recently in which it was referred to as the Foundation for the Improvement of the Commission of the European Communities! Perhaps such a foundation is required but the purpose of the new Foundation is somewhat different.

Community policies and activities in other sectors, such as transport, energy and the building industry, also influence human well-being in cities. Lack of space prevents extended description of them. I should not conclude, however, without referring to the development aid policy, which assists governments and people in developing countries to achieve the social and economic goals which they have set for themselves.

DEVELOPMENT AID POLICY

In 1975, a group of 46 African, Caribbean and Pacific countries concluded negotiations for a new, enlarged and deepened relationship with the Communities. The new ACP-EEC Convention of Lomé, which came into force on 1 April 1976, represents not just an extension of the former association policies but marks a significant step in the rapidly evolving relationship between the developed and developing countries.

A large European Development Fund (the fourth in the series and amounting to 3,500 million u.a. or about $ 4375 m) will be deployed, as in the past, in the form of non-repayable grants aimed at the development of production, infrastructure, social services, trade promotion, etc. Particular emphasis will be placed on the provision of infrastructure (especially health facilities) in rural areas. In addition, ACP goods, with the exception of that tiny fraction of ACP trade in areas covered by the Community's common agricultural

policy (where a preferential arrangement applies) will be accorded free entry
into the Community. Innovatory features of the Convention include an
imaginative scheme to seek to stabilise earnings from exports on which ACP
economies are particularly dependent.

By these means the Community is making its contribution to the world-wide
effort to achieve "social progress and better standards of life in larger
freedom" for all peoples.

SECOND ENVIRONMENT PROGRAMME

Eurobarometer, the twice-yearly public opinion poll carried out for the
Commission, continues to show public support for action to protect and
improve the environment. The Commission has ensured that there will be no
slackening in the Community's effort to respond to public concern and
support, by preparing a second Programme of Action for the period 1977-1981.
This programme, which has been submitted to the Council for decision and
published*, continues and extends the first action programme.

HOUSING CONSTRUCTION AND MODERNISATION

The Social Action Programme gave priority to work on behalf of migrants and
handicapped persons. A sociological survey of the housing conditions of
migrant workers in Member States has been completed, as has a general study
of the cost-effectiveness of housing aids in benefiting those groups of the
population in greatest need and a study of urban renewal has also been
completed. The results of those studies will provide a basis for policy and
action in response to the problem of migrant workers, where prejudice is frequently reinforced by associating migrants with bad housing conditions.
In the field of housing for the handicapped, the Commission has prepared the
ground for the establishment of agreed standards and for the launching of a
programme of pilot schemes which will link the removal of architectural
barriers with the integration of handicapped persons into a normal productive
working life.

The Community involvement in housing construction dates from the beginning
of the Coal and Steel Community. To date, the Community has assisted the
construction or modernisation of over 140,000 dwellings for workers in the
Coal and Steel industries. In the experimental modernisation programme,
800 houses in 9 different places were improved, at a cost equal to 25%-40%
of the cost of new dwellings. A comprehensive report on this programme has
been published.*

REGIONAL DEVELOPMENT

To narrow the gap between the Community's prosperous regions and backward
areas was one of the goals set by the EEC Treaty. The richest areas in the

---

* Bulletin of the European Communities, Supplement 6/76 : Office for Official
  Publications of the European Communities, Luxembourg.

* Modernisation des logements, Office for Official Publications of the
  European Communities, Luxembourg, 1975.

Community have an income per head about five times that of the poorest.
Certain regions have always had high levels of unemployment and there has
always been sizeable migration from some Community regions, in particular
from those at the periphery.

In its "Report on the Regional Problems in the Enlarged Community" (1973),
the Commission pointed out that the physical poverty of the underprivileged
regions is matched only by the mounting environmental poverty of the areas
of concentration.

The Community is far more than an inter-governmental organisation, as its
institutions have power to legislate on matters falling within their competence.
The Commission has proposed, and the Council has adopted or is actively
considering, legislation to reduce several forms of water and air pollution
and of noise, to control the disposal of domestic and industrial wastes
and to regulate the composition of certain products and the activities
of polluting industries.

Community legislation to reduce pollution will improve the quality of
life for everyone but particularly for urban dwellers, who are now
subjected to the dangers and nuisances resulting from the concentration
of people and activities in cities.

IMPROVEMENT OF THE ENVIRONMENT

The Programme of Action on the Environment firmly declared that "qualitative
improvement of living and working conditions is now a fundamental task of
the European Communities" and continued: "an environment programme for
the Community cannot therefore be limited to protecting the physical
environment by combatting pollution but must also make an active contribution
to improving the quality of life".

Among the problems selected for particular attention were those connected
with urban development and the geographical distribution of human activities.
The Commission began by engaging consultants to study the environmental
problems specific to city centres, to coastal areas and to open spaces.
The final reports have recently been received. The megalopolis in formation
in North West Europe has also been studied. An assessment of urban policies
in Member States is in progress. The reports of these studies will be
examined by the Commission, with the assistance of experts from the Member
States, with a view to deciding what action should be taken at Community
level.

In addition to the studies described above, a Community urban research
programme is in preparation. This programme is focussed on the growth of
large urban concentrations and will be implemented as a 'concerted action',
in which a number of research projects in the Member States related to
this theme will be coordinated at Community level. The aim of the programme
is to carry out a comparative analysis of the causes, dynamics and consequences of the development of large urban concentrations in the Community.
It is expected that this research programme will begin on 1st January 1977
and will continue for a period of two years.

The results of work in progress on two other fronts will be of particular significance for land use planning. These are the development of a method of mapping the ecological characteristics of the Community territory and the introduction of environmental impact assessment procedures,which is discussed by Dr. N. Lee in another chapter in this volume.

ENVIRONMENTAL IMPACT ASSESSMENT IN THE EUROPEAN ECONOMIC COMUNITY

Norman Lee
University of Manchester, Manchester, Great Britain.

ABSTRACT

The protection and improvement of the environment of human settlements presumes a policy instrument capable of ensuring that the environmental impacts of poss- ible future activities affecting urban areas are adequately taken into account in planning and decision processes. The United States system of environmental impact statements is examined with this purpose in view but it is concluded that certain of its features may not be appropriate to a number of European countries.

The elements of an alternative, more modest system, still adhering to the prin- ciples of the American system, are discussed. This alternative, it is sugges- ted, might have wider international appeal and might therefore justify some international co-operation in training personnel in environmental impact assessment methods, in the preparation of project and plan assessment manuals, and in the development of environmental-land use models for urban areas.

INTRODUCTION

There is now widespread agreement that the efficient and economical attain- ment of environmental policy objectives in human settlements requires that potential environmental impacts should be taken into consideration during the early stages of selecting and preparing plans and projects. For this reason a comprehensive environmental policy needs to supplement controls over the environmental impacts of existing activities by an instrument ensuring that the environmental impacts of possible <u>future</u> activities are adequately taken into account in planning and decision processes. In this connection, the Council of Ministers of the European Economic Community has accepted both the general principle that "effects on the environment should be taken into account at the earliest possible stage in all technical, planning and dec- ision processes" and the more particular objective that "more account is taken of environmental aspects in town-planning and land use" (1). The European Commission is currently investigating the most appropriate means by which this principle and objective might be implemented.

ENVIRONMENTAL IMPACT STATEMENT PROCEDURES

By the provisions of the National Environmental Policy Act (1969) each U.S. Federal agency is required to "include in every recommendation or report on proposals for legislation and other major federal actions significantly affecting the quality of the human environment, a detailed statement by the responsible official" covering:

(a) the environmental impact of the proposed action;

(b) any adverse environmental effects which cannot be avoided should the
proposal be implemented;
(c) alternatives to the proposed action;
(d) the relationship between local and short-term uses of man's environment
and the maintenance and enhancement of long-term productivity; and
(e) any irreversible and irretrievable commitments of resources which would be
involved in the proposed action should it be implemented.

This environmental impact statement (EIS) forms an integral part of an EIS
procedure of which the essential features are:

(a) a draft EIS should be prepared and made available prior to the first
significant point of decision in the agency's review process;
(b) the agency should consult with, and (on the basis of the draft EIS)
obtain the comments on the environmental impact of the action, of the public
and of other agencies; and
(c) a final version of the EIS should be prepared, incorporating the sub-
stantive comments received, and this should accompany the proposed action
through the remainder of the agency's review process.

By June 1974, statements on 5,430 federal actions had been filed with the
Council on Environmental Quality and, by the same date, 21 states and a num-
ber of cities had adopted EIS requirements similar to those contained in the
NEPA legislation (2).

The implementation of this EIS system in the United States has generated a
great deal of interest in a large number of countries in N. America,
Australasia and Europe and in such organisations as OECD, ECE, the Council
of Europe and the World Bank. Within the European Economic Community, a
number of Member States have initiated their own investigations of EIS procedures or are proposing to take action enabling some form of environmental
impact assessment system to be implemented.

In the case of the Federal Republic of Germany, the Federal Cabinet Order of
9th September 1972 provided that the Combined Rules of Procedure of the Federal Ministers be extended in the following ways:

(a) in the case of draft laws, regulations and administrative provisions
which might have a bearing on environmental protection, the Federal Ministry
of the Interior must be called upon at an early stage of the preparatory work
to ensure that an examination for environmental compatibility is carried out
to avoid or counteract damage to the environment; and
(b) it must be stated in the preamble to all draft laws and regulations
whether or not there are likely to be effects on the environment.

Subsequently the Federal Ministry of the Interior prepared a Model Procedure
to provide a standard system for examining proposals for environmental compatibility. Federal cabinet approval has since been given to the application
of the Model Procedure to all federal actions.

In France, a draft bill relating to the protection of the environment is
currently being considered by the National Assembly which proposes that works
and planning projects which are undertaken by a public agency or which
require a licence or other form of authorisation must observe environmental

requirements. A National Assembly Commission on the Draft Bill (3) has recently proposed strengthening this provision so that:

(a) a special environmental impact study must be prepared in relation to
each of a wide range of proposed public actions and this study must be taken
into account in reaching a decision on each proposed action; and
(b) the study must be available for consultation by the public.

In Ireland the Local Government (Planning and Development) Bill proposes to
require the preparation of a 'written study' of the effect each proposed
large development will have on the environment. This 'written study' would
then form an integral part of the Irish development control procedure.

The United Kingdom government has commissioned two studies relating to the
possible use of environmental impact assessment procedures as part of its
development control system. The first study is an internal investigation at
the Department of the Environment and is due to be completed by the end of
March 1976 (4). The second study, which is directed to the preparation of
an impact assessment manual, is jointly commissioned by the Scottish Development Department and the Department of the Environment and is being conducted at the University of Aberdeen (5). The report of this work is expected
to be published by the Department of the Environment by Easter, 1976.

In the Netherlands the Ministers of Health and Environmental Hygiene and of
Economic Affairs have invited the Central Advisory Council on the Environment
to study the EIS procedure as it operates in the USA and to advise them on
its possible application in their country. The final report of the Council
is expected to be completed in July 1976.

ATTITUDES TOWARDS THE UNITED STATES SYSTEM

It is clearly too soon to specify, in any definitive sense, the views on the
American EIS system which are held within the Member States of the European
Community. However, certain attitudes are forming and issues are being
raised which it would be appropriate to examine in this conference.

There does appear to be broad support within the Member States, including
those States which are not currently undertaking specific studies or proposing action in the area, for a more systematic approach to environmental
impact assessment and for its integration within certain planning and decision
processes. However, for reasons that will shortly become apparent, there is a
clear preference favouring the introduction of an environmental impact assessment system in a phased manner and, to the extent that is practicable, of
incorporating environmental impact assessment procedures into existing planning and decision processes rather than creating entirely new ones.

There are certain aspects of the United States EIS system which are a source
of some concern amongst those forming views on its operation. The principal
concerns include the following:

(a) that it may result in considerable delays in decision making, due to the
length of time needed to produce a satisfactory draft EIS and due to the
additional time taken up by the agency consultation and public participation
process;
(b) that it may disrupt existing decision and planning processes;

(c) that providing a public statement of details relating to a proposed action
may prejudice the commercial interests of the applicant;
(d) that gaps in scientific knowledge may prevent a reliable assessment of
environmental impact being made; that insufficient trained staff may be
available to prepare a large number of statements; and that statements may
not be of a sufficiently high standard.

In certain cases these concerns may be exaggerated or arise from misunderstanding - for example, delays may be due to other factors (6) - but in
other cases they indicate that modifications to the American system may be
necessary.

AN ALTERNATIVE SYSTEM OF ENVIRONMENTAL IMPACT ASSESSMENT

In devising an alternative system which alleviates the above concerns but
still contains the essential principles of the US system, special consideration should be given to the scope and phasing of the introduction of the
system, to the required content of statements and to the embodiment of
environmental impact assessment within existing planning and decision processes. Each of these is now briefly examined.

Scope and phasing of the system

Many of the concerns previously mentioned are related to the varied types
and large number of actions for which environmental impact statements might
be required. For this reason there is a widely-held view that a new system
of environmental impact assessment would have greater chance of success if,
particularly in the early stages, it was restricted to a much smaller quantity of actions than under the United States system and if these actions
were of a kind for which the methods of environmental impact assessment were
currently most developed.

In considering the possible phasing in the introduction of an environmental
impact assessment system, it is possible to distinguish five main categories
of action to which such a system might apply:

(a) draft laws and application decrees (legislative assessment);
(b) approval of land use, sectoral and other plans (plan assessment);
(c) authorisation of specific new developments (project assessment);
(d) approval of research and development projects and programmes (R & D
assessment); and
(e) approval of new products.

Logically, one might argue, a phased introduction of an environmental impact
assessment system should commence with legislative and plan assessment before
proceeding to project assessment. Ideally, legislation and plans should provide the previously-evaluated framework within which the more detailed environmental impact assessment of individual projects is undertaken. However, it
is almost certainly the case, given the present state of knowledge, that the
environmental impact assessment of projects can be more reliably undertaken
than the corresponding assessment of draft legislation and plans. Therefore,
it may be necessary to consider the initial application of environmental
impact assessment procedures to projects whilst developing the capability
for the more reliable impact assessment of legislation and plans. The con-

siderations involved in developing this capability in relation to plans are
discussed later in the paper.

Even if the first phase of an environmental impact assessment system is
restricted to projects one would not wish to apply a full assessment procedure to all projects. The United States system is restricted to major
actions significantly affecting the quality of the human environment, but
such terms as 'major' and 'significant' are not easily translated into measurable criteria. The criteria most frequently mentioned in determining the
scope of the environmental impact assessment of projects are the type, size
and location of proposed developments. The Conference might consider
whether more specific guide-lines based on these criteria can be developed.
This is a task of some importance since it will determine the number as well
as the types of developments falling within the jurisdiction of the proposed
assessment system.

Content of impact statements

A number of the statements produced in the United States (particularly in the
early stages following the introduction of the EIS system) have been of
great length, involved considerable preparatory work and yet been considered
less than satisfactory (2), (7). The proposal to restrict the number of
statements to be prepared should enable greater attention to be given to the
quality of statements. The lack of preparation, however, is also affected
by the type of statement that it is decided to prepare. In this context,
the following questions deserve consideration.

(a) How wide a range of impacts should an environmental impact statement
    attempt to assess? Should it, for example, include impacts on employ-
    ment, the social structure of communities, personal life-styles, etc. or
    should it be restricted to impacts on the physical and natural environ-
    ments of human settlements? The conclusion reached may not only affect
    the volume of preparatory work needed but also the nature of the tech-
    nical problems involved in statement preparation.

(b) Should the statement be a decision-making document, containing a recom-
    mendation on the desirability of the project to which it relates? If
    so, it will need to balance environmental impacts against other (e.g.
    financial) impacts as in cost-benefit assessment. Apart from the
    technical difficulties involved, this may encroach upon the decision-
    making responsibility of the authorising agency. Alternatively, the
    EIS might be viewed in the more modest rate of a documentary input
    (possibly alongside other documentary inputs) to the decision-making
    process.

(c) Should all possible impacts associated with a project be examined in the
    same degree of detail? Screening procedures can be used to narrow down,
    at an early stage in the preparation of an EIS, the number of impacts
    and types of receptors which are to be studied in detail.

Relationship to existing decision processes

Within the Member States of the Community there is a clear preference to
incorporate any new procedures for environmental impact assessment into
existing planning and decision processes rather than to establish new areas.
This is understandable to the extent that provision already exists for some
form of environmental impact assessment within a number of existing decision

processes. This is particularly the case in the authorisation of new industrial developments in the private sector.

Each Member State in the European Community has some existing legislative
provision (often, originally introduced many decades ago) for authorising the
siting, building and operation of industrial establishments. Special legislation normally covers nuclear installations but there are usually more
general provisions covering important industrial developments in the private
sector which may have a significant impact on the human environment. Examples
of this more general legislative provision are contained in the following
table.

TABLE 1   Examples of Legislative provision for the authorisation
           of new projects in the Member States of the Community

Belgium	General Regulation for the Protection of Labour (origi-nating from Law of 1888)
Denmark	Environmental Protection Act 1973
Federal Republic of Germany	Federal Immission Control Law 1974
France	Law of 19th December 1917 relating to dangerous, insani-tary etc. establishments (frequently revised – Draft Law 138 (1975) currently before the National Assembly)
Ireland	Local Government (Planning and Development Act) 1963 (to be amended by Local Government (Planning and Develop-ment) Bill 1973)
Italy	Various provisions, including Law 615 (1966) on air pollution
Luxembourg	Grand-Ducal Order of 17th June 1872
Netherlands	Air Pollution Act 1970, Nuisance Act 1952, Surface Waters Pollution Act 1969 (further legislation on chemi-cal and other wastes is pending)
United Kingdom	Town and Country Planning Act 1971 (separate legislation applies in Scotland and Northern Ireland).

Subject to a small number of exceptions this legislation provides for the
supply of certain documentation by the developer which is relevant to the
assessment of the project's likely environmental impact; for some degree of
agency and public consultation; and for the consultation findings to be considered in the later stages of the authorisation process. In other words, an
embryonic system of environmental impact assessment of projects already
exists in a number of countries. However, the system may not apply to all
appropriate developments (particularly all appropriate public sector developments); the documentation required may be insufficient for an adequate environmental impact assessment; and the provisions for consultation may be too
limited or insufficiently formalised. To this extent there is a need to
strengthen and extend existing provisions for the environmental impact assessment of projects.

ENVIRONMENTAL IMPACT ASSESSMENT OF PLANS

Although the systematic environmental impact assessment of major projects
should make a significant contribution to the long-term improvement in environmental quality in urban areas, this contribution could be greatly enhanced
by subjecting urban and related plans to similar forms of assessment. Some
of the issues involved in extending the assessment system to planning processes are now considered.

Area of application

Within each of the Member States of the Community a relatively large number
of plan-making activities are undertaken. There exist a variety of land-use
plans relating to geographic areas of different sizes - regional, provincial,
conurbation and local. Generally speaking, the land-use plans covering the
larger areas are of a more strategic nature (and involve elements of economic
planning) whereas local plans tend to pay greater regard to land zoning.
However, in addition there may be sectoral plans relating to such matters as
transport, energy, water supply etc. which can exercise an important influence on land-use plans for urban communities.

Therefore, as in the case of project assessment, it is necessary to establish
the criteria for determining which plans should be subject to an environmental
impact assessment procedure and whether there should be a phased introduction
to plan assessment, applying the procedure to certain types of plans in
advance of its application to others.

Content and form of assessment

The term 'environmental impact statement' may not necessarily be the most
appropriate term to describe the written input on environmental assessment to
the plan-making process. In the case of local land-use plans, whose primary
objectives are often already of an environmental nature, all the documentation should be concerned, explicitly or implicitly, with environmental considerations. Therefore, provided this documentation is of an acceptable
standard, a requirement for a separate environmental impact statement may be
superfluous. This conclusion, however, may not be valid in the case of sector plans which have different primary objectives.

The requirements relating to the content of an environmental impact assessment may need to be adjusted to take account of the type of plan concerned.
For example, the assessment of a sectoral plan for energy would probably
examine different types of impact (or, in certain cases, the same impacts at
a different level of generality) than a local land-use plan. The former might
involve a more strategic assessment of physical, pollution and energy resource impacts whereas the second might pay greater attention to the local
spatial distribution of physical and pollution impacts.

If the environmental impact assessment of plans is to be developed, then a
strengthening of the methods and techniques of assessment is needed. In
the past, certain types of environmental impact (for example, pollution
impacts (8)) have received insufficient attention in plan-making studies.
Also, greater precision is needed in measures of the environmental impact
 of different patterns of land-use development. In the longer term we look
to the development of land-use - environmental methods to complement the
land-use-transportation models already used for planning purposes (9). In
the meantime worthwhile progress can be made in using environmental monitoring

data to map existing and trend levels for different parameters of environmental quality in relation to pre-determined planning norms for particular urban
areas (9).

Structure of the environmental impact assessment procedure
It would seem most appropriate to attach the environmental impact assessment
procedure to existing plan-making systems, thus paralleling the suggested
arrangement for project assessment. In the case of many local land-use
planning systems there is already some provision for the preparation of documentation on environmental impact assessment, for agency and public consultation, and for the findings of the consultation process to be utilised in the
later stages of plan-making. Where this is the situation, one would be seeking a strengthening of existing practice. In the case of sectoral plans
where both the preparation of documentation on environmental impact assessment and direct consultation with the public are less developed, greater
changes in existing practice may be needed.

CONCLUSION

An integral element in protecting and improving the environment of human
settlements is the adoption of an instrument ensuring that the environmental
impacts of possible future actions in urban areas are adequately taken into
account in planning and decision processes. The United States system of
environmental impact statements is one possible instrument to achieve this
purpose but certain of its features may not be sufficiently appropriate to
a number of European and, possibly, other countries. Nevertheless it
should be possible to develop an alternative system which still adheres to
the basic principles of the American system. Such a system would be introduced in phases, it would be restricted to a smaller number of actions, the
range of impacts assessed in depth would be reduced, and it would be incorporated into existing planning and decision processes.

Such an alternative system, given its more modest demands on time and personnel, may provide a framework within which the environmental impact assessment of projects and plans for urban areas in other types of economy may
be developed. If this has wider international appeal then some international
co-operation may be justified in:

(a) training of technical personnel in the methods and techniques of environmental impact assessment in urban areas;
(b) preparation of impact assessment manuals for projects and plans; and
(c) research on urban environmental quality monitoring, environmental mapping in urban areas, and the development of land-use-environmental quality
models.

REFERENCES

(1) Commission of the European Communities, Declaration on the programme of
       action of the European Communities on the environment, Official
       Journal of the European Communities (20.12.1973)

(2) Council on Environmental Quality (1974) Environmental quality: annual
       report, U.S. Government Printing Office, Washington.

(3) National Assembly (1975) Report of the Commission on the draft law relat-
     ing to the protection of nature, (No. 1765), Paris.

(4) Thirlwall, C.G. and Catlow, J. (1975) Environmental impact analysis,
     Proceedings of the Symposium on Environmental Evaluation, Canterbury
     PATRAC, Department of the Environment, London.

(5) Clark, B.D. (1975) Project appraisal Proceedings of the Symposium on
     Environmental Evaluation, Canterbury, PATRAC, Department of the
     Environment, London.

(6) Goldsmith, B.J. (1974) Delays in initiating construction of energy
     facilities in the United States, due to environmental review pro-
     cedures OECD, Paris.

(7) Greenberg, M.R. and Horden, R.M. Environmental impact statements, some
     annoying questions, Journal of the American Institute of Planners,
     40, 164 (1974).

(8) Lee, N. and Wood, C.M., Planning and pollution, Journal of the Royal
     Town Planning Institute, 58, 153 (1972).

(9) Wood, C.M., Lee, N., Luker, J.A. and Saunders, P.J.W., (1974) The
     Geography of pollution: a study of Greater Manchester, Manchester
     University Press, Manchester.

A COMPUTER SYSTEMS APPROACH TO AN INTEGRATED REGIONAL PLANNING PROJECT AND ENVIRON— MENTAL PLANNING

T. Shiina, President
IBM Japan, Ltd.
2-12 Roppongi 3-Chome,
Minato-ku, Tokyo 106, Japan

ABSTRACT

Japan has been faced with serious environmental problems associated with a rapid regional development. Several counter measures have been taken to cope with some of problems, such as a concentration regulation and a total emession control. However, those alone are not enough to resolve the complex problematique. In view of this, the Environment Agency of the Japanese Government is preparing a bill to be proposed to the National Diet which will establish a government basic policy on a total Environmental Impact Assessment.

In this paper, we are going to propose a systems approach along this direction. Regional development projects are to pass, first of all, a basic filtering system to be cleared in environmental standards and land use regulations, etc. Then, the selected development plans should pass a regional effects prediction system with a result which will be processed through the assessment system that follows. The plans are to be open to the public to get regional consensus among related bodies.

Experiences in case studies are presented which are carried out jointly with Local Government of Japan - Hyogo Prefecture.

INTRODUCTION

Japan has attained the highest degree of affluence and prosperity in its history as a result of the great strides made by its economy in recent years. This fast growth of the economy, however, has created various social strains. For instance, environmental pollution has become a nation-wide problem, jeopardizing the living environment and the health of the people.

A system of environmental assessment is indispensable to study and determine in advance the environmental impact of such

activities which affect the environment as regional development.
However, experience with environmental assessment is still
limited and many points concerning methodology, factors to be
checked, etc., await further study.

In June 1972 the Cabinet approved the idea of making preliminary
assessment, when necessary, of how various kinds of public works
and regional development would affect the environment. This
idea is even closer to being implemented now that the Seto Inland
Sea Conservation Law has been enacted. In FY 1974 efforts will
be made to develop the techniques and set the guidelines for
such assessment.

A SYSTEMS APPROACH TO AN INTEGRATED REGIONAL PLANNING

A multi-stage assessment concept is proposed for regional development projects to be assessed aiming at the resolution of societal
conflicts among several business bodies including regional
people.

A multi-level hierachical systems concept in modern control
methodologies is the basic idea of this approach.

Applied systems analysis methodologies are utilized assisted by
modern computer technologies such as interactive handling of
data and models representing generated informations on a graphic
display system in order to enhance communication between a computer system and policy planners. And an organizational system is
to be designed in such a way that systems flexibility should be
maximized in an operational environment. Among systems analysis
techniques, prediction methods of various kinds play very
important roles, on the basis of data stored in a well-structured
manner in the computer system. Adverse effects as well as
positive socio-economic effects are projected for the necessary
time period. Assessment system model is one of the most difficult ones to be developed and operated. The concept to overcome
this difficulties is an iterative and spiral use of a total
assessment system with the participation of the concerned people.
Gaming concepts are implicity implemented during these procedures.

Societal Conflict Resolution by Multi-level Assessment Concept

Figure 1 shows a conceptual input-output relationship in a
regional management system for a regional development project
planning.

Objective and major concept. We have designed the system in such
a way that an input regional development plan will be decided
upon in regard to its own peculiar goals with the consensus of
apparently conflicting concerned bodies. A major underlying
concept is "a societal coordination through multi-stage assessment process".

Plan with an augmented information. During the regional plan
moves from left to right, plan element is broken down into
several consituent elements. At the same time, uncertainties
associated with the plan will be minimized by, human intervention
in the process.

Thus, a conceptual regional development plan from a conceptual
idea evolves gaining its maturity to attain regional concensus,
eventually.

Basis Role of a Computer Assisted System

As described in Fig. 1, a computer system is playing a supporting role. Timely informations will be supplied to each stage
interactively.

The Regional Development Planning System is composed of Regional
Development Project Impact Assessment System (PIAS) as an applied
system and Computer Assisted Regional development Planning System
(CARPS) as a tool of Regional Development Planning System. The
PIAS and CARPS are the system to prepare project information for
the coordination activities. The PIAS is the operating system
which is assisted by CARPS (Computer System) and in this system,
human factors and mechanized factors are well combined. Some
functional characteristics of the system are shown in Table 1.

The CARPS must have the following functions.

Geo-data handling and display. It loads, accumulates, retrieve
and display geo-data. With this function, the System can assist
a plan with areal expanse. Geo-data are assumed to consist of
"Map", which expresses geographical relations and "Regional
Information", which are the attributes of maps. Geo-data processing is given flexibility by dividing maps into "regional division",
"expression of divided area" and "Expression of Boundary".

Processing of geo-temporal data for model operation
It makes models, such as the impact prediction of a composite
project and assists simulation. It also input, retrieves and
process geo-data and time-series data effectively and flexibly.
It provides data as exogenous variables of models and assists
geo-data retrieval, as well.

Model Operation Function that assists modelling and simulation
allows planners to use various models easily and to link various
models conversationally by such a variety of functions as
description of model structure, description of data, quotation of
other models, quotation of data outside model, specification of
a part of model definition at execution time, conditional simulation, and sequential simulation.

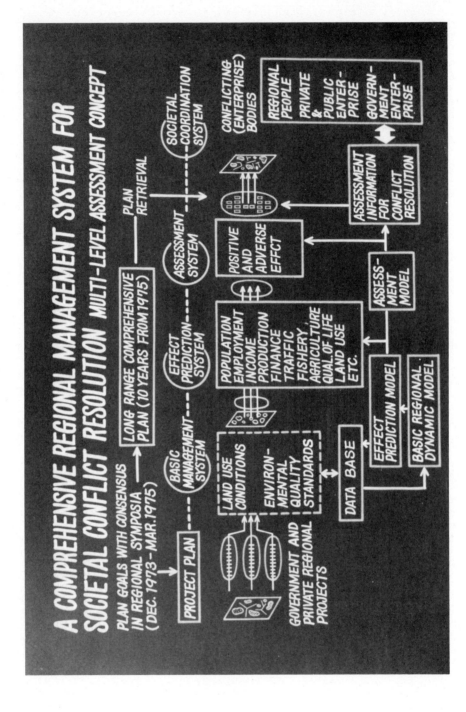

Fig. 1. A comprehensive regional management system for societal conflict resolution

Flexible system operation. It assists the organic linkage of the systems constituting the Regional Development Planning System according to users' problems and assists integrated system operation. Users give instructions to a computer through Conversational Operation Function and calls out the functions that assist the solution of problems and links the functions organically.

The Interrelation between PIAS and CARPS is shown in Fig. 2.

A Prototype Systems Development

A prototype system is under development jointly by Tokyo Scientific Center, IBM Japan and Hyogo Prefectural Government.

Table 1 Functional Characteristics of Regional Management System

Subsystem	Functional Characteristics
Basic Management System	- for preliminary screening and filtering - from financial, land use condition and environmental quality standard point of view - handling spacially distributed regional data - supported greatly by human judgement
Effect Prediction System	- for interrelated regional project impact estimation - on the basis of dynamic regional behaviour - referring to socio-economic status at the national level
Assessment System	- to evaluate positive and negative (adverse) effects simultaneously - in a multi-dimensional fashion
Societal Coordination System	- for conflict resoltion - among interested enterprise bodies - by citizens' participation

Note:

Input regional development project plans should pass an above series of subsystems consecutively and spirally to be finalized.

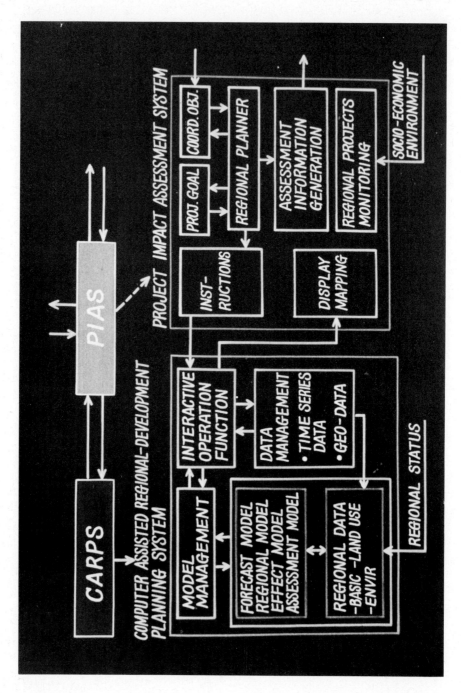

Fig. 2. Project impact assessment system and computer assisted regional development system

CASE STUDIES

Since 1972, we have jointly developed planning support system for
the local government of Japan - Hyogo Prefecture. This local
government is located about 550 km west by south west of Tokyo,
with her population of about 4,990,000 as of June, 1975 in an
area of 8,373.5 km^2. 70% of the area is mountaneous covered by
forest. The heart of the District is Kobe City with the population of 1,350,000.

Hyogo, as a miniature of Japanese island is suffering from
regional problem complex as is described in Fig. 3.

Some case studies are introduced which have been carried out in
an integrated regional development project.

An Assessment of a Long Range Comprehensive Plan by a Hyogo Dynamic Model

Hyogo Prefecture has set its sights on the realization by 1985 of
a "New Comprehensive Plan" that would result in the creation of a
welfare state. This plan will replace and complement an earlier
plan which proved to lack a sufficiently concrete and systematic
attitude towards human life, social welfare and cultural requirements. The Hyogo Dynamic Model has been developed as an information system to assist work on the New Comprehensive Plan. The
activities are being carried on with the participation of both
the Council for the Comprehensive Plan which is an advisory body
to the governor, and the general public. The Comprehensive Plan
consists of a basic plan and a regional development plan. In
drawing up the basic plan, consideration had to be given to the
long-term possibilities and limitations of important societal
elements. (Fig. 4.a)

In the regional development plan, regional management concepts
require the establishment of multi-dimensional assessment criteria
so as to enable the responsible planners to make sensible decisions under uncertain conditions. This is realized in PIAS-CARPS.

Hyogo Dynamic System is identified as an upper system to regional
management system.

A new comprehensive plan being formed. The output results of a
series of computer simulation had been submitted to regional
symposia after compilation and editting for presentation. The
presentation to the regional people had been made in a sophisticated manner equipped with a conversational approach. The
symposia were held in 52 different subregions of Hyogo District.
80% of the opinion amounting to 2,000 gathered through these
processes were reflected in the draft of the new comprehensive
plan for the coming 10 years.

The governer, Mr. T. Sakai decided to adopt the new plan supported
by Hyogo Dynamics in March, 1975.

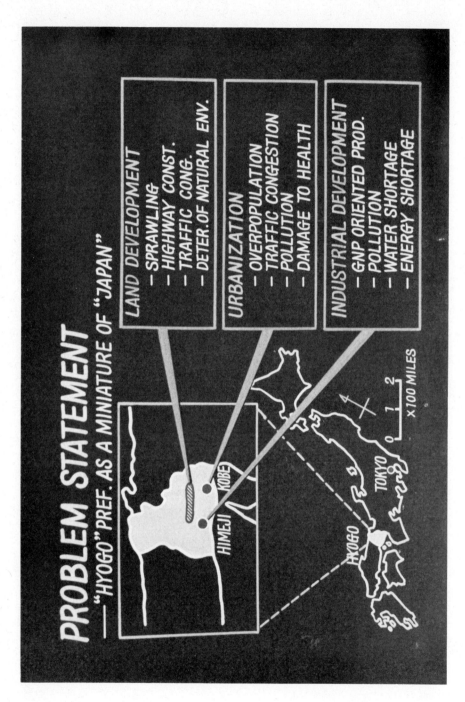

Fig. 3. The problem statement in HYOGO Prefecture (Japan)

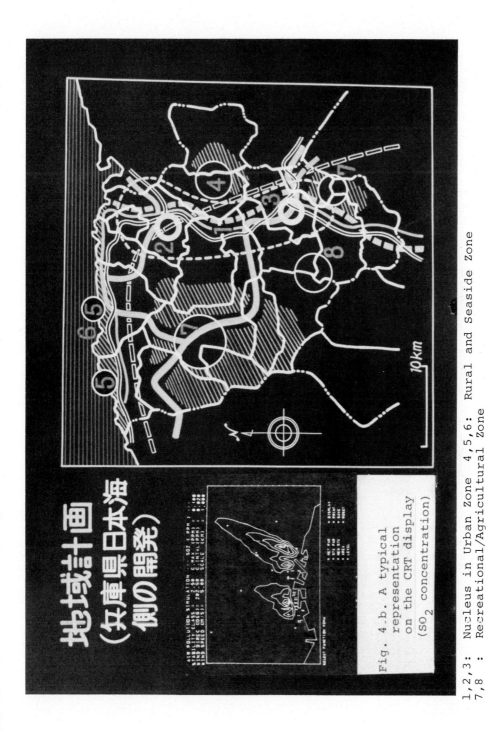

Fig. 4.b. A typical
representation
on the CRT display
(SO_2 concentration)

Fig. 4-a. Integrated regional development program in Hyogo

1,2,3: Nucleus in Urban Zone 4,5,6: Rural and Seaside Zone
7,8 : Recreational/Agricultural Zone

A Conversational System for a Plant Site Evaluation

Himeji, with its population of 420,000 is the hub of the bustl-
ing Harima industrial region facing the Inland Sea in Hyogo.
The city is bordered by hills to the north and slopes gently
southward to the coast where steel mills, thermal power plants,
petro-chemical and manufacturing industries dominate the skyline.

A conversational approach through computer graphics. A man-
machine systems approach is employed to assist the planner in
assessing the projects impact on the regional environment. The
graphic display system is introduced as a communication medium
among planners and the computer simulation system. Our system
is designed in such a way that a human decision is assisted by
investigating the air pollution concentration patterns at the
ground level over the subject area. Gaussian plume model is
used on the basis of a well established statistical method.

Through computer graphics, it is now possible to determine in
advance the pattern in which pollutants will diffuse - in
direction, density, and so on - under any combination of conditions. And it is possible to obtain a diffusion pattern not
only for the area, but for each individual smokestack as well.
This kind of information will make it possible to determine, for
example, not to permit the construction of a new plant at site
'A' because its smokestack emission will contaminate area 'B'
which is a residential section, or to reduce factory operation
during certain hours in certain months when prevailing wind
currents could otherwise carry contaminants over dense population areas. (Fig. 4.b)

ACKNOWLEDGEMENT

The author would like to appreciate assistance and cooperative
efforts in carrying out project activities by staff members of
Hyogo Prefecture, Tokyo Scientific Center and many other concerned organizations.

REFERENCES

1. Environment Agency, Quality of the Environment in Japan, 1974.

2. Shiina, T., A Systems Approach to Human Survival, Life
    Science Symposium, Tokyo, 1974

3. Shiina, T., A Computer Assisted Long Range Comprehensive
    Planning System for a Regional Project Impact Assessment in
    Land Use Planning, IFAC Sixth Triennial World Congress,
    Boston, 1975

4. Matsuzaki, T., Sawaragi, Y., A Computer Systems Approach to
    the Assessment of Regional Project Impact on the Environment
    Proc. of International Congress of Scientists on the Human
    Environment, Kyoto, 1975

REGIONAL MANAGEMENT AND SOCIAL CLASS: THE CASE OF EASTERN EUROPE

Ivan SZELENYI - Department of
Sociology - University of Canterbury at Kent -
Canterbury (Kent) - ENGLAND.

INTRODUCTION

Urban and regional phenomena have attracted the interest of sociologists both in the West and in Eastern Europe during the last fifteen years - we might be witnessing the birth of a "new urban sociology". It is increasingly realized, that the urban and regional system is directly related to the structural problems and processes of our societies. Herbert Gans in his pioneering essay on urbanism proposed to explain urban differentiation in terms of social stratification, and convincingly questioned the usefulness of urban sociology - dominant during the late forties and fifties, focusing on "urbanism as a way of life", on the specific character of urban value system, attitudes and behaviour. Gans was interested more in what is characteristically "social" rather than what is "urban". Certainly there is a long way from this proposition to the position of contemporary neo-marxist urban sociology, which is based on the hypothesis that the urban question can be understood only from an analysis of the mode of production. At the economic level at least, there are no specifically "urban social relations" (M. Castells and F. Lamarche), there are only class relations in cities, but despite ideological differences the distinguished representatives of the new urban sociology, from the liberals of the early sixties to the French radicals of the early seventies do have at least one thing in common : they were looking at the urban phenomena as an expression of the structural conflicts in the society.

Most empirical research in urban sociology in the sixties was focused on the question of social inequalities, trying to measure to what extent social inequalities created elsewhere (mostly on the labour market), are expressed in the urban system, and whether the urban and regional system merely reflected these inequalities in terms of differential access to housing, to the means of collective consumption etc. or whether these inequalities were affected - increased or counter-balanced - by urban policies.

Thus the new liberal urban sociology accepted an active role in shaping urban policies, in making policy recommandations to planners and State or local authorities as to where and how to intervene into "spontaneous" market processes, to create more equality, more social justice.

Regional planners and State authorities welcomed this new
research orientation since the urban and regional economy
became more centrally controlled anyway, an increasing proportion of the surplus for infrastructural development (for
housing, investments into communal infrastructure, into the
"means of collective consumption" etc.) was redistributed by
the State, in forms of grants to local authorities.

Sociologists were invited to committees working on the reforms of local governments, regional plans etc. and many of
us - both in the West and in Eastern Europe - believed that
we might bring more social justice in the urban and regional
system by improving the mechanisms of State redistribution.

We, in Eastern Europe, who were interested in the social
class implications of urban and regional processes, started
to wonder about the nature and social class character of
State regulation of urban and regional processes, and since
the answer to this question we could borrow from an orthodox
marxist theory - namely that the Socialist State is a "worker's
State" - contradicted too sharply to our empirical findings
we also had to focus our attention on the very system of regional management in trying to relate it to the general social
reproduction process. But here we were confronted with the
empirical facts of a functioning redistributive economy which
has been an ideological notion to our Western marxists colleagues, and even to most of the Western liberal reformers.

To formulate the problem more empirically I would like to
refer to my research carried out in Hungary during the last
decade. I found that the redistribution of surplus through
the urban and regional system creates its own inequalities.
Our research falsified the hypothesis of the Western new left
which suggested that social inequalities in Eastern Europe
are created or maintained by the survival (or revival) of
market forces. For example, the State allocation of flats
leads in fact to the redistribution of surplus in favour of
the more qualified, of the white collars and especially professionals. I become convinced that socialist redistribution
produces social consequences, unexpected by tratitional leftish ideologies.

This paper represents an invitation to conduct comparative
analysis of different regional management systems and the system of social conflicts built upon them and conditioned by
the social reproduction process. I will try to define the
contemporary East European redistributive system as a distinct model, different in principle from the market based
Western system, and I will try to show how socialist redistribution is creating its own conflicts by solving some of
the contradictions inherent in market conditions.

In this paper I will try to identify social relations, in fact
social class relations behind the urban scene. Urban and regional processes are interesting to me as long as they express
structural conflicts in the society and this way I share the
interests of those I called "new urban sociologists"earlier.
On the other hand, I try to identify social conflicts created
by those redistributive institutions which are widely regarded as the remedies of social class conflicts. Both liberal
reformists and even more revolutionary socialists might find
my arguments ideologically disarming. Although I do not have
ideological ambitions, and I try to make my analysis more
ideology-critical than ideological, I hope the contrary is
true and the demystification of certain elements of the "social ethos of redistribution" might stimulate more thinking
and research about alternatives to the dichotomy of private
ownership based market and State redistribution, which after
all might not offer an exciting choice.

I. <u>TOWARD A TYPOLOGY OF REGIONAL MANAGEMENT SYSTEMS</u>

1. <u>The Weberian ideal types of urban management.</u>

When I first tried to elaborate a theoretical model for the
description of the contemporary East European regional management system I found the distinction made by Weber between
Eastern and Western urban development the most stimulating.
First of all the weberian distinction offered a methodology
to relate the problems of "urban management" to societal
processes, namely to the problems of social reproduction and
power structure, secondly I was struck by the distinct character of the contemporary East European system from both of
the ideal types suggested by Weber.

In his historical sociology Weber wondered why capitalism
developed in the West and why its development was blocked in
Asia, when the level of economic growth, the state of "productive forces" were not significantly different between
European and Asian societies at the time when they started to
diverge from each other. Obviously he was dissatisfied with
the marxian proposition that the development of productive
forces determines changes in social organiz tion and he was
looking for "intervening variables" of social change. Among
these intervening variables he identified the protestant
ethic, rational law and bureaucracy ..... and the Western
system of urban management.

According to Weber's description, the Eastern urban management
system was dominated by the strong centralized Asian bureaucracy. Asian cities were not autonomous in economic, legal
or in a political sense. City governments were not elected,
but appointed. The Western paradigm of "Stadtluft macht frei"
was not valid for Asian urbanization, which did not represent
an alternative to feudal relationship, and urban-rural

migration did not alter the status in the feudal system.

This urban management system served the purposes of the Asian
type of expropriation of surplus, the amount of expropriated
surplus being maximized and channelled into the state bureaucracy. Surplus was centralized and later redistributed for
societal purposes. The basic function of the redistributive
institutions was to assure simple reproduction and when the
surplus exceeded its requirements it was used for the strengh-
tening of the very redistributive structure rather than for
enlarged reproduction.

The Western urban management system already started to diverge
from this pattern under European feudalism. Cities questionned
the legal and economic power of the feudal lords upon themselves. Cities looked on their inhabitants as their citizens,
developed their own jurisprudence and legislation. They were
willing to pay taxes to the feudal lords but as legally autonomous units they paid their taxes as units.

Western cities started to have their representative governments. The city government represented local interests against
the interests of the feudal lors, or later against any interests of "central government".

Weber described this Western system of urban management as a
pre-condition of the development of capitalism.

If we would try to re-interpret the Weberian analysis in terms
of urban political economy, we would have to point out the
crucial importance of private ownership, especially the private ownership of land which is the basic economic institution of the self regulating regional management system.

This is clearly in contrast with the prebendal ownership,
where land does not have a "price" since it cannot be expropriated and accordingly it cannot have a rent either.

Higher concentration of capital in cities led to a differential ground rent of urban land which not only exploited the
urban proletariat through especially high rents but also
channelled more surplus into urban development. This basically determined the character of urbanization in Western
Europe, where, in the period of extensive industrialization,
it was a specific feature of West European development that
the creation of infrastructure even preceeded industrial investments in contrast with contemporary East European-urba-
nization, which is caused by a delayed infrastructural deve-
lopmentcompared with industrial growth, and which has basically different social consequences as well as we will try to
show on the following pages. In market economies the self
regulating regional system serves the interest of capitalist

accumulation and industrialization in allocating the surplus
in favour of urban centres and consequently the regional
structure created by this system can be characterised by the
urban-rural conflict, by the exploitation of rural villages
by industrial cities.

2. Certain characteristics of urbanization and regional management and socio-economic change in pre-revolutionary
   Eastern Europe.

Since my major task is to present the East European "socialist redistributive system" of regional management as an
alternative ideal type to both the Asian redistributive and
the traditional West European self-regulating regional management system, I will be mostly concerned with the origine
of the present East European system.

Eastern Europe started to diverge from the Western model of
modernization long before the socialist revolution. The historical continuity of certain basic economic and social institutions, especially those of State intervention in the
process of social and economic change, is quite striking as
demonstrated by authors like Gerschenkorn, Nove, etc.

Notes on strategies of development and their impact on the
socio-economic system.

East European societies realized that the gradual introduction of market institutions was far too slow a process to
face effectively the economic and military challenge the
Western world presented. A higher rate of expropriation of
surplus and a faster accumulation of capital was needed that
was assured by the market and private ownership.

Contrary to the Western patterns it was not the full scale
development of the labour market which led to economic growth
but exactly the oppression of market forces. By the time of
Peter the Great the Russian State was in fact the largest
industrial entrepreneur and was supporting industrialization
not only by capital extracted from agricultural export but
also by the labour of the so-called "factory serfs", usually
state serfs sent to industrial work. I would argue that in
Eastern Europe from the sixteenth century on, we can observe
the emergence of new institutions of economic integration.
Strong centralized monarchies in the West did play a crucial
role in guaranteeing the development of market institutions
and encouraging economic growth, but the East European States,
especially Russia successfully adopted certain institutions
of the Asian redistributive economies(first of all, the land
tenure system) for the tasks of growth. This required a revolutionary transformation. Certainly pre-revolutionary East
European economies were mixed, they combined redistributive

and market institutions but only the socialist revolution
assured the final victory of redistribution. Before the socialist transformation of these societies the convergence of
these economies with the Western market economies always has
been a realistic alternative, but from the perspectives of
contemporary socialist societies the specific feature of the
East European development during these centuries is not so
much this mixed character of its economic institutions but
more the rationalization of the redistributive institutions.

Urbanization under the conditions of agricultural underemployment.

We would indeed suggest that urbanization and regional management diverged from the Western pattern also much earlier
than the socialist revolution, and this divergence can be
explained by the new agricultural structure ; the Prussian
system of regional management. In the Prussian mode of agricultural development the large estates were based on the
labour services of the serfs and not on hired labour, on the
lack of commodity producing peasant economy, and on the lack
of transformation of peasants into market oriented farmers.
Under this system the labour force was tied to agriculture,
both legal and economic means. In fact the economic determi-
nants became more and more important, so in the late nineteenth century, after the legal abolition of serfdom, economic
forces were strong enough to maintain the existing agricultural system and to hold back the labour force in agriculture
and in the rural villages as well. Permanent migration to the
city or into urban industry even if legally possible was too
risky, so when the labour force migrated, this move was regarded more as a temporary solution, as a way to support the
family financially which stayed back in the rural village as
well.

The population in Eastern Europe was kept in rural villages
and near the agriculture. Industry in the pre-revolutionary
period cannot be described simply as backward ; this industry
was extremely concentrated and based on a relatively advanced
technology. In certain branches of heavy industry, Russia was
an industrial World power as early as the eighteenth century.
Industrial development - based on a high level of productivity - needed less labour forces, was less dependent on urbanization. Furthermore, since industrial investments were not
directly influenced by the consumer market, and since the
growth of industrial production did not require the expansion
of purchasing power of the population, it did not require the
decline of rural subsistance economy and the mass transformation of the labour force into a commodity. Industry could
therefore develop with a large rural population for a long.
If the "illegitimate power" of cities in the Western world
has been one of the preconditions of capital accumulation

(in contrast to Eastern Europe where the accumulation of capital did not follow the laws of classical capitalism and was
not assured by the expansion of the market, but more by the
development of the institutions of State Intervention) we
might expect a different development in urban management as
well.

The analysis of any national system wold require much more
sophistication and this rather simplified distinction between
the "anglo-saxon" and "prussian" ways of managing urban and
regional development would not lead us very far in an empirical research. The nature of the State in France and consequently its role in local administration and "aménagement
territorial" is quite peculiar and probably there are as many
differences as similarities between England and the United
States etc. In Hungary, for example, the central government
never succeeded - at least in legal administrative terms -
to subordinate local interests to the central interests, and
the central-local conflict was built into the structure of
local governments on all levels, as expressed legally by the
fact that local governments were headed simultaneously by one
elected supposedly representing the "local" and by one appointed official (representing ex officio the central interest)
none of them subordinated to the other but whring their power,
and these types of national.

The purpose of the previous analysis was only to show that
certain institutions of the contemporary socialist redistribution regional management system (first of all, the
structure of local governments) developed already in pre-
revolutionary Eastern Europe.

3. <u>The "local Soviets" and the emergence of the redistributive
   system of regional management in early socialism.</u>

When local Soviets came into being and their very early ideology was formulated they were thought to represent a third
alternative, a radical solution of the conflict of local and
central interests so inefficiently handled by the "anglo-
saxon" system and so undemocratocally dealt with by the auto-
cratie Prussian State. Local Soviets started to operate as
the tools of direct popular power - an ever recurring theme
in leftish revolutions, more recently in Chile and in Portugal.

I am inclined to believe, despite the soattered empirical
evidence I could find, that these very early local Soviets
could be indeed conceived as the expressions of direct popular power in 1905 in Petrograd or during the Summer and Fall
of 1917 in Russia.

People has to govern themselves, and this iw why I would
regard the early Soviets as tools of direct popular power,
despite undemocratic elements in their way of functioning.

The system of Soviets solved - at least temporarily - in a
revolutionary manner the conflict of central and local interests, since the all-Russian congresses of the Soviets took
over most of the functions of the central government, there
were no separate bodies representing the "central" and the
"local", those who were locally elected took the central decisions as well and assured the execution of those decisions,
a functioning alternative to the anglo-saxon versus Prussian
way of handling local-central conflicts.

But this revolutionary experiment came to an early end. Soon
after the October revolution central State agencies, dominated
by the volsheviks, consolidated their power, from now on we
hear more about the evils of "spontaneous movements" and the
need for "revolutionary discipline" than about direct democracy and self government both from Lenin and from other leaders of the revolution. The "nationalization of local Soviets"
begins during the first grey week-days of bolshzvik power,
motivated not so much by ideological considerations than by
the requirements of a rationally and efficiently functioning
State. Laws are passed to curb the power of the local soviets
(see a detailed account of the story by Carr), to impair its
economic independance, almost unlimited before, to regulate
its taxation rights and to extract as much tax in money and
specially in kind as possible for the central government.

Very soon people have to learn that the construction of socialism requires sacrifices, the fruits of their labour cannot
be consumed, selfish (individual or group) interests should
be oppressed, and that more should be spent on the national
programmes of industrialization and modernization (the first
of them was the electrification programme soon followed by
others). The local Soviets which are aware of their revolutionary mission will extract as much surplus as possible from
their population and to transfer all of it to the State budget. They become sheer tax-collecting bodies of the central
government, with no revenues of their own at all and a new
ethos was so efficiently indoctronated that most local Soviets
officials would not dream of withholding or regaining part of
the surplus as such efforts would be regarded as betrayal of
the cause of the revolution.

When bolshevik power arrived after the War, to the Western
part of Eastern Europe this nature of the local government
organization during the "period of transition" was clear
enough and any attempt to transform local government organizations, into genuine organizations of direct democracy or

self government would be branded as "pretty-bourgeois illu-
sionism" if not troskyite deviation. The first socialist
local government reform happened in Hungary in 1951 which
introduced the system of local societs falls in the line of
the reforms of the last two hundred years and by no means
represents a revolutionary change.

The emerging new urban and regional management system and the
local government structure built upon it is by no means the
socialist one, but it is certainly a socialist system, shaped
as much by the necessities of economic growth and social
change as by ideological considerations. The system is functioning in societies where the private ownership of the land,
even if it exists, is strictly limited ; where the speek and
structure of economic growth is not regulated by the market,
where the labour force is not a commodity in the precisely
defined sense (in which the immediate producer is forced to
sell his labour power, but its price is not defined on the
market) and all these socialist economic characteristics do
have their imprint on the system or regional management.
Regional management in Eastern Europe is performing basic developmental tasks, in ensuring the maximization of surplus
used for productive investments, especially for extensive
industrialization, a re-allocation of surplus from agriculture into industry and the delay of infrastructural growth,
but it is doing so under socialist conditions. Local societs,
become integral parts of a planned economy, where the allocation of capital and labour was not regulated by the market
but was redistributed according to norms of central and scientific planning.

The function of the regional management system in the redistributive economy formerly of the regional management system
in the redistributive economy formerly was to secure the
maximization of the surplus and its orderly expropriation
mainly for the purposes of productive investments ; now the
emphasis is changing, and the task of allocation of the means
for infrastructural development in the urban and regional
system becomes fundamental. Local Soviet officials were more
concerned with finding the stocks of goods piled up by the
khoulaks and other counter-revolutionary elements, now they
have to learn more about budgeting and financing, regional
planning and urban renewel : they become more the local agents
of the Central Planning Office who are responsible for the
orderly execution of regional development plans.

This change not only requires the retraining of the "cadres"
into professional urban and regional managers but also the
reorganization of the governmental structure of regional
management. It is quite obvious that they will not be able to

divide indefinitely the increasing but still inadequate funds.
A mechanically equal distribution of grants among local authorities would lead to such a dispersion of investments that it
would be uneconomical. Thus since concentration of the soarce
resources for development is unavoidable, they would like to
deal with as few local authorities - as possible, preferably
with a well defined place for all of them in a scientifically
elaborated regional hierarchy. During the "siege economy"
period, when the control function of the local authorities
dominated, it was desirable to have as many local authorities
as possible to assure the presence of the "watching eye of the
Big Brother" in the smallest locality - and in fact the 1951
reform in Hungary for example created a great number of new
local authorities - now efforts were made to rationalize
local administration, to concentrate it as much as possible,
since the task of the regional redistributor becomes easier
as the list of localities among which the grants should be
distributed gets shorter and shorter. Such a rationalization
of local administration occurred during the last decade all
over Eastern Europe, and it is probably one of the most significant changes in the regional management system.

The shift of emphasis from the tax-collector role to the tasks
of managing communal infrastructural development left the
nature of local Soviets unaltered. They merely perform a new
function, but in their new role they are not expected to
articulate and fight for the local interests more than before,
on the contrary, they are local organs of the State redistributive machinery, and they operate on the assumption that local interests are particularistic and secondary to social
interests as they are defined by central planning. On the
other hand, the changes as they were briefly sketched above,
brought to the surface certain social conflicts such as why
it is necessary to expropriate the surplus and then redistribute   it with complicated scientific procedures and to finance a huge apparatus of administration and even scientific
research for this purpose, when even the poorest villages
could finance itself and probably invest more than at present,
if it was allowed to withhold at least a fraction of the surplus produced by its inhabitants.

Certainly the overall changes which took place especially
since the Great Depression in the Western did not leave unaltered the regional management system of advanced capitalist
societies. The Weberian description of the Western "self
regulating" system is obviously irrelevant for the analysis
of contemporary phenomena, and even in North America or in
England we could hardly find remains of the nineteenth century "anglo-saxon" institutions ; the self regulating regional management system of classical capitalism is gradually
being replaced by the regional grant economy of State monopoly

capitalism. These changes can be most directly expressed in
terms of transformations in the system of local government
finance, by the growing role of the central State in the
regulation of the circulation of capital in the regional
system when it is no longer assured by the ground rent mechanism. The expansion of central grants to support urban and
regional development is directly caused by the incapacity of
local governments to raise their revenues proportionately to
their rising expeditures, basically due to the relative
decline of rates, traditionally the major income resource of
local services (see the account of the reasons for the development of grand economy by D. Eversley). Certainly the
planners and "managers" of urban and regional development face
a number of similar problems and play a similar role both in
the East and in the West. In both parts of the world the
central State is covering most if not all of the expenses of
communal infrastructural investments, so central planning
needs similar scientific procedures in determining the proportions of allocation of surplus in the space. But from a
historical and structural analysis it must be sufficiently
clear that despite certain parallels, the socialist redistribution and the contemporary Western regional grant economy
were brought about by different socio-economic forces, and
because they operate in a different structural context they
will produce different social contraductions.

II. SOCIAL INEQUALITIES IN THE URBAN/REGIONAL
    SYSTEM....REDISTRIBUTIVE REGIONAL MANAGEMENT
    IN SOCIALIST EASTERN EUROPE

    ... Urbanization under the conditions of socia-
        list extensive industrialization.

a) Economic growth and urbanization - pre-revolutionary
   dilemnes and revolutionary perspectives.

In pre-revolutionary Eastern Europe over-urbanization was
practically unknown, the growth of the urban population by
and large kept space with the expansion or urban industrial
jobs, probably because the most desperate members of the
rural semi-proletariat chose the uncertainties in their own
cities. Furthermore, socio-economic ties of the rural population to the village communities were particularly strong
in Eastern Europe and the push effects of underemployment
were counterbalanced by the pull-backs of traditions, legal
and economic conditions. Consequently the major social conflict in pre-revolutionary Eastern Europe cannot be expressed
in terms of the contradiction between labour and capital :
it arose from the desperate situation of rural semi-proletariat and from its efforts to change the land tenure system
to introduce land reform, which in the first instance at
least would transform the masses of rural underemployed into

passants in the proper sense and not into real urban industrial proletariat.

But the relatively slow, even if supposedly more organic development of a "peasant rural socialism" was alien to the
revolutionary goals of bolsheviks. After 1905 Lenin realized
that the coming revolutions could and probably had to be
built on the "spontaneous movements" of rural masses in breaking up the political establishment, but he proposed only a
tactical alliance with these masses, to allow the bolshevik
avant-garde to take over the political power and to use this
power later to create the working class. In this early revolutionary stage the bolshevik avant-garde of the working class
not only represents the proletariat – its historical mission
is to create it. The State had to expropriate as much surplus
as possible from agriculture and to redistribute it for industrial investments and to transform (preferably quickly)
large masses of the for industrialization. The collectivization of agriculture was the major tool to reach this goal,
and the kholhoz was a well designed organization which assured the maximization of surplus which could be expropriated
from agriculture and freed sufficient labour force from the
agricultural production, still guaranteeing at least a certain
level of security of food production. This economic policy
resulted in an unprecedented decline in the agricultural population, and so the socialist redistributive economy could
re-allocate the labour force from agriculture to industry at
a much faster rate than any market economy. The ratio of the
agricultural population of those East European countries is
declining faster than in market economies because they can
operate with a smaller agricultural population on the same
level of economic development than the capitalist economies.
If we would like to calculate the real significance of agricultural population we should take into account the age structure and sex composition, since the proportion of females and
of those who are of pension age is disproportionately high in
contemporary East European agriculture. From a survey, representative of the rural population of Hungary, I estimated
that the proportion of those males who are under pension age
and who in fact do physical work in agriculture might be as
low as 10 percent, a strikingly low figure for a country with
about 1000 dollar per capita income.

b) Under-urbanization in early socialism.

In an earlier paper on urbanization in Hungary (Konrad-
Szelenyi) we proposed that this exceedingly sherp decline of
agricultural population was not followed by a similar acce-
leration of the rate of urbanization and consequently Hungary
(and we supposed that probably a number of other East European
countries) became under-urbanized. Data on the growth of urban

population, industrial development and occupational structure
for the last two decades indicate that the number of urban
industrial jobs has grown much faster than the urban population. Urban industry attracted a labour force with increasing
speed but cities did not offer accomodation to all of those,
who, following the collectivization of the agriculture, decided to take industrial jobs. As a result of this, the number
and proportion of commuters, especially of those who commute
from their village residence to urban industrial work places,
started to rise and it is still rising. Thus the term under-
urbanization was proposed to describe the relative delay of
urban growth in a period of fast and extensive industrialization, a fast growth in the number of industrial jobs in
cities.

Recently in a careful statistical analysis Jiri Musil and
Jiri Link proved that under-urbanization is quite a wide
spread East European phenomenon and is by no means a specifically Hungarian development. Musil and Link compared indicators of industrial growth, GNP, industrial and agricultural
population, with the size of urban population in a number of
East and West European countries, and they found, that urban
population is systematically below the level that could be
expected from the trends of economic development in most of
the East European countries, especially in Hungary, Czechos-
lovakia and East Germany, but also to some extent in Poland
and Rumania. The under-urbanization hypothesis was falsified
on the other hand in the case of the Soviet Union and Bulgaria, - that is for the countries with an extremely low level
of urbanization before the beginning of socialist industrialization. Much more research is needed to understand national
differences (in the case of the Soviet Union even internal
differences should be taken into account). But with the empirical evidence at our disposal it seems justified to suppose
that during the extensive industrialization period of early
socialism in most of Eastern European countries we can identify a rather specific pattern of urbanization, and that in
these countries some of the dilemnes and conflicts of economic
growth and urbanization are dealt within a different way than
in Western market economies. The social problems of urban
growth in contemporary Eastern Europe are qualitatively different from those of other non-socialist societies in the Third
World which are similarly struggling with the challenge of
industrialization. Under-urbanization is one alternative answer to the challenges of growth at a certain stage of economic development, but this alternative pattern of urbanization
expresses specific structural conflicts to the East European
socialist socio-economic system.

During the period of socialist extensive industrialization
the most striking structural change can be described in terms

of the creation of a new working class out of the previously
under-employed agricultural population and basically it is
this new class of industrial workers due to the economic forces which delayed urban growth which is kept out of cities
which remains a class of village dwellers. When cities grow -
they mainly receive the more qualified population white collars and especially professionals, basically those who in
migrating to the cities also change their class position -
those sons and daughters of rural workers' and peasants' families who became professionals or could move at least to "the
upper strata of the working class", who do not participate
directly in the production process, but more in its planning,
management and control, so that if we can make a distinction
between those who directly produce the surplus and those who
dispose with it and redistribute it, than they certainly
belong to the second category. Consequently during the last
decades the East European cities became more "white collars"
in character, urban population became more "middle class", to
use the terminology of American empirical sociology, in contrast with villages, which lost their peasant character and
became "proletariat". The urban-rural distinction is less
and less a distinction between agriculture and industry, it
reflects more social class differences.

Under these circumstances commuting is a qualitatively different phenomenon in under-urbanized Eastern Europe than in the
"suburbanized" parts of the Western World, in England or in
the United States for example, where characteristically,
although not exclusively, the white collar population commutes
from suburban residence to urban workplaces. There are commuters among professionals and white collars in Eastern
Europe as well, but mostly these are local government officials, medical doctors, agricultural engineers, teachers etc.
who live in cities and commute to their offices in villages ;
these are people who could not find jobs in cities, or in
the hope of higher income or faster promotion were willing
to take offices at least temporarily "in the countryside", in
the "provinces", but they were not willing to give up the
"advantages" of urban life. The advantages are not exclusively "culturel" but they assure also better accessibility to
State subsidized housing and communal infrastructure as well.
Even if we would accept that commuting, or to phrase it in
more general terms, the "separation of the place of work from
the place of residence" is an unavoidable consequence of
"urban-industrial society", we should analyse its class consequences, which might be of different nature under different
systems of regional management. As long as middle class commuting from the Western "suburbia" is a mechanism - built
into a "regional grant economy" - by which the more well to
do escapes the financial burdens of the maintenance and renewal of urban centres, East European working class commuting

assures the deprivation of the majority of the "new working class" from State subsidized urban housing and communal infrastructural development that is, it assures the redistribution of national income in favour of city dweller higher income groups.

c) <u>Social inequalities through the regional system</u>.

Under the redistributive egalitarianism not only cities "are more equal" than communities, but some villages are also "more equal" than other villages as indicated earlier in this paper. In my study on rural communities in Hungary I observed that the status occupied by communities in the redistributive hierarchy has a significant effect on the social processes which occur in the communities, and while the rank ordering of the communities by the central redistributive power is based on indirectly sociological criteria (like the size of the community, centrality of location etc.) it has unintended sociological consequences. These unintended consequences are the most striking in the "lowest statut group" of the communities, namely in those villages which due to their small size or geographical remoteness were identified by planners as "non-optimal" settlements for infrastructural investments and were accordingly deprived from the financial means of development. In the case of Hungary, about one third of the villages would belong to this category, with about one fifth of the rural-population.

Beside urban-rural migration, significant migration is taking place among villages. The population especially of the smallest communities, is sharply declining, and the more centrally located villages are gaining population. It was also observed that fast out-migration from villages belonging to the "lowest statut group" in the redistributive hierarchy is completed with a significant in-migration into the same communities, in fact the proportion of the population which migrated during the last decade is the highest in the villages with the largest loss in population size. From survey data it can be proven that this population change is a socially selective process ; the population which is migrating into the declining villages is less educated, less qualified and has less income than the average of the rural population, consequently the smallest and the least privileged communities, are not merely losing population but they are becoming poorer as well, and they are in the process of becoming "village-slums", the deterioration of their physical structure - caused by the redistributive mechanisms which withhold grants for development and even for maintenance from them - is followed by a sharp decline of the social status of their inhabitants. These village slums perform a double function : they are the last asylums for old and poor peasants, but at the same time they are the functional equivalents of the urban slums in the

industrial cities, created by the great "Landflucht" of
extensive industrialization.

The emergence of these villages slums is an expression of a
"syndrome of decline" which is built around the unequal allocation of surplus and which is certainly an unintended, but
perhaps a necessary, consequence of regional planning under
the redistributive regional management system.

Some of the unintended consequence of regional planning are
transmitted through the functioning of property market. The
property market is regionally quite diversified and very
sensitive to inequalities in the redistribution of grants
for communal development. Prices of houses and land are boom-
ing in growth centres, they are increasing much faster than
inflation rate. In the declining villages, on the **other** hand,
the housing market is depressed, and present house prices
hardly cover the costs of their construction ten years ago,
if houses can be sold at all. The redistribution of surplus
through the regional system does not only allocate national
income unequally, but it leads to a re-allocation of wealth
as well, and unquestionably further the interests of the more
well to do. Furthermore, the dynamics of the property market
might be responsible for the selective nature of the in and
out-migration. Declining satellite villages are probably
attracting low income population by their low house and land
prices, and these groups will buy and build houses in these
communities since they are unable to afford it elsewhere and
they will do so even if they are aware that they lose "capital"
by these investments in the long run. On the other hand among
the out-migrants we might expect to find more of those who
can afford to "economize" with their investments ; at least
some of them in moving to growth centres primarily intend to
transfer their property from a depressed market to a dynamic
one.

Thus changes through the regional system - changes which are
at least partially due to planning intervention and regional
redistribution - correspond to transformations in the social
structure.

d) The new working class and regional development.

In analysis regional development in contemporary Eastern
Europe, one always has to keep in mind that the new socialist
working class is to a large extent rural, and that socialist
industrialization in fact created not moraly a new proletariat, but a peculiar one.

An overwhelming majority of village-dwelling industrial workers is in one way or another involved in agricultural production ; many of them have at least one family member, wife or

daughter, father or mother-in-law who is member of the agricultural co-operative and this way they are entitled to a
"family plot", or a "minifundium" of about a half a hectare,
or they have a garden of similar size. Most village-dwellers
have some land which is cultivated by the work organization
of the family, and despite the small size of the land, it is
cultivated intensively enough to produce food for family consumption, and in some cases even for the market. The socialist
agricultural estate lives in a symbiosis with the intensively
cultivated small family plot, and about one third of the agricultural production comes from these "family entreprises",
which occupy anly about one tenth of the cultivated land,
and supply most of the food consumed by the rural population.
From this point of view the kholhoz system grew organically
out of the East European agricultural structure, and the
socialist collectivization was not such a new experience
after all in many respects for the East European peasants,
whose lands has, already, been taken away once during the
sixteenth and seventeenth century add who learned for many
generations the discipline of bureaucratic labour organization, and who were accustomed to a reward system in which low
wage level was compensated by the right to grow their own
food on a plot allocated to them by the landlord. Recent sociological research on agricultural co-operatives (P. Juhasz)
has proven the surprising degree of continuity in the organizational environment and organizational procedures, concerning both the labour organization and the allocation of
family plots and the regulations of production in the family
entreprise.

Despite all these continuities in the organizational structure
socialist collectivization brought at least one major change :
it freed masses of male labour power from the work on the
fields of the large estates, and made it available for extensive industrialization. The member of the new working class
exists between different worlds in many respects : he lives
in villages, but works in cities, works in industry but plays
a crucial role in agricultural production, sells his labour
power to the bureaucratic labour organizations at a statuo-
rily fixed price unrelated to the surplus he is producing,
but he also sells the products of his labour from the family
entreprise on the market, for a price which is fixed by market
forces. The real power of the working class in contemporary
Eastern Europe is based on this transitory nature of the new
worker, and the workers have counter-vailing power as long
as they are not totally dependent on the institutions of the
redistributive economy. The income of the "peasant workers"
steming from agricultural production on the family plot
(accordingly to recent calculations, about half of the family
income in villages if of this origin) is only one alternative
income resource to bureaucratically fixed wages, and the

success of the "spontaneous class struggle" of the urban
proletariat in industry depends to a large extent on its
capacity to find other alternatives.

The social conflicts of the contemporary under-urbanized,
regional system cannot be described merely in terms of inequalities in the allocation of grants by redistributive management, since also they reflect the conflict of interest
between immediate producers and the redistributive system.
The basic conflicts do not arise because the grants allocated to certain categories of the communities, or to certain
regions, are inadequate, or because the differences in per
capita grants are too large or too small. The basic conflicts
arise from the way, and principles by which surplus is expropriated and later re-allocated.

But I must conclude here, since the purpose of this paper
is not to offer an alternative ideology of urbanization and
regional management, but merely to describe some of the
unintended consequences of the contemporary East European
regional management system. Although I am not prepared to
draw any "lesson" from the East European case, my hope is that
through this paper I can make a contribution to the formulation of questions for comparative research on patterns of
urbanization and regional management in different socio-
economic systems.

REFERENCES

Bibo, I. : A harmadik ut. (The"third road") Nagy Imre Intezet
          (1961).
Carr, E.H. : The history of Soviet Russia, especially Volume
          Four : Foundations of a planned economy. London,
          Macmillan (1969).
Castells, M. : La question urbaine. Paris, Maspere, (1973).
Chayanov, A.V. : The theory of peasant economy . Irwin,
          (1966).
Eversley, D. : " Rising costs and static incomes - some
          economic consequences of regional planning in London ".
          Urban Studies, October 1972.
Eversley, D. : Reform of local government finance. London,
          CES, (1975).
Gans, H. : " Urbanism and suburbanism as ways of life ", in
          Arnold Rose (ed.)
          Human behaviour and social processes, Boston,
          Houghton Mifflin Co. (1962).
Gerschenkron, A. : Europe in the Russian mirror. Cambridge
          University Press (1970).
Gough, I. : " State expenditure in advanced capitalism ".
          New Left Review.(July - August 1975).
Haraszti, M. : Darabber (Piece-work). Unpublished manuscript,
          excerpts published in New Left Review. May - June
          1975.
Harvey, D. : Social justice and the city. London : Edward
          Arnold (1973).
Hauser, Ph. (ed.) : Urbanization in Latin America. Paris
          UNESCO (1961).
Hethy, L. - Make, Cs. : Differential incentives and the
          structure of interests and powers. Budapest :
          Institute of sociology, Hungarian Academy of Sciences,
          (1970).
Kemeny, I. : " Restratification of the working class " in
          Industrialization, urbanization and ways of life.
          Budapest : Institute of Sociology, Hungarian Academy
          of Sciences (1972).
Kochan, L. : The making of modern Russia. London, Penguin,
          (1963).
Konrad, G. - Szelenyi. I. : A kesleltetett varosfejlodes
          tarsadalmi konfliktusai (Social conflicts of under-
          urbanisation). Valosag, December 1971.
Lamarche, F. : " Les fondements economiques de la question
          urbaine ". Sociologie et Sociétés (1972).
Lane, D. : " Leninism as an ideology of soviet development ",
          in E. de Kadt and D. Williams (eds.) Sociology and
          Development. London, Tavistock Publications.
Leemans, A.F. : Changing Patterns of Local Government. The
          Hague, IULA (1970).
Lenin, V.I. : The development of capitalism in Russia.
          Moscow, Progress (1964).

Marcuse, H. : <u>Soviet Marxism</u>. New York, Columbia University
        Press (1958).
Musil, J. - Link, J. : " Economic development and urbanization
        in the socialist countries ".<u>Szociologia</u>.1973.
Norman, P. : " Managerialism - a review of recent work ".
        Paper presented at the York Conference of the CES,
        1975.
Nove, A.L. : <u>An economic history of the USSR</u>. London, Penguin
        (1969).
Pahl, R. : " From urban sociology to political economy : the
        case of urban and regional development ". Manuscript,
        March 1975.
Pickvance, C. : " Housing : reproduction of capital and
        reproduction of labour power - some recent French
        works ". University of Manchester, 1975.
Pirenne, H. : <u>Medieval cities</u>. New York, Doubleday (1956).
Polanyi, K. - Arensberg, C.M. - Pearson, H.W. : <u>Trade and
        market in early empires</u>. Glencoe Ill. (1957).
Ronge, V. - Schmieg, G. : Planung und Demokratie - <u>Futurum</u>.
        1970, n° 2.
Smellie, K.B. : <u>A history of local government</u> . London (1968).
Vagi, G. : Mit er egy kozseg - mit er egy mogye ? (The
        criterions of the distribution of grants among
        communities and counties). <u>Kozgazdasagi Szemle</u>
        <u>1975,n° 7-8</u>.
Weber, M. : The city - New York, The Free Press (1958).

FIRST RESULTS OF THE UNESCO RESEARCH ON THE PROTECTION OF CITIES AND HISTORICAL NEIGHBOURHOODS

G. Fradier

Coordinator UNESCO, Paris, France

Mr Fradier. — Thank you, Mister Chairman.

First I want to thank the World Environment and Resources Council for inviting Unesco and myself who represents this organization very humbly today. I would also thank them for having listed as my subject Historic Cities rather than anything which Unesco does in the field of human settlements, which will have probably exceeded the fifteen minutes limit.

And yet, although I would love to talk about historic cities, I am sure that it is almost impossible to talk about those things without talking about anything which concerns planning, public participation etc.

Well, anyway, when one mentions these words "historic cities", "historic centres", "historic quarters", usually one has the image of beautiful monuments in antique or medieval or baroque cities and that is true, we started that way.

As far as Unesco goes, if we did some work in those fields, it was because governments thought that it was very important to safeguard this cultural heritage and that is why we cooperated very closely, for instance last year and the years before, with the European Community, with the Council of Europe, the Economic Commission for Europe, the O.E.C.D. etc.

although historic cities are not the cultural heritage or Europe and they are to be found absolutely everywhere.

When we do some operational work as they say, we always start, at the request of governments, with monuments, with particularly beautiful cities or particularly beautiful squares which are of so great interest and which we are told development or developers are putting in danger.

Very soon we see that these small areas usually cannot be preserved as such out of their context. You have to enlarge the so called quarter, or centre, or village, you have to view these historic parts in their environment, which usually is also historic although from a different period.

In other words, the approach which is necessary to safeguard a couple of streets or a few hectares of historic land has to be multidisciplinary or interdisciplinary from the start.

It is not the business of restorers, architects specialized in historic monuments etc. — at least it is not only these people's business, it is also a question of knowing what are the economic resources of that place, what is the social habit, who are the people who live there and what they want.

When Mr Atkinson was talking this afternoon, I realized that Bradford, which

I don't know, is a typical historic city in that sense, not only because some of the houses which were shown date from the early 19th century, for instance, but because it is a central core which people wanted to preserve as such. The problems which he let us understand were very simply that either they would rehabilitate that city or do nothing, which means renovate it, which means destroy it and then build over. They chose to keep it and to rehabilitate it. And other consequences will be drawn from that.

The main one is that obviously for an ancient historic city — let us say perhaps, to give a broad definition of an historic city nowadays that it would be a town or city or whatever human settlement, built, organized either in pre-industrial or pre-automobile age, which means that it would be a place to live, a place where you meet people, a place where centres are never too far away and a place where it is nice to be — being consequently a place which people want to keep, they want to be there rather than in other places.

The best example, known of course by all the planners in Europe, is for instance Bologna in Italy and here again I was reminded of Bologna a propos of Bradford. Mr. Atkinson said that he would have much to say about public participation and I am sorry he didn't and that I'll be away when he talks about it, because obviously two things were necessary — at least two : one was a political decision at the top, local and national to keep Bradford. The same thing happened in Bologna. This very extraordinary decision which was taken to help and develop that city of 500,000 inhabitants inside instead of going outside. But as in Bradford, this was only possible because the people who live in that medieval and renaissance city have an active interest in their city, because they want to stay there and they accepted — sometimes somehow cheap, because when you rehabilitate a house, sometimes you have to move away and come back again — that was possible in the case of Bologna for particular reasons which are of political origin certainly, but apparently in a very different context and with a very different political approach that was also possible in Bradford.

One might take another example : this city, which I personally like very much. It is probably the city in Europe which suffered the hardest aggression in peace time. Further it was destroyed in the last eighteen years for reasons which are very well known, international reasons shall we say. And when I mean destroyed, it is simply that very nice section of town, where it was good to live and that has been replaced by office-towers, roads, no man's lands, etc.

That happens everywhere, but what is particular to Brussels is that at some point, citizens said : no, we don't want that to keep on. So, in another section of town, south rather than north, people decided that they did not want to have their section destroyed, that they liked their houses, although that was not a particularly historic part of the city, without any beautiful monument except for that famous little statue. They organized in such a way that in that case they won the battle and their section has been preserved, and as you probably know, there are now more than a hundred committees of neighbourhoods in Brussels which are actively involved, not only in fighting the destruction and building, but involved in the management of their city or communes which is not easy and they don't succeed all the time. Still the fact is that they are at it.

That again is explainable in terms of Belgian politics and it would be very difficult elsewhere and in my country, for instance, it would be almost impossible to achieve that.

I could give more examples but I'll give simply one more to finish with my speech and also to show another aspect of it.

All cities in developed countries like those I mentioned, pose certain problems which are difficult to solve, because citizens usually do not oppose authorities as such but capital and money. In developing countries it is a bit different. The ancient city also is in danger, not so much of being destroyed because the land is expensive and valuable — it is, but not that much and you can always build somewhere else — but because, and that again has been known in Europe, the peoples, the families, the traditional bourgeois classes who had built these centres and used to be there, leave those. The way of life changes and instead of a big patriotical house in a small street, someone prefers an apartment on a large street.

The result is that the centres of cities become a haven for unemployed people, poor people and the process of decay is very rapid.

So, what to do? It is almost impossible to ask the people who used to own or who still own and rent their houses, to come back.

We believe that the answer then is again public participation but in another sense. Instead of having the people interested in their cities, participate in the process, fight, win, lose and so on — what we need then is to have the authorities participate with the public. That public being the inhabitants, the tenants which do make some money since in fact they have to pay a rent and if they are helped they can rehabilitate their own houses.

It is an economical and social process. I cannot go into details but simply to finish with I would give you of course an idea of another aspect of Unesco's work in the field of historic cities, it is a more legal or normative aspect as an international recommendation to member states will be adopted this year.

On the safeguard of historic cities, quarters and villages in a changing environment.

It is a more or less unofficial text, it is perhaps less dull than most and what will be interesting for you, I think, is that not only it gives principles, it says that mankind wants to save its heritage etc., not only it gives in detail a series of technical measures, economic and administrative measures which are absolutely necessary — I mean it would be extremely necessary that all authorities concerned with such heritage would have a common approach — but in addition they insist on the social aspect of it, so much though that when you read some of the articles you will think that, let's say the world community would decide that it is imperative to keep historic cities and centres, but that if it is at the cost of moving out people and sending them away perhaps it is better not to do it.

I'll simply leave it at that and perhaps we have time for a few questions. Thank you very much.

PARTICIPATION IN SMALL AND LARGE TERRITORIAL DIMENSIONS

R. Guiducci
University of Milan, Milano.

Many cities around the world have reached the critical threshold of being unlivable, ungovernable, and in the impossibility of having sufficient means to face past and present
needs. The most critical point is established when to a further increase in the population, costs grow in an exponential
manner to such a degree that there no longer exists "technological remedies" which are compatible with available resources.

Population
increase

Costs increase

Owing to this now paroxysmal and pathological "crisis" of the
city, many countries are attempting to use "decentralization".

In synthesis, the models that were put and are still being
put into practice are two :

1) The model of satellite cities. This is in process in New
York as in Moscow, in Tokyo as in London, to cite some of
the larger examples. The first endeavor is to create "new
towns", where new population immigrations can take root and
where natural increases or already existing surpluses can
be exported.

It is a known fact that these centres have always been in
serious need of habitability and identity, being void of any
social consistency and aleatory in their qualification.

Therefore, where ithas been possible, as in London, the "graf-
ting" of decentralizations has been used on small pre-existing
towns, which in some way are already characterized by historical centres or which are however coming alive with a first
germ of "character".

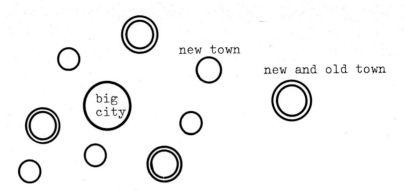

However the initial or modified model brought with itself
its evils as it was inexorably <u>hierarchical</u>. The same word
"satellite" conferms the presence of a hegemonic "planet",
<u>destined</u> "a priori" to maintain its leadership and powerful
attraction.

This is how after more than half a century of using a policy
of "new towns" and "old and new towns" in London, the only
fruit gathered was a decentralization of approximately
600,000 inhabitants on a whole of a population of 12 million
in Greater London, which is gradually becoming a megalopolis
with a population of 14-16 million.

Consequently, the hierarchical model is presented as the
following :

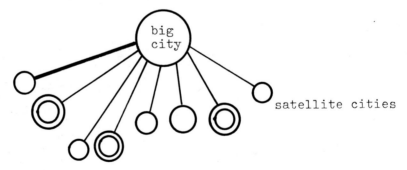

Satellite cities are found in hierarchical situations at various distances both for a question of size and of socioeconomic influence. Little or no connection exists between them
and the system of reference remains the great metropolis upon
which they depend.

2) The model of development directrices. This deals with the
attempt to create a "series" of cities or "linear cities"
along pre-arranged axes, destined to absorb growth pressures,
assimilating these within themselves.

This model is applied from the United States to the U.S.S.R.,
and is presently undergoing great experimentation in Paris
with the Defence axis.

The model is presented as the following :

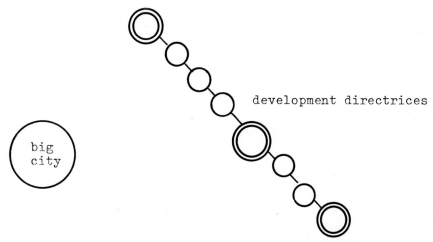

development directrices

big
city

The smaller cities, either new or comprising pre-existing
centres, have the appearance of something entirely new, but
in reality these cities are of different socioeconomic importance, resting completely separated among themselves, even if,
often, they are alike for their irksome uniformity and repe-
titiousness. They continue to refer and depend from the principal, dominating city which created them and remains the
"mother".

This is how, in another form, the same hierarchical model
advanced earlier reproduces itself again with all its evils
and inconveniences.

In fact from a point of view of actual socioeconomic influence
we have the following :

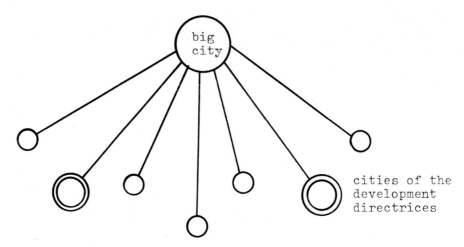

cities of the
development
directrices

Confronted with the increasing failures of decentralization
and the contemporary growth and unlivability of crowding,
from many parts there is an appeal for a participation from
below. The city should assume its own management responsibilities, dividing the zones and districts which are most crowded, in order to promote and support the decentralization
processes in smaller centres, wherever possible, voluntarily
favoring this phenomenon.

In other words the "body" of the city would be attributed with
responsibilities that the "head", which has governed from
above, was not capable of resolving.

However the request for participation accomplished, precisely,
from above frequently encounters a scarse reply from below
with astonishment from the top. Viceversa, this "resistance"
has a very precise motivation. The sociologist, Michels, had
already warned that you cannot participate but among equals,
as, otherwise, you would not have participation as such, but
only greater consent to subordination, reinforcing it right
when the top is no longer in a position to exercise, alone,
its traditional coercion.

Nevertheless, from a sociological viewpoint, urban decentralization is a variable depending on the decentralization of
power. And an equalitarian distribution (and, therefore,
decentralistic) of the urban structures is directly propor-
tional to the democratic-equalitarian distribution of power.

In territorial terms power is made up of decision-making and
administrative institutions of different activities : primary
sector ; secondary sector ; and the traditional tertiary sector (linked to the other two : from offices to private trans-

portation) ; the social tertiary sector, make up of a set of
services (research, education, health, welfare, housing, free
time and recreation, etc.). A leveled and indifferent distribution of all the elements in every point would therefore
be impossible (and, as we will see, if it were at all possible it would be both mistaken and counterproductive). The
problem becomes that of allowing each urban aggregate to
select a mixture of different activities, the sum of which
however, having equal parts of socioeconomic and decision-
making power.

$$P_1 = F_2 + F_4 + F_{12} \ldots\ldots + F_h \qquad\qquad P = \text{influence}$$

$$P_2 = F_1 + F_3 + F_5 \ldots\ldots + F_k \qquad\qquad F = \text{specific functions}$$

$$\ldots\ldots\ldots\ldots\ldots\ldots\ldots\ldots\ldots$$

$$P_n = F_6 + F_7 + F_9 \ldots\ldots + F_w \qquad \text{where } P_1 = P_2 \ldots\ldots P_n$$

Thus we come to a third model :

3) <u>Polycentrical model with equalitarian aggregations.</u>

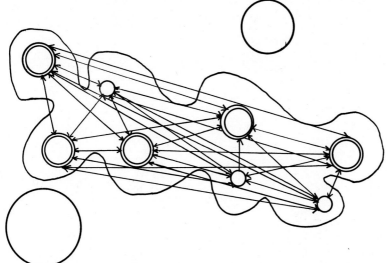

In this model the major centres P_1 and P_n have the same
influence as the aggregation of smaller centres representing
P_2.

And the smaller centres are not disconnected among themselves
and subordinated by the larger centres, nor on a hierarchical
scale among themselves inside the aggregation P_2.

Therefore, not only $P_1 = P_2 = \ldots\ldots\ldots P_n$, but also
$F_1 = F_3 = F_5$ etc., (coordinated and complementary among
themselves).

It should be noted that the F's do not depend on the quantity
of population, nor on any other solely quantitative economic
factor, but on the urban <u>quality</u> achieved, or the "urban effect" determined by many complex social causes.

The aggregation P_2 will not even be a "antimetropolis" in the
sense that on the whole it includes the same functions as P_1
or P_n, and on the contrary, it will have <u>other</u> and <u>distinct</u>
characteristic functions.

Urban nuclei or the sum of many identical nuclei, do not
produce the social <u>dynamic</u> which is indispensable in order
to have an intense "urban effect".

It has been demonstrated both by the sociologist and anthro-
pologist, Levi-Strauss, and by the most advanced sociological
and anthropological studies that a civilization which is
completely uniform in all its parts, or likewise many identical civilizations, have a tendency to not develop and are
likely to become stagnate and decadent. While civilizations
which are internally diversified and different in comparison
to others, tend to elevate the social dynamics, discoveries,
changes and transformations. In this model the aggregation
P_2 will, therefore, be internally diversified and dynamic
and in comparison with the different aggregations P_1 and P_n.

Consequently, instead of the hierarchical scheme we would
have the following :

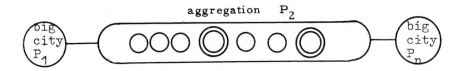

This model is not abstract, but is already in part being
applied in the Dutch Randstadt, where Amsterdam and Rotterdam
are P_1 and P_n and all the chain of smaller cities are P_2.

Even London could tend to have a systematic aggregation differ-
entiated by the new towns and the towns which are in part old
and in part new found in the peripherical crown, until reaching the influence of central London.

Likewise the scheme could be used for further aggregation
of Swedish and Russian new towns, and in certain areas in

Germany and the United States.

In Italy this model has presided over several hypotheses for terrirorial planning.

For instance, in Lombardy, there is an attempt to block the urban growth of Milan and to create a crown of eight provincial cities within the Region and three outside of the same, in order to obtain a circular "second city" equal in influence to Milan, with different and complementary functions. The same scheme was successful for Rome and Lazio ; Naples and Campania ; Florence and Toscany ; Turin and Piedmont, etc., etc...

Italy could actually be particularly favored with the application of this model as there are many small centres that would be a support to aggregations capable of having an influence equal to that of larger centres which are not yet considered very big.

We were forced to start with the "large dimension" in order to consider the problem of participation because if we would have limited ourselves to the big cities, as seensseparately, we might have reproduced the same phenomenon as Pericles' Athens, free cities, or medieval republics, which were internally more democratic and dynamic, but, which nevertheless, became, unfortunately, hegemonies over other "polis", creating conflicts and not cooperation, leading entire systems, though polycentrical, to decadence.

Once this problem has been met, the other must be faced, and namely how is it possible to obtain a participation on a lower level either in the big cities, or in the aggregations of smaller cities. This problem becomes further complicated withing the limit in which once reaching the smallest terri- torial dimension (the zone or district), it is exactly here where the maximum power of choice is needed for all problems of every dimension, from the biggest to the smallest.

However one wonders : how can the smaller dimension under- stand and select also for the larger one, where problems of national and international communications must be resolved, from industrial and social centres at a transnational level, etc... ?

This question is put forward by who attempts to confirm the necessity of decisions coming from the top.

The answer could be : it is precisely the decision from the top that has brought chaos to the cities, from their unbea- rable growth patterns, to physical and social pollution, etc.

Therefore the top is not suited to managing the cities. However the answer in terms of territorial planning which is
both possible and democratic, is more difficult, and this
must not be forgotten.

The fundamental problem here is also of method.

In many countries, as also in Italy, a decentralization process was first attempted at the regional level, and then at
the district (sub-regional areas), and municipal and zonal
levels (quarters within the city).

The problem always occurs identically in relations between
State and Region ; between each single Region and district ;
between districts and municipals, and municipals and their
zones.

So far the systems applied have come up with the following
"cluster" scheme, where the various nuclei are unequal in
power among themselves, as there is still often a certain
degree of hierarchism from the top and now and then they are
in conflict with themselves (from which stems the pretence
from the centre as being the sole equilibrator and reconciler
at the outbreak of conflicts).

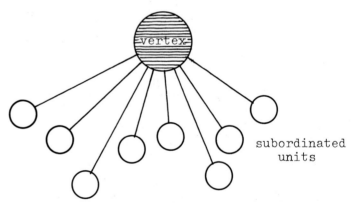

subordinated
units

The mistaken thesis of delegating only some secondary functions to decentralized levels without entrusting those more
principal functions, originates from this unequal and varying
starting condition (which would have been criticized not only
by Rousseau, but also by Tocqueville).

Thus the decentralized organs, invested with only subordinate
functions, do not participate because of the contradiction
brought up by Michels. However, does a model exist that would
really provide both decentralization and participation ?

The model would cease to be a "cluster", but a group with sub-groups or a system with sub-systems.

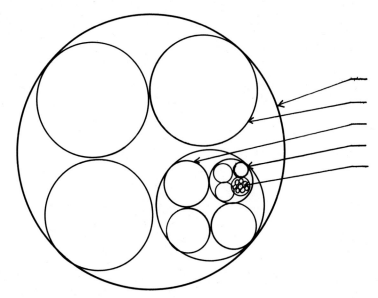

As you will note this diagram is no longer hierarchical in a cluster and, potentially, power could be completely reversed. If the faculties of power were entrusted to the zones, the municipal would <u>only</u> have the task of coordinating them ; the district would coordinate the municipals ; the Regions the districts and the State the Regions.

Modern models of simulation of processes, with simplified alternatives, would offer the global possibility of permitting fundamental choices on more general problems on behalf of institutions on lower levels.

However the essential would be the Tocquevillian formulation of having analogous conditions at the outset, because, otherwise the games would already function on behalf of the existing and unbalanced powers.

This is exactly what happens in the development of the Italian Regions, where the stronger Regions have greater faculties and those much weaker end up marginated, while the authority vested in the central power is incapable of overcoming this lack of balance.

And the same happens at the level of the districts, municipals and zones. However, as said earlier, confliction between decentralized unequals only helps to strengthen the powers on a superior level, even if the latter are absolutely incompetent of resolving the contradictions that arise.

Thus impotent powers are conserved, decentralization takes place with no positive effect, and there is an insufficient rate of participation.

In this way an implacable logic leads the urban structures to the disasters we all know too well.

Nevertheless, problems in contemporary societies will no longer be able to be dealt with, even in a coercive manner, from the top, and on the other hand, pressure from the regional, districts, municipals, and above all, zone levels, is continually becoming more stronger, authoritative, mature and by this time, unsuppressable. For instance in Italy, committees and zone councils are growing both in number and stature in many large and small Italian cities. In fact, it is becoming more than clear that only a concordant and capillary responsibility from all citizens could have faced such problems such as limiting the birth rate in this gradually shrinking world ; careful use of space which is forever more limited and limiting ; saving raw materials which are near exhaustion ; management of the cities in all those aspects which have escaped even the most organized and scientific police forces ; resolving the problem of pollution which comes not only from the big industrial centres, but also from acts performed by a single individual and multiplied millions of times, etc. etc.

Consequently, the resolution of the problem of the cities now depends not only on the degree of physical decentralization, but also on that of power. Participation is the daughter of direct powers, and she does not grow in a vertical or autocratical system.

At this stage, however, it is important to demonstrate a pragmatic and concrete possibility in order to support this model.

In the business field, theoretics have reached a high degree of sophistication permitting to coordinate, for instance, processes in decentralized industries with different products and with particular schemes. (1).

It is unfair that the result of long and complex studies as well as the use of electronic calculators is only of use for the industries and that it cannot be applied to urban structures.

---

(1) See Franco Momigliano, "Economia industriale e teoria della impresa"
    (Il Mulino, Bologna 1975, Appendice III, Modello generale di simulazione gestionale multinazional, "multiproduct" e "multiplant").

The city is also an industry, and can be a social industry
with decentralized units : her product are the industrial
and residential zones, and those of services and infrastruc-
tures. Given certain resources it might be possible to apply
the model advanced earlier using macro-choices so as to
determine the standards, considered as concrete objectives,
to achieve in the various fields, reserving space for future
objectives.

If, at this point and with this mechanism, even simplified,
the zone committees and councils were entrusted with an effective responsibility for decisions and the management of the
process of general territorial planning, the maximum respon-
sibleness and effective participation would be attained.

The municipal, district, regional and state levels which
today are at the vertex, would necessarily become places of
executive coordination.

It is evident which "long march" will be involved for a
concrete victory of this model.

Our task here was only to demonstrate that without a distribution of powers, serious decentralization as well as an
effective and efficient participation in the urban process,
cannot be achieved. And such distribution and participation,
today, are no longer impossible, keeping in mind the maturity
reached by the citizens and the availability of models for
democratic programming.

Thus, what was effectively the "missing link" between "large"
and "small" dimensions remains revealed.

Against the opinion of many, the problem at hand is not one
of intrinsic incapacity of the "particular" to understand
the "general", if the exact opposite is verifiable by all.
Therefore, as Wright Mills upheld, the incapacity of the top
to program for everyone the city for everybody, the "citizens' city", because the top follows a social "rationality
without reason" or on the other hand only for particularistic
reasons and therefore, irrational.

The "general" can only coherently come from the "general".
However, the "general" is still repressed in the subordina-
teness of the "particular" which is segregated in the zones
and quarters, but is nevertheless, made up of the great majority of citizens who are by now educated, informed, prepared
and capable of self-management.

The "missing link" is therefore revealed as the restitution of
the "general" to the "general", in a manner so as to manage

the "particular", rightly avoiding that the latter, at the
top, continues, without any result in respect to the complexity of the problems, to try to arbitrarily and disastrously
manage the "general", namely the problems and responsibilities
of all.

THIRD WORLD HOUSING: SPACE AS A RESOURCE

C. M. CORREA

249, Dadabhai Naoroji Road, Bombay 1.

1.1 Some time ago, at the Environmental Conference in Stockholm, our Prime Minister said that in countries like India the most serious pollution of all is poverty. And one can go further. For it is not just poverty, but the particular _forms_ which poverty takes in our urban areas. Rural poverty in India is a different thing. The people are as poor - often in fact poorer - but they are not as de-humanised. Obviously there is very little relation between the way our cities are built and the way people use them. Not having the proper range of spaces they need in order to live, people merely mis-use what they _do_ have access to - hence the thousands of families cooking on pavements, defecating along railway tracks, and so forth.

1.2 The scale of the problem is staggering. By Government count, a few years ago, there was a back-log of almost twelve million housing units required in our urban areas alone. To this must be added the four-fold increase in urban population expected over the next three decades. In contrast, our resources - both financial and material - are minimal. About 25% of our urban households earn less than Rs.200 per month. The next 50% earn between Rs.200 and Rs.500. Even if we assume a rent-paying capacity of a quarter of this income (high by Indian standards for this economic level), then, using brick and concrete, very little can be constructed for this money - somewhere between two and five square metres per family - and this for 75% of the population ! Furthermore, it is not merely a question of financial budgeting; there is not enough cement and not enough steel in the country to deal with our millions of urban homeless in this way.

1.3 Yet will self-help schemes provide the answer? Granted that simple mud and bamboo houses are very much cheaper, but since densities anywhere near the city centre are extremely high, these "sites-and-services" schemes are usually located on the periphery of cities, far away from the mass transport lines. With the result that they tend to become ghettos of cheap labour, at the mercy of one or two local employers. Putting in a mass transport system can be expensive - as is the augmentation of other existing municipal services.

1.4 This then is the dilemma we face: On the one hand, multi-storey tenements cost more to construct yet save on transport and other infrastructure costs; on the other hand, low-rise housing costs less to construct but occupies more space. The question is: What is the point of trade-off between these two? To answer this, we must of necessity examine the entire system we call "city" and try to arrive at a solution which is the most economical in its _total_ cost per family - including roads, services, schools, green areas and mass transportation systems.

1.5 Let us begin by taking a look at what housing a family in a city really means. Now, even in spatial terms, providing housing involves much more than just building houses. The room, the cell, is only one element in a whole hierarchy of spaces a human being needs in order to live in a city.

1.6 This hierarchy is determined by many factors, such as climate, culturally-defined life-styles, and so forth. For instance, under Indian urban conditions, it appears to have four major elements:

(A) The space needed by the family for exclusively private use, such as cooking, sleeping, storage, etc.

(B) The areas of intimate fine-scale contact i.e. the doorstep where children play, you chat with your neighbour, etc.

(C) The neighbourhood meeting places (e.g. in our villages, the village well) where you become part of your community.

(D) Finally, the principal urban area - e.g. the maidan - used by the whole city.

1.7 Each element in this hierarchy can consist of covered spaces and/or open-to-sky spaces. For example many of the private activities at the micro end of the scale, such as cooking and sleeping, need not be exclusively indoor but can - and do - take place in an open courtyard (provided of course that the families privacy is reasonably assured). In fact, depending on the cost of building construction this trade-off is automatically adjusted - each society (and each family within it) finding its own balance. This adjustment is of the utmost importance, particularly in developing countries, because they are usually in warm tropical climates where a number of activities can indeed take place in the open.

1.8 The second important fact about the elements in this hierarchy is that they are mutually inter-dependent. That is to say, less space in one area can be adjusted by the provision of more in one of the other three. For example, smaller dwelling units might be compensated by larger neighbour-hood community spaces. Or vice versa. (New Delhi provides about 1.5 hectares of open space per thousand people; that is, about 75 square metres per family. The question is : Would we be better off trading some of this public area for more private space - say a courtyard of 10 square metres per family? Exchanging monumental public vistas for greater individual privacy - specially for the poor - may not be such a bad bargain. And we might even save some land area in the process).

1.9 To re-cap briefly, we perceive housing not as cells in isolation but as a hierarchy of activities and spaces; secondly, within each activity there is a trade-off between spaces which are covered and those open-to-sky; thirdly, the activities themselves are mutually inter-dependent and there can be spatial trade-offs between them.

2.1 To identify the hierarchy and to understand the nature of these trade-offs is of course the essence of the task of providing housing. Without this, one is in grave danger of formulating the wrong questions. For instance, most attempts at low-cost housing perceive it only as a simplistic question of trying to pile up as many dwelling units, as many cells, as possible on a given site, without any concern for the other spaces involved in the hierarchy. With the result that in much of the Indian urban scene today, what we are observing is the desperate attempt of people - especially the poor - to try and somehow work out a pattern of living within the totally inadequate context provided for them.

2.2 And tragically enough, piling people one over another does not in fact
"save" much land for the city. For in most urban areas around the world,
only about 15% of land-use is devoted to residential building sites. The
rest is in other space-extensive uses, such as industry, ware-housing, and
so forth. For instance, transport is usually between 25% to 35% of land-
use (higher in Los Angeles!). Even with the inclusion of local distributory
roads, tot-lots, and so forth, housing occupies about a third of most cities.
Thus we see that doubling the number of people on each site does not "save"
much land for the whole city (though it could mean much higher profits for
the individual developer - which is of course the reason it gets done). On
the other hand, halving the density on residential plots could mean only a
marginally larger city.

2.3 But then the question arises: Will lowering the densities increase
disproportionately the cost of the service infrastructure? In particular,
of the travel time and travel costs involved in the public transport
systems? This is indeed an important question. Without transport there can
be no mobility, therefore no job choice - in fact often no job at all - and
for the poor, mass transport becomes as crucial an urban prerogative as
housing.

2.4 Now a mass transport system - whether a tram, or a train, a bus in
mixed traffic or on a reserved track - is essentially a _linear_ function.
It only becomes viable in the context of a land-use plan which develops
corridors of high-density demand. The distance that a person is willing
to walk to the transit station depends on the mode of transport and differs
from country to country, indeed very often from city to city. Thus the
cost and convenience of the mass transport system is not merely a function
of overall densities, but depends also on the structure of the city -
namely that it be a linear system, or a combination of linear sub-systems -
with each station having a sufficient hinterland of commuters.

2.5 Let us take an example. Assuming a dwelling unit of 32 square metres
carpet area and a communal space at 30 square metres per family (for some
of the activities in the hierarchy mentioned earlier and the social infrastructure therein contained, e.g. tot-lots, health centres, etc.; the
school playfields and other space-extensive uses are just outside this area),
we find that ground floor houses on individual sites (each 4m x 11m) will
accommodate about 25,000 people in an area of one km. square (8 to 10
minutes walk from a station); 5-storey walk-up apartments would send up
this figure to 40,000; 10-storey buildings (using elevators) would
accommodate 55,000. (Density is not a direct function of the height of the
buildings. This is partly due to the fact that the taller the buildings,
the further apart they must be; and partly due to the social infrastructure area per family being constant, at 30 square metres). In all
three cases, there are a sufficient number of commuters in the hinterland
of the station to make viable an economic mass transport system, though of
course the actual cost per passenger will vary.

2.6 And though these density variations in the residential areas will not, as was pointed out before, make a great deal of difference to the overall size of the city, they will make crucial mutations in the living patterns - really the life-styles - of the people. Furthermore, they can also make a decisive difference to the cost of constructing the dwelling units themselves. For again, in developing countries, there is a great variety of simple materials (mud and brick and thatch) and existing vernacular technology in which the ground floor house can be built. Furthermore, any open-to-sky space left on the site is really an extra room, obtained at no cost, usable at least three-quarters of the year for essential family purposes, e.g. for grinding masala, or sleeping at night; thus saving on the cost of constructing an extra room; and thus, of course, making operative exactly the kind of trade-offs discussed earlier.

3.1 Understanding these trade-offs, and identifying the various options available to us, necessitates an over-view of alternate land-use patterns, taking into account a number of crucial variables, e.g.:

A. The cost of providing mass transport

B. The cost of service infrastructure, i.e. roads, water supply, sewer lines, etc.

C. The cost of social infrastructure (schools, hospitals, etc.)

D. The construction cost of the units

E. Some usability coefficients for open-to-sky space, both private and communal.

F. Some weightage against using nationally scarce materials (steel, cement, etc.)

G. Some weightage in favour of configurations and densities wherein it is possible to re-cycle human and other wastes (gobar-gas and bio-gas plants, etc.).

3.2 Considerable research has been undertaken in recent years on this basis, and from the work we have done so far, it appears that in most third world urban areas, these trade-offs would decisively favour a pattern of medium density ground floor housing on plots of between 45 to 100 square metres. It must be again emphasised that the gross residential area required for this kind of "carpet housing" is not much greater than that required for multi-storeyed housing. Unfortunately, the notion of low-rise housing is associated with the kind of urban sprawl we see in the suburbs of our cities; but this, of course, is not what we are talking about. In its concentrated form, low-rise housing is the optimal and classic pattern of residential land-use. For it has a number of advantages, to wit:

(I) An individual building his own house is a highly motivated person; this motivation engendering an increase in per capita savings - so that housing is built without sacrificing other national investment targets.

(II) A low-rise building has a much shorter construction period. Thus the interest cost of capital tied up during construction is considerably less.

(III) It is incremental, i.e., it can grow with the owners requirements and his earning capacity. Eventually, the owner may want to add an additional floor or two, either for rental or for his grown-up children's families. (This would have the additional advantage of increasing the housing densities; though it would entail a certain flexibility in the pattern of infrastructure provided).

(IV) It has great variety, since the individual owner can design and build it according to his own needs.

(V) It need not use high-priority construction materials. Multi-storeyed buildings must of necessity use steel and cement - commodities which are in excruciatingly short supply, in developing countries. On the other hand, the individual row house can be constructed out of anything, from mud on up. The recent advances in paper technology open up a world of new possibilities.

(VI) Of course, if the house in its early stages is constructed of brick, mud and country tile, then it will not have a life span of more than 10 or 15 years - as compared to an RCC structure which will have a life span of, say, 70 years. But this impermanence is really an advantage. For after 15 years, when our economy improves, we might presumably have more resources to deal with this problem of housing. As Prof. Charles Abrams has pointed out "renewability" should be one of the prime objectives of mass housing in developing countries; for as the nation's economy develops, the housing patterns can change. The 5-storey concrete tenement slums built by housing boards all over this country are really the work of pessimists; what they really are saying is : we aren't going to have any future.

4.1 Of course it is one thing to be able to identify optimal residential patterns and densities; it is quite another matter for the authorities to be able to stabilise densities at these levels. This is of course a crucial question. And it is here that strategies must be developed, strategies which would, in all probability, involve the mass transport system. For instance, if we could install a transport system to open up new areas for residential use, we would in effect be subsidising low-cost housing indirectly through a subsidy on the transport system. This might well be preferable to a direct subsidy on housing, as that contradicts the actual market value of the housing, and leads - at least under Indian conditions - to illegal transfers of the tenements.

4.2 In any case, one wonders whether the critical issue in third world cities is not so much a question of increasing densities, but rather one of lowering them. For instance if we can bring down the density in the residential areas to 80 to 100 persons per hectare, it may become feasible to dispense with a central sewage system and instead recycle waste matter (both human and animal) to considerable advantage (cooking gas, fertiliser, etc.). Under Indian conditions this would have the additional advantage of allowing the people a pattern of life they are accustomed to; as though Mahatma Gandhi's vision of a rural India had an almost exact urban analogue.

4.3 Which brings us to some very important considerations. In most urban areas, a surprisingly large proportion of the people prefer to be tenants rather than land owners (in Bombay this proportion runs as high as 80% , but this may well be due to the distorted situation). If we assume that the ratio works out to say 50%, then each plot of land would house two families: one the owner-family, and the other the tenant-family. (In India this could easily happen because of the migration pattern in the joint family system). If we include this assumption, we find that even in urban areas of relatively high land values (Rs.300, or thereabouts), the plot size for the poorest sections works out to about 90 square meters. Now a plot of 75 square meters to 100 square meters is a viable proposition for even the highest income groups; in fact you can build an elegant town house (like you find in Amsterdam or Greenwich village) on a plot of 100 square meters; (i.e. 40 square meters on the ground floor, 40 square meters on the first floor, and 20 square meters in a barsati room on the terrace.)

4.4 Thus we see that our optimal- sized plot - or let us call it a standard-sized plot - will cover upto 97% of the urban population ! This is indeed a concept with profound socio-political implications. One which would constitute a crucial step towards defining a truly egalitarian urban society, totally different from that prevailing in the vast majority of third world cities - where the surrealistic contrast of rich and poor is formalised and made permanent in the totally unequal amount of urban space they each command.

4.5 In too many third world cities, (e.g. Bombay or Dacca), the residential densities in the poorest sectors are extraordinarily high. And these densities are not achieved through high-rise buildings; no, they primarily result from the (criminal) omission of play spaces, hospitals, schools and other social infrastructure in these areas.   (For instance in Bombay city, open space is about 0.10 hectares per 1000 persons - and this includes the "green" of the traffic islands ! Then again, road coverage is about 8% of land use; that is, less than a quarter of what it is in New Delhi. Which goes a long way towards explaining the great crowds we see on Bombay's streets - as compared to the empty boulevards of Lutyen's Delhi).

5.1 In conclusion it must be emphasised that any investigation of optimal densities is largely determined by the scale of the context we establish. For instance, to a developer looking at an individual urban site, the trade-off between cost of construction and marketability will lead to a somewhat higher level of density, since he is not responsible for the schools, roads, and other infrastructure involved in his decision. To an authority responsible for a larger context - say the whole neighbourhood district - this trade-off will certainly give another answer. To anyone looking at the whole city, in fact at the nation and its resources, the answer will change again. Given the awesome scale of the urban growth that lies ahead, there can be little doubt that it is within the larger dimensions of this third context that we should view this problem.

5.2 For too long we have allowed the land-use patterns and densities of
our cities to be determined in the narrowest context by the random (and
self-interested) decisions of individual commercial developers; higher
densities triggering off higher land values, and vice versa, in an
increasingly vicious spiral. Today almost the entire building industry in
all our major cities is turning out a product that only the middle and
upper classes can afford - three-quarters of our society falling below the
price-line ! In their confusion and desperation, Architects and Engineers
start searching for new "miracle" technologies (rather like the elusive
medieval touch-stone which would convert dross into gold). But the
problem of housing the vast majority of our urban people is not one of
finding miracle building materials or construction technologies; it is
primarily a matter of re-establishing land-use allocations. We have
squandered far too much time in a fruitless quest for architectural and
engineering answers, when all along the Planners have stated the question
wrongly to begin with. Even a cursory glance around the indigenous towns
and villages of the third world, will reveal that people - without benefit
of Planners or Architects, or Engineers - have always made marvellous and
ingenious trade-offs between open-to-sky space and built-up construction,
indicating to us a lesson of decisive importance : Namely, that in a warm
and tropical climate, space itself is a resource. It is imperative that
urban planners in the third world begin to use it that way.

MEGALOPOLIS NORTH-WEST EUROPE PRELIMINARY CONCLUSIONS AND OPEN QUESTIONS

Jacques ROBERT, Head of Research
European Research Institute for Regional and Urban
Planning (ERIPLAN) - The Hague.

Macro-urbanization policies are of particular significance
in densely populated regions, like the megolopolitan regions
of North-West Europe. They can be justified by the fact that
urban society is more and more dominating the non-urban spaces
while the dependence of urban society upon the availability
of open spaces is similarly increasing. These reciprocal and
cyclical relationships between ur an and open spaces reveal
the exist nce of equilibria, mainly of ecological character
which can easily be disrupted. They reveal also the existence
of human nd social needs, mainly for recreation purposes
which must be respected and even developed. These reciprocal
relationships are themselves confronted with the productive
function of open spaces for agriculture and forestry.

I. TRENDS OF MACRO-URBANIZATION IN NORTH-WEST EUROPE

The measurement of trends of macro-urbanization in the North-
West European context is a particularly difficult exercise
due to the great divergence of statistical concepts among
countries. An attempt, however (1), has already been made,
based on relatively simple criteria.

1. The first step of this attempt consisted of the delimi-
tation of areas of population densification. The pattern
revealed by this analysis conducted for the decade (1960-1970)
shows a peripheral extension of urbanized areas (those with
a population density higher than 500 inh./km2.' Long distance
deconcentration of the existing urban regions does not play
a major role. Densification is progressing in the areas adjacent to the urban regions, rather irrespective of the type
of economic evolution affecting the urban regions themselves :
population moves are taking place from the Ruhr area (old
industrial structure) towards the Rhine axis Düsseldorf-Bonn,
in the same way as from the Randstad Holland (where major
tertiary activities are located) towards the east and south-
east of the Netherlands.

----

(1) "Prospective study on physical planning and the environ-
    ment in the megalopolis in formation in North-West
    Europe" - ERIPLAN in cooperation with other national
    institutes, EEC, 1975.

Projections available in official reports reveal that future demographic concentration is likely to occur at proximity of existing concentration areas : in the South of the Netherlands and the North of Belgium, in coastal and estuarine areas (northern Germany near Hamburg, in France along the axis Calais-Dunkerque, along the lower Seine valley between Paris and Le Havre, along main valleys (Oise, Aisne, Rhine) and around the largest agglomerations (London, Paris, Brussels).) This pattern of macro-spatial concentration of population revealed by the projections does not differ widely from the trends analysed over the last decade.

The impact of this pattern of densification on the North-West European open spaces will therefore continue to be significant : it is leading, among other pressures, to the convergence of three of the main urban regions : Randstad Holland, Rhein-Ruhr, Central Belgium. The metropolitan open space situated between these urban regions is of key importance for the maintenance of a certain quality of life in North-West Europe, particularly because of its regulative and recreative capacity and the high quality of its landscapes.

2. The second step of the analysis consisted of the evaluation of space consumption through urbanization and transport infrastructure.

The increase in the consumption of space through urbanization and transport infrastructure is much faster than demographic increase : the results of a preliminary land use survey show that between 1960 and 1970 the increase of population in the megalopolitan regions has been 8%, while the increase of urbanized space in the same period was as high as 17%.

Important consumption of space through urbanization occured particularly in Belgium and in the Netherlands during that period : while the average rate of increase was 17%, it was 44% in North-Brabant, 38% in Limbourg, 36% in the Belgian Brabant and 28% in the Antwerp region. In comparison, this rate was only 7% in Northern Germany and South-East England. The greatest urban land use pressures are found in the Northern half of Belgium and in the Southern half of the Netherlands, i.e. in the wider Delta-Region.

The most important indicator explaining these divergence is the increase in the standard of urbanized space per inhabitant. The highest increase took place in Belgium (165 sqm/inhabitant in 10 years). Its amount has been in the same period 50 sqm/inhabitant in Northern Germany, 28 sqm/inhabitant in the Netherlands, 11 sqm/inhabitant in Nordrhein-Westfalen and only 4 sqm/inhabitant in South-East England.

These diverging figures show that consumption of space through
urbanization does not reflect directly the trends of macro-
spatial demographic concentration : it reflects more the results obtained by the various countries in their management
of spatial resources.

3. The third step consisted of the analysis of the expansion
of the residentail function at metropolitan level. Despite the
fact that the heterogenity of the statistical material severely hampered the value of this analyses, the general conclusion is that the metropolitan deconcentration of residential
popouation is progressing rapidly. An important decrease
(absolute or relative) of population is occuring in the central municipality (or municipalities) of the metropolitan
areas, particularly for those with a size larger than 250.000
inhabitants.

This deconcentration of the residential function and the related suburbanization are generating a series of problems :

- the increasing concentration of tertiary employment in the
city-centres of the metropolitan areas are inducing increasing
movements of commuters, both in distance and intensity. These
are generating a decline of the quality of the urban environment due to the congestion of traffic and an over-consumption
of material and human energy.

- the centrifugal movement of residential population has been
accompanied by an increasing social segregation in accordance
with, among other factors, the varying quality of residential
environments.

- as far as environmental aspects are concerned, high density
residential areas generate usually residual effects such as
the rapid development of week-end homes and important flows
of week-end traffic.

- sprawling sururbanization, more or less planned, affects
considerably the quality of landscapes and open spaces.

In conclusion of these three steps of the analysis of macro-
urbanization trends, one may assume that macro-urbanization
is the result of two main components :

- Key forces of macro-economic development are favouring certain locations and induce therefore the formation of axial
or diffuse densification (i.e. coastal areas or the Rhine
axis) ;

- On a smaller scale metropolitan explosion which is the main
expression of macro-economic development, is leading to great
damages for our environment.

II. THE NATURE OF MACRO-URBANIZATION POLICIES IN NORTH-WEST EUROPE

The response of policies to the above-mentioned problems is rather difficult to analyse in the North-West European context. At first urbanization policies have many facets : land-use control, containment, renewal and improvement, integration of urban functions, development of new and expanded towns, etc. Secondly, the results obtained vary widely among countries.

In the field of land-use planning it must first be stated that not all countries in North-West Europe have elaborated structure plans or schemes at the regional or national level, and this is particularly true for Belgium. Here, the largest scale used for land-use planning is that of the so-called "plans de secteurs". The recent decision to envisage the elaboration of a national plan for transportation infrastructure can be considered as a very preliminary step in the direction of a more comprehensive large scale land-use planning. The same could be said of France, where the regional schemes are more regional strategies for economic and social development than constraining land use plans.

Urbanization policies are very much affected by some major sectoral policies : the attribution of incentives or disincentives to enterprises by the ministries of economic affairs, the attribution of grants to municipalities by the ministries of public works, housing, education, social welfare etc. have a large impact on the pattern of urbanization.

Three main characteristics can be drawn for the definition of macro-urbanization policies :

1. Macro-urbanization policies are long-term policies. This does not mean regidity but rather the elaboration of a framework to ensure the compatibility of sectoral objectives and the integration of micro-scale policies. Here, large-scale schemes can play a major role.

2. Macro-urbanization policies are not conceivable without a high degree of coordination. Horizontal coordination (of administrative nature) must be ensured at the inter-departmental level. Vertical coordination (mainly of political nature) is necessary for the compatibility of plans drawn at

various scales and for that of the decisions of the public
sector affecting the choices of the private sector. In some
countries in North-West Europe efforts towards coordination
have already lead to sophisticated planning structures. In
others coordination is still some sort of long-term objective.

3. Macro-urbanization policies are more likely to be implemented there where they are sustained by a political willingness or political control possibilities. However, in some
countries, regional schemes have been elaborated at scales
which do not allow such control possibilities. There, the
trends are mainly influenced by the competition between metropolitan authorities.

III. SOME EVALUATIONS OF MACRO-URBANIZATION POLICIES

Policy evaluation is a difficult exercise, particularly on
the supra-national level. It can be largely facilitated by
referring to the opinion of well-known national actors and
observers of urbanization policies. Some examples will ve
chosen among countries where the planning systems can be
considered as rather sophisticated.

Urbanization policies in England have been mainly characterised by the principle of containment. However, it has been
observed that "containment is only partly the product of
conscious planning. It is also the result of the failure of
the planning system to react quickly enough to the persistent
upward revisions in population projections in the 1950's and
early 1960's. Containment reflects the power of the agricultural and rural preservationist interest groups. Containment
has to some degree been achieved because of the reluctance
of urban local authorities to loose population. But the most
important single factor resulting from - and in turn, rein-
forcing- containment has been soaring land prices". (1)

In the Netherlands "since the fifties the aim of the Government has been to preserve the central open area of the Randstad, to concentrate urban development on the ring and to
find room for growth - which is essential as bearer of the
quality of the centres within the ring - through a process
of outward radiation. This policy has been generally accepted
and the pattern of the Randstad can be clearly visualized by
everyone concerned. This pattern constitutes in particular
the background of the provincial approval policy for municipal allocation plans" (2). A policy of "concentrated decon-
----
(1) Peter Hall et alia : The containment of Urban England -
      1973 - Vol II - p. 395.
(2) Prof. L. Wijers - Director of the Department "Urban re-
      gions" - National Planning Agency - The Hague - In :
      "Pays-Bas, étude de la Randstad" ; Colloque : Les Mégalo-
        poles dans l'Europe du Nord-Ouest - Bruxelles, March 1975.

centration" was advocated as governmental guideline in 1966, which aimed at the expansion of medium-sized towns. "Despite all this, the central open area is gradually filling in. For a lot of people the need to escape from the city and to go and live outside in smaller communities is so great as to produce a pressure, thus giving the rural municipalities in this central area the chance of growing much faster than the urban municipalities on the ring, in spite of the national and provincial politicies". (1)

In the Ruhr-area, a region with the longest physical planning tradition in Western Germany, the strategy defined by the Ruhr Regional Planning Authority attempts to "channel migratory movements primarily to the established settlement cores of the vast agglomerations, the target being to achieve functional zones and urbanized cores offering improved supply conditions and contact possibilities. To attain this goal, the planning board has developed the concept of urban growth poles in the Ruhr. However this strategy is just the reverse of what many local authorities are looking forward, i.e. decentralization. The positive migration trends towards the smaller towns and rural districts located in the fringe zone cannot be exclusively explained in terms of economic progress due to the attraction of industries and manufacturing plants, but must be attributed as well to the numerous newcomers taking up residence there but continuing working in the core zone. These people prefer living in natural and healthy surroundings not to be encountered in the core zone". (2)

These few examples of policies, chosen amongst the most famous in North-West Europe show which kind of difficulties may be encountered in the implementation of macro-urbanization schemes and will have to be faced by countries hardly engaged in such exercises.

IV. A PROSPECTIVE VIEW OF MACRO-URBANIZATION IN NORTH-WEST EUROPA

Prospective thinking could be defined as the attempt not to confer a deterministic view to the observed trends, but rather to pay a greater attention to the key forces underlying the trends, to elaborate conjectural alternatives and to deduce their spatial impact.

---

(1) L. Wijers - Ibidem
(2) Dr. L. WIERLING - Former Deputy Director of the Ruhr Regional Planning authority - In :"Etude de la région Ruhr-Rhin"- Colloque : Les Mégalopolis dans l'Europe du Nord-Ouest - Bruxelles, March 1975.

In the field of macro-urbanization, two main components seem
particularly interesting for long-range prospective thinking :

- as far as the key forces of economic development are concerned, one should explore the ability of North-West European
regions to attract quaternary activities and enterprises ela-
borating and using advanced technologies. The spatial impact
of such evolutions should be scrutinized.

- in the field of the spatial organization of metropolises,
factors of mutation should be looked for which may counteract the actual prevailing trends of suburbanization.

1. The actual economic crisis has strengthened the belief
that economic prosperity in Europe, if any, could mean a
greater productive specialization in the sectors of quaternary activities and advanced technologies. The location of
enterprises belonging to such sectors is mainly dependant
upon the availability of high skilled labour force and numerous services which can only be found in large urban regions.
It may appear banal to assume that the North-West European
regions, being situated in the middle of the European urbanized axis "Manchester-Milan", are really favoured in their
ability to attract such enterprises. Actually, more than 40%
of the headquarters of the 500 largest industrial enterprises
of the E.C. are located in the following 7 towns : London,
Paris, Hamburg, Francfort, Munich, Essen, Milan. London and
Paris together totalize more than 30% of them (1). It has
also been shown that, in the context of progressing European
integration, international traffic flows would tremendously
benefit to the North-West European regions (2). More elaborate analyses on the topic of potentialities for these regions
lead to the same conclusion (3).

The concentration of such sectors of activity in North-West
Europe could possibly mean a tremendous challenge to metropolitan planning, as their location would strengthen the
expansion of city-centres which already resulted in the rather

----

(1) R. Lee "Integration, space and regional relationships
    within the E.C." - Paper presented to the First Convention
    of the Authorities of Peripheral European Regions -
    Galway, October 1975.
(2) Mögliche Entwicklungen im europäischen Fernverkehr. St-
    tus-Seminar-Programm Angewandte Systemanalyse. DFVLR.
    Köln, February 1976.
(3) Scénarios européens d'Aménagement du territoire - DATAR,
    Paris 1974.

damaging metropolitan explosion observed during the 1960's.

2. However the factors which determined the pattern of metropolitan expansion during the 1960's are not all immanent.
Certain factors of mutation in location preferences, able
to counteract to a certain extent the actually prevailing
trends, have already been observed. (1)

On the operational level, in various countries, actual policies are being directed towards a better integration of employment and residences, by limitation the expansion of city-
centres and promoting housing improvement programmes (2).
This is particularly sensible in the Netherlands. In Western
Germany, concern is being developed about the impact of the
expansion of tertiary and quaternary activities on the urban
structure of the concentration areas. Actually, medium-sized
growth-centres are being selected, which may be attractive
enough to locate such activities and to avoid a further congestion of the largest agglomerations.

In conclusion, it must be said that the process of macro-
urbanization which has developed through North-West Europe
during the sixties has been rather damaging for the open
spaces, the landscapes and the quality of life. The risk
still remains that the factors which determined it continue
to reproduce the same pattern, affecting other metropolitan
areas, possibly smaller ones. However, in the field of metropolitan policies, a great awareness about these problems
can actually be observed. It must simply be remembered that
the continuation of the actual trends of macro-urbanization
could in the long-range rather affect the prosperity of
North-West Europe.

----

(1) J. Remy, L. Voyé : "Aspects socio-culturels de l'urbani-
       sation : avantages - inconvénients" - Colloque : Les
       Mégalopoles dans l'Europe du Nord-Ouest - Bruxelles, March
       1975.
(2) L. Klaassen : "Désurbanisation et ré-urbanisation en
       Europe" - Colloque de l'Association de Science régionale
       de Lanque française - Rotterdam 1974.

NATO AND THE HUMAN ENVIRONMENT

James George Sampas
Projects Officer for the Committee on the Challenges
of Modern Society, North Atlantic Treaty Organization,
1110 Brussels, Belgium

ABSTRACT

NATO has been actively concerned with environmental protection
and related issues concerning urban areas since 1969. The
constitutional basis for NATO's concern is Article II of the
North Atlantic Treaty. In late 1969, NATO established the
Committee on the Challenges of Modern Society (CCMS). NATO has
since developed a cost-effective pilot study technique (funded
on a national basis) to stimulate action. The present paper
briefly gives a history of CCMS and describes those pilot studies
which are especially concerned with problems closely associated
with urban areas. It concludes that non-NATO nations could
benefit greatly by studying the NATO experience and drawing on
these pilot studies.

The North Atlantic Treaty Organization, founded in 1949, has been
engaged in the field of environmental protection and related
issues concerning urban areas since late 1969. There are some
who question NATO's legitimacy in non-military, non-political
areas. That questioning attitude reflects a lack of knowledge
or a misunderstanding of NATO's genesis and its constitutional
basis. There is no doubt that the founding of NATO was a response
to the Soviet Union's threat to all of Europe and its absorption
of the countries of Eastern Europe. When NATO was created by
the North Atlantic Treaty, the emphasis of necessity had to be
on defense. Thus, it is that Article 3 of the Treaty speaks of
maintaining and developing the individual and collective
capacity of the members to resist armed attack, Article 4 calls
for consultation among the members when the political independence
of any member is threatened, and Article 5 describes the undertaking of each member in the event of an actual armed attack.

But the North Atlantic Treaty also recognizes that peaceful and
friendly international relations are promoted by "conditions of
stability and well-being". This recognition is given in
Article 2 as well as in the preamble of the Treaty. However, in
fact, for the substantial portion of its first decade of
existence, NATO continued to be concerned with defense and
political problems. When one recalls the weaknesses of the
defense forces of the countries of Western Europe at the time,

this preoccupation is understandable.

It was not until 1956 that sufficient attention was paid to the
role which NATO might play in the non-military areas.   During
the Spring Ministerial Meeting of the NATO country Foreign
Ministers, "Three Wise Men" (Mr. Gaetano Martino of Italy,
Mr. Halvard Lange of Norway and Mr. Lester B. Pearson of Canada)
were requested to submit recommendations to the North Atlantic
Council, NATO's highest body, on how to improve and extend
co-operation among the NATO countries in non-military fields.
These Three Wise Men strongly urged the necessity for scientific
co-operation among the NATO countries, a necessity underscored
by the Soviet launching of the first sputnik on October 4th,
1957. But in spite of the report of the Three Wise Men, NATO
was still not concerned as an organization in major questions
dealing with the human environment and the quality of life.

NATO did not look at environmental issues seriously until 20
years after its birth when, at the April 10th-11th, 1969 Spring
Ministerial Meeting of the NATO countries, the American
President, Mr. Nixon, proposed the creation of "a committee
on the challenges of modern society ... to explore ways in which
the experience and resources of the Western nations could most
effectively be marshalled toward improving the quality of life
of our peoples" and to help 20th Century man to learn "how to
remain in harmony with his rapidly changing world." The
American President pointed specifically to the fact that the
United States could learn from the "new towns" policy of the
United Kingdom, "the great skill of the Dutch in dealing with
high-density areas; the effectiveness of urban planning by
local governments in Norway; and the experience of the French in
metropolitan planning." He stressed that the "work of this
Committee would not be competitive with any other work being
carried on by other international agencies," nor would the
"benefits that flow from it" be restricted to the NATO countries.
Rather, benefits and ideas would be shared in recognition that
the problems to be dealt with have no geographic boundaries.

The reaction of the other NATO countries to the American
proposal was positive. The communique issued at the end of the
meeting stated, in part: the "members of the Alliance are
conscious that they share common environmental problems which,
unless squarely faced, could imperil the welfare and progress
of their societies. The Ministers recognise the important
work on these problems is already being carried out within other
international organizations." Finally, the Ministers instructed
the North Atlantic Council to examine the question of improving
the exchange of views and experience among the NATO countries in
the task of improving the environment of their societies.

The result of that study was the creation in late 1969 of the
Committee on the Challenges of Modern Society (CCMS) under the
Chairmanship of the Secretary General of NATO with all 15 NATO
Governments represented on the Committee. The Committee's
terms of reference may be summarized as follows:

1.   To examine how to improve in every practical way the
exchange of views and experience among the NATO countries
in the task of creating a better environment for their
societies and in so doing consider specific problems of the
human environment with the deliberate objective of stimulating
action by member governments.

2.   To collect information and make assessments of selected
activities of common interest planned or pursued by member
governments domestically or internationally.

3.   To make suggestions and recommendations to the North
Atlantic Council in order to:

   (a)   improve existing arrangements for information
          exchange on work being done nationally on
          environmental problems,

   (b)   draw attention to the need for governmental action
          on recommendations made by other international
          organizations on methods dealing with particular
          environmental problems,

   (c)   propose governmental action when national or
          international bodies have done work on particular
          problems without making recommendations for action

   (d)   where studies have not been adequately carried out
          or co-ordinated, indicate how important gaps might
          best be filled.

4.   To examine the advisability of co-ordination among NATO
members regarding activities pursued in international
organizations,

5.   To make recommendations to the North Atlantic Council on
co-operation between member and non-member states, on the use
to be made outside the Alliance of the Committee's findings
and on any publicity.

In its operations, the Committee has developed a unique cost-
effective approach to stimulating action which encompasses a
number of concepts. The principal tool is the pilot study.
The study is directed towards determining the scope of a
specific problem, breaking it down into its components,
ascertaining the best scientific, technical and economic data
available and then producing resolutions and recommendations
which are submitted to the North Atlantic Council for approval.
Efforts are not directed towards research but rather towards
the application of existing knowledge through solution of
questions relating to policy-formulation and legislation.

The pilot country, in collaboration with other countries,
volunteers to undertake a particular study, finance it, and
generally be responsible for it. It goes without saying, that

unless a country feels it will do a good job, it is not likely
to volunteer to undertake a particular study.

Unlike the understandably classified nature of some NATO
activities, the studies are treated openly. The results of the
pilot studies are freely available to non-NATO countries and
non-NATO countries are invited to participate in the expert
meetings.

Since its establishment in late 1969, the Committee has sponsored
16 pilot studies. A listing of these studies will show their
wide range:

Completed Studies:

Environment and Regional Planning (France)(1)
Coastal Water Pollution and Ocean Oil Spills (Belgium)
Disaster Assistance (United States)
Road Safety (United States)
Air Pollution (United States)
Inland Water Pollution (Canada)

Current Studies:

Advanced Health Care (United States)
Advanced Waste Water Treatment (United Kingdom)
Urban Transportation (United States)
Disposal of Hazardous Wastes (Federal Republic of Germany)
Solar Energy (United States)
Rational Use of Energy (United States)
Geothermal Energy (United States)
Air Pollution Assessment Methodology and Modelling (Federal
Republic of Germany)
Automotive Propulsion Systems (United States)
Nutrition and Health (Canada)

These are the pilot studies, each study comprises a number of
projects.

Environment and Regional Planning

The basic objective of the study on Environment and Regional
Planning was to develop guidelines on regional planning. Some
18 case studies were investigated in an effort to define general
principles that might serve as a basis for establishing national
rules of action using a "whole environment approach" rather than
the sectorial approach which has left many problems unsolved.
The study, in fact, developed a set of proposed guidelines to
serve as a constant reminder that geographical considerations
and the regional dimension are the sine qua non of any
environmental policy. The guidelines were endorsed by the

(1) The pilot country of each study is indicated in parenthesis.

Foreign Ministers of the NATO countries on December 11th, 1973.
The professional planner perhaps may have viewed the guidelines
as merely a restatement of recognized principles, but NATO's
endorsement of the guidelines undoubtedly gave them more weight
and authority than would have been the case otherwise. Certainly,
the pilot study afforded the other countries of NATO an
opportunity to benefit from the French experience. Perhaps a
drawback in the conclusion of this pilot study was an absence of
follow-up by NATO to assess how countries were doing in following
the guidelines. But when one considers the complexities
encountered in this area, the competing and overlapping
jurisdictions in some countries (especially in the United States),
it can be understood that provision for immediate follow-up action
might not have been viewed as practical. What was expected was
that the guidelines would be studied and considered by those
in the NATO countries responsible for environment and regional
planning.

Conference on Cities

In 1971, CCMS co-sponsored an international Conference on Cities
held at Indianapolis, Indiana. The purpose of the Conference
was to afford participants an opportunity to "exchange ideas and
experience to approaches to urban problems". The theme of the
Conference was "innovation in the cities" with the intention of
focusing on finding ways to encourage "the development of
innovative approaches to urban problems through international
co-operation."

Some   500   delegates from 18 countries attended the Conference.
In addition to representatives from all the 15 NATO countries,
there were participants from Austria, Japan and Mexico. These
delegates included local government officials, cabinet ministers,
other national government leaders, many mayors, experts in urban
affairs from the academic and research communities as well as
private organizations (unions of municipal employees, private
tenants' associations) and groups concerned with environmental
issues.

The Conference undoubtedly did a great deal in focusing additional
attention to the innumerable major problems that face the world
in a period of massive urbanization - waste disposal and treatment, urban transportation, delivery of health care, rehabilitation of drug addicts, air and water pollution. More specifically,
the Conference made a number of recommendations including the
establishment of an International Cities Institute, periodic
international conferences of mayors, and a pilot study on urban
transportation. The latter two recommendations have been
implemented.

Air Pollution

The study on Air Pollution leant itself to immediate follow-up
follow-up which is continuing. The study was a massive one and
took over four years to complete. Many volumes of technical

reports were issued. The main purpose of this study was to promote the setting up of air quality management programs in NATO and non-NATO countries. The essential tasks undertaken by expert groups were:

1.   Assessment of ambient levels of sources of pollutants in one major urban region in each of the three participating countries, including projected growth of air pollution during a 20-year period.

2.   Selection of appropriate mathematical modelling techniques to relate source emissions to ambient air quality levels.

3.   Promulgation of control technology documents.

The experts completed all their tasks. Assessment guidelines and specific assessment studies were completed on Ankara, Frankfurt, St. Louis, and Oslo. Assessment studies were also completed on Milan, Turin, and Rotterdam. Criteria documents were produced on sulfur oxides, suspended particulates, carbon monoxide, oxidants-hydrocarbons, nitrogen oxides, and oxidants. These criteria were later used by the Experts Committee of the World Health Organization in determining long-term air quality goals. There were also published control technology documents on stationary-source emissions of sulfur oxides, particulates, nitrogen oxides, hydrocarbons, organic solvents and carbon monoxides.

The final report that issued from the study contained 15 recommendations approved by the North Atlantic Council in 1974. The recommendations called for action in such areas as general assessment of air pollution, standard-setting, establishment of air quality monitoring systems, and suitable systems for retrieval and storage of data, the use of recognized methods for monitoring and institution of uniform procedures for conducting emissions inventories. Moreover, it was decided that there would be follow-up on eight of the fifteen recommendations to assess how nations are doing with respect to implementing these recommendations. This follow-up consists of annual national reports collected and collated by the pilot country, the United States. The follow-up indicates that the effect of the pilot study is indeed positive and is helping to nudge national authorities to do more in cleaning up the air.

As part of the Air Pollution pilot study there was also developed a project on Low-Pollution Power Systems Development (LPPSD) centered on developing low-pollution power systems for automobiles. One product of this project was conclusion of a Memorandum of Understanding by agencies of six countries of NATO providing for co-operation "to ensure that the total resources available internationally for **developing** and bringing into use vehicles with low-pollution pwer systems are developed to the best advantage" by information exchange. Another product is the institution of a periodical international symposium on automotive propulsion systems designed to quicken

the pace of international exchange of views and pertinent
information.

Air Pollution Assessment Methodology and Modelling

The pilot study on Air Pollution Assessment Methodology and
Modelling stems from the experience in use of air pollution
assessment methodology and modelling gained in conducting the
study on Air Pollution referred to above. This study is designed
to permit NATO countries to pursue and carry out the recommendations of the Air Pollution study which call for co-operation to
develop standardised methods for emissions data storage and
retrieval to support requirements in the conduct of national
air quality management programmes, and co-operation to develop
standardised techniques for projecting emissions and predicting
future ambient air quality. Moreover, by means of the study, a
review of assessment investigations with respect to the
application of assessment methodology is being carried out. Also
the study is developing standardised models for various air
quality management application programmes to improve modeller/
user communication and serves as an information forum on new
modelling concepts and techniques. Two panels have been
established to conduct this study.

Advanced Waste Water Treatment

The Advanced Waste Water Treatment pilot study has as its
principal objective the demonstration and assessment of pilot
plants using physical-chemical and direct oxygen processes
for waste water treatment. The physical-chemical work is being
carried out by the United Kingdom with the United States
providing certain technical data. Oxygenation work is being
conducted by the Federal Republic of Germany and France. As
part of this pilot study, the United Kingdom has constructed
a pilot plant near Birmingham to treat both municipal and
municipal-industrial sewage. At that pilot plant, it is
expected that the United Kingdom will develop a methodology
for evaluating the comparative results of these pilot plant
processes. It is hoped that the exchange of experience and
data gained in conducting these pilot plants will show the most
cost-efficient ways of treating waste water.

Urban Transportation

In this study, the NATO countries are studying in depth such
questions as urban goods movement, low-cost bus priority systems
and their impacts, intermodal consideration and evaluation of
existing short distance transport techniques, collection system
evaluation and urban travel forecasting.

$$* \quad * \quad * \quad * \quad * \quad *$$

As one can readily see, the range of CCMS activities is wide,
but nearly all the studies and activities are concerned with
problems associated with human settlements for some of the

greatest challenges of modern society are those encountered in the ever-increasing urbanisation of our world. The efforts of €CMS to help achieve acceptable responses to these urban challenges are an important contribution to making our world a better place to live in. Non-NATO nations would undoubtedly benefit greatly by studying the NATO experience and drawing on the NATO studies.

ABOUT THE RELATIONS BETWEEN POLITICIANS AND PLANNERS IN THE FEDERAL REPUBLIC OF GERMANY

Elmar Wertz, Fachbereich Orts- Regional- und Landesplanung, Universität Stuttgart FRG

When I was asked to put on paper a few words on this theme my first reaction was to answer polemically: this depends on what kind of politician and what kind of planner you have in mind and who would be interested in the question at all.

But the persistance of my Belgian friends convinced me that there could be something particular about the relations between politicians and planners in my country, something I have probably been blind for. I do not deny that there are quite a few analytic publications about planners, planning administration planning politics etc. But as I understood, the interest is focused more on informal or semiformal relations than on the formal set-up.

In this sense I shall try to communicate subjectively my observations and their subjective interpretation rather than a analysis scientificly valuable avoiding nevertheless to furnish to much of a feuilleton.

I don't remember who said that it was one of the characteristics of mankind to make plans or to plan by which the author meant that man is aware of the future and that he acts accordingly, I don't know whether it is true that only men are aware of the future but I do know that they do not act accordingly. I should like to change the characteristic by saying that men have illusions about the future and that they act accordingly.

After this first axiomatic statement I come to another
preliminary one: one of the most existential questions for the
planner is how to please the politician and for the politician
how to please his potential electors. Notice the difference in
scale: for the planner there are only a few politicians to
please whilst there is a great number of electors to be pleased
by the politician!

There is a third statement of axiomatic nature: unfortunately
politicians and planners are not the only people in the observed
field; there are two more, and I sometimes fear that they are
even more important than the two we focus on, i.e.: the
administrator and the jurist.

And finally, I should like to mention a fourth axiom: It is not
always easy to distinguish politicians from planners as there
are politicians having become planners because they thought
planning had more influence than politics and planners having
become politicians because they thought politics had more
influence than planning. (This statement is based on a duality
model constructed for the purpose of explanation only. But the
fact of changing from planning into politics and vice versa is
characteristic for the Federal Republic since about 10 or
12 years.)

Looking at the four selected axioms one may come to the
conclusion that the relations between politicians and planners
are complex and inscrutable. They are, but they still could be
described and at least partially commented. To do so, I try to
apply that sort of simplifying typology architects are
proverbially unscrupulous about. Undoubtedly the different types
of planners and of politicians sharpen their profile mutually
so that very often we find a certain type of planner in relation
with a certain type of politician. This is not only the result
of selection but also of adaptation and of profil-carving. So,
in another step of simplification one could reduce the wanted
description to a typology of relations. These again are based on

legal and administrative standards some principles of which
should be outlined:

The planner in the civil-servant-status is free to have and to
show political colour, he can be member of one of the political
parties and, in the last few years it became nearly the rule that
civil servants, not only planners, were members of political
parties or showed at least certain sympathies.

This is quite different from the situation for instance in
Great Britain though some other points are comparable: the
planner does not participate in decision making, he is, if ever,
responsible vis-à-vis the Council or whatever the authority is.
The planner (still the civil servant is meant) is considered as
a technical adviser, advising on demand. The German system of
dissemination of competences is very complicated and leaves
interstices and informal paths to take influence. The
hierarchical system is marked by scale levels in town and
country planning and on the contrary a "going-through-competence"
(from the top straight down to the basis) in the case of
sectorial planning. Hence, the system allows sectorial planning
(traffic, water supply, educational faculties etc.) much more
stringency than the overall planning of communities for instance.

The planning profession can also be exercised as a liberal
profession which is open to individual planners as well as to
planning firms. Their relations with politicians and with
administration have some particular traces to be dealt with
later.

So far, I abstained from describing administration and jurists
having been mentioned above as very important elements of
planning and politics. Confining myself again to simplification
I tend to say that these represent something like the solid and
unchangeable building of social organization making me doubting
the astonishment about Fouchet's stability in spite of the
changing regimes. It did much more astonish me that regimes

could change in spite of the stability of administration and I
wonder if they really changed as much as we thought they did.

The first type of realtionship between planner and politician
could be named the magic-circle-type in which the planner is
what the French call the illusionist. The magic circle rests
upon the illusions men have about the future, that growth will
always be possible were it is wanted: of quality and of quantity,
of intelligence and of knowledge, of the number of inhabitants,
of food and water and that decrease will always be possible
were it is wanted of hunger, analphabetisme, underemployment ...

Illusionist-planners have good relations to politicians in
so far as they provide optimisme and promises. Illusionist-
planners prepare spectacular fireworks in exhibitting plans and
models showing what this dirty world could be like if it was
given to planners and politicians. This sort of plans are
masterworks as far as presentation is concerned. Even if they
are unusually modest they offer modesty as new type of optimisme.
Illusionist-planners in the Federal Republic like to say that
they "have to sell their plans to the politicians". The word
"to sell" is used synonymously for "to seduce them to accept".
The travelling salesman's attitude has very well been adopted
by this sort of planners, no matter whether they are of civil
servant or of liberal status. The illusionist-planner is given
access to the political scene on the stage of which he acts side
by side with the politician. Their relations are marked by the
fact that in theory politicians and planners share responsibility.
"In theory" was put in because there is very little
responsibility due to a relatively high degree of non-
explicitness of the plans. Consequently this type of magic-
circle-relations increase the more you go up from the lower
planning level of community planning to higher levels as regional
or national planning. In any case relations show signs of
conspiracy.

Another type of relationship between politicians and planners

may be indicated by the partnership between playwright and
actor: the planner still works for the scene but he is not
admitted on the stage. The politician takes most of the
responsibility with the exception of merely technical elements
of the plan. The playwright-planner is not a reduced illusionist-
planner because he tries - perhaps provoked by the non-admittance
to the scene - to persuade the politician of how the system of
values needs to be changed. Here, we have come to the crucial
point that the system of values of politicians and of planners
differ if not for other reasons than for the one mentioned
already: the politician addresses himself to a great number of
potential electors, whilst the planner - in this sort of
relationship - addresses himself to the politician only. This
means in practice that the planner inclines to defend what he
believes the interests of minorities could be, no matter whether
he does so for romantic or other reasons. The politician is
bound to majoritary voting, the playwright-planner to the
defence of the underpriviledged.

Conflicts produced the indicated way are not really malicious as
they can be smoothed by the "talk-much-but-say-little-technique"
as long as plans are not explicit and detailed. Things become
worse as soon as it comes to physical consequences of planning.
In many larger communities two or three groupes of planners
fight each other permanently, even more than politicians do,
tricking out each other, setting up coalitions etc.

Internal guerilla wars are quite usual in public (and private)
administration, but between planners of the playwright type they
are limited to indirect passage of arms. These "administro-
social" conditions may occassionally lead to absurdities as for
instance when a service for long term planning was installed to
controll the short term planning service. They use to fight each
other in presence of the council in a way comparable to a match
on the playground. Both spokesman (being politicians) defended
respectively the interests of developpers, architects and their
clients and on the other hand what we may call public interests.

Such staging of political alternatives takes into consideration
the fact that you cannot shake hands with a chimney sweeper
without them getting black or grey at least, by which I want to
say that the daily contact between the authorities responsible
for building permits and the applicants entailes a certain
companionship we sometimes find similarly between policeman and
crooks. The planning scene is remarkably influenced by traditions
and actual conditions of the building trade which is known as
being rather generous as far as strict obedience of the law is
concerned. Conterparts of the traditional building control
authorities are the departments for urban and regional research
and planning, a kind of brain trust attached to the
administration headquarters installed since about 10 years in all
larger towns and counties, not far away from what in the military
trade is called general staff which is known as being rather
generous as far as strict obedience of the rules of the
democratic game are concerned. Born during the past days of
expansion and growth this sort of "public" service has quite
well fulfilled its task. Criticized since expansion has come to
its end, authorities come back to more transparence and
strictness in their administrative decisions which may also be
true for the relations between politicians and planners.

Strictness also rules a relation between politicians and
planners which I prefer to name by characterizing the role of
the planner as being comparable to the one of a plumber. If you
agree to the hypothesis that the plumber is a craftsman doing
generally more repair work than new installations (even if this
hypothesis is wrong statistically) we may be also unanimous
about the plumber-planners typical features: he does not do much
planning himself but repairs what other people thought they
planned or what other people - namely politicians - decided
avoiding intentionally to plan. Planners being thus restricted
tend to clandestine planning, two well known versions of which
are the initiation of public partizipation by giving information
to newspapers secretly and the correction of a "plan" during its
realization pretending technological constraints. The reduction
of the administration planner to an administrative excuter has

provoked that planners try to strengthen their technical
monopoly by declaring modern techniques (data-banks, computers,
gaming simulation etc.) as indispensable. In my eyes, something
is good about these changes: public participation has at least
potentially become reality due - at its origine - to the reduced
planner's desire for compensation of lost competences and to the
coalition resulting therefrom with contesting groupes of
citizens. It was only much later that the idea of participation
has been taken up by politicians now being aware of losing
parts of their competences.

In order to keep away from too much simplification some
observations should be added: the relationship between
politicians and planners in the Federal Republic is stamped on
the planner's side by his architectural and engeneering heritage
and on the politician's side by reminiscences of authoritarian
attitudes. The traditionally reactive administration of which
planners are part very often must be considered as another
element influencing their relationship with non-administrative
people.

But, what about the "free" planners, members of a liberal
profession? Their number is decreasing as one can easily imagine
thinking for instance of the plumber-planner's advances. The
more the free planner is thus endangered existentially the more
he looses distinction. Hence, he seems to be reduced to the
maker of expertises ceasing then to be a planner.

To close up, some more details should be given on the "sectorial"
planner, already mentioned above, whose relations to politicians
have been developped historically: the sectorial planner
dealing with narrowly defined planning objects attaining
nevertheless much more penetration than the global planning
normally does. Objects of planning can be: roads, localisation
and programmes of schools, railways, programmes and distribution
of hospitals, airports, telephonlines and -exchanges etc. Their
planning is effective because they possess the most indisputable
knowledge. I don't know very much about the relations between

these planners and politicians. Interpreting my observations I
should come to the conclusion that there is no relation at all
because these planners do what they want without any visible
control. They can only indirectly be stopped by lack of money.

Many jurists are in a similar position as they possess the most
indisputable arguments. Many of the politicians in the Federal
Republic are jurists by education. Statistics say that their
number is increasing.

WELL BEING IN ESTABLISHED RESIDENTIAL AREAS

Vera I. van der Does
General Secretary International Federation of
Pedestrians*

After one of the squares in the centre of Vienna had been re-
designed as a pedestrians-only square, the planners were surprised to find that the noise meter was still showing a substantial degree of "noise". Upon going further into the matter,
they found that this time the cause of the noise was the happy
voices of children at play!

The man in the street is now beginning to form a different
picture of what constitutes "well-being". Ten years ago well-
being was represented for many by a car outside the front door.
But for a number of years now there has been extensive publicity for cycling, walking to keep fit, and selective use of the
car.

In some countries groups of parents no longer accept the unsafe, unhealthy environment in the street in which they live,
where their children cannot safely play out of doors and meet
their little friends, where cars have priority over the most
vulnerable road-users: children, elderly persons, handicapped
persons, whether young or old.

In my country you can see indignant, protesting parents waving
banners as they march to the Town Hall or to the Houses of Parliament to make it quite clear that they will dig up "their"
street if steps are not taken to tame the motor car in residential areas.

Ten years ago cars still tended to be regarded as the greatest
contributor of all times to human happiness. It is true that
society can no longer function without the motor car. But this
does not mean that it may dominate our residential streets or
our shopping streets, taking priority over man's happiness,
health and well-being, killing or maiming our children.

What are we to think of the "well-being" of families that have
to put up with a huge lorry parked all weekend in front of
their living room window because the driver has nowhere else to
leave it? Or those who live in streets where the pavements are

---

* Secretariate: Passage 61^{III}, The Hague, Netherlands

littered with parked cars so that mothers with prams or invalids
in wheel-chairs are obliged to take to the carriage and drivers
cannot see the small children playing around the stationary
cars, unaware of the danger?

This is the environment that hundreds of thousands have to en-
dure, failing to realize that their environment might be one
without danger, noise and polluted air, inhaled in the first
place by the toddlers nearest to the exhausts.

Public Opinion

If public opinion were outraged by the ever-increasing toll of
injury and death on the road, and especially the high proportion of injury and death to pedestrians and cyclists, means would
very quickly be adopted for instituting the technical measures
that have already proved effective in eliminating many accidents. It is well known that the great vulnerability of young
children and old people needs special measures.

Since the Second World War pedestrians in many countries have
been organizing themselves into Associations. Not to go hiking,
but in protest against the deterioration in traffic environment of the street in which they live, of the parks and natural
playgrounds that have been converted into car parks and against
the heavy toll that motorization has taken of high-risk groups.
In 1963 these associations organized themselves into the International Federation of Pedestrians (FIP). This body does not
wish to turn the clock back, but is actively opposed to the
evil side-effects of the motor car. It has a very definite
opinion on the changes that the authorities have to make to
rescue human well-being today. However, this task is not con-
fined to the authorities; it is also YOUR task and mine.

Modern town planners were the first to see what should be done.
In Stevenage New Town Eric C. Claxton built the first town under
the New Towns Act, a place for PEOPLE. In the USA Jane Jacobs
wrote her magnificent book "Life and Death of Great American
Cities", while Victor Gruen, the well-known Viennese town planner, later active in the United States, described with sharp
irony the victory of the "free flow of traffic" in residential
streets.

In 1962 the first results of the sophisticated research done by
Professor Stina Sandels at her Institute for Child Psychology
in Stockholm were published. From then on those concerned got
the message that even the best road safety education cannot
adapt a child to modern traffic, so that the traffic has got to
be adapted to the child.

Soon a number of modern town planners who agreed with this axiom
and the International Federation of Pedestrians, which under-
wrote the principles involved and published the articles of
Professor Sandels in every edition of her International Bulletin, met on common ground with Professor Sandels. Not that the

battle was won in 1964 or 1965. It is a long and bitter struggle
that has to be waged every day, with the aid of many wide-awake
experts fighting for the common cause. It needs the backing of
public opinion, based on a new philosophy that the priorities
in urban planning no longer have to go to machines but to people
for the greater good of the latter.

In my country my association, which has several town planners
on its board, no longer has to fight alone. And my International
Federation is better understood today when we plead for priority in residential areas for what Professor Sandels has called
the three handicapped groups in traffic: the young, the elderly
and the disabled pedestrians.

The inhabitants of Stevenage are lucky; even a toddler can go
to nursery school by himself in safety, since he never has to
cross a road at ground level. The same applies to bus passengers, who make use of an underpass, and motorists have freedom
of movement too: they encounter neither pedestrians nor traffic
lights. Homes have two front doors, one opening on to the road,
the other on to the footpath system.

For years now thousands of people have visited Britain's new
towns. Did their home towns immediately profit from these visits? The answer unfortunately is no. Many a town planner had
to fight a bitter fight to attain his end. Many authorities
went to see for themselves, but even so decisions are often
political ones.

The Dutch Way

In Holland the tide turned about ten years ago. The new town of
Lelystad, in the North-East Polder, was built largely on the
example of Stevenage. Hardly any child has been involved in
a road accident in Lelystad.
Elsewhere in Holland too, new design principles are being applied. Their basis is that people must have continuous, clearly
indicated systems of footpaths and cycle tracks, linking dwellings, schools, shops, offices, factories and recreational
areas. There is also room for the motor car in such systems,
but only if it is subordinated to the safety of pedestrians and
cyclists.

This new town planning movement began as early as 1960 in
Kampen, where gutters were laid across some streets to force
motorized traffic to slow down. At the end of the Sixties old
residential streets in Delft were given a face-lift. Cars may
enter them but can drive only at very low speeds. They are obliged to behave like guests. Priority goes to the pedestrian and cy-
clist. Similar principles have been applied in the design of
new residential streets too, not only in Delft but also in Emmen,
Gouda and many other Dutch towns and villages.

To illustrate the above, let me take Delft as an example. An official description of the city informs us that all designs are

made by the city planning department in close cooperation with
the department for general maintenance, the parks and gardens
department, the traffic department, the welfare department and
the local traffic police. The Ministry of Culture, Recreation
and Social Work subsidizes part of the costs in areas of the
city dating from before 1945.
A major endeavour in Delft is to convert roads that do not
function as main roads (a maximum of 300 vehicles during
peak hours) into "residential streets". The social and recreational function of such streets should prevail over their
function as a route for through traffic or as parking. To a-
chieve this, the design of the street itself should invite
use by pedestrians and playing children.
"Private" property in front of each door, such as trees, posts.
benches, playgrounds, is essential. Such elements at the same *
limit the physical influence of the motor car by creating "unexpected" barriers for drivers.   *time
Parking should be strictly limited to those areas clearly marked
as such; the design and function of the street must prevent
high speeds (maximum for instance 15 - 20 km per hour) and not
allow large lorries to enter.
Special legal rules should be instituted to protect such functions. (This the Ministry is now doing.)
When Delft streets are on the verge of being redone, a letter
with a plan for the improvement is distributed among the residents. They are told in this letter that "in various parts of
your city streets have been improved in a rather special way.
We have tried to make the street more of a pleasant and normal
place for pedestrians and children". The letter also includes
the following: "Mostly something had to be done to prevent cars
from driving too fast. Every car should behave like a guest in
your residential street, which is in a way your territory. Fast
driving can be made difficult by creating ramps, planting trees,
installing posts and making narrow passages. Long, unbroken
lines of cars parked by the kerb may make it difficult for you
to cross the street or even reach your home. The parked cars
also prevent drivers from spotting your children at play. If
the lines of cars are broken by open spaces at regular intervals, crossing the street can be made safer and opportunities
for play are created for your children. Having parking on alternate sides of the street may also help to slow down cars, since
nobody can zig-zag down a street at more than a slow pace.
Social and all other residential uses of your street should not
be prevented by any car. When possible, each house will be given
a small area of its own in front of the door. This will mark
your "private" property. When there are no conduits underneath,
residents are allowed to use a small stretch of ground in front
of their home to plant shrubs or flowers. The letter ends as
follows: "Our plan for your street is presented to you with
this letter. If you have any questions or suggestions, you are
welcome at the Department of Public Works. The explanation on
the plan tells you whom to ask for when contacting my office".
The letter is signed by the Director of Public Works.

Children and Road Accidents

I should now like to draw your attention to a real misunderstanding that is firmly rooted in the minds of millions: "The way
to prevent accidents with pedestrians is to educate the pedestrians. As soon as the right method has been found we'll be rid
of most accidents involving this group".
But research amply shows that even the very best education can
not make a young child safe on the road. Since 1960 Professor
Sandels' institute, in cooperation with research-workers from
other disciplines, has been performing a searching and refined
investigation of the possibilities and difficulties of children
up to the age of ten in traffic. Other Swedish research in the
field of urban planning is being done by the SCAFT Group,headed
by Professor O. Gunnarsson of Chalmers University of Technology,
Göteborg.
In one of its studies this group argues that, from the point of
view of the accident, the wrong actions of the pedestrian,grown-
up or not, are of secondary importance. The primary cause is
that the traffic environment creates situations through which
wrong actions cause accidents.
In all countries, as far as children on foot are concerned, the
age groups between three and ten years are hit the hardest. For
this reason it is urgent that we take a closer look today at
the protective measures at our disposal for these high-risk
groups. As Professor Sandels remarks: "Often it is said that a
traffic accident has been caused by lack of carefulness by the
child, wrong traffic behaviour etc. The grown-up then compares
the child's ability to cope with traffic with his own ability
to do so. This identification of children with grown-ups leads
to difficulties in some countries when the judge has to determine the damage, and declares the child guilty". She often appears in court as an expert in this type of lawsuit, and argues:
"The child is never responsible for the accident, it is the
victim of that accident, because the grown-up has not been able
to understand its situation and adjust to it". Fortunately, a
change in jurisprudence is also noticeable in Holland.
For example, we read that a District Court held the parents of
a toddler of $4\frac{1}{2}$ responsible for damage because it is not jus-
tifiable to send a child through traffic all on his own.

Investigation in to the "Traffic Maturity of Children

Professor Sandels makes the point that children function in
every respect, and therefore also in traffic, in accordance
with their age. Scientific research into the traffic maturity
of children in various age groups shows how their traffic environment has to be accommodated to protect them from road accidents.
I shall now quote 12 theses developed by Professor Sandels on
the basis of her investigations:
1. Adults and children do not experience "the same" situation
   in the same way. There are also considerable differences between the experiences of children of different ages.
2. The diminutive stature of children limits their vision: small
   children cannot see what is on the other side of a parked car.

Moreover, we "see" with our whole personality. Small children try to observe every object in order to learn as much as possible about it, or to get a vague overall view of a situation. The adult tries to grasp what is essential. Grasping objects in motion and judging their correct speed requires long training and experience.

3. Children find it more difficult than adults to judge from which direction a sound comes. This can be a severe handicap for them in traffic.

4. Road signs are not always understood by children. Sometimes they are directly misunderstood.

5. Children are often run over on zebra crossings. This is connected with their inability to master relevant rules.

6. Also children often believe that drivers can stop their vehicles instantaneously.

7. Many children believe that the safest way to cross the road is to run.

8. Even among 9-year-olds, children often have no working knowledge of left and right.

9. Misconceptions about even common traffic expressions are frequent, which means that we may give a child a "perfectly clear" instruction, but the child may understand it another way than we meant and act accordingly.

10. The ability to concentrate is much greater in adults than in children.

11. The child is by nature a playful being. Since its body is growing fast and the body proportions are continually changing, play is often another term for violent physical movement.

12. Children are impulsive, spontaneous beings, more undifferentiated than adults. This unity is especially noticeable when they are seized by some violent emotion. And what produce strong emotions in children often appears insignificant to adults. "Dashing-out accidents" are often caused by sudden emotions.

The Best Method for Protecting the child

Although good training in road safety has to start as early as possible and should be continued all through school, it may never be assumed that a child is able to apply even the best of training at all times. Traffic training takes a long time before it bears fruit. In traffic children can never be raised to a level with grown-ups. Adjustment of the environment to the child is a primary requirement for protecting the child effectively.

The problem of old people in our roads

What goes for the young child also goes for the other two high-risk groups. Both our old people and the physically handicapped of every age are entitled to a safer environment just as much as our children are.
Provisions should also be made for the practice of safe walking habits by old people, and it is essential to impress upon motorists the special problems of the young, the old and the infirm, who together form the three handicapped categories.

Drivers recognize the limping invalid or the blind man with his
white stick. They need to learn to recognize the other two
groups.
An unsignalized pedestrian crossing over a road with heavy traffic or where fast driving is possible gives no protection for
these groups. They have a right to cross in complete safety.

Good News for the Blind and Visually handicapped

In New South Wales the Ministry of Transport (F.R. Hulscher
B.E.) is engaged on research of great importance into means of
helping the blind at signalized crossings. Twenty-four European
countries are involved in the painstaking research by Mr.
Hulscher and his team.

From this research we learn that buzzers at traffic lights to
help the blind are no new invention. Israel was already using
them in 1963, and various Australian cities can profit from
experience extending as far back as 1967.

Congress

The subject will be discussed at a congress to be held in Perth,
Australia, from 23 to 27 August 1976. In the meantime the same
group of research workers is looking into the question of standardization. It will not be possible to opt for one specific
type of buzzer, since different situations require different
solutions.

Standardization

Anyway, you will be interested to hear that a standardization
congress will be held in Sydney in October 1976 as part of the
Vibration and Noise Control Engineering Conference (Australian
Institute of Engineers).

Well Being in Established Residential Areas

If we really want to make the world a better place to live in,
if we want to join in the battle against polluted streets rendered unlivable by cars racing through them, we shall have to
create a safe and healthy environment for all, young and old,
handicapped or free from handicap.

The OECD held a conference on the theme: "Better towns with less
traffic"and published the report last year. (OECD's Urban Division sent a questionnaire to towns with more than 100,000
inhabitants in 19 countries, three hundred answered the questionnaire).

"Cells"

In Göteborg, Stockholm, Bremen and Nagoya experience has been
gained with "cells" of about one square kilometre. There is an
entrance and an exit in each area, but cars cannot drive from
one cell to another, but have to return to the road they left to
enter a cell. It goes without saying that this new structure
must benefit the well-being of the inhabitants.

Let us bear in mind that, as far as traffic is concerned, changing a policy of welfare into one of well-being makes particularly heavy demands of care for our young children and for the elderly and the disabled.

Every municipality will have to admit that these categories have the same claims to SAFE use of public roads as do motorists. More and better provisions are required for this.

We shall therefore keep on pointing out to all authorities what their primary task is, namely:

Always side with the weakest party in any conflict situation.

ROLE AND IMPACT OF GREEN SPACES IN URBAN PLANNING

Robert IMPENS[*], Karine STENBOCK-FERMOR[†]
[*]Biologie végétale, Fac. Sciences Agronomiques de
l'Etat, Gembloux
[†]Et.& Rech. Conditions de vie des arbres en site urbain
(ERA/IRSIA)

ABSTRACT

Green spaces are of great importance for man's urban well-being. The
green spaces of our cities are exposed to many different pressures. They
are much more than ornaments that give a pleasant picture of towns, as
usually extolled by city-planners. A definition of the ecological characteristics of the urban medium and of the place of green spaces in it is given.
An investigation carried out in Brussels concerning the living conditions of
city trees is discussed.

INTRODUCTION

All over the world, urban areas are expanding through migrations and
natural population increases: 30 percent of the world's population live in
towns with 5000 inhabitants and 18 percent in cities with 100,000 inhabitants
or more.
In 1800, 2 percent of our country's population lived in towns. In 1950, 20
percent of the population was living in cities and it is generally admitted that
by the year 2000 this will be in excess of 60 percent.

In nearly all the industrialised and developing countries, towns are expanding,
taking into use more and more land. This urban growth has embodied, like
a hungry amoeba, a lot of green spaces such as forests, fields and meadows,
parks, and historical or private gardens.

An appreciation of the green spaces in larger European towns is difficult
due to the varying appraisals of its meaning. This appreciation differs
following a study of the historical center of the city or the surrounding
districts or even the suburbs. Other problems lie with the differing conceptions as to the inclusion of cemeteries and playgrounds or the estimation of
the surfaces that street trees represent.

It is generally admitted that Brussels with its 19 districts and one million
inhabitants has a quota of 28 square meters per inhabitant.
In the city center of Paris with its 2.6 million residents, each enjoys 7.5
square meters of green space. When the surrounding districts of Neuilly,
Vincennes, Boulogne-Billancourt and others are taken in account, this
increases to 18 square meters per inhabitant.

The green spaces of our cities are exposed to many different pressures. It
is not so much the pressure of traffic, air pollutants or climatic changes
as the pressure of city expansion and economic value of building sites.

Green spaces are much more than ornaments that give a pleasant picture
of cities as usually extolled by city-planners.

We intend to give a definition of the ecological characteristics of the urban
medium and of the place of green spaces in it. To this end we shall briefly
describe an investigation carried out in Brussels about the living conditions
of city trees.
This investigation has been assisted since July 1975 by a subsidy granted by
the IRSIA.

ECOLOGICAL PROPERTIES OF THE URBAN MEDIUM

Protection and extension of green spaces need first of all as perfect as possible a knowledge of their layout conditions. Among ecological properties of
urban environment we can note:

-Physical Structure of the City:

It concerns the relief, the number of rivers, channels and ponds, the importance and distribution of thoroughfares, etc.

-Spatial Structure of the City:

The distribution in concentric areas with different population densities, the
divisions in sectors of various socioeconomic destinations (residential, industrial or business sectors), the situation of the dormitory towns and the
importance of the daily migratory movements in their direction.

-Urban Climate:

In built-up areas, the particular aerodynamic roughness parameters, the
thermal and hydrological properties of the landscape, the heat from metab-
olism and from the various combustion processes, and the chemical composition of the atmosphere create a climate which is quite distinct from that
of extra-urban areas.

Strong winds are decelerated and light winds accelerated as they move into
towns. Turbulence is increased, relative humidity is reduced, the chemical
composition of the air is changed, receipts and losses of radiation are both
reduced, temperatures are raised, fogs are made thicker, more frequent
and more persistent, and rainfall is sometimes increased (Ref. 5).

-Air Pollution:

Undoubtedly, the best-known aspect of urban atmosphere is the generally
high levels of pollution.

Man has always treated the atmosphere as an open sewer. Smoke and sulphur
dioxide might be called the traditional pollutants. Petrol engines also emit

poisons: carbon monoxide , oxides of nitrogen, polycyclic hydrocarbons, inorganic lead, bromides and chlorides. Heavy-metal contamination of urban trees is also reported (Refs. 10, 12, 6, etc.).

-The Soil's Conditions:

In cities, natural landscapes are greatly changed by urban works - cuts and fills, laying of pipes, etc. - with consequent great variations in the subsoil composition.

Planting on flagstones or in containers is used more and more for what is named "framing green spaces". The reduction of space available for the roots needs a specially well-improved soil.

Finally, urban soil is characterized by the presence of many pipes. These are sometimes broken through vibrations and pressures caused by traffic. This results in underground overflows of waste-waters, gases or other toxic substances (Ref.4).

-Water Contributions: .

Water cannot get into the soil because of macadam and asphalt. Bare soils may be trampled and hard, and the water flows away without soaking in. If we add to these phenomena concrete's high level of potential evaporation, we can understand how much plants are suffering from underwatering in the cities.

-Energy Contributions:

The surface of the town is of a rocky nature: brick and concrete can be considered as storers of heat and the warmth is concentrating between the big buildings.

In spite of the dust dome over the city, solar radiations are very important and increase heating of the atmosphere.

We can note too the warmth resulting from domestic means of heating, from traffic, etc. Because of all these factors, the city is like a "heat island" which is warmer than the surrounding country.

All these properties of the urban medium are unfavourable for the plants, for animals, and for man who knows many other psychological stresses.

Before asking for the protection and the extension of green spaces in towns, we are going to define their essential roles.

ROLES OF GREEN SPACES

-Influence on Urban Climate

Green spaces are the only effective natural means of transforming the un-natural climate of cities and of improving it.

In Frankfurt, Germany, green belts (even though they were not larger in

width than 50 to 100 meters) had an important effect in reducing the temperature by 3.5°C compared with that in the center of the city (Ref. 2). The
relative atmospheric humidity showed an increase of 5 per cent in comparison with that in the city center.

Another important feature is the reduction of wind speed in avenues and
parks, which can enhance the air-filtering effect of vegetation.

-Dust-reducing Effects of Green Spaces:

Airborne dust will settle on the leaves of grasses and trees in parks and in
avenues. Comparative experiments on the filtering effects of different
canopies have been made (Ref. 14, 15).

Theoretical aspects of the use of green belts in cities and in industrial
areas have been studied by BERINDAN (Ref. 1) and POPOV (Ref. 11).

-Fixation of Some Toxics:

In addition to carbon dioxide fixation by photosynthesis, plants are able to
occlude atmospheric pollutant gases through their stomata. In this way they
contribute to air cleaning in cities. Of course, the pollutant's concentration
must be sufficiently low not to cause vegetal tissue lesions.

-Noise Reduction:

Noise reduction by plant screens is very debatable, though it is not impossible to reduce traffic noise on a very crowded street by joint action of the
removal and the use of artificial or plant screens (Ref. 13).

-Other Functions:

Meeting places, suitable for relaxing, and leisure green spaces are really
special quiet and restful areas for the people. The role of colour in psychic
reactions has been verified by experiment. Green and blue have a calming
effect on the nervous system. From an aesthetic point of view, trees, along
the street or all together, effect a good integration of monuments and big
buildings in the town.

Marking the progress of the season and introducing into daily life the notion
of biological renewal, they illustrate natural cycles and may be considered
as a good teaching method for the observation of nature. They shelter too
many varieties of insects and birds.

By their reactions to the urban environment trees and other plants constitute
extremely precious pollution indicators. The introduction of very sensitive
plants against a particular agent permits this unfavourable factor's evolution
to be followed in a much more shaded way than by any other apparatus
because plants react by integrating all the medium's factors.

Convinced of the necessity of protecting green spaces in towns, the ERA
has directed its researches towards the pathology of urban plants, applying
itself first to street trees because they are the most threatened plants. This
investigation began at the end of 1972 in Brussels and it is now expanding to
the cities of Gent and Mons.

SURVEY OF STREET TREES IN BRUSSELS

Street trees are defined as being those trees which are separated from the general traffic and planted not more than 5 meters from the road. Thus are included, for example, trees on footpaths, on central reservations, on roundabouts, on little squares, etc. The survey undertaken by the ERA includes a number of points (Refs. 3, 7, 8):

Figure 1 shows how the 75, 000 trees are distributed in the city. This type of representation allows the comparison, by sectors, of the densities of different trees.

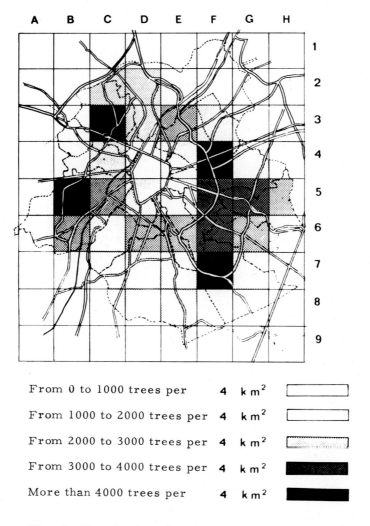

From 0 to 1000 trees per   **4**   k m²

From 1000 to 2000 trees per   **4**   k m²

From 2000 to 3000 trees per   **4**   k m²

From 3000 to 4000 trees per   **4**   k m²

More than 4000 trees per   **4**   k m²

Fig. 1. Distribution of road bordering trees examined in the Brussels area in 1974.

-The Inventory:

There was no precise inventory in Brussels and the first job was then to
mark and to compute all the street trees. This checking revealed more
than 80 species distributed into Brussels' 19 districts and adding up to
about 75, 000 trees.

The best-represented species are Prunus serrulata Ldl. (9551 trees),
Platanus acerifolia (Ait.) W. (x) (8941 trees), Robinia pseudoacacia L.
(6612 trees), Acer platanoïdes L. (5604 trees), and Tilia platyphylla Scop.
(4750 trees).

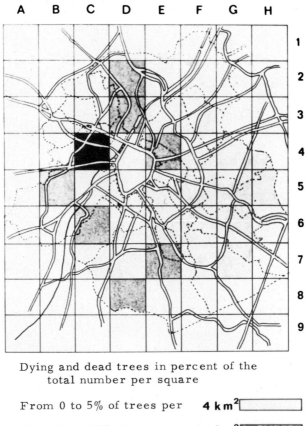

Dying and dead trees in percent of the
total number per square

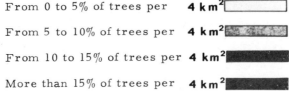

From 0 to 5% of trees per   **4 km²**

From 5 to 10% of trees per   **4 km²**

From 10 to 15% of trees per   **4 km²**

More than 15% of trees per   **4 km²**

Fig. 2. State of health of Platanus acerifolia
in the Brussels area in 1974.

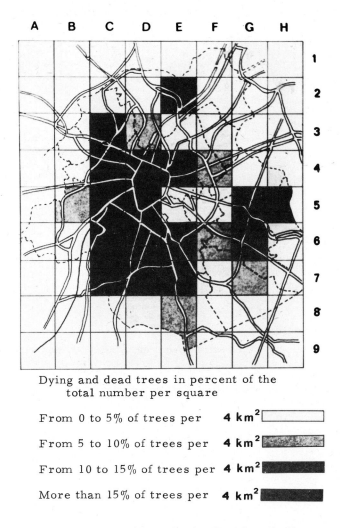

Dying and dead trees in percent of the
total number per square

From 0 to 5% of trees per   **4 km²** ☐

From 5 to 10% of trees per   **4 km²** ▨

From 10 to 15% of trees per **4 km²** ▦

More than 15% of trees per   **4 km²** ■

Fig. 3. State of health of <u>Filia platyphylla</u>
in the Brussels area in 1974.

We note, for example, the low concentration of street trees in the heart of
the city and their large numbers in the outlying residential sectors. This
distribution is not the best because most of the houses in these parts of
the town are surrounded by gardens which are playing perfectly their role
of dust filters. And it is precisely in the middle of the town that green spaces
would be necessary for cleaning the atmosphere.

-Survey of Trees' Health:

The survey of trees' health includes the determination of the precise species,
the noting of the dates of budding, flowering, fruiting and leaf-falling, but
above all the observation of the trees' health. These are classified in three
health classes: healthy trees, decaying trees, and dead trees. We generally

obtain around 3 percent dead and 5 percent decaying trees.

These observations have shown that species behave very differently towards
the medium. And now, after 3 years' study, we might choose some resistant species of trees that we could recommend for new plantings. We can
quote, for example, Populus nigra L., different species of Malus, Platanus
acerifolia, and Ulmus glabra Huds.

The most fragile species have been recognised in the same way; let us quote
Quercus rubra L., Acer saccharinum L., and Tilia platyphylla. These
observations have been put on maps for some species. Figure 2 describes
the health situation of the plane tree (it is a resistant species) and Figure 3
describes the health situation of the broad-leaved lime (a fragile species).
This type of representation makes clear each species' different sensitivity
and permits the marking-off of zones where living conditions require particular attention.

-The Soil's Physical and Chemical Analyses:

Major elements absolutely necessary for plant growth are titrated for
healthy, decaying and dead trees. The alkaline or acid reaction of the soil
is measured. Anaerobic condition indicator elements are tested for and
put in relation with the soil's redox potential (sulphides and nitrites).

-The Soil's Atmospheric Analyses:

Flagstones, the soil's compactness and gas pipe leakages hinder normal air
diffusion in the soil. A great number of the soil's atmospheric analyses are
made giving the percentage of oxygen, carbon dioxide and methane. Anaerobic soil conditions, whatever their causes may be, are specially disastrous for the trees.

-The Soil's Humidity:

The soil's humidity is checked monthly and assessed in relation to the
amount of rainfall. Shortage of water during the summer is generally very
troublesome for urban plants, especially if the winter's rainfall contribution
was less than average. Chemical properties of this water are tested too.

-Foliar Diagnosis:

Minor elements indispensable for plant life are titrated for the detection of
any deficiency. Indicators of pollution by heavy metals are reported too
(lead and cadmium, for example). There are very close relationships between the amounts of lead on the leaves and the effect of traffic on the
sampling point (Ref. 9).

- Young Trees' Behaviour:

Young trees' behaviour is examined during their first year in the city: their
rate of growth is measured each month.

Particular note is taken in the case of young trees planted to replace dead
trees where the soil has rarely been removed and planting conditions are
as bad as they were before. That is why such a high death rate among these
trees is noted.

-Planting Conditions and Maintenance:

Different planting and maintenance systems are experimented with and
practical information is distributed among the various arboreal authorities.
We also transmit lists of strong species to be planted in the critical sectors.

Finally we recommend the introduction into parks and public gardens of
very fragile species whose behaviour and reactions would be closely observed. These fragile species or bioindicators will be very useful for determining standards for urban and industrial pollutants. They are the first defen-
sive line against environmental hazards to people's health.

The results acquired by the ERA after 3 years' study have indicated several
species that we can consider actually as resistant ; they have determined
some important reasons for the decaying of city trees. First of all, there
are the soil's asphyxic conditions due to trampling, compacting or gas pipe
leakages. Water deficiency also plays a big part in the decaying of trees.

To these factors we can add several features connected with the expansion
of towns: road-widening with the cutting of roots, pipe-laying, excessive
clipping, injuries resulting from accidents, etc.

This investigation which is restricted to street trees will develop into
a more extensive examination of Brussels' green spaces and of other cities
of the country. It hopes to attain practical and scientific objectives and to
be a basis for new urban planting projects.

DISCUSSION

This investigation carried out in Brussels shows how complex are the
ecological and technical factors affecting the safety of urban vegetation.
There are, besides, a large number of economic problems depending on
land prices in towns and on speculative builders' appetites.

An objective report by the administration on the usefulness of green spaces,
on their role as air cleaners and bioindicators of environmental deterioration, would result in very important decisions being made. Thus existing
green spaces could be saved and perhaps new green belts or new public
gardens might be created.

The costs and benefits of such an operation can be compared.

On the debit side, we must think of the costs of land and plants, of the laying out and planting costs, and finally of the upkeep expenses. These can be
reduced by a judicious choice of well-adapted plants and by as natural a
layout as possible.

On the credit side, we must note the beneficial effects on climate (temperature and humidity), air cleaning, security for children and for pedestrians,
the relaxing effect on people, and lastly the pleasant aspect that clumps of
trees give to towns. Too often people only take note of this last aspect in
the defence of green spaces.

In conclusion, the protection and extension of green spaces in cities need not only financial contributions but also good laws protecting existing areas. As for technical problems of layout, they must be dealt with by multi-disciplinary teams where ecologists and experts would work with engineers and planners.

Then it will be possible to get 40 or 50 square meters for each citizen. We consider, indeed, that this quota is an essential for the urban well-being of people. But we are now very far from it; however, we must remember that a tree needs 40 years to grow to maturity, and it is now that we must plant trees for the year 2000. We cannot forget, either, that bad plantations are worse than no trees at all.

REFERENCES

(1) C. Berindan, Interrelation pollution atmosphérique et espaces verts en tant que principe protecteur des villes industrielles.
Poll. atmosph. 43. : 143-153 (1969)

(2) A. Bernatsky, Zur praxis der Begründung von Schutzpflanzungen,
Proc. 1st Eur. Congr. Influence of Air Poll. on Plants and Animals Wageningen C.A.P.D. : 383-395 (1969)

(3) J. Boulanger & R. Impens, Enquête sur les conditions de vie des arbres dans l'agglomération bruxelloise.
C.R. Sem. d'Etude Agriculture Environnement, Gembloux 2-6 sept. 1974 pp. 559-568

(4) B. Boullard, l'Ecologie en Milieu Urbain
C.R. Sem. d'Etude Agriculture Environnement, Gembloux 2-6 sept. 1974 pp. 527-537

(5) T.J. Chandler, Urban Climatology - Inventory and Prospect
W.M.O. Technicol note n° 254 TP 141. : 1-14 (1970)

(6) E. Delcarte, P. Nangniot & R. Impens, La détermination d'éléments métalliques dans les sols et les végétaux en sites industriels et urbains.
Ann. Gembloux, 79, 141 (1973)

(7) ERA, Rapport de l'année 1973
Ed. Lancelle Bruxelles (1975) 109 p.

(8) ERA, Rapport de l'année 1974
Ed. Lancelle Bruxelles (sous presse)

(9) R. Impens, J. Deroanne Bauvin & J. Tilman, Les dépôts de plomb sur la végétation en tant qu'indicateurs de la pollution par la circulation automobile.
C.R. Sem. d'Etude Agriculture Environnement, Gembloux 2-6 sept. 1974 pp 605-617

(10) M. Maeno, Effects of air pollution on trees (VIII). Heavy metals in leaves of street trees : lead, nickel, chrome and cadmium
J. Japan Soc. Air Pollution, 6, 159 (1971)

(11) B.V. Popov, Making a city verdant - translated in
AICE Survey of USSR Air pollution literature - II : 60-75 (1969)

(12) D. Purves & E.J. Mackenzie, Trace-element contamination of parklands in urban areas,
J. Soil. Sci. 20,288 (1969)

(13) G. Reethof, Effects of plantings on radiation of highway noise

J.A.P.C.A. 23, 185-189 (1973)

(14) L. Steubing & R. Klee, Vergleichende Untersuchungen zur Staubfilterwerkung von Laub und Nadelgehölzen
Angew. Botanik, 44, 73 (1970)

(15) A. Willam, Fixation des poussières atmosphériques par les végétaux,
Ann. Gembloux, 79,11 (1973)

TRADE-OFF ANALYSIS IN URBAN WATER RESOURCES PLANNING

Yacov Y. Haimes[1], Daniel H. Hoggan[2], and J. Paul Riley[2]

Abstract

Planning in the context of urban water and related land resources should be responsive to a diversified set of objectives and goals which often are in conflict and competition with one another. Because of the interactions and couplings that exist between objectives and uses, it usually is essential that the planning of urban water and related land resources be conducted in a broad metropolitan context and that it involve the consideration of multi-objectives. Thus, urban water resource systems create special problems that make the application of classical optimization methodologies quite difficult and, unless they are treated with considerable insight, quite meaningless, if not actually misleading. It is proposed by this paper that the problem of trade-off analyses in urban water resources planning might be approached by the formulation and application of a macro-scale planning model. This model would incorporate many of the desirable features of existing design models, would be hierarchical in structure, and would be capable of addressing the multi-objective planning problems encountered in urban water resource systems.

Introduction

The constant increase in the unpredicted environmental impacts due to man's activities is of a major concern in achieving a better human settlement. The enormous problems that our society faces today in air, water and noise pollution, solid waste disposal, and other areas is a manifestation of the close interaction among environmental system components. This paper concentrates on one part of the system, namely, water and related land resources. Otherwise, its scope would be too large for any meaningful discussion and analysis.

---

[1] Professor of Systems Engineering, Case Institute of Technology, Case Western Reserve University, Cleveland, Ohio 44106

[2] Professor, Department of Civil and Environmental Engineering, Utah Water Research Laboratory, College of Engineering, Utah State University, Logan, Utah, U.S.A. 84322

201

Water use within the urban environment entails many interactions across a broad spectrum of disciplines and other areas of resource use. For example, a dam might be constructed to provide flood control, electric energy, and recreation benefits to an urban settlement. However, the construction of the dam might well have adverse impacts on other social uses, such as transportation and human settlement within the reservoir area. A modification or change of use at any point in a system initiates a whole series of adjustments throughout the entire system until a new equilibrium condition is reached. These adjustments produce both physical and social impacts, some of which are positive, some negative, but all of which need to be anticipated and assessed by a program of system management.

The following is but a partial list of environmental impacts of various urban activities on the water resources system:

(i) Domestic wastewater consists mainly of organic wastes which require oxygen decomposition processes. The decomposition of organic wastes may deprive the fish and other aquatic life of needed oxygen. Bacteria and toxic materials which also may be found in domestic sewage can cause diseases such as cancer and other unknown health problems.

(ii) Industrial wastewater may contain organic and inorganic wastes, including heavy metals and other toxic materials. These also may cause severe health problems.

(iii) Electric generating plants discharge heated water which destroys some fish habitats and reduces the suitability of the water for other uses. Valuable cold water game fish may be replaced by warm water scavenger fish, thus both sport and commercial fishing may suffer.

(iv) Urban runoff consists of oil washed from roads along with suspended undissolved solids. These runoffs, often known and referred to as non-point or area source pollution, undoubtedly present one of the most difficult problems that our society is facing today with respect to water quality.

(v) The combination of reduced dissolved oxygen and increased temperature in a water body may lead to eutrophication accompanied by excessive growth of algae and other aquatic plants. Phosphorus from domestic sewage contributes to this problem by providing nutrients for the algae. Large algae blooms then further reduce the level of dissolved oxygen.

Trade-Offs in Multi-Objective Planning

Real world systems, large and small without exception, are characterized by having multiple objectives and goals which are often in conflict and/or competition with one another. This is particularly true in water resources and environmental systems in which there are many users with different preferences (11, 12, 13, 14, 15, 16).

The kind of chain reaction which is triggered by a change or modification at some point in a system is illustrated in Figure 1 (25). Some of the possible

impacts of developing a water collection, storage, and distribution system
to supply water to an urban area are shown. In this example, the physical
or hydrologic system is altered in order to better accommodate a water
supply use. However, alteration of the system also produces effects which
might adversely affect other social uses, such as stream fishing and land
transportion links.

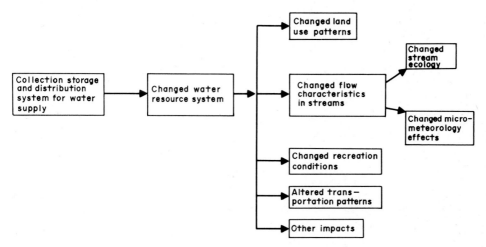

Figure 1.   An example of possible impacts, produced by modification of the
            hydrologic system to accommodate specific uses by the urban
            society.

A Definition of Interactions Involving
Urban Water Resources

A general representation of the interactions between water uses within an
urban context, and interactions of these uses with outside uses is shown in
Figure 2 (25). Included in the representation is a monitoring system, including
both remote and on-site sensing, which samples the various components
of the system and provides essential information for management purposes.
In Figure 2 the parameters which characterize both the effects of water use
and the effects on water use (and therefore all interactions involving the water
resource system) are water quantity and quality. The two directions of the
arrows shown in the diagram are intended to indicate that urban uses of water
affect other resource uses and that those other uses, in a reverse sense,
have an influence upon urban water uses.

Some of the specific items which might be included within each of the four
major system components of the total system represented by Figure 2 are
listed in the left hand column of Table 1 (25). This table also indicates a relative
importance to the interaction or impact of each water use with each of the
two basic characteristics of the water system, namely quantity and quality.
The relative values of the interactions are indicated by numbers between
0 and 4, with 0 indicating no interaction and 4 suggesting a highly significant

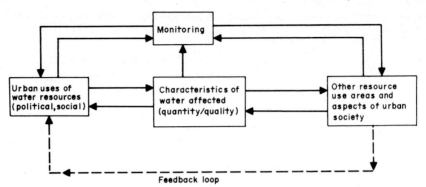

Figure 2.   A representation of the interactions involving the urban water
          resource system.

relationship.   The rectangle at the intersection of each column and row in
the table contains two numbers, one to the right of the diagonal slash and one
to the left.   The right number indicates the relative importance of a particular water characteristic (quality or quantity) on a specific water use.   The
number to the left of the slash indicates the magnitude or relative importance
of a specific water use on the water quantity or quality parameter.   For
example, water quantity is shown to have a significant effect on an industrial
water supply (rated 4), whereas an industrial water supply is shown to have
a rather minor impact (rated 1) on water quality.

An Evaluation of Interactions through
a Multi-Objective Approach
It might be noted that, as shown by Figure 2, the two basic characteristics
of water quantity and quality link or relate the impacts between all uses and
monitoring activities related to the urban water resources system.   For
example, energy generation (whether hydro-electric or thermal electric)
can have a major impact on water quantity (rated 3 in Table 1).   In turn,
water quantities are moderately important to public health (rated 2).   Thus,
a moderate interaction is indicated between energy generation and public
health.   Similarly, Table 1 suggests that a broad spectrum of problems
associated with the urban water resource system could be analyzed in a
multi-objective approach.   Indeed a multi-objective, systems approach, such
as the Surrogate Worth-Trade-Off (SWT) method (11, 12, 13, 14, 15, 16),
may be essential to their solution.

Trade-Off Analysis Procedure for
Multi-Objective Planning

In the process of planning and managing the development and utilization of
urban water resource systems, the decision-maker needs to find answers to
hydrologic, water quality, and other technical questions.   Several mathematical models of the urban runoff system already have been developed, and
these are capable of answering some of the questions.   However, these

Table 1.   An assessment matrix for urban water resources system interactions.

System Components (refer to Figure 2)	Rating of Impacts or Interactions	
	Water Quantity	Water Quality
Urban Water Resource Uses		
Municipal Water supply	1 \ 4	4 \ 2
Industrial water supply	1 \ 4	4 \ 2
Local agricultural use	3 \ 3	2 \ 2
Recreation	1 \ 3	3 \ 3
Energy generation	3 \ 3	1 \ 1
Navigation	3 \ 4	3 \ 1
Flood Control	3 \ 4	2 \ 1
Other Resource Use Areas and Aspects of the Urban Society		
Land use	3 \ 3	2 \ 2
Energy use	2 \ 2	2 \ 2
Communications	0 \ 1	0 \ 0
Climate	4 \ 1	3 \ 0
Public Health	1 \ 2	1 \ 3
Transportation, land	1 \ 1	2 \ 0
Science, Technology, Government	2 \ 0	3 \ 2
Socio-Economic	1 \ 1	2 \ 2
Urban development	2 \ 2	2 \ 3
Monitoring Systems		
In-situ sensing	2 \ 0	2 \ 0
Remote sensing	2 \ 0	2 \ 0

answers usually pertain to system component design rather than to planning.
There is a need for a centralized or macro model(s) which incorporates many
desirable features of existing design models, and which thus would be capable
of dealing with a broad range of urban planning and management problems.
The problem, therefore, is essentially one of (1) developing a macro model(s)
which manifests this kind of capability and (2) assisting local decision-makers

in the application of the model(s) to a study area. This problem should be approached by implementing the following four steps:

1. the identification of those characteristics of existing urban runoff models which are responsive to planning and management needs in the context of urban water resources,
2. the construction of a macro model(s) on the basis of existing models which are identified as being useful in step (1) above,
3. the testing, verifying, and demonstrating of the utility of the model for potential users through a case study in a selected urban region,
4. the transfer of the model to a group of users.

All of the above four steps should be conducted in full cooperation with appropriate government officials and citizen groups within the case study area.

A Strategy for Model Development

A hierarchical-multilevel approach is essential for modeling a large-scale system, which a total urban water system would be. This approach is capable of taking into consideration the muliple objectives and goals involved, as well as all system interactions. The concept of the multilevel approach is based on the decomposition of large-scale, complex systems into "independent" subsystems. This decentralized approach, by utilizing the concepts of strata, layers, and echelons, enables the system analyst to analyze and comprehend the behavior of the individual subsystems at a lower level and to transmit the information obtained and integrate it at a higher level, (3, 4, 5, 6, 7, 8, 9, 10, 11, 12, 13, 14, 15, 16, 17, 18, 19, 20, 21, 22). Whenever more decentralization is needed, the system is further decomposed.

In order to proceed in an orderly manner with an evaluation of existing design models, the matrix format shown in Figure 3 is proposed. In this matrix, desired planning characteristics of a model are identified on the vertical axis (rows). For each design model to be examined (represented by the depth dimension) the attributes of each model could be listed (horizontal dimension). Thus, the elements of the matrix would indicate the degree to which the various desired planning characteristics could be satisified by the particular attributes of each model. Some typical planning characteristics which might be identified for inclusion in the macro hierarchical model are as follows:

A. Land use and its impacts on quantity and quality
B. Water recycling and/or sequential use
   (i) impacts on streams
   (ii) impacts on the groundwater system
C. Trade-offs for multi-objective planning
   (i) impacts of the treatment efficiency on downstream quantity and quality
   (ii) point sources versus area sources
   (iii) stream standards versus effluent standards
D. Treatment types
E. Assess infiltration of pollutants to the groundwater system

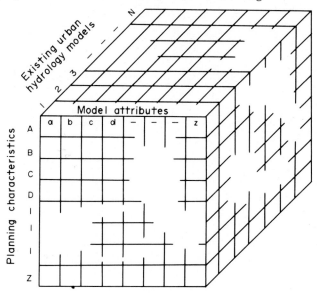

Figure 3.   Three dimensional matrix for the development of the macro
model.

F.   Flood plains
G.   Development environmental impact
H.   Economic evaluation
I.   Non-structural management
J.   Energy development and its effects on urban supplies-impacts on
municipalities
K.
:   Zoning implications
.
Z.

For an evaluation of existing models it is suggested that each model be decomposed into its component parts.   Model characteristics, such as input
data requirements, real world processes represented in the model (i.e. the
system of equations), coefficients required, and types of output responses,
are summarized on the top of the matrix (Figure 3).   The following is an
example of the kinds of attributes which might vary among urban models:

A.   Flow rate
B.   Variable boundary conditions
C.   Conveyance structure location and dimensions
D.   Storm sequences
E.   Structural costs
F.   Default options or characteristics
G.   Runoff versus land use relationships
H.   Rate of release of pollutant load

I.   Sediment load (erosion and/or transport)
J.   BOD/COD
K.   Grease and oils
L.   TDS
M.   Choliform
N.   Nitrogen forms
O.   Phosphorous
P.   Toxic materials
Q.   Heavy metals
.
.
.
Z.

Included in the depth dimension of Figure 3 would be a list of models such as
the following:

1. STORM   10. CBM - Australia
2. SWMM   11. Gerald I - France
3. AVCO   12. Tank I - Japan
4. HYDROCOMP   13. Tank II - Japan
5. MIT   14. IMH2-SSVP - Romania
6. UWRL - USR   15. SSARR-Corps of Engineers, Portland
7. QUAL-II   16. NWSHM - National Weather Service,
8. HEC   Portland
9. UWRL-SSAM   17. SRFCHM-National Weather Service,
                                       Portland

Urban hydrology models invariably contain three basic components:
      (i)   a hydrologic submodel,
     (ii)   a water quality submodel,
    (iii)   a control program and solution technique
These submodels are linked in order to provide an integrated response that is
sensitive to both the system hydrology and water quality characteristics. The
resolution of each of the two submodels may be developed to a high, moderate,
or low degree.

General differences in resolution among models are associated with the degree
of time and space resolution, with the number and types of water quality
parameters included in the model, and with the mathematical solution techniques. The best combination for a particular application depends on the characteristics of the system and the objectives of the study. A comprehensive
review of urban hydrologic models (primarily design models) is provided by
the American Society of Civil Engineers (1).

Model Applications
An example of the kinds of trade-offs which might be evaluated by means of a
comprehensive multi-objective planning model as applied to urban water resources exists in the area of water quality in reconciling level of dissolved
oxygen (D.O.) with treatment costs. This example is of major interest in
light of the U.S. Water Pollution Control Amendments of 1972, (Public Law

92-500) (23).   The net benefits from most wastewater treatment processes
are subject to severely diminishing returns due to the exponentially increasing
loss in treatment efficiency.   For example, cleaning up the last one percent of
pollution may be double the cost of eliminating the first 99 percent (23).   The
cost of achieving the known discharge goal should be viewed in terms of the
sacrifices society will be compelled to make in other social demands and in
terms of the large amounts of energy and natural resources which will be consumed.   The elimination of the last increment of water pollution is likely to
have serious, upsetting, waste disposal impacts on air and land.   These adverse impacts may be more damaging to the environment than the retention
of some small amount of water pollution, particularly in areas where the
self-purifying capacity of water is great and where its other users are not
adversely affected.

 Specifically one may want to minimize the total cost of wastewater treatment
on the one hand and minimize the dissolved oxygen deficiency in the stream
at the outlet of the treatment plant on the other hand (see Figures 4 and 5).
Even though the two objectives are measurable in different terms, through
the utilization of a macro planning model and trade-off analysis, a trade-off
can be generated showing how much the cost of treatment increases with the
lowering of D. O. level.   Through attitudinal surveys, public preferences can
be determined and reflected in a public "indifference-curve".   These two
curves can be used to assist planners and decision-makers in determining
alternatives that have a high level of public acceptance (see Figure 5).

The use of the natural capacity of water to purify itself of some kinds of wastes
in limited quantities does not preclude alternatives of sequential use of the

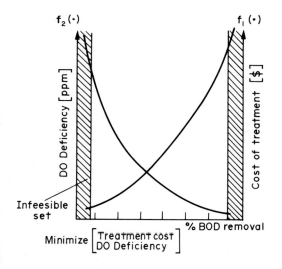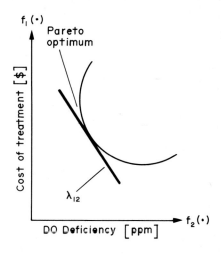

Figure 4.   Treatment costs and DO   Figure 5.   Treatment costs vs. DO
            deficiency in the decision   deficiency in the functional
            space (after 11)).   space (after (11)).

water for other purposes. Water quality standards should vary depending on the alternative uses desired for the water. Water quality control programs should try to find the economically desirable and socially preferable uses of specific water bodies and set quality standards in relation to the preferred uses and well-being of the aquatic environment.

Thus, depending on the purposes and on the users of the water body, different trade-offs and corresponding Pareto optimal solutions may be determined. For example, where the assimilative capacity of the stream is high and where that part of the stream is not used for recreational purposes, then a lower treatment efficiency may be feasible and even desirable while minimizing overall treatment costs. On the other hand, if the water quality is low in a particular stream reach, then it might be necessary to improve the treatment efficiency with its accompanying higher cost for the advantage of environmental quality. The point in this example is that a trade-off analysis is inevitable when considering treatment costs versus environmental quality. A planning model which would be capable of addressing the multi-objective planning problems encountered in urban water resources management would help to alleviate the increasingly more complex role of the urban decision-maker.

Selected References

1. ASCE urban water resources research program. 1975. Technical memorandum No. 1Hp-1, "Urban mathematical modeling and catchment research in the U.S.A." American Society of Civil Engineers, 345 East 47th St., N.W., NY 10017.

2. Great Lakes Basin Commission, 1974. Planning for water and related land resources of the basin MRB. Series - No. 3 and 4, August.

3. Haimes, Y.Y., 1975. Hierarchical modeling of regional total water resources system, Automation, Vol. 11, pp. 25-36. Pergamon Press

4. Haimes, Y.Y., 1971. Modeling and control of the pollution of water resources systems via multilevel approach. Water Resource Bull. 7, 104-113.

5. Haimes, Y.Y., 1975. Decomposition and multilevel approach in modeling and management of water resources system. Decomposition of large scale problems. (D.M. Himmelblau, ed.), pp. 348-368. North-Holland Amsterdam.

6. Haimes, Y.Y., 1975. Multilevel dynamic programming structure for regional water resource management. Decomposition of large scale problems, (D.M. Mimmelblau, ed.), pp. 369-378. North-Holland, Amsterdam.

7. Haimes, Y. Y., F. Foley, and W. Yu. 1972. Computational results for water pollution taxation using multilevel approach. Water Resources Bull. 8, 761-772.

8. Haimes, Y. Y. and D. Macko, 1973. Hierarchical structures in water resources systems management, IEEE, Systems Man and Cybernetics, SMC-3, 396-402.

9. Haimes, Y. Y. and W. S. Nainis, 1974. Coordination of regional water resource supply and demand planning models, Water Resources Research, vol. 10, no. 6, 1051-1059, December.

10. Haimes, Y. Y., M. A. Daplan and M. A. Husar, Jr., 1972. A multilevel approach to determining optimal taxation for the abatement of water pollution, Water Resources Research, vol. 8, no. 4, 761-772.

11. Haimes, Y. Y. 1975. Technology assessment in environmental systems: Trade-offs in multiple objectives. Invited paper presented at Penary Session III, International Congress of Scientists on the Human Environment (HESC), Kyoto, Japan, November 16-26, 18 pp.

12. Haimes Y. Y. and W. A. Hall. 1974. Multi-objectives in water resources systems analysis: The surrogate worth trade-off method, Water Resources Research, Vol. 10, no. 4, pp. 615-624.

13. Haimes, Y. Y., W. A. Hall, and H. T. Freedman. 1975. Multi-objectives optimization in water resources system, Elsevier Scientific Publishing Company, Amsterdam.

14. Haimes, Y. Y. 1976. Hierarchical analyses in water resources systems. McGraw-Hill International Book Company, New York (in press).

15. Haimes, Y. Y., and W. A. Hall. 1975. Analysis of Multiple objectives in water quality. Journal, ASCE, Hydraulics Division, vol. 101, no. HY4, pp. 387-400.

16. Hall, W. A., and Y. Y. Haimes. 1976. The surrogate worth trade-off method with multiple decision-makers, to appear in Multiple Criteria decision making. Kyoto 1975, edited by M. Zeleny, Springer-Verlag, Ing., New York.

17. Kaplan, M. A., 1973. The planning and operation of a regional water quality management system: A multilevel approach, M. S. Thesis, Systems Engineering Department, Case Western Reserve University, Cleveland, Ohio.

18. Lasdon, L. S. 1971. Optimization Theory for large systems, Macillan Book Company, New York.

19. Lefkowitz, I., 1966. Multilevel approach applied to control system design, Trans. ASME 88D, 2010.

20. Mesarovic, M.D., D. Macko, and T. Takanhara, Theory of Hierarchical and multilevel systems, Academic Press, New York.

21. Nainis, W.S. 1973. Multilevel approach for regional planning and capacity expansion in water resource systems, Ph.D. Dissertation in Systems Engineering. Case Western Reserve University, Cleveland, Ohio.

22. Nainis, W.S. and Y.Y. Haimes. 1975. A multilevel approach to planning for capacity expansion in water resource systems, presented at the 1972 International Conference on Cybernetics and Society, October 19-12 1972, Washington, D.C., IEEE Systems Man and Cybernetics, SMC-5, no. 1, 53-63, January.

23. Public Law 92-500, 1972. To amend the Federal Water Pollution Control Act, October, 18.

24. U.S. National Water Commission, 1973. Water policies for the future, U.S. Government Printing Office, Washington, D.C., June.

25. Wolff, E.A. (editor), 1975. USERC environment resources and urban development workshop, Proceedings, November 14, 1975, USERC, Inc., Silver Springs, Maryland.

THE ROLE AND IMPACT OF WATER RESOURCES IN HUMAN SETTLEMENTS

Crook, Leonard T., Co-Chairman
Summary of the Water Resources Panel at the USERL
Workshop of Washington.

1.0 Discipline Description

Water resources is the field which addresses all aspects of water, including occurrence, measurement, preservation, conservation, utilization, distribution, development, and disposal; in fact it is concerned with an understanding of the complete water cycle.

2.0 Discipline Objectives

2.1 Definition of a Successful Human Settlement

Judged from the viewpoint of water resources, a successful human settlement must achieve the following objectives.

1. There must be an adequate quantity of water to meet all reasonable needs.

2. The bacteriological and chemical quality of water supplied to a community must meet both health and aesthetic standards. Less strict standards may be applied to water for industrial and agricultural use, but these should also be based on scientific reasoning.

3. The supply should be obtained by means that leave source areas, particularly natural streams and lakes, in an ecologically sound and minimally disturbed condition.

4. Treatment methods for wastewater should use recycling to the maximum extent consistent with economic operation, protection of health, and minimum disturbance to natural systems.

5. Pricing of water to users should reflect both internal and external costs of water supply and wastewater treatment, and should be allocated equitably among different classes of users.

2.2 Good and Bad Features of Human Settlements

Judged from the viewpoint of water resources, human settlements may induce either "good" or "bad" effects on water resources. Some of the "bad" effects are as follows.

1. Human settlements require the commitment, often far in advance of the time of actual use, of large, reliable supplies of high quality water from the stock in nature. This stock is at any time a fixed, limited quantity, even though it represents a renewable natural resource.

213

2. Settlements require wastewater treatment, and this involves construction of capital-intensive equipment which does not provide a direct economic return to the community, but generally protects interests outside the community. For settlements which are too small or too large, wastewater treatment is frequently less than optimal both from performance and economic standpoints.

3. The taking of water from natural source regions to supply settlements may have adverse impacts on the source region and its downstream ecosystems ranging from slight to very bad. Frequently, the operation of a water resource facility may disturb land in a relatively natural state, and therefore, interfere with percolation, storage, and recycling of water which might offer greater benefits than   the designed facility. Because of the naturally very slow response of underground water systems, benefits of such development of water resources may be sensed quickly, while adverse impacts are recognized only after a long time period.

4. Human settlements with complex, highly developed water supply and treatment systems, become vulnerable to any interruption of supply or wastewater removal, man-caused or natural. For example, natural extremes such as floods recur with cyclic, random periodicity and are essential to preserve overall ecosystem stability. At the same time, these violently disturb the stability of systems intended to serve man's settlements.

5. The water resource needs of human settlements frequently are met by aesthetically unpleasant means, as by the use of reservoirs that fluctuate to leave shorelines and vast areas of silty flats exposed and sewage treatment plants with odorous products.

6. Because water is too often treated as a free commodity, its use and disposal are often handled carelessly; for example, water bodies are permitted to become at least temporary breeding grounds for unpleasant insect species.

Some of the "good" effects on water resources induced by human settlements are as follows.

1. With proper planning and development, water resource systems can provide a stable supply in an efficient manner, meeting multiple objectives of water use, making conjunctive use of surface and ground water supplies, and permitting sequential use and reuse so that the quantity of water needed and the impacts on the environment are held to reasonable minimums.

2. Wastewater can be collected so that treatment needed to protect public health and to avoid adverse environmental impacts becomes an efficient, reliable process.

3. Water can be recycled and maximum use made of its resource content. In particular, nutrients in wastewater can be used in a beneficial way rather than wasted. Aquaculture is an example of this type of use.

4. With proper planning, settlements can permit the shared or common use of a water resource in ways which reduce per capita needs and costs. This diminishes adverse impacts on natural ecosystems.

5. Water is a natural and desirable aesthetic component of man's habitat,

and proper use of both natural and man-made water systems can enhance that environment and the quality of life which depends on it. Thus, for example, settlements may provide a better recreational environment and simultaneously provide for essential utilitarian needs.

6. The presence and use of water can modify climate. For example, large bodies of water may alter the climate, or water may be used to ensure a comfortable indoor climate.

7. Human settlements, by proper location and design, benefit from the use of water-borne transportation.

Changes can frequently be made within industrial processes to minimize the amount of new water required, to improve processes, conserve catalylic materials, and to reduce wastes.

3.0 Estimate of Future State of Human Settlements

The most obvious prediction for the future of our human settlements is that nothing of particular long-term significance in planning will occur at all, i.e., the current policies and modus operandi will continue to ebb and flow in response to the short-term emergencies and value structures of the population and its leadership. With respect to water resources, such behavior would result in piecemeal solutions haphazardly promulgated and financed. The continued overlap of agencies with resulting duplication of effort and waste of time and money would be perpetuated in the attempts to respond to whichever demands were the most pressing or politically attractive. As with other resources, overall quality and quantity of water for the myriad uses of an urban society would be uncertain and in a perpetually deficit condition.

3.1 The Eight Scenarios

If, in the scenario scheme, cities as we know them should be abandoned or dispersed, the changes in requirements for and use of water would be immense. The demands on the system for quantity would be lessened and less concentrated. Stresses of disposal, percolation and recycling, for example, would also be more equitably distributed. However, the proliferation of supply and disposal systems necessary for a scattered population would materially increase costs and be less manageable, and be of more overall harm than the benefits to conservation would justify.

Should a transcendental approach to urban revitalization be taken and an intensive program of education, incentive and punishment structures, and mass behavior modification be undertaken and successfully achieved, i.e., a reverence for the fragile and transient qualities of our natural resources and their interrelationships universally accepted, most of our concerns about our water would be specious. Citizens would of their own accord in recognition of needs and relative values—conserve, protect, and willingly pay for meeting their water requirements as they occurred.

Conversely, should we enter an era of benign neglect in our cities, removing all constraints and allowing the laws of supply and demand free rein, economic competition would result in waterfront exploitation, eutrophication, and the like, with a doomsday effect on the quality of fresh and salt water alike.

Small changes within existing urban areas, thoughtfully carried out, would have at minimum cost a beneficial effect on the water resources of such an area. Such changes presuppose attention to long-neglected water-bearing systems, reappraisal of the water supply and quality in general, and provision for some added aesthetic or recreational water use.

The scenario postulating encouraged growth in peripheral towns should also have a beneficial effect on the water picture in that such a strategy allows for long-range preparations for expansion before the fact instead of after it. With care, adequate provision for the multiple needs of a projected population may be made before the population actually occurs.

Building a new town within the urban center has all of the virtues of a micro-revitalization program multiplied by the economies of serving and refurbishing many facilities with fewer contracts and a concentration of capital--reevaluating whole segments of the urban water cycle at one time.

While expanding satellite communities may make fewer short range demands upon water resources of the larger area than the more densely populated city core, long-range regional foresight is necessary in developing satellite communities to prevent repetition of water-related mistakes that have occurred within that urban core.

Of all the scenarios, perhaps the idea of a free-standing new city, perfectly situated and planned in virgin territory--a modern Oz--is the most enticing to all planners, as well as to water managers. Should such a dream actually become feasible, the potential and urgency for planning every facet of water use, such as beneficial supply, usage, and conservation, is challenging and exciting for theoreticians who perceive the possibility of actual solutions to the vast problems of protecting a finite commodity.

3.2 Method of Describing Future Human Settlements

Describing future human settlements can be accomplished by directing attention to impacts upon water resources resulting from proposed settlement patterns. Impacts must, however, be examined in relation to time of implementation and how they are manifested in these time periods. Results of these impacts help form the character of the settlement and land around it.

The future of human settlements rely upon our capabilities to understand our environment and manage factors which may alter it. In a highly developed society a prominent factor affecting change is water and its distribution. Water supply and wastewater disposal play major roles in the commercial, industrial and residential distribution within our society. Therefore, it is necessary to examine trends in developing future settlements and their effect upon water resources. To accomplish this, each scenario will be trended for water resource impact in the short range (10 years), intermediate range (25 years), and long range (over 25 years) future in the following actions applied to future human settlements.

3.2.1 Elimination

The elimination of settlements could provide opportunity for ever expanding water distribution and wastewater collection systems or the elimination of the same. Because the elimination of these systems would create obvious health problems, it will be discounted as a possible event, and expansion will be addressed.

Expansion in the short run poses severe risks of a health hazard in the event of system failure, and exponentially rising costs with distance from treatment and source; hence cost/unit of development increases. In the intermediate run, land use patterns will change distribution of land uses and ground water recharge will decline rapidly. The long range reveals: 1) critical land allocation, 2) cost increases from limited supplies and recycling of water, 3) availability of many floodplains for alternate uses, and 4) increased opportunities for water access.

3.2.2 Transcendental

Transcendental or behavioral changes project little change in the near future. In the intermediate period water quality would increase, consumption per capita would decrease, and water users would increase in number and diversity. In the long range distribution costs would decline, land use would become rational, thus improving water quality, and ground water recharge would improve in quantity and quality.

3.2.3 Benign Neglect

Benign neglect in the short run proposes a gradual decline in water quality of surface and ground water as populations of users both change and decline. Further decline in quality and quantity of ground water would occur in the intermediate run. In addition, costs would rise with concurrent unequal cost sharing of distribution, access to waterways would decline, types and number of users would continue to decrease, potential health hazards would develop where opportunities for systems failures occur, and land use changes would increase quality and cost of water. Long range projections would show a continuing decline in the availability and quality of water throughout society.

3.2.4 Micro-Revitalization

Micro-revitalization in the short run would provide opportunity for establishment of permeable surfaces for ground water recharge, improve water quality by reduction of stormwater runoff, and increase the opportunities for surface water usage. In the intermediate range of 25 years, ground water would continue to increase in volume and surface water would improve in quality. In addition floodplains would be reclaimed, resulting in reduced pressures being applied to land use changes elsewhere. Long range enhancement in water quality, quantity, and overall utility is inevitable with proper management in micro-center development.

3.4.5 Growth Centers

Growth centers would produce immediate cost increases by duplication of systems. These increases would continue in the next 25 years. Concurrent with this cost rise, water quality improvements would occur and efficient water resource use would begin. The efficient usage of water resources would continue in the long range with increased problems of maintenance, operation, and monitoring

3.4.6 New Towns in Town

Short run advantages of new towns in town are similar to micro-revitalization. Available facilities would prove to be cost effective, ground water recharge would begin to improve, and surface water usage would increase. During the intermediate range, developments would display a reduction of land use changes which affect water quality and quantity, floodplains would be reclaimed, ground water recharge improved, and surface users would increase. In the long range, cost of water resources usage would be minimized in its cost/unit while maximizing its utility.

3.4.7 Satellite Community

Satellite community developments display short run and intermediate run problems in increased costs for distribution, reductions in ground water recharge, decreasing water quality in surface and ground water, and rising costs in management of water resources.

3.4.8 Free Standing City

Free standing new cities would initially show high costs for water distribution and systems development. The intermediate period gradual cost effectiveness would improve in water resource management. In the long range, these costs would decline, ground water recharge would improve, and water quality would be enhanced with proper water resource management.

4.0 Needed Tools and Information

4.1 Trend Analysis

Many of the great, near great, and opportune men of commerce from the Bible on down the ages to T. J. Watson have said that we must analyze the past, concede the present, and visualize the future (with hope). We now call this trend analysis or systems analysis or use other terms appropriate for special uses.

Relative to the synergistic congregating of peoples into human settlements or cities to satisfy their needs, and more particularly relative to the condition of and needs for water resources, we agreed that the present situation is being viewed in a subjective and fractionated fashion. The past is being analyzed by confident experts and documented with verbose legal and technical jargon. However, there seems to be much less confidence expressed when visualizing the future--wherein the results of all actions must be considered and decisions will be taking place in various disciplines and in the professional and public leadership. Why is it that "Mankind is continually changing--but Man (proud man) never does?"

The conclusion that people live with people because of mutually recognized, if not mutually valued, interdependencies leads to some not very profound premises and conclusions about settlements and water:

Man, whether as an individual, a family supporter (member), or in a society,

depends on soil, sun, oxygen in steady state, and food and water in necessarily
changing states within a steady cycle. Therefore, each person has been, and will
continue to be completely dependent on water for their own bodily existence,
plus satisfaction of any other personal and social functions.

Most agree with the laws of the conservation of energy and matter that
energy and mineral resources can be neither created or destroyed - only
changed in form and utility.

All people will live by waterways and the larger the waterway, the more
it shares boundary with other nations, the more people will congregate. Eighty-
five percent of the people of the United States live in the coastal zone (i.e.,
within 50 miles of the national water boundary).

The more people congregate (along waterways), the more they will be
interdependent and then dependent on others (witness governmental welfare
for food, transportation, security, barter points (markets), warmth, and even
entertainment and education).

The more densely people live together, the more anomic, psychologically
and sociologically, they become (i.e., no plan or goal, nonacceptance of personal
responsibility, more spectator than participant, social distance, the inverse
of physical distance, between them).

Earlier and more primitive man did think and operate with a total interactive
systems concept though not as "an island." Family and organizational leadership
has moved from local owner-management to impersonal corporate ownership that
is too far removed from the people and conditions its decisions affect.

As small organizations with their more singular purpose and product
and simple effluents started up, they honestly believed that the waterway and
its wildlife was both infinitely available/replenishable and an infinitely
deep sink, capable of assimilating all wastes. However, anything in bulk or
concentration (even water in flood form) becomes dangerous and polluting to the
biotic ecosystem, including man who has taken rights of dominion or private
ownership over it.

The great bulk of land along waters is increasingly in private hands,
inaccessible to the public and very threatening to large and small species
of biota living and propogating in that ecosystem. Its economic and aesthetic
values have been increasingly growing and in the hands of a few.

National and international laws have made the waters open to all. Nationally,
they have been maintained by public taxes and management by Federal agencies.

Food and water to sustain the people had formerly been brought out of and
turned to the earth directly by the consumer. Now the remoteness of the
consumer results in an energy cost of production and utilization that has
increased to large proportions.

The profits and thereby taxes of free enterprise industry and marketing
have virtually paid for everything in our way of life. Free enterprise and profits
will continue if the piper is to be paid to continue to play.

Ground water quality and quantity have become increasingly threatened. This is because of few related laws and concerns, unabated drawdown, diminishing land (especially along the waters) into which rain water can percolate and salt water infiltrate.

We have evidence of this American progress and these general and specific urban problems. We can now identify some more specific water resource programs' problems and successes. Essentially, these have dealt with urban consumption of rurally generated water and food to feed the gluttony of people and industrial process.

1. In the past, industries have located very close to or on waters that provided hydropower or were commercially navigable. Although ships still carry the majority of international cargo, the waterways are now of greater value to industry as a source of cooling or process mixing water or as a deep sink into which to discharge or carry process wastes.

2. Past location of urban multi-unit housing has been along the waterways also. That is where less skilled manipulable people could be employed or serviced by industry and shipping. This was initially where the great owners of industry had their homes, but with industrial pollution, increasing floods, and the value of that land for commercial purposes it became occupied by either multi-family homes or sold for commercial use on large concrete foundations. Human wastes therefrom were handled in the old "septic" way, i.e., pits or drain fields in the ground that then percolated and were carried by rain into the underground aquifers and/or the waterway itself. As the ground along the waterways was concreted by buildings and streets, rapid rainwater runoff caused wastes to be inadvertently discharged to the waterway along with sediment and a myriad of wastes from the air and streets. The ancillary problems were not quite this evident. The nutrients of wastes no longer went back into the land, the water no longer went into the ground or the deeper aquifers; in fact, the ground frequently dried, shrank, and subsided. Bacteria, viruses, and other toxic materials went unpounded and insidiously into the waterways where they could grow and be transported in unknown ways and distances to do unrecognized harm not only to other people, but to the health and very existence of numerous species of biota, flora, and wildlife.

Many of the deleterious effects of the above conditions, problems, and trends on the quality, viability, preservation, and propagation of human and nonhuman life are now being recognized. Much legislation, more regulations, and some enforcement and meager zoning restrictions are being generated at the federal and state levels to maintain the quality of our waterways. Land use and ground water protection legislation has only recently been considered and inadequately understood and placed in statute. The rights of eminent domain or private ownership have continued to restrain or lobby against much essential laws, while the rampant ignorance of the public about such invisible issues and the public's 'other' interests have resulted in no countervailing forces against the power, avarice, and wealth of the current landowners and heirs.

The trends of public health and recreation indicate the need for a possible right of public ownership of waterways and immediately contiguous lands. Much of these can be, are, and must be decentralized or moved back from the water's edge at least to above the highwater mark of respective 100-year floods and storms.

3. Large capital and land intensive opportunistic pork barrel projects for flood protection are one type of well intentioned or rationalized public projects in this and other countries. Could the dollars involved in this concrete, street, and stream flow alteration plus the costs of frequent rebuilding from flood damage be better spent? Are not these floodable lands the domain of wildlife or the public--after all, are they not part of the original stream? These lands are prime alluvial deposits rich for agricultural production, but they are generally out of that production. The latter is particularly true around urban centers that also have related food and water shortages. If we could accelerate the use of these lands as actual floodplains rather than channeling and increasing the rate of flow-off (and downstream destruction) of fresh storm waters, we could realize multiple values to many, not just a favored few. Examples of new trends, uses, and recognized needs are:

a.   open or green space for urban peoples
b.   agricultural use such as food and fiber, production, and grazing
c.   educational-aesthetic opportunities and wildlife preservation
d.   recreational lands for environmentally clean low-energy consuming activities such as sailing, canoeing, hiking, and picnicking
e.   more land to absorb storm water runoff, thus preventing erosion for ground water percolation, etc.

4.2   Strategies to Increase Success

The improvement of water resources is contingent upon the responses which society displays through time. A programmed effort becomes necessary in a dynamic state both in microadjustments and long range trend planning. The potential for implementing this necessary control must begin with the development of strategies to insure change capability. These strategies must be established in the time periods previously established and with realism for accomplishment.

The early approach to water resource management in human settlements would best be served in incremental changes of existing conditions. Micro-revitalization and new towns in town offer the best short run approaches to water resource improvement by reducing distance of distribution for service and treatment. Existing improvements can provide a base for this redevelopment. In addition the application of natural drainage and recharge concepts could reduce volumes in drainage. The cost benefits to users will provide a more equitable distribution of capital improvement costs. New concepts in water resource management can be employed with minimum investment and impact. As technology improves, adjustments can be employed with minor disruption of existing systems. Micro-changes will also provide an opportunity for social attitude changes, which are traditionally more resistent to change. Accomplishments in social and cultural areas will occur more quickly if built upon guarantees or incentives. These, in turn, can only be developed systematically through incremental changes which will erode established systems.

During the intermediate period from 10 to 25 years, different strategies may be employed while reshaping the existing system. These strategies include the development of sound land use planning to enhance water quality and water quantity.

1.   adopt improved methods of analysis to judge merits of proposals

2.   establish hieriaechy of goals and objectives among urban decision-
makers and residents concerning social, economic, land use, institutional,
taxation, transportation, and water resource factors

3.   integrate local, regional, state, and national planning programs and
projects to improve efficiency, reduce duplication, and allocate resources

4.3 Improvement Expected from Strategies

1.   reduced costs

2.   improved effects in predicted manner

3.   better service

4.   more amenities

5.   happier populace

6.   lower taxes

7.   less government

8.   lower product costs

9.   improved international
     posture and relations

5.0   Interdisciplinary Interactions

Water use within the urban environment entails many interaction areas, a
broad aspect of disciplines, and other areas of resource use. Problems which might
exist for a particular water use might be resolved by modification of the system so
as to better accommodate the use. For example, a dam might be constructed to provide flood control, electric energy, and recreation benefits to an urban settlement
However, the construction of the dam might well have adverse impacts on other socia
uses, such as transportation and settlement within the reservoir area. A modification or change through use at any point in a system initiates a whole series of
adjustments throughout the entire system, until a new equilibrium condition is
reached. These adjustments produce both physical and social impacts, some of which
are positive, and others of which are negative, but all of which need to be anticipated and assessed by a program of system management.

The kind of chain reaction which is triggered by a change or modification
at some point in a system is illustrated by the diagram of Figure 1. This figure
illustrates some of the possible impacts of developing a water collection, storage,
and distribution system to supply water to an urban area. In this example, the
physical or hydrologic system is altered in order to better accommodate a water
supply use. However, it is speculated that the new system also produces effects
which might adversely affect other social uses, such as stream fishing or transportation links.

A general representation of the interactions between water use in an
urban context and other areas of resource use and aspects of the social system is
shown by Figure 2. Included in the representation is a monitoring system, both
remote and in-situ sensing, which samples the various components of the total
system and provides essential information for management programs. Figure 2 also
indicates that those parameters which characterize both water use and the subsequent effects of water use (and therefore all interactions involving the water
resource system) are water quantity and quality. The two directions of the arrows
shown by the diagram are intended to indicate that urban uses of water affect other
resource use areas and that these uses in turn have an influence upon urban water
uses.

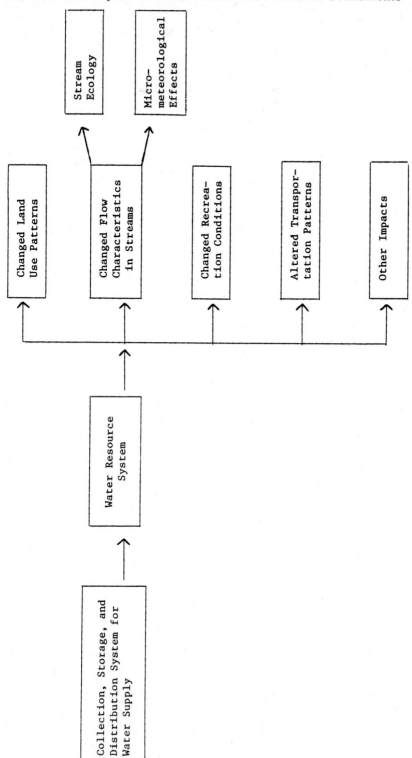

FIGURE 1:   An example of possible impacts produced by modification of the hydrologic system to accomodate specific uses by the urban society.

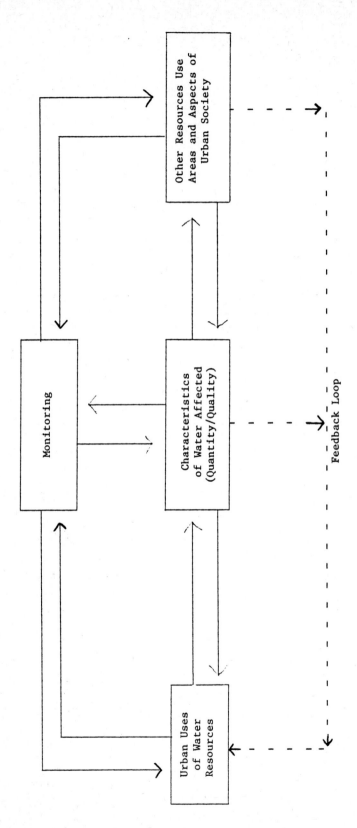

FIGURE 2: A representation of the interaction involving the urban water resource system.

TABLE 1: An Assessment Matrix for Interactions Involving
the Urban Water Resources System.

System Components (Refer to Figure 2)	Ratings of Impacts or Interactions	
	Water Quantity	Water Quality
Urban Water Resource Uses		
Municipal Water Supply	1 / 4	4 / 2
Industrial Water Supply	1 / 4	4 / 2
Local Agricultural Use	3 / 3	2 / 2
Recreation	1 / 3	3 / 3
Energy Generation	3 / 3	1 / 1
Navigation	3 / 4	3 / 1
Flood Control	3 / 4	2 / 1
Other Resource Use Areas and Aspects of the Urban Society		
Land Use	3 / 3	2 / 2
Energy Use	2 / 2	2 / 2
Communications	0 / 1	0 / 0
Climate	4 / 1	3 / 0
Public Health	1 / 2	1 / 3
Transportation, Land	1 / 1	2 / 0
Science, Technology, Government	2 / 0	3 / 2
Socio-Economic	1 / 1	2 / 2
Urban Development	2 / 2	2 / 1
Monitoring Systems		
In-situ Sensing	2 / 0	2 / 0
Remote Sensing	2 / 0	2 / 0

Some of the specific items which might be included within each of the total systems represented by Figure 2 are listed in the left hand column of Table 1. This table also attempts to assign a relative importance to the interaction or impact with the two basic characteristics of the water system, namely quantity and quality. The relative values of the interactions or impacts are indicated by numbers between 1 and 4, and 0 indicating no interaction and 4 suggesting a highly important relationship. The square at the intersection of each column and row in the table contains two numbers, one above a diagonal slash and one below. The upper number indicates the relative importance of a particular water characteristic (quality or quantity) on a specific system component. The number beneath the slash suggests the magnitude or relative importance of a specific system component on the water characterizing parameters. For example, water quantity is of major importance for an industrial water supply (rated 4), whereas industrial water supply is considered to have a rather minor impact (rated 1) on water quantity.

It might be noted that, as shown by Figure 2, the two basic characteristics of water quantity and quality link or relate the impacts between all uses and monitoring activities involving the urban water resource system. For example, energy generation (whether hydro-electric or thermal electric) can have a major impact on water quantity (rated 3 by Table 1). In turn, water quantities are important for public health. Thus, a strong interaction is indicated between energy generation and public health.

6.0 Conclusions and Recommendations

In the consideration of alternative forms of human settlements, certain conclusions and resulting recommendations have become apparent to this panel.

1. Water is a finite commodity at any one time essential to all life and facets of human activity.

a. A continued effort to educate the public to an awareness of the privileges and responsibilities of living within the constraints of this limited supply of water.

b. In particular a clear illustration of the trade-offs inherent in water use, i.e., social versus economic versus aquatic biology, should be kept before the public mind.

2. Any consideration of water resources is a highly risky, multi-disciplinary activity. Any projections of human behavior regarding water and its rational use is speculative.

a. Intermodal approaches to water problems should be encouraged.

b. Conjunctive uses of ground, surface, and waste waters should be required.

c. The international community should be a party to any national planning for overall water strategies.

d. An informational agency and retrieval system should be available to affected water agencies to prevent duplication of effort and disseminate research and development information to the field.

     e. An effort should be made to streamline and combine existing agencies and lines of authority dealing with national, regional, and local water questions so that urban revitalization projects are examined with the total water resource in mind.

    3. Water is a finite commodity, and if we are unable to manage population growth, total demands upon quantity will continue to increase.

     a. Some equitable charge must be borne by all segments of society for what at present are both internal and external costs of water usage.

     b. Emphasis must be given to the quality and quantity of ground storage facilities.

     c. Priority must be given to new applicance designs in all sectors which design alternative mediums or a reduction of water use.

     d. Continuing efforts and research in recycling techniques at economical costs should be encouraged.

     e. Recycling should proceed on a premise of sequential use of water, thereby cutting costs.

     f. Consider constraints on agricultural water use based upon efficiency considerations.

     g. Encourage reduction in solid waste generation and promote local disposal having minimum environmental effect.

    4. Clean, ample water is a necessary aesthetic benefit to mankind as well as a domestic and commercial necessity.

     a. Quantitative measurement techniques to assess the subjective qualities of water enjoyment should be developed.

     b. High priority should be given at all levels of government to retaining open land, waterfront, bodies of water, etc., in a natural state for the public enjoyment--visual as well as physical involvement.

     c. Similar consideration should be given to increasing the possibilities of water for aesthetic and recreational use within the city where it may not already exist or is inadequate.

    5. Water needs are closely coupled with energy consumption.

     a. Energy conservation should be practiced both to conserve energy and the water required for its development and use.

     b. Since alternative sources of energy to those in common use today have substantially different requirements for quantity and quality of water, evaluation of future energy sources should consider carefully the parallel water requirement commitments.

    6. A high value is placed by society on water-related recreation.

     a. Human settlements should be planned to include such recreational facilities nearby.

7. Floodplains are natural water courses.

    a. Flood management must be practiced with recognition that extreme flows are necessary for energy flow across the ecosystem and thus for long-term ecosystem survival.

    b. Man must learn to recognize and live with occasional extreme flows of water.

8. We do not yet understand all that is needed about quantity and quality of water in the hydrospace.

    a. We must continue to explore and monitor to improve our information base for decision-making.

9. Water provides an avenue for the transmission of disease.

    a. Priority must be given to public health concerns in maintaining high quality.

10. The water medium holds the possibility of many new uses ranging from aquaculture to a site for industrial and housing activities.

    a. Careful monitoring of such uses should be encouraged for beneficial possibilities to the society.

11. Water is an essential component of many economic activities and controls some. The water quality required for various uses varies widely and improved quality involves added cost.

    a. The water quality should be matched to the use required.

12. Transportation by water is historically low cost, energy efficient, and has a minimal adverse effect on the environment.

    a. Existing systems should be maintained, encouraged, and expanded.

13. Water is vital.

14. Water strongly interacts with most other urban activities.

15. Wastewater is a resource out of place which can be profitably used with proper control and distribution.

16. Urban-revitalization water projects should be analyzed on a with and without comparison which considers all future impacts.

17. Urban-revitalization projects should be examined with the total water resource in mind so that as many related functions as practicable may be favorably affected and as few functions as possible adversely affected.

18. Lands and improvements within the limits of floodable areas should be managed in ways suitable to economically and socially accommodate occasional flood flows.

19. Consideration should be given to public ownership and management of lands adjacent to water courses for open space, green areas, food production, and infiltration, and minimize areas used for industry to those benefitted by a water course location.

20. Maximize reuse of water.

21. Modify water-using processes to reduce water demand, recover process, and catalytic materials, and reduce wastes.

22. Price water to include all costs to induce efficient use.

23. Consider total surface and ground water management, including conservation, recharge, reuse, waste use, and weather modification.

24. Increase research on health hazards from contaminants in water.

25. Establish and monitor systems to abstract urban effects on area ecosystems for advance warning of major or important changes.

26. Localize goals determination, management strategies, and monitoring results within broader state and national guidelines and financial assistance.

27. Utilize amenity values of water and water bodies.

28. Emphasize water recreation use with minimum energy and pollutional effects.

29. Improve efficiency of water use in agriculture to provide water for use in industry, energy, and urban areas.

30. Recognize need for water in energy development, conversion, and conservation.

31. Recognize the relationships (conflicts, complimentarities, and trade-offs) in uses of water.

32. Encourage international cooperation to achieve world goals and meet world needs in water protection and food production.

33. Encourage waste reduction, generation, and local disposal with minimum impact on the environment.

ALTERNATIVE POLICIES IN WATER POLLUTION CONTROL

A.P.Grima
Erindale College/Department of Geography/Institute for Environmental Studies
University of Toronto, Toronto, Canada.

LIKELY FUTURE OF URBAN WASTEWATER CONTROL

The world's urban population is expected to increase from 1 billion in 1960 to 3.1 billion by the year 2000.[1] This rapid increase in the process of urbanization creates pressures on the supply of housing, health services, education facilities and jobs. Basic to all these needs is the municipal water supply, the effluent disposal system and the quality of the ambient water resources in general. The need for water pollution control in maintaining a high quality environment may be illustrated with reference to Canada. The total water withdrawals for municipal industrial and agricultural purposes were estimated at some 10 million acre-feet in 1956 and 22 million in 1970; they are projected to reach 56 million by 1990. In addition much larger volumes of water are used for non-withdrawal purposes such as recreation, fishing, transport and hydro-electric power generation. Of the amount withdrawn about 25% are consumptive uses; significantly, water pollution in Canada and the boundary waters with the U.S. has been estimated to affect three times as much water as is withdrawn.[2] Cass-Beggs estimates that 50% of minimum flow must be allowed for effluent disposal.[3] This is partly due to industrial effluent and partly due to lack of municipal wastewater treatment plants; of the major Canadian cities only Toronto has 100% secondary treatment and the next best served city is Edmonton with 54%.[4] Even in a country with ample water resources in relation to population, regional shortages and conflicts are already developing in areas of concentrated water use away from large lakes, e.g. Grand River Basin in Ontario[5],

1 U.N. Economic and Social Council (Population Commission) World Population Situation: Note by the Secretary General (Doc. E/CN 9/231), 15th Session, 1969.

2 Prince, A.T., "National Report on the Status of Canadian Water Resources Activities and Development", Proceedings, International Water Resources Association, First World Congress on Water Resources Chicago, 1973.

3 Cass-Beggs, D., "Water as a Basic Resource", in Nelson, J.G., and M.J. Chambers (eds.), Water: Process and Method in Canadian Geography, Toronto: Methuen 1969, 22.

4 MacNeill, J.W., Environmental Management, Ottawa: Information Canada, 1973, 104.

5 Ontario Water Resources Commission, Middle Grand River Region, Water Supply Study, Toronto: 1966

and the St. John River Basin in New Brunswick.[6]

The main legislative thrust in Canada has been in the direction of national and provincial regulation and subsidies for building water pollution control plants. Examples of blanket regulations are those for chlor-alkali and pulp and paper mills. An example of the emphasis on subsidies for hardware is the Onatrio-Canada agreement under which some $170 million of federal assistance are guaranteed over a 5 year period for the upgrading of municipal sewage treatment facilities including nutrient removal in those parts of the province draining to the Lower Great Lakes.[7] The cost on the American side of the Lower Great Lakes was estimated to be $2 billion for comparable improvements.[8]

On the basis of available data it is not possible to provide projections of total expenditures required in Canada if urban areas are to catch up with their backlog and treat the waste discharged by municipalities and industry to secondary standards. The annual investment for treatment plants only is estimated to rise from just over $100 million in 1966 to between $240 and $380 million in 2001. The annual cost of operation, maintenance and capital amortization is projected to rise to between $765 and $904 million by the year 2000 from a level of $100 million in 1966.[9] Other options for water quality management should be urgently considered.

TOWARD MORE RATIONAL WATER POLLUTION CONTROL POLICIES

Subsidies and grants have encouraged the building of more municipal treatment plants while regulation, persuasion and court action have reduced at least some of the worst abuses. Nevertheless, it is pertinent to ask whether the progress has been fast enough and also whether other institutional mechanisms would not result in (1) a more efficient allocation of scarce capital and even scarcer tax dollars and (2) in a more equitable allocation of costs and benefits.

Although the criteria of equity is a basic ingredient in successful environmental management, a full discussion of the ethical rights to environmental resources is precluded by reason of space.[10] Suffice it to say that there are many potential uses of environmental resources and it is not intuitively

---

6 Policy Planning Directorate, Department of Environment, Canada, Water Quality Management and its Application to the Saint John River, vol. 1, Ottawa: 1971.

7 Prince, A.T., "National Report on the Status of Canadian Water Resources Activities and Development", Proceedings, International Water Resources Association, First World Congress on Water Resources Chicago, 1973.

8 Report in The Toronto Star, May 12, 1973, p. 25.

9 MacNeill, J.W., Environmental Management, Ottawa: Information Canada, 1973, 102-3 and p. 105 (Table 14).

10 For a fuller discussion see A.P. Grima "Sins of Emission", a paper read at the Toronto meeting of the Canadian Association of Geographers, 1974.

obvious which uses have prior ethical claims. The pulp mill that overloads
the stream with oxygen-depleting material has no incontrovertible claim on
this resource; nor do the conservationists who would pre-empt the use of a
valuable waste-removing stream.[11] The issue is political. Society - particularly its elected representatives - could decide whether to give a high
priority to the preferences of the recreationists or of the mill operator
(and consumers of newsprint) on purely political grounds.

This decision could also be made on the grounds of efficiency. In this context "efficiency" refers to the allocation of common environmental resources
in such a way that the welfare of the community is maximized. In practice
there are severe limitations on the accuracy of measurements of welfare;
measurement in dollars could only be a useful first approximation. Let me
take again the example of the allocation of the assimilative capacity of a
stream which recreationists would like to use and a pulp mill also wishes to
use. It is proposed to reduce the B.O.D. level by one ton per day; suppose
that the benefits to recreation from the reduced pollution level exceed the
costs imposed on the mill; the welfare of society as a whole increases.
Further reductions in effluent load would be justified until the last addition
to benefits is equal to the last addition to cost. At that point the community maximizes the total utility for all users of the stream. After that
point further reductions in effluent load would result in a lower total social
utility (or welfare).

If the parties concerned are able and prepared to negotiate and to agree on
compensation, they may discover that their mutual interest is best served by
an agreed reallocation of the water resource; for example the mill may be
able to pay compensation to the recreationists and still run a profitable
mill or the recreationists may subsidize the mill to reduce effluent loads
and still feel better off. In such instances a more preferred (i.e. a more
"efficient") reallocation of uses has emerged. If such negotiation and compensation is not possible, public intervention is justified and alternative
choices must be considered on their merits in each case.[12] Five main alternative solutions are outlined below.

Status Quo

The do-nothing lobby is normally strong because there are many whose vested
interests would be eroded by any change in policy. Whether the status quo
requires some state intervention or not, depends upon the cost incurred by
users of environmental resources (e.g. clean water). Let me assume that a
pulp mill's cost of creating a "nuisance" (i.e. polluting water) to others
is zero. Then the status quo requires public intervention. Since the present
users (polluters) of clean water must attach some positive value to this use
of clean water, they would be prepared to pay for this use. The public

---

11   In a seminal paper Coase has questioned the prevalent approach that
pollution should be reduced simply because it causes damage to other users
of environmental resources. See Coase, R., "The Problem of Social Cost",
The Journal of Law and Economics, 3, 1960.

12   There are no obviously superior prescriptions. This view is elaborated in Turvey, R., "On Divergencies between Social and Private Cost",
Economica, 30, 1963.

would be better off because it would require some monetary compensation which may well be spent to further reduce the level of water pollution. Alternatively the polluter may choose to respond to public pressure by spending some money on reducing the level of nuisance and still make a profit; again the public has profited from a change in the status quo. Such preferable outcomes are precluded by the status quo.

Prohibition and Regulation

Prohibition is one form of regulation that is appealing to policy makers. Outright prohibition of pollutants is only justified in those instances where there is a direct deleterious effect on human health or a serious problem for waste-treatment (e.g. heavy metals and arsenic produced in some industrial processes).

A regulatory agency must first decide on a water quality standard that would be acceptable to the present and potential users of the water course or lake. This is made difficult by (1) lack of precise knowledge of the impact of an effluent load on the lake or stream and (2) lack of information regarding the benefits and costs associated with a choice of a water quality standard. The next problem is to translate ambient standards into specific directives for each source of emission. Must each polluter instal the latest available technological controls, irrespective of other options open to the individual firm? Should the directive be in the form of a uniform percentage cutback (e.g. 50%) for all dischargers irrespective of initial levels and costs of in-plant treatment? In times of high assimilative capacity do the regulations allow the firms to take advantage of this increased capacity of the water body to cleanse itself?

Other major shortcomings of regulations are the costs of policing the points of emission and the cost of litigations. The administration of a regulatory system lends itself to postponements due to political pressures and pleading of "special cases"; any infractions which land up in courts are subject to slow legal processes.[13] Regulatory efforts to curb water pollution are inefficient since they are not primarily related to the cost of reducing pollution; they are inequitable because the cost of reducing effluents varies among polluters; they are ineffective in the long run because there is no incentive towards continuing improvement in effluent control.

Grants and Tax Incentives

Subsidies seem a sensible way to help industry reduce effluent loads particularly with industries that are somewhat marginal in their profit and employ a large number of workers in small towns. Tax write-offs or grants suffer from a serious defect: they are most easily administered when directed to installation of equipment and may lead to misallocation of resources because there may be other less costly options open to the firm to reduce pollution e.g. changes in product mix, recycling of waste water. Another shortcoming of subsidies is that they transfer the costs of pollution control from the firm and its customers to the general tax payer.

---

13 For a useful review see Environmental Law Institute, Effluent Charges on Air and Water Pollution, Washington, D.C., 1973, 87.

Effluent Charges

The main advantage of effluent charges is that each polluter may be expected to choose the least expensive way to reduce emissions; therefore a least-cost solution is likely to be attained. Another advantage is that administrators enforcing regulations would be faced with the simpler task of assessing a charge rather than the task of charging a polluter with an offence. In international water resource management this advantage may be of vital importance. A third advantage is that the principle of "the polluter pays" applies.

The main difficulty of effluent charges is the large amount of information required. The effluents of each producer have to be measured. The level of charges would depend on the cost of regional (or municipal) treatment plants or on the cost of stream flow regulation or of other pollution control options. So information on these costs is also required.[14]

The effluent charge should be related to damages imposed on other users. Choosing the correct level of charges is complicated because the impact of effluents on water quality is often unknown; the cost of pollution control may also be difficult to obtain. Under such circumstances the setting up of a charge can only be considered to be experimental and subject to change as more information becomes available regarding the sensitivity of polluters to the charge and of the improvement in the water quality to reduced levels of pollution.

Assimilative Capacity Rights

The costs of pollution control are known (at least to producers) but the damage imposed on others are not so easily ascertained. Dales argues that since the worth of pollution abatement to the community is so difficult to estimate, it would be preferable to decide as a political matter how much more or less pollution the community is prepared to tolerate and allocate this amount of pollution rights to those users who are prepared to pay the most for them.[15]

Social benefits would result if ownership rights to water use were strengthened and formalized by instituting a market in transferable rights to the assimilative capacity of water. The government could decide how much of each pollutant may be dumped into the waters of a region. As long as the permitted level of each pollutant is less than the amount being discharged at present, the issue of rights or "shares" for using the assimilative capacity of water would command a positive price. These rights would be acquired (through the government) by those individuals, groups or firms who value them

14 Roberts, M.J., "River Basin Authorities: A National Solution to Water Pollution", Harvard Law Review, 83, 1970; Freeman, A.M., and Haveman, R.H., "Water Pollution Control, River Basin Authorities, and Economic Incentives: Some Current Policy Issues", Public Policy, 19, 1971, 53-74; Kneese, A.V., and Bower, B.T., Managing Water Quality: Economics, Technology, Institutions, Baltimore: Johns Hopkins Press, 1968.

15 Dales, J., Pollution, Property and Prices, Toronto: University of Toronto Press, 1970.

most. Existing polluters would have an incentive to reduce pollution levels
and sell some of the shares at a profit while newcomers would have an incentive to get by with the lowest amount of effluence (and effluent rights)
possible. The administrative machinery for policing discharges above the
level acquired by the buying of rights would be of the same type required to
levy effluent charges. The difference is that there is no need to pretend
that the incentive mechanism is specifically related to damage imposed on
others as it is for effluent charges.

In conclusion, the systematic consideration of several policy options would
have two important effects. Firstly, the information generated to compare
the advantages and disadvantages of each alternative could provide a deeper
understanding by the community of the damages inflicted by polluters as well
as of the changes in social welfare following from changes in water quality
and emission control. Secondly, the involvement of the community through
public hearings, briefs from special interest groups, and the electoral
process would assist in setting "reasonable" standards and in choosing
policies that do not unduly penalize any single section of the community.

DESIGN AND THE PHYSICAL ENVIRONMENT

Carl Auböck
President International Council of Societies of Industrial Design
Austria

Design is today gaining recognition as among the most vigorous diverse
and provocative disciplines in the world, it is not surprising that
scientific advances, economic struggles, social development and the
continuing pressures of urbanisation have all contributed to the emergence of new directions in Design.

Design, as we know, is a social art. Consequently, the responsible Designer assumes a vital rôle in shaping our physical environment. However,
suffocating subways, traffic jams, parking problems, foul air and polluted waters are now the facts of urban life. It does not seem to help much
that capricious Design elements are occasionally injected, mainly because
they are considered good for public relations.

It is therefore not surprising that responsible Designers have internationally become more and more concerned with the relevance of the Design
contribution to solving urban problems. ICSID's purpose and policy over
the last term of office was to help find, clarify and define the elements
central to the Designer's thought and work, and thereby contribute to an
international forum for the examination of the great issues of contemporary Design.

The concern for social development, environmental education, the search
for significance in Design, and the formulation of beliefs were and are
central to ICSID's approach. But although notable individual results in
Design have been achieved, the positive impact of Designers as a whole
on urban environment seems inconsequential. Unfortunately too, work of
quality is the exception, not the rule. If one were to deduce standards
from works of Design being conducted today, the inevitable conclusion
would be that a sweeping and dramatic upgrading of those standards would
be one of the principal challenges of the profession. However, the complexities of the Design process no doubt create formidable barriers in
achieving results of quality. The efforts of many are required to bring
this about, including a client or committee who often only have a limites
appreciation of the values which the Designer is seeking to create.
Concern for meaning and dignity, concern to elevate and celebrate life
seem very remote and not considered practical, regardless of socio-
economic or political structure. Unfortunately, this is the cultural
climate within which the committed designers work.

Therefore, the needs for more viable design processes, ones which
respect complexity and are scientific ptential, are naturally related
to the type of world we see in the future. It is not surprising at this
stage, that Designers seem to have little more than the most fragile
areas of agreement of what the physical nature of the new world might be.

237

Consequently, self-education processes among Designers internationally
try to lead to a new and better understanding of values, or recognition
of objectives and an agreement on principles for purposeful action.

All these considerations as well as a special uneasiness with the
current motives of professional expression and exchange of views in seminars and the like, led Designers to try and find other means of working
together successfully on an international level. This is how ICSID Interdesigns came into being, and I would like to say that in idea as well as
in method, they have proved successful beyond expectation. We were lucky
to have with us today Ms. Mary Mullin of Kilkenny Design Workshops in
Ireland who was involved in and has helped to organize several interdesigns
and who informed us about these particular contributions and their impact
on urban design problems.

Planning as we know, means many things to many people. It certainly need
not constitute an imposition on individual freedom, but should much rather
be seen as a process to enable us to move from where we are to where we
would ideally like to be.

Designers who can translate a society's needs into a meaningful vision,
and the politicians and leaders in the community who can establish the
necessary legislation must, as we know, collaborate to this very end.

On this tone, I would like in summing up, to thank all the participants
at todays session for their interesting and valuable contributions, and
I would also hope that the contributions of the individual Designers as
well as ICSID, will on an international level, help to contribute in developing a better and more human urban environment.

DESIGN FOR SMALL COMMUNITIES — INTERDESIGN '74 ONTARIO

Frank E. Dudas.

Perhaps one of the most interesting facets of Interdesign'74
Ontario was the somewhat unique approach taken to make sure
that the people of the "case-study" area, Port Hope-Cobourg,
Ontario, became in every sense of the word, the designers'
clients. In more traditional approaches to community design
there are few opportunities for the citizens of the human
settlement to be involved directly in the design process.

The Interdesign process became essentially a two-way system
 of education in human settlements. The designers achieved
a much greater awareness of the needs of people and the
people were exposed to the processes of the design approach.

Some of the conclusions that came out of this innovative
design workshop were :

- People are very aware of the detail factors that
  affect the quality of life of their own communities
- In smaller communities it is very rare to find
  a citizen who is a professional expert in human
  settlement design
- Small communities have to rely on outsiders for
  expertise who more usually live in larger centres
  and do not have a personal understanding of the
  needs and aspirations of smaller human settlements
- People who live in smaller communities are not
  aware of the design alternatives that are possible
  and have little direct experience of the design
  process

239

- There are few tools available to inhabitants of
  smaller communities to help them understand the
  implications of design and planning
- There is a great need for education on human
  settlements at the citizen level
- For design solutions to be valid for communities
  there is an obvious need for a closer and more
  intimate relationship between the experts and the
  people.

During the first few days of the Interdesign workshop the
designers were put into close and informal contact with the
inhabitants. The attempt was to expose each participant to
as many individuals and their opinions as was practical in
a short period. Every attempt was made to create the impression that the designers were sympathetic friends interested
in understanding needs and aspirations rather than visiting
"experts" bringing formula solutions.

THE PROBLEM

The two towns, Port Hope and Cobourg, are only 10 kilometres
apart and they are approximately the same size (about 10,000
population). Yet they are entirely different with different
economic bases, aspirations and tangible differences in traditions, culture and attitudes. The physical environments
are not the same either and the visitor would never mistake
one town for the other after first acquaintance. Nor would
he have any difficulty, after a short stay, to distinguish
the inhabitants of one town from the other even though there
are no differences in appearance, dress or accent. On the
outside there is no difference but on the inside each citizen reflects attitudes, priorities and aspirations that are
unique to his own community.

People in smaller communities share a feeling of community

identity, a close and personal relationship with other
people who live there, a fondness for the way of life of
their place and a concern that the qualities they like and
suit them could be destroyed by either pressures for growth
or the lack of opportunity for development. They mostly share
a conservative view towards change which represents a threat
to an accepted and preferred way of life.

The overall problem that affects the Port Hope-Cobourg area
is that it is a small-town and rural environment located less
than 100 kilometres from the expanding major metropolis,
Toronto. The area is within worker commuting distance of
the big city and its suburbs and as a consequence is seriously threatened by an inundation of people and development.
Unchecked, the pressures for growth destroy completely the
existing way of life and the uniqueness of character which
marks the individuality of these communities. Recognizing
that some change and development is inevitable, and has to
happen or the towns would atrophy, the people of this area
wish to see the future alterations happen in a controlled
and rational fashion. To them something has to happen which
will strengthen the nature of their human settlements so
that impending change will not destroy those elements which
are suited to their style of living.

The process of Interdesign'74 not only stimulated the close
initial contact between designers and inhabitants but also
maintained this liaison throughout the period of the workshop and ended up with a presentation to the public of its
results. In the short two weeks period, the forty participants created over three hundred drawings along with many
written and photographic reports and numerous sound and
television tapes. What is described below is the material
that was edited and selected for the published report and
is the essence of the creative ideas that grew out of the

very close relationship between the designer-participants and the people of the Port Hope-Cobourg area.

A SENSE OF IDENTITY

The Interdesign participants generally agreed that the concept of community identity plays an important part in preserving the life-style of human settlements. It is largely a community's sense of its own identity that determines the nature of its connection with the outside. The less well defined the identity, the more likely is the community to be overpowered by unsympathetic outside influences. If the Port Hope-Cobourg area is to remain a unique entity, its individuality must be nurtured and its citizens must develop a greater sense of belonging to the collective purpose of maintaining a small town life-style. It is clear that one of the keys to community building is community identity.

THE SILENT PEOPLE

A community is no more than the sum total of its residents, but the strength of its identity is dependent on the extent to which those inhabitants are able to share in the normal course of day-to-day life. Frequently the victims of exclusion from the mainstream are the aged and handicapped, the silent people.

The large city, especially, tends to ignore the silent people, to push them into the background. The small community often offers a better human environment for them since it tends to allow more personal inter-action, more caring attitudes in its residents, a slower pace and easier mobility. It is important to provide adequate amenities for this segment of the human settlement and to facilitate its integration into the full spectrum of community life. Community designers must consider the entire population if a solid sense of identity with the community is to be encouraged.

SENSORY ENVIRONMENT

From a participant's notebook :

> "At no time in our lives can we avoid the influences
> of our physical environment. Whether we are cons-
> cious of it or not, our surroundings stimulate or
> depress us, put stress on us or allow us to relax.
> They make us discontented or fill us with joy. The
> happiness of the community is built not only on
> good technical planning which guarantees the citizen
> water, electricity, garbage collection and other
> services. The shape and form of the community - its
> colour, texture, scale, sound and smell - play a
> dynamic role. These elements create the communal
> garden in which personal and social relationships
> grow and mature.
>
> The role of the designer is to give physical form
> to environment and to things which satisfy the
> needs of human beings both as an individual and as
> a social being...
>
> The ultimate aim of all community design is an
> environment which leads the citizen to think new
> thoughts, create new things, to follow new dreams."

INHERITED PROBLEMS

The most serious threat to a community's identity arises not
from isolated action of individual corporations, but from the
combination of forces exerted by the whole range of external
corporate and government decisions. To protect itself from
the impact of corporate power, the small community has no
defence but the determination of its citizens to assert

themselves in their desire to maintain and create the kind
of community they want.

THE PARACHUTE DEVELOPER

When an outside developer brings the promise of growth he is
often welcomed by small communities and attracted by profer-
red economic advantages. The community sometimes fails to
consider the total impact on its quality of life. The community's identity is in danger when it overlooks long-term
environmental affects in favour of short-term economic gains.

AREA DESIGN COMMISSION

Interdesign'74 proposed that an effective method for the
creation and maintenance of community identity is the establishment of a Design Commission responsible to review all
development proposals. The Design Commission should be composed of concerned citizens supported by experts in settlements design. Its responsibilities could include :

1. to establish design criteria and to publish guidelines
2. to examine development proposals in relation to
   established guidelines
3. to negotiate any necessary changes to new proposals
4. to present these revised proposals to municipal
   authorities for ratification.

In order to manage their development small communities should
have a greater say in the way in which land is assembled by
private developers and governments.

COMMUNITY TREES

It was suggested that living trees could be used as symbols
of the environment to welcome new residents to small communities. New arrivals would be invited to plant a community

tree in private or public spaces and the program would include both corporations and individuals. As a symbol the
tree would represent both the vitality of the community and
concern for the environment.

A further use of the tree symbol might be a "Silver Tree
Award", an annual award program for excellence in community
design.

A SYMBOL FOR THE COMMUNITY

A direct approach to foster a strong and cohesive identity
for the Port Hope-Cobourg area was recommended through the
adoption of a community symbol. Broad application of the
design to area signage, street furniture, and other elements
of the physical community would do much to create a unique
identity. The concept was designed to be able to represent
individual communities while at the same time providing a
form that could represent the area when linked together.

TO PROTECT AN ALTERNATIVE

The small community is seen increasingly ofter as a clear
alternative to living in crowded cities. The pressures for
growth in large urban centres also affects small nearby communities. The designers, looking at the problems of growth
for the specific study area, arrived at general conclusions
which relate to small towns everywhere.

-   There is little virtue in the idea that growth can be
    imposed on an existing community by an arbitrary formula.
-   If new growth areas are developed alongside established
    communities, great care must be taken to ensure social
    and economic harmony between the two.
-   Growth need not follow traditional patterns.

MANAGING AREA GROWTH

The pressures of growth as an overflow from the nearby large
city could inundate the small towns of the area and destroy
the character, identity and quality of life of the communities. It was therefore recommended that growth be deflected
away, as much as possible from the existing communities to
a properly planned new town. The creation of the new town
would have to be planned in such a way that the needs and
aspirations of the established communities would be incorporated in the planning process.

A major question is how can regional growth be integrated so
that people feel connected to others who live in the same
area. The need for regional interactions becomes very clear
when one looks at the problems of land use and public services.

It was proposed that land use controls are necessary to maintain a suitable balance between urban, recreation and agricultural uses. These are vital concerns to the local inhabitants, but they are also concerns of the larger society
which needs to maintain valuable foodlands in production.
Legislation and tax incentives are needed to encourage developers to use non-agricultural land.

HELPING TOWN AND COUNTRY MEET

The growing world food shortage underlines the need for a
better understanding between urban dweller and farmer. An
experiment is proposed through the assembly of a number of
farms for the purpose of bringing together experienced farmers and young townspeople in a working farm situation. Just
as the farmers would benefit from closer personal contact
with townspeople the converse would also be true. The value
of farm to urban land can be appreciated better when citi-

zens come to understand the environmental interdependance.
The land for this program might be operated on a joint basis
by farm owners and local government with encouragement from
higher governmental levels.

Throughout the industrialized world there is the simplistic
notion that waste is dealt with by moving it from one place
to another. While some encouraging steps have been taken by
communities through re-sorting garbage in order to salvage
specific materials, a more comprehensive solution still
awaits. In fact the only real answer is to design garbage so
that it fits into a waste disposal system while at the same
time recognizing that the problem goes right back to products
and packaging. These things should be designed so that there
is conservation, longevity and re-use with minimum throw-
away components. It was proposed that a comprehensive research program aimed at developing an efficient system of
garbage disposal would be a valuable contribution to the
world-wide problem of garbage.

> "The time has arrived for man to economize with space
> as never before in history. We must encourage compact
> urban development in harmony with the landscape.
> Where possible, industry should be integrated with
> the urban areas by making fullest use of modern
> technology. If industry must be located outside the
> urban area, it should use as little space as tech-
> nology will allow".

From a report by one of the Interdesign participants.

RE-USE OF WASTE SPACES

It was proposed that communities should look at existing waste
spaces for possible development. The example given is the
potential use of exhausted gravel pits in the Port Hope-

Cobourg area as the location for future industries and development.

THE ROLE OF INDUSTRY

It was suggested that industry must take responsibilities for
its presence in the community. Ways have to be found to persuade industry to fit into the range of community goals.
Industrial firms should explore the possibilities inherent
in containerization, in multiple storey operations, in new
processes which make better use of space. If industry were
to adopt the most logical approaches to technology, there is
no reason why its physical plant could not become an acceptable part of the landscape. One proposal was to prevent the
development of vast industrial parks through defining zones
in the community area that would be best to use such as poor
land, waste-land, or destroyed land such as gravel pits. What
is needed is a more than usual comprehensive approach to the
industrial problem by small communities and a greater awareness
of community and human needs on the part of industry.

A CLIMATE FOR LOCAL INDUSTRY

The small community with a heavy concentration of branch-
plant industry makes itself extremely vulnerable to outside
influences. By their very nature, branch plants are unlikely
to become closely integrated with the community fabric. It
was recommended that small communities should find the ways
to foster a climate where smaller concerns with local loyal-
ties can become established and grow. The community that
attracts and develops new small industries is investing in
the future. However to create the right climate, ways must
be found to gain support from higher levels of government.
A positive step would be the creation of "incubators" for
new ventures where the use of shared and common facilities
under partial subsidization would encourage people, particu-

larly the young to start new businesses with a minimal capital investment. Government assistance would be desirable to
provide low-cost or rent-free space, to underwrite the capital cost of renovating old facilities and the cost of shared
services such as design, promotion, etc... It is also essential that banks and other lending institutions take a more
active role in the support of new local industries.

It was also proposed that every small community should look
at its unique geographic location, markets, human and natural
resources as a guide for the types of new ventures which
would be compatible with its environment and potential. For
instance the Port Hope-Cobourg area is ideally suited to
develop an industry related to the expanding sport of cross-
country skiing. The manufacture of skis, poles, boots, clothing and other sport accessories requires a technology well
within the capabilities of the region. A growing interest in
sailing in Lake Ontario and other lakes suggests further possibilities since this particular area is so closely tied to
the economics of the tourist and recreation industry.

THE JOY OF BEING SMALL

As an alternative technology, small or craft based industry
offer both the individual worker and the community many advantages. Given the smaller scale of the operation, its impact
on the environment is less than that of large industry. For
the worker there are many opportunities not to be found in
the mass-production plant. The worker is more able to use
his full creative potential in every stage of production,
each of which he understands.

There are advantages to the community as well because small
industry can more easily adapt to local objectives and needs.

TOOLS TO INVOLVE THE CITIZEN IN COMMUNITY DESIGN

At Interdesign'74, the participants saw a need to help residents of the study area, and of small towns generally, become more aware of the problems of community design. They agreed that the fundamental choices of design concern must be made by citizens themselves. The following are a number of tools proposed to increase awareness and the capability to participate in community design.

EDUCATION FOR COMMUNITY

Education aimed at preservation of a community's identity and quality of life must begin in early childhood. It is the responsibility of the parents, teachers and community at large. The Community Educational Tool requires the organized participation of all the parts that make up the community including the business and industry sector. It is suggested that there would be no difficulty to have visiting experienced planners, architects and designers talk about typical human settlements problems and solutions.

SNOWBALL : a Global View of Community

SNOWBALL is the Interdesign name given for the phenomenon that happens when as suggestions arise from the community, one idea will inevitably lead to another.

It was proposed that through a series of public meetings the local government would invite residents to contribute ideas. Citizens' committee would be formed to study feasibility of these ideas. At a certain point of development, professionals might be brought in to implement the concepts.

The SNOWBALL program would allow citizens to examine their own needs and explore the ways in which their communities serve or fail them. The resultant knowledge would naturally

place the citizens in a solid position from which to influence politicians, planners and developers. Perhaps the most
important feature of SNOWBALL is that it would encourage
a "global" view of the community's potential and an all-
inclusive catalogue of priorities and objectives. The effect
would be a more integrated community with a strong image.

THE ENVIRONMENTAL PLANNING GAME

This is proposed as a tool to bring the citizen more directly
into the process of community design. It is seen as a metal
map of the town or area with modular magnetic pieces representing various types of land use, amenities, functions and
services. Members of the community are invited to make their
own decisions about where various elements should go and
which things should be incorporated in the community. Each
participating citizen can move pieces around, add or remove
modules and work in concert with his fellow citizens. Both
amusing and enjoyable, playing the game in a group could lead
to better perceptions of the opportunities and potential for
the community. The object is not to win but to arrive at a
result which is agreable to all participants.

ALMANAC : a Self-Help Compendium for the Small
Community

ALMANAC is simply the collection of material and information
on all facets of community design into a clear instructional
catalogue for the lay person. It is meant to take all the
mystery out of the planning and design process and give the
citizen and community a manual, similar to the old fashioned
Farmer's Almanac, that gives people a good understanding of
the factors of community design and what can be done about
them. It would prepare the citizen to be able to deal with
experts better, to understand the alternatives available, to
be aware of the processes of implementation and the sources

of funding and assistance.

However, ALMANAC is not conceived as being only a book. It
should be designed to use all existing communications media
from local newspapers to television. It provides easy access
to human settlement information, whatever the original source.
The ALMANAC Handbook would instruct people on how to participate in the detail design of their community. The fundamental belief of the Interdesign participants was the idea that
the more that people know, the more planners, architects and
designers can achieve realistic results for the people they
serve.

CONCLUSIONS

The intimate co-operation between the people of Port Hope-
Cobourg area and the Interdesign'74 participants leads us to
think that would be worthwhile to recreate in a different
form elsewhere. It is therefore proposed that communities
should consider bringing together volunteer human settlements experts within their own national region to participate in an intensive planning and design workshop. It is
suggested that the participants should represent the full
spectrum of human settlements experts from social to physical planners.

Finally it is worth lokking at the results of Interdesign'
74/Ontario and its possible implications for any urban situation. Even large cities and metropolises are comprised
of neighbourhoods and human villages.

INTERDESIGN '72 — DESIGN FOR TOURISM KILKENNY, IRELAND. MAY 1972.

Mary V. Mullin
Kilkenny Design Workshops, Kilkenny, Ireland.

THEME

How can a country cater for tourism to benefit both visitor and host, without damaging the environment and character which both want to preserve ?

PARTICIPANTS

Twenty designers from twelve countries formed the working group. They came from Australia, Austria, Belgium, Bulgaria, Finland, Great Britain, Israel, Japan, Kenya, United States of America and Ireland.

HOSTS

Sponsoring organizations:- Kilkenny Design Workshops, Irish Tourist Board and Irish Export Board.

INTRODUCTION

While Ireland was the subject of the study it was recognised at the outset that the issues involved were widely applicable; that variations from country to country would tend to be particular rather than general.

The Brief was divided into four sections:-
Holiday Accomodation
Transport
General Equipment
Colour and Materials

Before proceeding to a detailed examination under each heading, some general matters of agreement were formulated in preliminary discussion.

Tourism is a social phenonomen arising from the development of industrialised society. It is a product of the following:-

1.   The wealth, earning capacity and increasing amount of leisure time in developed countries.

2.   The development of rapid mass transport systems.

3.   The possibility of escape from familiar routines, and surroundings particularly from urban areas in industrial countries, to countries promising unspoilt natural landscapes.

4.   The possibility of contact with other lifestyles and exotic customs languages, and environments.

These factors are intensified by the commercial development of tourism by transport operators, hotel chains and the authorities within potential host countries which have a direct interest in increasing the revenue from tourism. This results in an increasingly large scale need for tourist accomodation which in turn intensifies the demand for the best sites in both towns and countryside and encourages peripheral service network of facilities and amenities geared to the tourist, not to the residents, and consequently frequently destructive of the essential qualities of the area.

The resulting imbalance creates a new kind of consumer society in undeveloped areas, a tourist consumer society. A conflict therefore arises between the needs and wishes of tourists who live and work in an industrial society and the economic benefits that tourism can bring to a developing society. This conflict was expressed in the form of a triangular diagram, the apexes representing the tourist, the residen t and the environment.

The impact of tourist (who is seeking an undeveloped environment)
The impact of resident (who is seeking to preserve the undeveloped environment)
The impact of both tourist and resident on the environment.

The education of the public about the conflicts which can arise between the demands of tourists and the requirements of the local residents was regarded as fundamental to any successful approach to design in the industry.

Information/Education

Tourism was seen as a continuing social and educational process. Guide books, brochures and other forms of tourist information should be considered as devices which condition the tourist to 'see' the country through the eyes of promotional material, but they should be regarded as no more than components of a wider system of communications. Information for children, teenagers and adult travellers should be co-ordinated with planning for national and regional development and with the objectives of the tourist authorities.

Policies and action for developing and catering for tourism should be included within existing planning frameworks, rather than imposed from outside afterwards.

Resource allocation and management, were not seen as products for tourism to be indiscriminately distributed throughout the countryside. "Not a 'good design' label everywhere, but rather a 'design not necessary' label."

The natural environment, complete with its man-made activities, is the fundamental resource for tourist needs. For tourist satisfaction to prevail tourism must remain, or appear to remain, secondary to some primary activity or resource. In other words, the environment does not exist for the sake of the tourist.

Applied to Ireland the tourist expectation would probably be in terms of the picturesque, the historical, the romantic and the enjoyment of landscape, the uncrowded living conditions. The expectations of the Irish people, by contrast, would be a wish to see Ireland with an improved standard of living, to feel a sense of important identity, and not the inhabitants of a tourist museum.

Methodology

A system was worked out whereby certain criteria would be applied to each of the separate aspects of tourism that came under study.

An understanding of the system, developed for the purpose of scrutiny analysis and recommendation, as applied to the different aspects of tourism, is difficult to describe without recourse to the actual charts drawn up for the purpose. There were four charts:-

1.   Key Interaction Network sets out national aims and goals as applied to tourism. It is subdivided into various blocks of information which shows the relation between them and the bodies or organizations which are responsible for them. On this chart is listed all the data which a tourist authority might be expected to take into account.

2.   <u>Performance Criteria</u> depicts the interactions between the tourist, the environment and the residents, the people who live in the country, who shape the environment and who are shaped by it. (The aim at all times being to achieve a balance between economic and social objectives and environmental considerations).

3.   <u>Network of Tourist Services</u> sets out the various headings of tourist activity and is so designed as to bring to the front the information necessary for the tourist authority to form a policy.

4.   <u>Description of the Design Process</u> illustrates a way in which a planning team may be expected to relate to a tourist authority.

These charts provide an ingenious reference, so presented, as to enable vital information to be read off by tourist authorities and planners in any context.

ACCOMODATION

The full range of tourist accomodation, hotels, motels, guest houses etc,. were sampled by the participants.

Evaluation of, and recommendations on, the existing situation were made with particular reference to furnishing and equipment, opportunities for further development, alterations, etc,. Design proposals were sought. Check lists were made which applied to the different types of accomodation thus enabling the owners to assess their strengths and weaknesses.

The group considered the suitability or otherwise, in their various contexts, of large international hotels, motels, family run hotels, farmhouse accomodation, furnished cottages and condominium units. The following points were made:-

<u>The International Type Hotel.</u> Described as catering for a wide variety of tourist needs such as sleeping, eating, entertainment, shopping, recreation, sports etc,. and having a large number of rooms (300-500) and usually situated in an area of great natural beauty where these hotels are a relatively new phenomonen. Their attractions, from the tourist's point of view, their effects on environment and on local residents were dealt with in some detail.

<u>Family Run Hotels.</u> It was felt that this type of hotel could be developed in small towns and villages. Its merits were investigated and recommendations made.

<u>Farmhouse, Cottage Accomodation and Condominiums.</u> These were also examined in detail and their respective merits weighed in accordance with the criteria established for the district and the type of tourist to be catered for. A case study was made of one farmhouse and detailed proposals for a three phase development plan were made.

Observations

Amongst the general observations on tourist accomodation were the following:-

The group felt it is of greater benefit to a town, from a social and planning point of view and to the tourist industry to reconstruct existing buildings and plants (old mills, warehouses etc,) than to put up new structures outside the town or village. When, as is common, a new hotel is built on the outskirts of a town or village, tendency is for the social centre to move with it, to the detriment of the life of the town or village. While making this recommendation it was acknowledged that the reconstruction of such buildings would be expensive, less productive of revenue and requiring greater effort and co-operation between planners and developers than exists at present. But it was also felt that the planning authorities, local and national, have an overriding responsibility in this matter.

TRANSPORT

Ireland it was noted, is a destination country, unlike most European countries, which are transit countries. July and August are peak tourist periods in Ireland. This produces a high demand for transport during the period and a contrastingly lower demand for the rest of the year. The situation is further complicated in that the Irish road network was planned for local business, commercial and recreational use, but the large increase in the number of tourists in recent years (many coming from overseas who bring with them their own cars, caravans, dormobiles, etc.) has brought problems of a technical, economic, aesthetic and environmental nature.

The group drew attention to the unsatisfactory nature of the system of jurisdiction by local authorities and emphasised the need for a single planning authority for roads.

Some of the most important recommendations made were the following:-

An extension of the tourist season, thereby reducing the seasonal traffic peaks; encouragement of tourist traffic away from the fast, main traffic routes by highlighting attractive alternative routes with well serviced lay-bys, picnic sites, camping sites etc,.

Surprise was expressed at the lack of basic environmental safeguards such as:-

The siting, screening, design and furnishing of lay-bys, picnic sites, car-parks, filling stations, caravan and camping sites, public footpaths, signposting.

In addition to the comments on the existing situation, detailed illustrated suggestions were put forward for the improvement and development of these facilities.

GENERAL EQUIPMENT

Points of tourist interest require a great deal of miscellaneous equipment such as refreshment kiosks, lavatories, information and directional signs, seats, shelters, litter bins etc,. Using the performance criteria chart, design principles were formulated which would meet the requirements of the tourist while respecting the landscape. An underlying principle to be observed was that there should be no man-made intrusions in the environ-ment except where appropriate and absolutely necessary.

A study of an Irish country town, Ennis, Co. Clare, was carried out to explain, by way of detailed illustration, the general principles recommended:

Our object was to explore the town with a view to developing the character already there rather than to suggest sweeping and expensive changes. Emphasis was placed on small scale projects which one could expect local communities to organize and that demonstrates how such schemes enhance the town itself.

Ennis is the county town of Clare - a principal market centre and a logical centre for touring the main attractions of the county. It is a pleasant town to explore - a maze of lanes and narrow streets, full of interesting commercial congestion, lead into market places, a small public space, the Abbey ruins and, inevitably to the river which runs through the centre of the town.

The main emphasis is centred on the river Fergus. In common with many Irish towns and villages Ennis is built with its back turned to the river and so a principal attraction is ignored and wasted. The town is fortunate in that a great length of the riverbank has been opened up through demolition, but only to provide car parking space instead of emphasising the river itself. We propose that a walk be created to Club Bridge. This would have obvious benefits for the local population. If the derelict mills were converted to hotel accomodation a pleasant pedestrian access to the town would be provided for the tourist.

We suggested the tidying up of the market and development of the space
around the monument, intensifying its role as focal point of the town.
We noticed that the townspeople gather there throughout the day, and by
re-siting the Tourist Information Office there along with such services as
a cafe, souvenir bookstall etc,. and with the addition of some landscaping
an attractive oasis could be formed, again to the great benefit of the
local people and the visitor.

COLOUR AND MATERIALS

The brief required an examination of the more tangible qualities of the Irish
landscape and the presentation of these in a form which would guide
designers working in Ireland.

Industrial development and modern travel disturb the balance of the
landscape by introducing elements that are out of scale. Tourism and
temporary residents who have no vital attachment to the region also
disturb the balance.

Industry and tourism usually involve large-scale financial involvement.
Such investments are not easily regulated. On the other hand, damage to
the natural balance can go beyond the point of no return.

If new man-made elements which modify the landscape are to be
introduced these elements should proceed from the organic whole, be born
from it, and so fit into the life of the region.

The group defined its objectives:-

To make information available to local inhabitants, national and foreign
tourists that would make them aware and respectful of the country by
showing how the beauty of the landscape is the result of all ecological
interactions into a unique, well-balanced organism.

To create a tool that will help local authorities, designers, architects and
persons responsible for local equipment, conservation and information to
be conscious of the country as an organic whole, so that the result of their
work should be born from an understanding of this total organism.

Analysis of the General Landscape
Attention was paid principally to the constant features of each
distinctive region, noting the characteristic elements.

Travel was perceived as a continuous experience of landscape and
surroundings in contrast with place to place movement (tourism).

Landscape was perceived related to movement in space (wind, clouds, waves) and in time (light, hours, seasons).

The group attempted to understand the interactions and relations of the observable elements as an organic whole.

Attention was given to the fact that the distinctive aesthetic quality of a region or landscape was due to the constants and not the exceptional elements, to the life as a whole, to changes of light and atmosphere.

These constants were grouped and distinguished as follows:-

<u>Atmosphere.</u> Prevailing wind, light, weather.

<u>Geology.</u> Kind of rock, slant of rock layers, colour and quality of soil, general line of hills, rivers, beaches.

<u>Botany.</u> Plant life at different levels - wild and planted.

<u>Human Elements.</u> Roads, paths, gates, stiles, bridges, harbours, canals, fords.

<u>Farming.</u> Crops - sizes, types and situation of fields, animals, hedges and fences, carts, tools, haystacks, manure heaps.

<u>Architecture.</u> Walls, cottages, farms and barns, colour and buildings, materials.

<u>Sports and Leisure.</u>

<u>Examples of External intrusive, non-constant elements.</u> Industrial buildings, signs, rubbish, litter, electric poles, mining, hotels.

<u>Assumption.</u>
That tourism is about Ireland's own people, Ireland should aim at attracting the type of tourist which will appreciate, respect, and have sympathy for the people and the country.

<u>Behind the Landscape.</u>
To be able to appreciate a country, you need to understand why it is as it is.

Usually only the most <u>unusual</u> things are pointed out to tourists - castles, monuments, specially shaped or picturesque rocks or mountains.

Attention should rather be given to characteristic features which may
not necessarily be seen as interesting by local people. These
closely interlinked characteristics should be regarded as a whole:-
Climate, geology, crops and cattle, architecture, sites of villages,
plant and animal life, industry, roads.

In other words, we should begin by observing the constants of the
landscape in an area. We should try to understand the internal
mechanics of these constants, or understand how they are linked
together to form a whole. We should try to explain how future
developments and equipment can fit into that whole by internal logic.

The team produced a series of diagramatic drawings which tried to convey
the essence of the landscape in graphic terms. The text which
accompanied these drawings identified certain general principles which
go to determine the whole visual quality of the landscape yet whose
influence is not always recognised or appreciated. These principles lie at
the root of the work of designers and architects.

CHILDREN

Some special proposals in relation to children as tourists were put forward.
It was rightly stated that they are the tourists of the future and that they
deserve consideration now. They should be made aware of their
environment for it is through education of the young that the tourist of the
future is formed.

A series of folded paper games was designed to encourage children in
observation and enjoyment of the countryside. The idea has potential in
many countries of the world, being inexpensive to implement and being of
enormous value in educating children in the appreciation and
conservation of the countryside.

Comments were made on stereotyped solutions to hotel facilities - if there
are any at all - for children. Most were considered an adult's answer to
how he thought a child might like to play. Little thought was given to the
development of pictorial maps of the area which could, for instance, turn
the grounds of any hotel into an immediate treasure hunt area. Inside the
hotel there should be a room set aside for children for use on a rainy day
or for when parents are having a meal. This could be equipped to include
creative activity for the children. Comments and suggestions were also
made for the provision of childrens' play areas in Airport terminals which
could be of great use during the inevitable flight delays.

A full report of the event has been prepared and will be published by the
Irish Tourist Board and Kilkenny Design Workshops with the aid of funds
from UNESCO in May of 1976.

ICSID INTERDESIGN '75 — BRUGES

G. des CRESSONNIERES.
Avenue Montjoie, 127
Brussels - BELGIUM.

The theme of the "Interdesign", held in Bruges in August
1975, brought to light a problem common to those of our
ancient towns which form part of our artistic heritage.
This is : traffic.

Bruges, the celebrated Venice of the North, can be considered
a sort of prototype of this problem. Inside there is a narrow, formerly, walled city of 600 hectares (1,500 acres),
begun in the 10th century, now known as the "oeuf de Bruges".
Here winding back-streets criss-cross canals, giving way
to the Market Square - the focal point for the tourist traffic. During the high season there is a daily invasion of
70,400 cars and 86,800 bicycles within this perimeter.

The increasing strangulation of the city creates a dilemna :
either the city centre is adapted to automobile traffic,
or cars are to be excluded. The first solution would be the
mutilation of our artistic heritage, and the second would
be to transform the centre into one vast pedestrian area
and so condemn Bruges to being one big museum, from whence
all activity would soon vanish. For small traders and crafts-
men, schools and even private dwellings could not exist without transport, both public and private.

It was this alternative - and the search for solutions which
would harmonise two diametrically opposed demands - which
was suggested as a subject for reflections to the 29 designers from 18 different countries who came to Bruges from
6 till 20 August 1975.

Though each had his own fragmentary experience, it contributed
to the whole and the conference was backed up by the large
amount of information provided by the Head of the borough
finance department, the chief city architect and planner,
the Head of the police traffic department, constructors of
public transport equipment and delegates from the population.

It was soon evident that there was no miracle solution, but
there is A MEANS of stemming the present frightening trend
and proposing alternative solutions. The replies showed that
it is necessary to act simultaneously in four sectors :

- There must be a reorganisation of the public transport
  network.
- There must be an appropriate design of vehicles and equipment.
- An efficient system of visual communication must take place.
- There must be an area by area study to examine the possibilities of establishing pedestrian zones.

In their turn these measures depend on a <u>fundamental change</u>
in the attitude of the population and on the <u>political courage</u>
of the authorities concerned.

It was decided at the seminar that work should be grouped
within two different stages. The first, in the short-term,
would include rapid decisions destined to provide a progressive change in the urban system. The second, long-term stage,
would help to bring about a change in the attitude of the inhabitants. Two main objectives were pursued :

       (i)   Free the Centre
      (ii) Change the ideas.

I.-   <u>FREE THE CENTRE</u>

Let us bear in mind that the seminar was concerned with the
"<u>centres</u> of historic towns" and not "historic towns". It goes
without saying that the reorganisation of an historic city
like Paris has little in common with this study.

<u>Buses out</u>

On the whole the ancient streets are narrow and there is no
possibility of widening them without damaging listed buildings. Because of its size therefore, the bus presently in
use for public transport, is scarcely suitable. Moreover noise
and exhausts give rise to pollution, and a bus can only be
turned with difficulty.

The seminar proposed a number of solutions affecting the
urban network in general and buses in particular. A "loop
system" should be designed surrounding the city centre :
a circular one-way ring, reserved for buses and banning parking. The ring, formed out of adjacent existing streets,
would allow maximum commercial speeds to be maintained.

Buses would no longer come into the centre and the present
secondary routes bringing traffic from the outskirts would
stop at the loop, allowing buses to pass along the loop itself for another direction.

These secondary routes would also be one-way with no parking
permitted. Such a lay-out would allow the setting up of an
urban network conforming to the needs of a radial system,

instead of the present, diametrical one.

Careful placing of bus-stops would mean that no one would
have to walk more than 500 metres ; even within the city
centre itself the stops being spaced about every 300 metres.
Completing the system there would be a network of "soft
vehicles" and "pedestrian aids", explained later, available
at the bus-stops.

As a parallel study to the urban network the seminar proposed
the adoption of articulated buses, with one or more sections
according to traffic needs. This would eliminate the large
empty buses which block the narrow streets during quiet
hours, - buses which are never large enough during rush hours.

An alternative solution would involve the adoption of two
types of bus, consisting of 72 and 20 seats, which could be
used either alternately or in conjunction, depending on
traffic conditions. With both solutions, increased rationa-
lisation would cut down bottlenecks and create certain socio-
economical advantages such as reduced energy consumption,
increased frequency, higher mobility and cruising speed. The
"one sectioned bus" or the "small buses", during slack
periods, could even be used in a dial-a-bus system, where
the passenger telephones in the same way as for a taxi.

With improved bus services the population is naturally encouraged to use them, so abandonning their private cars. As far
as urban traffic is concerned a bus-passenger occupies 20
times less space than someone driving a car.

The fourth solution involves a new look at the movement of
passengers within the buses themselves. It is based on one
option : that the sale and control of tickets takes place
outside the buses at the stops. This would abolish the necessity for one-way movement of passengers and allow both doors
to be used for those both entering and leaving.

A mathematical analysis, first published in Poland in 1974,
has proved that directed passenger movement inside a bus is
only in the interest of the fleet operator. The shortest
stop-time is achieved when there are no "entrance" or "exit"
doors. In Bruges, the saving in time would be 65% in the case
where passengers only board a bus (e.g. near a factory after
work) and 30% when there is an exchange of passengers, such
as at a station.

Cars out

At the same time the seminar examined the problem of car parks, areas of dense traffic and alternative solutions to private vehicles such as "soft vehicles", "people-movers" and water transport.

Car-parks.

If traffic is to be drawn away from the streets two types of car-park are needed : one within the city itself for essential private vehicles and one at the periphery of the city centre both for tourists and inhabitants.

1. Semi-underground type for the inhabitants

The seminar noticed the fact that many dwelling blocks consisted of an outer building surrounding green spaces for gardens. It proposed that semi-underground car-parks be built under these gardens, for the use of the particular inhabitants. Access to the communal area, slightly raised to the 2.1 metres regulation heightof the car-park, would be achieved by a ramp leading from the street and two spiral staircases from the basement. The park formed by the assembled gardens would be supported by a structure of light steel and prefabricated concrete sections. An opening in the roof would provide lighting and ventilation.

This plan has taken   into account that it is impossible to dig down deep in Bruges, because underground areas become flooded.

2. Both for tourists and the residents, at certain strategic points in the city car- parks would
be coupled with information centres and pleasantly laid out green spaces where people could sit near bus termini.

3. On the periphery, so-called "deterrent" car-parks,
placed at the point of access of the main routes, corresponding with bus departure points and places where "soft vehicles" (small non polluting vehicles - see section on vehicles) could be hired.

Centres of dense traffic.

In historic cities the tourist information centre is frequently placed at the very centre. In Bruges, it is the "Grote Markt" or"Market Square".

The seminar's proposal is that all tourist information should be decentralised and spread among a number of strategic points.

1. At key points like the station or the airport, if there
is one. In Bruges, the station would become not only an
interconnecting point for different modes of transport
(trains, buses, cars and people-movers), but it would resemble
the tourist information centre, an area to relax with room
for picnics, where small non polluting vehicles, such as
bicycles, various "pedestrian aids" and horse-drawn calashes
could be hired.

2. At a number of secondary points, at chosen sites (in the
case of Bruges the "Vismarkt", "'tZand", the "Burg" and of
course the "Market Square").

Here one could find a map of the city, the departure times
of the boats and buses, taxis,hire of bicycles and "pedestrian aids", the sale of journals and tobacco, telephones,
litter baskets, benches and boxes of flowers, and an illumi-
nated pillar displaying information. During the tourist
period, one could add multi-coloured tents, fixed with wires,
which would disappear at the end of the season.

Alternative solutions to private vehicles.

1. Bicycles

In Bruges there are 86,800 bicycles, more than there are
cars, but there is hardly even the embryo of a system of
cycle-ways and no satisfactory equipment.

It would seem a logical policy for any town with a dense
urban structure to encourage the use of the bicycle.

In the case of Bruges the seminar studied an overall plan of
cycle-ways and well-distributed cycle racks, special signs
for cyclists and cycling maps - in other words a real "two-
wheels" policy.

2. "People-movers", vehicles as yet not developed,
which could be used in the long term. Example : an automated
platform moving slowly on a hidden guideway system which
passengers can step on or off without the system coming to
a full stop. Another idea is articulated systems where passengers can ask to be let off or on without reference to any
particular stopping place. (Something like those used in
Disney Land). Ideally a people-mover ought to be free of
charge.

3. Water-transport

Ancient historic city-centres like Rome, Barcelona and Genoa
were nearly all great ports at one time, which explains the
overriding importance of water.

At the present time water is often used as a sewer and not
with any utility or ingenuity.

The seminar proposes a profound study of water as a transport service, reinforcing this with examination of different
types of vessels. For example, during boat-trips passengers
could be protected against the rain by a removable transpa-
rent awning.

Pedestrians in

This section is the logical sequence of the two preceding
ones. The seminar investigates possible improvements in the
present situation : means to give the city back to inhabitants, make life easier for them by preventing waste of
time and unnecessary effort.

1. Pilot area

The principle was adopted of a close study of a pilot area
in St Gillis, the re-structuration of which should serve as
an example and an experiment, gradually extending to other
districts. Proposed steps do not involve revolutionary solutions but simple ideas carried out in close collaboration
with the population. It is the inhabitants themselves who
should recreate their city. Decisions can be aided by experts
but they can only be carried into effect with the willingness
of the interested parties. The overall plan envisages shutting off of certain streets for pedestrians only, while the
main routes surrounding the area would be made one-way. It is
planned to create axial routes linking the main centres of
habitation. The streets leading from the "loop" into the
centre will be reserved for local traffic. The existing,
generally ill-used, car-parks will be more logically organized, since it has been shown that by a simple intelligent
planning, these can absorb a number of cars hitherto parked
in the streets. The seminar also thought of an original
solution, consisting of semi-underground car-parks, above which
there would be communal gardens (explained in greater detail
in the car-parks section).

In streets and areas banned to traffic there are plans for
increased grassed areas, benches, play-areas and greater use
of the banks of canals. The conclusion is that, without a
large budget, but with close attention, taking into account
all the problems of a particular district, this district
can be largely given back to its inhabitants, allowing them
pleasant surroundings for walking, playing or life in
general.

2. Lay-out of urban space

This cannot exist without a structural plan. Bruges possesses

one thanks to the Planning Group under the direction of
Prof. Tanghe. This has formed a basis for the seminar's
work, organise the axial zone and divide it into two parts.

1. The cultural axis. Here tourists would find pedestrian
areas freely dotted with centres of cultural interest.

2. A suitably planned commercail axis with enclosed shopping streets, markets, restaurants, covered passageways, and
other social amenities. As concrete evidence, the seminar
showed in one block on a map of Bruges the space now occupied by car-parks - both those existing today, and, if something is not done, those foreseen in the short and long
term. The result was stupifying. The automobile will completely supplant the human being.

3. Pedestrian aids

Even if the pedestrian is given priority over others he is
not necessarily the happier for it. This is especially the
case in Bruges, with its rainy climate and its effect on
housewives burdened with parcels ; also the aged and the
handicapped people.

The seminar considered that an anti-car policy would only
be accepted by the population if it was compensated for by
a number of "aids" (for instance for transporting personal
goods), such as folding caddies which can be taken on to
buses, improved bicycles or tricycles (protected against the
rain), collapsible vehicles for easy and convenient storage.
Example : a small suitcase type vehicle for intra-urban
commuting/shopping which fold down flat and stand on end
when not in use.

There are enormous possibilities if imagination is used to
make the pedestrian's life pleasant.

4. Visual communication

The "pedestrian aid" is also visual. Visual systems of communication have a strong effect not only on the outer harmony of a city but also on general comprehension and safety.

As part of a rational policy the seminar first proposed that
the city should have a service whose job would be to clean
up old and often illegible signs and to unify the actual
design of them. It would also carry out a campaign against
visual pollution caused by the excess of existing signs,
their inadequate size and bad sitting.

On the other hand the seminar proposed more novel forms of
signing such as the use of flags, light projection on to
frontages, beacons for marking walk-ways... or the total

absence of signs altogether, which should at least make
people more helpful towards one another !

II.- <u>CHANGE THE IDEAS</u>

One of the most important basic arguments of the seminar was
that no solution could be achieved unless it came from the
inhabitants themselves. This implies a willingness on the
part of local authorities to integrate the population into
their actions. Too often decisions are taken outside by
councillors, then enforced by heads of police. The course
to follow is, by different means, to make the inhabitants
aware of their real interests, then to give them the chance
to participate in an action. The final aim is to change completely people's attitudes, so that they accept the well-
being of the community over and above their own individual
comforts. In other words there must be a new civic sense.

The seminar had studied the means possible for achieving this
aim and carried out a number of successful on-the-spot tests.
They were :

1. Direct contacts between the authorities and population,
   and public meetins ;
2. The issuing of questionnaires to sound out public opinion
   (In Bruges the group formed by the seminar used this
   method and obtained 50% of the replies in two days) ;
3. By provocation, i.e. certain traffic limitations in order
   to awake public consciousness and stimulate the crowd into
   reacting ;
4. Concerted action on the part of the inhabitants themselves,
   for example the shutting off of a street by legal means,
   so that communal activities, sports and green spaces could
   be developed ;
5. Limited experiments carried out in a pilot area, which
   should then spread outwards (to this effect, the seminar
   had studied the alteration of St Gillis) ;
6. At each stage, obviously, use would be made of the mass
   media ;
7. And why not in any case have an INTERDESIGN ?

INTERDESIGN '75/SERFAUS

Ernst Beranek and Charlotte Blauensteiner
Österreichisches Institut für Formgebung, Vienna

INTERDESIGN'75/SERFAUS, organised under the auspices of ICSID
by the österreichisches Institut für Formgebung, was held from
6 to 2o April 1975, at the Tyrolean village of Serfaus. The
sponsor was the Austrian Minister of Trade. The two themes
chosen for this event were " Local Identity" and " Safety in
Winter Sports". The common denominator of these two themes was
provided by conditions particular to Austria, and this report,
therefore, will be limited to " Local Identity" except for
some cases where close connections to the other theme recommend inclusion.

Identity was defined as the total of all features characteristic and unique for a specific phenomenon. In the first instance, identity is defined by two facts: appearance and behaviour.
Applied to " Local Identity" this would mean how a place looks
to the observer and what it is like to live there.

Local identity naturally has a particular meaning if tourism
is involved, not only in view of what visitors would find
there, but also how a place might develop given permanent contact with guests coming from very different countries with
quite different living habits.

While research into past and present evolutions could produce
important indications for the future and for possible measures
towards a positive development, such research at the same time
could offer a model - not only for similar places and similar
conditions elsewhere, but also, at least in its basic structure, for human settlements in general. This does not mean

that proposals worked out for a small alpine village, for instance, could be applied directly to urban problems.However,
the approach and fundamental insight into the interaction of
environmental problems might well be deduced from these.

The organisers of INTERDESIGN '75/SERFAUS believed that these
problems were exactly what seemed to be a task for designers
cooperating in the spirit and in accordance with the principles worked out for Interdesigns. When inviting participants,
their interest and experience in the described theme were made
important criteria for the choice of the selection committee.
Finally, fourteen designers from eleven countries (Czechos-
lovakia, Finland, the German Democratic Republic, Hungary,
Japan, the Netherlands, Norway, Sweden, the United Kingdom,
the United States and Yugoslavia) together with six colleagues
from Austria gathered for two weeks of intensive work.

The basic situation encountered by the designers was this:

Serfaus is a small village, situated in a high valley above
the Inn river. Altitude 1427 m.
Climate: monthly average of loo sun hours
         188 days of the year under snow.
Ideal for winter sports, but also very inviting in summer. The
summer season should be developed to economic purpose. It is
the intention of the mayor and the community to further any
development aiming at a harmonious balance between local traditions, local inhabitants, and tourism.
Local population of about 85o. History dating back to Roman
times, the mixing of Celtic tribes with Romans resulting in a
specific language, " raetoroman ", of which traces still remain in some names, and in particular housing features.
Peasants in this place were known to have been freed from bon-
dage as far back as the 14th century. Constant division of property - due to a peculiar legal system applied there - resulted
however, in bad living conditions and a draining away of the
population that reached its peak in the 19th century when many

people emigrated to the US. Only with the rise of tourism did
the situation improve, and now most families divide their activities between cattle breeding, some agriculture, and renting
rooms and providing other tourist services.
11 hotels, 12 boarding houses, 8o private rooms (with a total
of about 3,ooo beds), 5 inns, 2 restaurants as opposed to 77
farms. Tourist statistics show an increase from about 7,ooo
people staying for the night in 195o to about 35o,ooo in 1974.
Various sports facilities: funicular, skating, bob, tobogganing
in addition to skiing; swimming, skittles etc.

Generally it was agreed that the main objective should be to
balance the " grown" village structures with the requirements
of modern tourism. Serfaus and its immediate surrounding
(called " sun terrace " and including the neighbouring villages Fiss and Ladis) aim at creating an image which takes into
account present and future developments. Local identity, however, was not seen as being applied to visual appearance only,
but rather as the sum of all characteristic manifestations.
It was found that the typical visual impression was in danger
of being destroyed, and that the old heritage of culture, architecture and crafts should be preserved by every means - always
bearing in mind that a large percentage of the population earns
its living from tourism and that the tourist rightly could expect special facilities. But if the point was reached at which
nothing was left of the typical features tourists expected,
tourism itself would come to a standstill. In addition to other
measures proposed, better contacts between local people and
visitors, and communicative activities, would also help to stop
the alienating effect of purely commercial tourism.

WORKING PROCEDURE

Some weeks before the event, the participants of INTERDESIGN'75
SERFAUS had received a brief containing information on the
history and culture of Serfaus and some statistical data. However, part of the necessary information could only be provided

in the place itself, so during the first five days lectures
were given on regional planning, orientation, architecture and
landscape protection and excursions were arranged to neighbouring villages.

The working procedure that was adopted by the members of the
group dealing particularly with " Local Identity " was
a) to record the actual state of affairs; establish a visual
   impact; point out both positive and negative aspects in
   - environment
   - architecture
   - community services and
   - recreational activities/sports
b) to draw up proposals which may serve as a basis for consideration by the regional authorities as well as the community of Serfaus.

Of course the proposed actions would be overlapping in some
aspects. The method of investigation aimed at concentration on
the following features forming the complex notion of local
identity:

1) Visual elements:	site and settlement
	buildings- heritage and pre-sent -day necessities
	signs and signals -visual communication
2) Structural elements:	planning - by authorities or private
	traffic
	economy
3) Activities:	traditional and artificial
	tourist attractions
	educative measures

RESULTS

Some of the resulting proposals are intended for application
to the complete sun terrace area, some are focused on Serfaus
village only, but the keynote tendency was to stress the cor-

porate image of the region, particularly since financial problems could be more easily solved that way and for the tourist
a more significant impression would result.

This is the list of proposals worked out by INTERDESIGN'75
in accordance with the principles formulated above:

1) Visual elements

   o   a general development plan should be drawn up
   o   ideas and suggestions as to the shaping of a corporate
       regional identity for sun terrace, both visual and verbal,
       should be invited, involving
       - a representative symbol
       - a colour code, and
       - selected media to promulgate same (leaflets, TV spots)
   o   special points of interest in the visual village struc-
       ture should be carefully preserved and/or revitalised i.e.
       - village well to be removed and resited
       - village square with restaurant facilities
   o   planting of trees and shrubs throughout the village area
   o   preservation of monuments - inclusion of private buildings
   o   removal of junk and untidy objects
   o   improvement of the status quo by
       - reduction of wrongly applied architectural elements
       - curbing of billboard advertising
       - renovation of dilapidated barns and fences
   o   standardisation of direction signs and other indications
       for hotels, public services etc., so as to avoid an
       irritating visual impression
   o   redesign of street furniture

2) Structural elements

   o   development of a " regional consciousness" in the so-
       called sun-terrace area should be encouraged.
       The common features in all types of development should
       be stressed without damage to the specific identity of
       each village

o   competitions should be held with a view to obtaining
    proposals for regional concepts
o   a sun-terrace management body should be set up for the
    implementation of such concepts
o   improvement and enlargement of the footpath network for
    hikers
o   southern promenade: creation of a new development zone
    with terraced surfaces on top of new circumference road
o   year- round pedestrian area (presently only in Winter)
    extending to a future multifunctional building serving
    as car park, cafeteria, restaurant etc., to be put up
    in the so-called Apple Tree Gorge just outside the
    village
o   traffic free zones to be converted into a green area
    with community centres
o   extension of the postal motor-bus service
o   a new transport service to and from the sports centres
    (a new type of vehicle was designed)
o   extension of childrens playgrounds
o   unification of lift ticket system (at the moment there
    are too many different types of tickets in a rather
    confusing system)

3) <u>Activities</u>

o   setting up a regional Rent-A-Bike system
o   offering a specific holiday programme, for non-skiers
    also, covering
    - local handicraft and traditions
    - the study of nature and wild life
    - an introduction to local history
    - cooking of local food specialities
o   collecting folklore and samples of local arts and crafts
    for a permanent exhibition (" museum ")
o   putting up a common " kindergarten " for local people
    and tourists' children
o   ski-kindergarten at the departure points of lifts

o   putting new emphasis on local festivals, religious and
    otherwise
o   creating a special " Sun-Terrace Magazine " for tourists,
    including information on history, crafts, tourist events,
    weather and safety regulations
o   extension of sports facilities and programmes

On the final day of INTERDESIGN the fruits of a fortnight's
efforts - written reports, graphic documentation, sketches,
models etc., were shown to the public in an exhibition.

The various contributions - plans, recommendations, analyses -
were visualised on 18o sheets and submitted to the community
of Serfaus and to the authorities that sponsored the meeting-
These results were all " open ended " designs, proposals and
ideas that will need to be finalised.

In some cases, however, the mere fact that problems were discussed was a success. Those who are responsible for decisions
- local and regional - became aware of the importance of taking
an active part in keeping and building a satisfactory environment. The vivid interest shown by the local population - participating in meetings, inviting designers to their houses and
heatedly discussing the proposed solutions - was a first indi-
cation of the spiritual impact starting to work. By mass media
reports and coverage in international magazines - and the resulting feedback of information - a wider cross-section of
people was confronted with the problems involved.

Some suggestions have, in fact, already been carried out. For
instance, the mayor of Serfaus has introduced legal measures
for state participation in building the ring road. The idea
of a regional corporate identity is being negotiated in the
communities. The methods and organisation of this INTERDESIGN
are being investigated for application to similar situations.
The Ministry of Trade has promised to further all official proposals arising from the INTERDESIGN work. Several associations
- both federal and private - have shown interest in making use

of the results.

In view of the WERC objectives, INTERDESIGN'75/SERFAUS may
offer but little material contribution; still we firmly believe
that it is the idea of creating and maintaining the human scale
in all kinds of settlements and under the most extreme conditions that must be the basis also for WERC's work. And in that
sense the study of a small village and its problems can serve
as an useful approach to phenomenons encountered in cities of
many millions.

Fig.1. Serfaus today: characteristic view contrasting to
negative examples

STRESS IN CITIES

R.H. Ferahian
Consulting Engineer,
Montreal, Canada

ABSTRACT

To ensure the well-being of citizens under the ever accelerating
rate of urbanization on our planet, psycho-social stresses arising from urban living will become an increasingly important area
of consideration by planners of future cities. This paper enum-
erates the suspected stressors, considers some in detail, and
emphasizes the research needs to enable us anticipate emerging
conditions and plan for man's total health through education, legislation, and design.

INTRODUCTION

It took from early years of Christianity until the start of the
17th century for the population of our planet to double to 500
million. Only less than 250 years later in 1850, it had doubled
again to its first billion. By 1930, it had reached its second
billion and by 1968, its third(1). The present doubling time
for the world population is 33 years and for the urban population
is about 15 years. Today, about one and a half billion people
live in cities of more than 20,000 inhabitants. Two billion are
rural. By the year 2000, the critical change will have taken
place. There will then be 3½ to 4 billion living in cities, and
only 3 billion in the country. This will be our fateful change
to a different kind of planet--an urban planet(2). It is estimated that by then almost all Canadians will be living in cities(3).

Millions of years on this planet have formed man into what he is
today. For survival, he learned to live in harmony with the natural environment with a definite rhythm and pace of life. Since
the industrial revolution with all its blessings, however, man
has been subjected to an ever increasing rate of change in his
life mode, and for the first time in history he has acquired a
dimension of power which now makes his own activities the principal determinant of his future(1,4,5). Some studies(4) have projected rather alarming consequences within the next century if
man does not change his life style and his incessant demands on
the limited resources of our planet. Alarming though these unchecked consequences can be, the reality may well be even more
serious because practically all these studies have not taken into
account the psycho-social stresses man has been subjected to
as a result of this unprecedentally fast rate of change in his

life mode and the pressures involved in living in a highly industrialized urban society(1). Individual behavior depends far
more than previously assumed on the quality of the social environment which itself is affected by the physical environment. It
is with this in mind that we have to plan our cities(6).

URBAN STRESS

There is a great deal of speculation as to the causes of stress*
in urban life. Scientists such as Selye(7,10), Dubos(8) and
Levi(9-11) have concluded that stress arises from the clash of
man's age-old biological, psychological, and social make-up with
his technological, rapidly changing urban world; that the very
adaptive processes which enabled man to survive and thrive in the
past now elicit physical and mental distress and malfunction.
There are two suspected sources of this psycho-social stress:
the industrialized, urbanized society with its rapid rate of change, and the overcrowded, noisy, polluted urban environment that
today more than 1½ billion people call home(11-13).

The urban environment can act as a source of stress in a multit-
ude of ways through its settlement and population densities, through its urban structure, through the design of its supply systems and their side effects, and finally through the organization of the urban areas and the problem arising from specialization of groups and individuals, inadequate housing, co-operation
and integration of minorities and others. The urban supply systems and their side effects comprise: 1) Communication technology with its mass influence, information overload and overstimul-
ation; 2) Transportation technology with its tiring journeys, traffic accidents, difficulty of access to various facilities, noise
and air pollution and visual degradation of the countryside, and
3) Energy, water, sewer and garbage disposal systems with their
noise, air and water pollution(11-13)**. Crowding studies, for instance, have shown overcrowding to be a major producer of stress
leading to high rates of such physical and social disorders as infant mortality, psychotic behavior, sexual abnormalities, violent
aggression and others(14). Millions of dollars are spent every
year in hospital bills for the treatment of mental disorders and
the cost increases annually as we become more aware of the disorders.

---

*   Stress is defined according to Selye(7) as the nonspecific re-
     sponse of the body to any demand made upon it. It is one of
     the mechanisms leading to distress and disease.

**   These suspected stressors were first enumerated by Carlestam
     & Levi(11).

Seeking an Answer

Studies by architects, social scientists and psychologists have
shown the therapeutic effect of a properly built environment and
its effect on the morale, health and happiness of the occupants
as well as their work efficiency(15-18). So it is probably logical to assume that there must be a relationship between man's
behavior and the environment he lives in, perceives, responds to,
and acts upon(8,18-20). If so, should we not determine these relationships and make sure our built environment contributes to
our physical and mental health(18,21-24)? The urgency of this
issue is apparent when it is remembered that in order to house
and provide for population needs by the end of this century, the
volume of construction it is estimated will equal construction
from the dawn of civilization until today.

Interdisciplinary research is needed within the system comprising man, his health(physical, mental and spiritual) and the built
environment to identify the major sources of stress and work towards their elimination through education, legislation and design
(6,12-13). The need for this research cannot be overemphasized
and the need will increase exponentially with the increasing urban populations which are now globally doubling every 15 years.
Any system can stop functioning because of overload failures,and
this research is needed to anticipate emerging conditions and
correct them before it is too late.

Because of the complex interdisciplinary nature of the problems
involved and the paucity of conclusive published information a
detailed cause-and-effect treatment of all these stressors cannot
be presented within the short format of this introductory paper.
Of these factors mentioned earlier, the design of the urban structure and supply systems for projected settlement densities, and
environmental pollution come within the domain of the civil engineer and his concern for quality of life. Air and water pollution have been extensively covered but the environmental and social accounting principles and the regulatory legislation does not
seem to be coming fast enough. In what follows, some further observations will be offered about noise, transportation systems,
and the design of the urban structure. Environmental pollution
will also be treated within the context of Quality of Life Indicators needed to gauge the state of health of our cities and
society·

NOISE

In the technologically advanced societies, noise has increased to
such high levels that it is considered as serious a problem as air
pollution. From 1948 to 1963, the number of cars in Europe increased from 5 to 34 million and even at higher rate since then,
polluting and shattering the once enviable quiet of European Cities. It is estimated that more than 100 million people on the
North American continent may experience gradual partial deafness
due to noise. The incidence of hearing loss in children exposed
to high intensity sounds in their recreation environment is now
not only common but increasing at an alarming rate. Industrial

noise costs North America alone billions of dollars annually in
compensation payments in hearing loss, decreased efficiency and
loss of production. It is medically proven that loud sounds cause blood vessels to constrict, the skin to pale, muscles to ten-
se and adrenal hormones to be injected in the blood stream. It
is likely, moreover, that the psychological complications from
noise pollution will have a more profound effect upon people than
direct physical damage. According to W.H. Stewart former U.S.
Surgeon General: "Calling noise a nuisance is like calling smog
inconvenience. Noise must be considered a hazard to health
everywhere."

A Task Force discussion paper(25) published by the Canadian Council of Resources and Environment Ministers reached the conclusion that all three levels of government in Canada have not done
enough to provide adequate anti-noise legislation.Effective up-
to-date codes coupled with the use of acoustic engineers could
help planners, architects and engineers design better buildings
and cities. The slight additional cost of these acoustic designs
is negligible compared to the long-term national gain. The public must ask for better zoning and quieter machinery for industry , private transport, mass transit and the building trades. In
addition, mass transit should be given higher priority than in
the past to decrease the use of private cars in our cities. The
public will have to foot the bill to mute the ever-increasing
roar of its cities, but this will be a very small price to pay
for its health.

SETTLEMENT DENSITIES & OVERCROWDING

During an international conference on tall buildings held in
Bangkok(26) in 1974, the warning echoed that the world will run
out of agricultural land in 30 years if the cities continue their
present rate of expansion. Over the last decade, it is estimated that Toronto's growth has meant a loss of 30 acres of prime
agricultural land every day. The costs of sprawl especially its
encroachment on precious agricultural land cannot go uncontrolled.
With increasing urbanisation there will be greater pressure to
plan cities with higher densities because they also entail lower
personal, economic, environmental costs and natural resource de-
pletion(27).

Dense concentrations of people are one of the generators of flourishing city diversity. It is very hard however to determine what
are proper or optimum densities for city dwellings as this is very
much a function of performance of the city(28). Certainly there
must be some critical upper bounds to population densities. These
are set however not so much by physical but psychological, social
and cultural factors(11,29).

High settlement densities should not be confused with overcrowding. With appropriate planning and design high settlement densities can be achieved without overcrowding. Overcrowding occurs
only if by economic necessity of the occupants or design of the
housing project, the amount of space allocated per person is less
than an acceptable amount. In public places for short periods of

time less space is acceptable than that needed in private areas.
But what is acceptable is very much culturally and socially det-
ermined(11,29). Even though the census definition of overcrowding in Canada and the U.S. is 1.5 or more persons per room(the
room size is not defined), this will most probably not be so perceived by dwellers of a low-income housing project in Hong Kong.

Acoording to Chombart de Lauwe's studies(30) of the family life
of French workers, on the averge 16 square metres is an essential
minimum of space for each person. Disorders begin to appear below 14 square metres. Severe disorders and antisocial activity
are found below 8-10 square metres. In contrast, studies of the
relationship between population density and psychosomatic and social pathology in Hong Kong(31), a city with probably the highest residential densities in the world, indicate a corresponding
median crowding index of about 4 square metres with no comparable
'strains'.

Certainly overcrowding, as mentioned earlier(14,29) cand lead to
major physical and social disorders. Generalizations about the
threshold crowding indices are not possible, however, because
they are a function of such a diverse set of parameters and not
enough data is available to account for them. Although there is
published data showing mortality indices for some of the crowded
big cities are higher than those for areas of lower settlement
densities, there is not enough information to determine conclus-
ively the cause of these diseases. It is hard to determine, for-
example, whether these higher mortality indices are due to the
higher settlement densities or due to other causes such as pollution. Moreover, there are instances where the mortality indices
and the incidence of diseases are lower for the areas with higher
settlement densities(32). Similar uncertainties are apparent regarding criminality indices and suicide rates in cities(11). Long-
term research, possibly lasting for several generations, are needed to determine the correlations between incidence of diseases
and social pathologies and settlement densities and crowding
indices.

High settlement densities can be achieved without resorting to
wind swept canyons of tall gigantic buildings. It is a matter of
careful planning. Although some believe that living in high-rise
buildings is notconducive to mental health(23), tall buildings
are inevitable but they should not be allowed to proliferate and
care must be taken to ensure that they add to the quality of city
life(26). Good design with emphasis on human well-being, aesthetic needs, and harmonious integration in the environment are paramount because these buildiing'in no small way represent the destiny of the human race through the quality of living they will
help to shape'*.

---

* Quoted by Dr. E.K. Timby in the conference mentioned in refer-
  ence(26).

TRANSPORTATION SYSTEMS

The present form of the city and urban life in Canada and the U.S are to a large extent shaped and determined by the automobile. There is no doubt that the automobile made man freer and more independent in providing door-to-door travel in comfort. But with their increasing numbers, the machine that made North America mobile is now making it less livable. Some concerned transport experts wonder whether it is possible to be urbanized and motorized and at the same time civilized.

In North American cities, motor vehicles contribute a major part ,in some 75% if not more, of the air pollution and noise. They voraciously consume large quantities of land for parking,roads, and highways,breaking up neighbourhoods and uprooting residents. The loss of prime agricultural land to urban sprawl caused to a large extent by the automobile has been accelerating at a disturing rate as mentioned earlier(26,27). Moreover driving under the present polluted congested conditions is to many, if not extemely tiring, a cause of irritation and nervous tension. Lastly, the visual damage done by some roads, highways and car parks to town and country,though difficult to assess objectively, will be increasingly regreted by society.

'Motor vehicle accidents in 1974 caused over 6000 deaths and more than 230,000 injuries in Canada. The dollar cost is estimated at $1.3-billion in property damage, another billion in lost work time, and $250-million in medical bills.'* The corresponding figures for the U.S must be about ten times those for Canada, and similar ones can be quoted for Europe.

When these environmental and social costs are considered in conjunction with the energy costs of producing(33) and using(34) the automobile, the owner and user of the private automobile,especially when carrying no other passengers, must be responsible enough to realize that he is indulging in a dangerous luxury with great public costs. 'If we agree that we can not afford such scandalous waste of people and resources, then we must consider accepting a more reasonable balance between our freedom to own and drive a car, and restrictions on the way we use that car.'* For public well-being, the private automobile may well have to be banned from certain parts of the city. Taxes must be so levied to encourage the use of small, less polluting, energy-efficient cars. Most important of all,more emphasis must be placed on providing efficient,comfortable,and attractive public transportation with the aim first of increasing the efficiency of existing transportation facilities.

Urban planners have become increasingly concerned about the social impact of highway construction(35,36). These concerns have been aided by the public's resistance to the construction of new highways especially when they are planned to pass through the cities.

---

* Extracted from Prime Minister Pierre Elliot Trudeau's address to the Canadian Club in Ottawa on the 'New Society' reproduced by The Toronto Globe and Mail, January 20, 1976.

In the United States these concerns have been institutionalized in the National Environmental Policy Act(there is not an equivalent Act in Canada), which requires all Federal Agencies to submit a detailed statement which assesses the impact of any proposed change on the human environment. But still, the environmental and social, including the psycho-social, costs of transportation have not entered in the majority of the cost-benefit analysis models of transportation systems. They must be considered and the appropriate social and environmental accounting principles developed to realistically evaluate the costs of transport.

Maximizing Access

As the city is essentially a tool for communication, its transport services can be seen as part of the information system that comprises the city. As good transport services and high mobility are indispensible for the functioning of an industrialized society, it is essential that the transportation and communication systems be planned to optimize communication and access to urban services, thus minimizing the need for transportation(12,13).

Endeavors must be made to plan self-contained neighbourhoods where the inhabitants live, work and spend their leisure time. In the future people may not need to move from their residences to work, but work may be moved to them. Advances in cybernetics and computer technology may make this feasible in the near future, espcially for the workers involved in the research and information fields who could communicate through computer consoles available in their homes(3,13).

QUALITY-OF-LIFE INDICATORS

Indicators most frequently used for gauging the state of our society have been economic in nature such as the GNP and growth. But while unquestionably essential, these economic indicators do not adequately reflect many of the major dimensions of the social system. The calculations of the GNP overstate benefits and understate costs. The GNP of the nation is not a measure of the health of its population; nor is it a measure of the stability and quality of its environmental,including urban,systems and the degree of depletion of its natural resources. Moreover, the GNP is a measure of the activities of society based on the gainfully employed only; it does not account for the contribution of those who are not gainfully employed, e.g. mothers,families, voluntary workers,the unemployed and others.

The concerns of society have greatly bradened in recent years. The philosophy of economic growth as an end in itself is being challenged(4,37); the concept of the conserver and conserving society being explored; and environmental quality control demanded(3). For planning and policy formulation the financial and economic criteria, which business and government currently use, are being extended to include criteria for the environment,human beings and society(38). There is evolution from purely economic point of view and the GNP to the social point of view and the GSP, the gross social product(39). The GSP is based on the contribution of all members of society(gainfully and nongainfully employed)

discounted by the environmental and social costs of this contrib-
ution(39). Air and water pollution in some of our cities are
major health hazards and it costs nationally billions of dollars
in damage to person and property. Any indicator which does not
account for these costs can not be considered a measure of the
quality of life. Thus, the GSP is a more realistic measure of
the state of the society than the GNP.

Economic indicators are only a unit out of the quality-of-life
indicators needed to gauge the degree of satisfaction of society's basic goals- wellbeing and equity among its members. Environmental and social costs of these so-called 'economic' decisions must be evaluated and the corresponding accounting principles
developed and perfected. The 1974 Annual Report of the Economic
Council of Canada(40) included for the first time in conjunction
with the economic indicators selected environmental and social
indicators- housing indicators(crowding indices and rent or value
per room as a percentage of income), health indicators(life exp-
ectancy, infant mortality,and prime age mortality), and an environmental indicator to measure the levels of polluton in the cities.
This is the first step towards a comprehensive indicator system.

Stress Indicators

According to Selye(7):"As far as we know, our reserve of adaptat-
ional energy is an inherited finite amount which can not be reg-
enerated. Vitality is like a special kind of bank account which
we can use by withdrawals but not increase by deposits. The intelligent thing to do is to withdraw generously but never expend
wastefully". Boulding(41) advises in a similar vein:"The essential measure of the success of the economy is not production and
consumption at all, but the nature,extent,quality,and complexity
of the total capital stock,including in this the state of the human bodies and minds included in the system. ... I am inclined to
think of being well fed as being more important than eating,and
even to think of so-called services as essentially involving the
restoration of a depleting psychic capital". According to Schumacher:"The modern industrial economy lives on irreplacable capital which it cheerfully treats as income". He mentions that the
three categories of this irreplacable capital are our fossil
fuels,the tolerance margin of nature and human substance. He advises planning for peace,beauty,and permenance rather than continued material growth,domination,and change(37).

The present energy and fuel crisis has helped towards the realiz-
ation(hopefully not temporary) of the irreplacable nature of our
fuels and the need for conservation, but the tolerance margins of
nature and human substance seem to be taken nonchalantly. Very
little is known about the tolerance margins of nature and its carrying capacity and even less about man. How much change can he
adapt to and still remain human? A report released recently in
Nairobi by the UN Environmental Secretariat warns that human settlement patterns,like movement of people from the fresh air of
the country to the increasingly polluted cities,could lead to genetic mutations. Moreover, the psychological insecurity of living
in an unhealthy environment must not be underestimated as a stre-
ssor with possibly dangerous longterm consequences.

In the future,there will be an increasing need for a comprehensive system of quality-of-life indicators. With the increasing
percentage of the populace living in cities, there will even be
more need for criteria for judging the quality of the urban en-
vironment(42). There may very well be need for psycho-social
stress indicators. Will they be a measure of the rate of change
in man's living environment? How are they to be defined and
evaluated will require more research and information about the
suspected psycho-social stressors mentioned earlier.

DESIGNING HEALTHY CITIES

Even when large, a good city- well designed to the human scale
and planned to enhance human values- can promote not only economic but also social goals. One of the major problems is how to
create a physical structure that meets the demands of all its inhabitants, including individuals, groups(formed by age, sex,or
handicap), enterprises and others. To carry out effective environmental planning, it is necessary to specify the needs of each
group as well as the sources of satisfaction, malaise, stress
and maladaptation during each portion of their life cycle and
then finding ways of translating these life-cycle requirements
into the living environment. Although there has been some progress made in this area, especially in connection with user's requirements in buildings, the subject is virtually unexplored.

The discovery of the direct relationship between environment and
social behavior and its impact on the sense of responsibility,
happiness and total health of the individual is probably the most
important of present human tasks. The urban environment invades
all our senses. It has been shown that sensory monotony inhibits
the working of the higher brain; that with too many disorganized
sensations the brain system shuts down to preserve its equilibrium, and that organized sensory variety is a biological need as
real as hunger. We need,therefore,to make our cities beautiful,
integral and livable places. Our rivers must be cleaned and their banks designed for the enjoyment of the people. Streets must
not be just for flow of cars, cluttered with chaotic array of ad-
vertising signs and neon lights, but areas where people can walk,
sit, shop and enjoy life. The city must not be just a dormitory
of drab monotonous housing units and filing cabinets of offices,
banks, stores and schools from which people flee during the week-
ends to the ever-receding countryside. It must be a place where
man can live with dignity, security and harmony, where the great
achievements of modern civilization and the ageless pleasures
afforded by natural and built beauty are available to all. This
is not a romantic dream but an urgent need for man's sanity and
the survival of our civilization(12,13).

REFERENCES

1) Toffler, A., Future Shock, Random House, New York, 1970.
2) Ward, B., An Urban Planet, Ekistics 217, 428-33 (1973).
3) Kelly, F.(ed.), Science Council of Canada, Perceptions 1, Population Growth and Urban Problems. Information Canada, Ottawa, 1975.
4) Meadows, D.H., et al, The Limits of Growth, Universe Book, New York, 1972.
5) Mesarovic, M. and Pestel, E., Mankind at the Turning Point, Reader's Digest Press, New York, 1974.
6) Ferahian, R.H., Discussion to: A Society for the Built Environment, by Sir Ove Arup, Institution of Civil Engineers, London, 1972.
7) Selye, H., The Stress of life, McGraw Hill, New York, 1956.
8) Dubos, R., So Human an Animal, Charles Scribner's Sons, New York, 1968.
9) Levi, L., Stress: Sources, Management and Prevention - Medical and Psychological Aspects of Stress of Everyday life, Liveright, New York, 1967.
10) Levi, L.,(ed.), Society, Stress and Diseases: The Psycho--Social Environment and Psychosomatic Diseases, Oxford University Press, London, New York, Toronto, 1971.
11) Carlestam, G. and Levi, L., Urban Conglomerates as Psycho-Social human stressors. General Aspects, Swedish Trends, and Psychological and Medical Implications, Norstdet et Soner, Stockholm, 1971.
12) Ferahian, R.H., Discussion to: Desirable Urban Environments by Roy Sellors, Engineering Journal, 56/9, 31-32(1973).
13) Ferahian, R.H., Stress in Cities, Habitat, 18/2, 29-30(1975).
14) Martin, L.E., Mental Health/Mental Illness: Revolution in Progress, McGraw-Hill, New York, 1970.
15) Bayes, K., and Franklin, S.(ed.),Designing for the Handicapped, George Godwin, London, 1971.
16) Jourdan, A. de, Specialized Housing Helps Mentally Retarded, Habitat, 16, Nos. 1&2, 2-5,(1973).
17) Good, L.R., et al, Therapy by Design, C.C. Thomas Publishers Springfield,(1965).
18) Proshansky, H.M. et al(eds.), Environmental Psychology: Man and Physical Setting, Holt, Reinhardt and Winston, 1970.
19) Honikman, B.,(ed.), Proceedings of the Architectural Psychology Conference, Kingston, RIBA, London, 1970.
20) Lee, T., The Effect of the Built Environment on Human Behavior, Ekistics, 200, 20-24, (1972).
21) Lord Taylor et al, Mental Health & Environment, Longmans, London, 1964.
22) Moller, C.B., Architectural Environment and Our Mental Health, Horizon Press, New York, 1968.
23) Cappon, D., Mental Health in the Hi-rise, Ekistics, 196, 192-195, (1972).
24) Human Health and Human Settlements, Ekistics, 220, 37,(1974).
25) Canadian Council of Resources and Environment Ministers, Resources, 2, No.6, Part 1, Montreal, (1973).

26) Tall Buildings must Add to Quality of City Life, New Civil Engineer, London, February 14,(1974).

27) CEQ-HUD-EPA(Sponsors), The Costs of Sprawl, 1-2, U.S.Government Printing Office, Washington, 1974.

28) Jacobs, J., The Death and Life of Great American Cities, A Vintage Book, New York, 1961.

29) Hall, E.T., The Hidden Dimension, Doubleday Anchor Book, New York, 1966.

30) Lauwe, Chombart De, as quoted in Refs.(11) and (29).

31) Mitchell, R.E., Some Social Implications of High Density Housing, American Sociological Review, 36, 18-29, (1971). Quoted in Ref.(11).

32) Ref.28, page, 206.

33) Berry, R.S. and Fels, M.F., The Energy Cost of Automobiles, Science & Public Affairs, 11-17, December,(1973).

34) Hirst, E., Transportation Energy Use and Conservation Potential, Science & Public Affairs, 36-42, November(1973). (Some of the statistics are now rendered obsolete because of the increased prices of petroleum).

35) U.S. Department of Transportation, Social & Economic Effects of Highways, Federal Highway Administration, Washington, 1974.

36) Townroe, P.M.,(ed.), Social and Political Consequences of the Motor Car, David and Charles, London, 1974.

37) Schumacher, E.F., Small is Beautiful-Economics as if People Mattered, Harper and Row, New York(1973).

38) Simmonds, W.H.C., Bridging the Chasm-The Next-Step, Technological Forcasting and Social Change, 6, 267-276,(1974).

39) Simmonds, W.H.C., Industrial Behavior Patterns: A new dimension for planners, Futures, August(1975).

40) Economic Council of Canada, Eleventh Annual Report, Economic Targets & Social Indicators, Information Canada, Ottawa, 1974.

41) Boulding, K.E., The Economics of Coming Spaceship Earth, in Bell, G. de(ed.), The Environmental Handbook, 96-101, Ballantine, New York, 1970.

42) Blumenfeld, H., Criteria for Judging the Quality of the Urban Environment, Contact, 6, No.4/5, Faculty of Environmental Studies, University of Waterloo, Ontario,(1974).

INSTITUTIONAL RESPONSES TO THE NEEDS OF PEOPLE

Alberto Cannetta, Architect
National Research Council, Milan, Italy

I firmly believe that this conference and the world conference in
Vancouver can be an important step forward down the road to   an
effective democratic management of our environment in our cities;
a step that leads to that process called citizen participation
which we think is the only possible alternative to the disastrous
management of all or almost all the cities of the world.   The
city is a machine that no longer functions either because it is
often badly planned or because it is badly used.   Its structures
and its infinite possibilities attract thousands of new citizens
each day in every part of the world, but the majority of these
citizens then discover that these services are unattainable in
their cases due to economic, cultural and social reasons.   Even
those citizens who have always lived in the city, but who belong
to those less privileged classes who would therefore be the most
needy or most conditioned for the quality of their lives by these
services, are for economic reasons slowly pushed toward those
parts of the city which offer only the form and disadvantages of
the actual city.   One can verify here how our materialistic
society has created more problems that it is able to resolve for
the vast majority of its citizens.   However the citizen who is so
frustrated in his aspirations becomes a potential enemy of those
who actually manage the city, rendering even the most correct solutions almost impossible.

His state of dissatisfaction is transformed into a battle against
everything.   Often, as we can witness in all our cities, this
frustration becomes civil violence.   Even the quiet, model citizen, and sometimes the most progressive in his public requests
conditioned as he is by the consumer society, can be extremely
reactionary in his private choices.

It is very easy to say that only a city which meets the needs of
its citizens can be defined a "livable" city, but do we really
know what these needs are if the citizens themselves do not know?
We can even say that only a city planned with the collaboration
of its citizens can be governed with the same collaboration.   But
how can this process of public participation come about - also
when the structures have been created - if the citizens do not
realize the actual dimension of the problem concerning human
settlements?   Consequently information and extended knowledge to
all social strata becomes one of the fundamental problems.   It is

precisely for this reason that I believe that this conference, as well as that in Vancouver, will be of great importance within the limits of knowing how to leave this tight circle of technicians in order to comunicate and involve all those on the outside who are the real managers of the solutions we are examining and without whose participation such solutions would certainly not give the desired results.

Information and especially the monopoly of such information has been in the past, and still is, one of the principal points on which power is based. If we want this power to be governed in a democratic manner, then we must destroy this monopoly of information. However the problem of socialization of information is not only, in my opinion, tied to the fact of a more vast dissemination of information, but more to a different system of comunication. We must actually pass from an illuministic culture that comunicates only through ideas to a culture that can comunicate with the evidence of facts, that knows how to distinguish the fundamental parameters so that experiences can be analyzed and comunicated. This, so as to create a series of alternative models that actually permit the citizens to choose, with the clearest possible knowledge, the results of the hypotheses being advanced and knowledge of the facts reached. I am in full agreement with Harold Chestnut when he points out that the city is a system in which information can be gathered, analyzed and compared with the other system-cities in order that any negative experiences are not blindly repeated by other groups.

This will also allow the citizens to better understand the impact between public and private needs --- we have requests for quiet urban areas and the blind habit of always having to use the car. But also the desire for a house that privately reproduces what, up to a few years ago, was public and in many civilizations still is a social space, without useless multiplications that often create an unbearable economic weight for society. This, in my opinion, is one of the most important problems to be faced with citizen participation and would certainly be a very dangerous one if faced without their collaboration. The reduction of private housing standards is of absolute necessity in all those countries that today find themselves face to face, as my own country, with the problem of housing millions of citizens with absolutely inadequate financial means. But after fifty years of consumer models that have helped to create in us the desire for a house as a place to isolate ourselves from social life, this reduction can not be accepted without a profound requalification of social services that produces an alternative to private isolation and above all without having given the woman who today, in many of our societies is still a prisoner within the home, all those structures which will allow for her to fully participate in the city. We must pass from housing standards to social standards.

The citizen who sees his buying power diminishing with each pay check due to the continual rise in prices, should be guaranteed a kind of "social salary" as Roberto Guiducci would call it. This salary would include services, facilitations, alternative possibilities for a simpler working life. Therefore breaking away from the routine that today makes up our lives and what the French students in 1968 referred to as <u>metro-bulot-dodo</u>; all this in order to begin a positive process in which participation in a social life is one of the principal factors in the quality of life.

For many of our cities this is a step that must be taken. As many have repeated many times over, our cities are finished. Finished in the sense that even only for a question of lack of space, any extension on their part has become impossible, rendering them ungovernable. However, within our cities everything is still to be done to meet the needs of our citizens. We must invent new structures as instruments which allow for a real participation on behalf of our citizens in the transformation and governing of our cities. We must substitute the old myth of the development plan, the town project, as an instrument that only regulates the exploitation of certain areas, with instruments of analysis of the municipal budgets in order to include not only the phase of the actual project for services but also the phase of governing, which considers renovation and transformation as new needs arise. We must invent new instruments that permit us to analyze all experiences even and above all those which are considered negative.

All this in order to reach a consciousness and knowledge of the result of our actions which only permits unanimous agreement. Unanimity which is indispensable for a correct use of our cities. We must also go beyond the concept of democratic decisions by the majority because a minority in dissent can put any project in crisis. But unanimity can be acquired only if we can comunicate at all levels with the evidence of facts. This information process is the principal aspect of our work.

Only when we have learned to work together with our citizens for other citizens will we be able to win the battle which, alone, up to now, we have been losing.

Modern Technology for Cities of Today

Transportation in cities is considered as very important to their life. Heavy automobile traffic is much questionned as opposed to public transport.

Ms . F. DUESBERG shows as an example how separate lanes for public transport are part of a solution. She stresses that traffic problems in our cities cannot be solved by using traffic techniques only but these must be in accordance with a general traffic policy and a general planning policy defining objectives for the whole city. The values of traffic and transportation techniques resting in the purpose they serve, "soft" or light solutions, having following characteristics, must be emphasized : low costs, low energy consumption, short execution delays, no harm to the city, flexibility, attractiveness to users. Among existing techniques, one immediately available is the use of reserved lanes and streets for trams and buses which can be a precious tool if they are integrated into a complete and diversified traffic and transportation system and are created with the aim of faciliting the movements of pedestrians, cyclists, public vehicles, whatever the sacrifices imposed to automobilists. A clear choice between priority to public transportation or the car must be done. The fondamental of the matter is likely a transformation of mentalities. This can be helped.

Ms . DUESBERG was asked

> by FERREIRA for the amounts of people transported in Belgium on
> private and public transportation and the expenditure of money for
> these five modes of transportation by the community, and which are
> the pedestrian benefits.

The figures requested are given in Miss DUESBERG's answer here below:

1. Data concerning trips to work, Belgium, whole country

| | % of the active population | |
	Men	Women
Private car	65.91	58.71
Public transportation	18.84	25.85
Walk—Bicycle—Motor—cycle	15.24	20.44

The relatively high proportion of people using a car to go to work
should not be considered as a norm — as a good reason for investing
more money into road works. We should not forget that there is no
real free choice : many people are "prisoners of the car", because
they have no adequate public transportation at their disposal. And
many others are captive of public transportation because they do not
have the financial means or the abilities to drive a car.
(N.B. Belgium : 2.5 million cars for 10.5 million people).

2. Data concerning investments.

State budget 1974, budget of communication 104 billion Bfr:

Tramway, subway, buses	9,4 %
Railroads	19,0 %
Roads	43,2 %
Others	28,4 %

So, in the budget devoted to both roads and public transportation, there is about 60 % for the former and 40 % for the latter.

The rate of growth of investments in favour of the car is also higher
than in favour of public transportation. And the trend is very difficult
to change, because it is unthinkable for the government to go backward,
even if many authorities recognize that the planned road investments
(highway) are harmful and/or unnecessary

Mr. W. OWEN develops similar conceptions, insisting on the need to
have both technologies and systems of management that supply transportation and the design and location of community activities that generate
the demand for transportation. On the transportation side, focus should
be on low-cost solutions that organize existing facilities more effectively
and rely primarily on surface public transit, with exclusive rights of
way when necessary. Such solutions include improving bus transit and the
public automobile or group-riding taxi. An integrated traffic management
strategy should include pricing policies that charge the motorist his
full costs, preferential treatment for buses, computerized signal systems
and other uses of electronics, street parking prohibition, pedestrian
zones, street enforcement of traffic rules, routing of through traffic
away from the center staggered work hours and staggered days of work.

On the side of design of community activities, a serie of clustered
activities that provide easy access by local transport or pedestrian
pathways to neighborhood markets or centers, and that are provided with
nearly employment opportunities and recreation, seems preferable.

Mr. GAMBLE was asked

by Mr. FERAHIAN for "noise-impact" and for property loss figures
for which the answer was that 35 dB (A) would be the limit above

which "impact" will be belt and property loss occurs.

by Mr. BREMNER for the terms of reference and comments whet should

be done to abate noise. Gamble's answer indicated both education

and legislative measures to be taken to curb the noise.

by Mr. ARORA about the effects of noise in case of more than one lane;

this question was left unanswered.

by Mr. DORNBUSCH about the isolation of the noise influence from other

covariant influences such as visual impact of the highway, visual

muisance, etc. The answer gave the impression that the speaker

stuck to the noise only in his paper.

by Mr. COHEN for the public sector's role in reducing the pollution

not only by noise but also by trash, emissions, sewage, etc.

Technical solutions are not valid alone; we need attitudional

education also. In his answer Mr. GAMBLE stated that out problmes

are both technical and social (economic, political, socio-

psychological) in their origin. Consequently, all these aspects

have to be addressed simultaneously.

Mr. FUNK was asked

by Mr. JONES whether he has given any thought at all to the energy

demand of his purification systems. In his answer Mr. FUNK indicated

that in all three presented cases there is really a firm economical

background and the processes can be operated with profit in each case.

Mr. KAS KALBA was asked

by Mr. POLUMIN for the possible reduction of the individual travel

and transport by telecommunications technology. In his answer

Mr. KALBA indicated the very complexity of the problem, in certain

cases telecommunications will increase travel, in some decrease, in every case telecommunication will increase demand for all forms

of information.

by Mr. FERAHIAN for the energy increase caused by modern telecommu-

nications. In his answer Mr. KALBA indicated that all forms of

telecommunication tend to decrease the common demand for energy.

In the "Ecological Basis of the Urban Situation", Mr. A. BOURNE,

the author, indicates that the live of human species being based on energy

provided by the ecosystem, the availability of this energy is an absolute

limitation to existence and growth of mankind. Homo sapiens can only

maintain his population growth if he can increase his energy base. However,

he absorbs more land through urbanisation that can be rought into cultivation.

To maintain the present production of the agricultural base, additional

fossil fuel energy imputs in the form of fertilizers pesticides and irrigatior

are required but the ressources in fossil fuel energy will be exhausted

within a few generation. A new equilibration has to be reached if mankind

is willing to find a solution to this dilemma. In the long term, it seems

certain that the human population will be either voluntarily or

involuntarily reduced. In the short term, the pressure of population

will increase the disruption of the urban way of life : its very vulnerabi-

lity makes this certain unless swift remedial action is taken. Mr. BOURNE

suggests that the answer is the establishment of much smaller settlements

sited close to their food-producing land, water and energy supplies with

less dependance on supplementary energy. Concomitantly, population policies

must ensures settlements are not living beyont their maons.

Future of man lies in his ability to design a way of life within

the constraints that Nature imposes. If he does not, growing disenchantment,

higher costs of maintening our urban civilisation and lastly escalating intra-

specific competition with its accompanying violence and destruction will
occur.

Mr. R. NOVICK makes a review of the environmental factors associated
with ill health in human settlements, health problems and remedial actions.
Among these are methods for improving the state of imbalance between
population and ressources.

Mr. NOVICK was asked

by Mr. FERAHIAN whether WHO include psychological or mental health
in their investigations. The answer was yes but indicated limited
amount of information being now available. References were given.

Summary of the Monday Sessions By U. Luoto

Modern technology and its application to our development, which so much
has expanded society's possibilities in many ways, has on the other hand
created innumerous new problems. For example technical development has
caused an enormous amount of pollution, espacially in our urban habitat.

Automobiles cause traffic congestion, noise and air pollution.
Factories pollute the air and water and in many cases also the soil. Waste
management is utterly inefficient. We are not returning valuable raw
materials contained in the waste back to the circulation but rather dump
them in places where they remain inaccessible and cause only pollution.

Not understanding the natural balance of our ecosystem we have
created havoc with our environment. Chopping down complete forests, we
have created man-made deserts and reversed climatic conditions completely.
Overburdening the ground water system we have created sinking cities.
Current urban development makes the automobile not only a necessity but

also a status symbol and we have effectively restricted the accessibility
of our cities.

   We now need a really hold program in order to avoid an irrevocable
climax condition in many sectors of our environment. We have to learn to
see our environment as a large scale system controlled by the feedback laws
of nature. To reverse today's trends means, in many cases, economical
difficulties. Yet society, the community, industry and trade in many cases
concentrates only on the short run profitability of their operations and
behaviour at the moment.

   It is far cheaper for a pulp mill not to treat its waste water and
not to collect the raw materials contained therein. It is far more economical
for a brewery to bottle its beer in fancy non-return bottles than to wash
and re-label returned standard bottles, and, for the general public it is
far easier to discard all the modern packages than to collect, classify
and return them for retrieval of their raw material. But only in the
short run!

   We have to start using available deep scientific knowledge and
all our experience to stop this waste-based economy of ours and try to
return our development to within the stability boundaries of our ecosystem.
We do have all the possibilities there. Our modern technology gives us
all the tools and means for this. Our highly developed telecommunications
technology can help us in many ways if properly used. Our computers can
be programmed to predict coming trends and situations and our measuring
technology can give us all the necessary indications and warnings. Today's
waste processing technology can provide us for the separation of valuable
raw materials otherwise wasted permanently. Proper planning of the human
settlements can circumvent the choking of our population centres. Learning

to reuse efficiently our waste by returning it to the ecosystem – something
our forefathers instinctively knew – can save us from depletion of our
natural resources.

All this has to be taught to the people, especially in the third
world, in a sensible way, by confessing our heretofore mistakes and by
proving that reversal of certain practices of ours is really necessary
in order to stabilize our environment and our whole ecosystem.

Discussion and Summary of Session No. 2
Tuesday April 6, 1976

Decision-making for Human Well-being in Cities

Political, Legal and Economic Considerations

A question posed by Mme. CAPEL-BOUTE, addressed to Mr. MAXWELL and
Mr. McSWINNEY, concerned the possibility of a "clean-air act" being
enforced inside working premises in the United Kingdom, or the Commission
of European Communities. Mme. CAPEL-BOUTE reported that air inside
offices in urban areas may well be more impure than outside offices.

Mr. MAXWELL pointed out that industrial hazards are dealt with by
legislation and that most other sources of pollution within urban offices
are caused by individuals. Personal rights are not usually infringed
upon by politicians for political reasons. Mr. McSWINNEY replied that
under the social programme of EEC studies are now underway concerning
health protection and safety of workers and the general public under
a variety of areas. One area being nuclear irradiation ; secondly, major
pollutants ; thirdly, safety, hygiene and health protection at work ;
fourthly, risks in manufacturing hazardous chemicals ; and finally,
medium term objectives for social research.

Other speakers pointed out that in some municipalities in the U.S.A.,
smoking is forbidden in certain public places and Mme. CAPEL-BOUTE
pointed out this also was the case in some parts of Vienna.

Mr. R.H. FERAHIAN commented that the taxation systems still, in many
countries, favours the tobacco industry and encourages smoking. In
Denver, Colorado, everything is taxed, including books, but not ciga-
rettes and tobacco. He also pointed out that there is culturally an
imbalance in protecting the rights of the smoker more than the non-smoker.

Mr. FERAHIAN went on to ask Mr. MAXWELL if there are any changes
contemplated in the laws of the United Kingdom to permit a private
citizen to bring a case against polluters in the name of a community.

Mr. FERAHIAN pointed out that our laws, both common and civil, are more
designed to protect properties than health on a personal basis. Mr.MAXWELL
agreed and said that there must be a large number of bills designed to
protect property for each bill designed to protect persons. In the United
Kingdom, of course, there is no Bill of Rights; all laws are based on
the ancient common law. However he pointed out that in permitting an
individual the opportunity to bring a case against a large corporation,
or the Crown, practice has shown that many of these cases turn out to
be private vendettas or personal feuds. The law should not be amended
to permit this kind of activity to encumber the already encumbered
court system.

Mr. Y. FUKUSHIMA posed the following question to Mr. MAXWELL. There
are very serious legislative problems associated with after-effects
of discontinued activities of factories or mining operations. Residual
wastes frequently give dangerous effects to the inhabitants long after
the corporate activity has ceased to exist and there is no longer anyone
or any corporate body that can provide restitution for those people
affected. Is there any legislation being developed in the United Kingdom
for such cases ?

Mr. MAXWELL replied that to the best of his knowledge there was not.
He did, however, suggest that long-term solutions may be developed on
the basis of the export credit guarantee scheme which provides that
industry pay a premium into a fund which could be used to satisfy
judgements at a later date. The editor believe that such an unsatisfied
judgement fund might be applicable to many countries and provide a
solution to a very vexatious problem.

Mr. H.F. FUNK asked Mr. MAXWELL if the Clean Air Act was in fact
linked with planning of district heating and incinerators, etc. Mr.MAXWELL
said, yes, it most certainly was.

Dr. A.P. GRIMA asked Mr. MAXWELL if indeed, under the U.K. Clean
Air Act, municipalities had the option of enacting local by-laws
regarding air pollution. If this was the case, how many municipalities
have not yet enacted such by-laws and why has the progress been
universally slow. Mr. MAXWELL replied that indeed not many municipalities

had enacted these by-laws and that he felt that the shortage of finances
from the central government, which were intended to assist the municipalities with these by-laws, would probably have accounted for the
tardy enactment of such legislation.

A comment which was made by Mr. GRAHAM KING was addressed to
Mr. MAXWELL and it concerned the difficulties in reconciling long-
term and short-term political horizons. Mr. MAXWELL stated in the
U.K. he felt it difficult for politicians to reverse administrative
development plans. At the local level in the U.K., Mr. KING says, he
doubted this. Development plans are often out of date and invite
pragmatic treatments. The new two-tier local government system has
tended to institutionalize conflict between district and county
planning authorities, breaking up the old monolithic British planning
system and making it more pluralistic like the Americans. Economic
austerity has enforced a major 're-think' of all road construction
programmes, industrial sites, etc., in high unemployment areas. This
presents difficulties and complex decision of the long-term and short-
term kind. Again, the Community Land Act is a political shuttlecock
causing further uncertainty for developers and planners alike. Mr. KING
indicated that, while he would agree with Mr. MAXWELL's comments in
relation to the British planning of the 1950's and 1960's, he did not
agree that this applied equally to the 1970's.

Dr. CHESTNUT then posed a question to Mr. McSWINNEY asking if there
were more details, including people to write to with their addresses,
regarding the CEC Foundation located in Ireland to study general problems.
Mr. McSWINNEY indicated that the foundation will ultimately have a building in Dublin but this is not yet a fact and, therefore, for details
one should write to the Commission which address is now : 200 rue de
la Loi, 1040 Brussels.

Dr. POLUNIN then asked Mr. McSWINNEY if the many "Common Market"
activities, which sound very much like those of the Council of Europe,
overlap in any way since the countries concerned are very much the
same ones. It was therefore hoped by Dr. POLUNIN that the two organizations worked in concert. Mr. McSWINNEY reported that they did try
to accomplish that. Dr. A. FALUDI then asked Mr. McSWINNEY if he agreed

with the observation by the Honourable Margaret SCRIVENER, emphasizing
that decision-making is the single biggest source of problems, and if it
does, does the CEC engage in or commission research on decision-making
with respect to environmental questions, especially on local matters.
Mr. McSWINNEY said that certainly part of the studies commissioned
examine institutions and decision-making processes as part of
their mandate.

Following the presentation of these papers, Mr. R.H. FERAHIAN asked
both Mr. LEE and Mr. SWAN if the long-term consequences of pollution
have somehow got to be considered in the cost benefit analysis for
environmental impact assessment. How do we define this "long-term"
duration ? Is it 5-10 years, and indeed how far into the future can
we plan for ? Dr. SWAN indicated that it was certainly not a legal
question to define a long-term. Undoubtedly, it could be defined in
economic terms or others but certainly not in legal terms. Professor
D.N. DEWEES then asked Mr. SWAN, since he suggested (Mr. SWAN) that
the courts have refused to consider any secondary economic issues such as
job loss in environmental cases, are you saying that economic considerations are inappropriate for judicial evaluation or that the law has
not so far required courts to address economic issues ? In Anti-Trust
and Anti-Combines law, courts are asked to probe complex economic
issues and to speculate upon the economic consequences of certain
events. Can't we legislate that certain polluting acts shall be un-
lawful unless justified by substantial economic benefit ? Professor
SWAN replied that courts can be given power to analyze complex
economic factors. They often, however, regard such enquiries as
irrelevant and then such evidence may become inadmissible under the
order of procedure followed by that court.

Professor DEWEES further asked as follows : "You express concern
about the problems of rapid change in environmental legislation yet
tax laws are in constant flux and corporations find the tax lawyers
to give them the sensible tax avoidance advice". Professor SWAN reported
that indeed tax laws do change frequently to the profit of lawyers and
accountants. Tax laws are a part of a game really and not a law. That
is to say, it's certainly not as important as the question of the
environment and losses can be corrected the following year in the case

of taxes, whereas environmental repercussions may go on for generations.

Mr. van WUNNIK asked Dr. SWAN if it is not a fact that one of the main
difficulties in control of environmental pollution, etc. is that law
(and environmental theory) expresses itself in concepts of the prevalent
culture (ideology perhaps). Power and property in feudal Europe are an
example. The property that counts, land property, could in most cases
not be sold. Feudal property was very different from modern "property".
Among other things, it would seem that present stress on individual
(including companies etc.) property responsibility is not appropriate.
As a subsidiary question, Mr. VAN WUNNIK asked if law could not in fact
be used as a tool for changing the dominant ideology. Dr. SWAN responded
that in fact he agreed with this position that we were in fact prisoners
of our own cultural values. Laws rapidly became dated simply because
laws cannot lead society. The examples of where the law has tried to
lead society, such as prohibition in the United States, produced disastrous side effects which are known to all.

Mr. Mark HALLE questioned Mr. LEE as follows. The environmental
impact assessment is very important as a tool for environmental management
However, such assessments relate to specific activities or plant projects.
A much wider concept is being proposed by UNEP, this is "Ecodevelopment",
or planning for development of a natural region or ecosystem so as to
integrate environmental concerns with economic, social, cultural, political and administrative factors in planning. Is there a similar follow-up
being envisaged within the European Communities ? Dr. LEE replied that
this was really a question of phasing in various concepts. He believed
that the most practical approach would be to first of all introduce
environmental impact assessments to project level activities rather than
to planning level activities in the immediate future. Clearly, as an
outgrowth of this, the planning phase should be subject to environmental
assessment when the tools are more refined and then from the planning
phase to the operational or project level would be the follow-up to that
second stage. However, he suggested there were practical reasons why the
project oriented statement would be more easy to manage for the moment
and, therefore, this is what he recommended.

Mr. Ray BREMNER addressed a question to Dr. LEE. "You used the

expression "public" in connection with the circulation of draft
environmental impact statements. To what extent do you feel the 'public'
is to be circulated and do you consider it possible to limit the involvement of the 'public', particularly when pressure groups and self-seeking
politicians can easily agitate the 'public' ? " Dr. LEE agreed that the
methods used to get effective public participation generally tend to
overstimulate one section of society. This section is frequently the
articulate middle class section and perhaps this is the one which most
frequently is against most things. He did, however, agree that a strict
timetable should be followed to prevent the introduction of the
"infinite study".

Dr. Y.Y. deRUITER said Dr. LEE had expressed the idea of building
the environmental impact statement on existing procedures. Dr.deRUITER
asked if there is both environmental and physical planning legislation,
would he have a preference for one of these fields of legislation.
Dr.deRUITER suggested that environmental legislation would permit a
more detailed study and so better evaluate the impact. A further possibility would be to have the impact statement in several phases of decision-
making starting with a more global stage when the plans are being prepared
to the more definitive stage when the specific project, such as a motorway or an industry, etc., are more definite. Dr. LEE agreed that assessment
should be introduced into all areas and all phases and, of course, the
planning stage is the logical phase where it can be done but the particular
implementation phase is the most important phase when it should be
examined in great detail.

Mme. CAPEL-BOUTE asked Dr. CHESTNUT if the analogy between human
settlements and the feed-back system, while surely a very attractive
method for decision-making, probably masked the fact that it needs
quantitative data to produce related driving forces for adaptation.
Mme. CAPEL-BOUTE indicated that she didn't feel this was possible for
low energy information factors changing the trigger effects and the
adaptive forces required for the survival of any living organisms such
as human beings. The quality of life is not expressed by purely quantitative values. Dr. CHESTNUT agreed that this was most certainly the
case, that there were many other values that would be developed as the
feed-back system tool was developed. He cited other scientific information

which we were not able to evaluate until comparatively recently.
Previously we had no need to evaluate it so we did not devise a method.

Mr. Graham KING made the following comment. "Harold CHESTNUT wants
a comprehensive way of looking at cities generally agreed so interested
parties can sort out a better future for us. As a practising planner,
count me out of any attempt to see cities based on electronic feed-back
systems. I do not believe it is possible or desirable.

a) Fragmented and partial views of the city is, and will remain, a fact
   of life for the majority of those living in or taking decisions for
cities. Each will invent their own city.

b) Systems view is too narrow. The theory can never be built or tested,
   the date will never become continuously available, the interactions
and variables are too difficult to predict. Man, thank God, is too random.

c) Even with such data, the platonic ideal of publicly interested men
   of goodwill sorting things out on behalf of people is not on. In my
view, efforts should be in the other direction. Define the quality of
life at the grass roots in a fragmented way perhaps and then use politics".

Mr. MARTINEAU asked Dr. CHESTNUT if his view of his proposal of the
input/output models would ultimately become the basis for a working
method for planners and other decision-makers ? Dr. CHESTNUT replied
that he believed it would be but that added efforts would obviously be
needed and that, in addition, other groups should be involved.

Dr. MARTINEAU then asked what is the involvement or the role of the
citizens in the proposed work. In other words, how are the voices of the
urban dwellers to be heard? Dr. CHESTNUT indicated here that the urban
dwellers should be a part of the planning and the decision-making process
of course.

Dr. MARTINEAU finally asked if Dr. CHESTNUT felt that his proposal
may eventually lead to the formulation of scientifically based urban theory?
Dr. CHESTNUT stated that he hoped that this would be the long-term
objective.

Mr. FERAHIAN then asked Dr. MATSUZAKI how many pollution monitoring

stations we used in the study reported in his paper. Dr. MATSUZAKI
responded that ther were 30 stations in an area of about 10 x 20 miles,
43 major stacks out of 200 were used to validate the model used in the
simulation.

Case Studies in Urban Environment

Dr. CHESTNUT asked Mr. ATKINSON if any of the cities adjoining or
neighbouring Bradford took similar approaches to restoring their ancient
environment and wether they, too, profited from Bradford's experience.
Mr. ATKINSON pointed out that the neighbouring cities of Sheffield and
Leeds certainly profited generally but, while Bradford is essentially
a city of stone, Leeds is a city of brick, and therefore could not
gain the same aesthetic improvement.

To the question of financing of the improvement of Bradford,
Mr. ATKINSON replied that there was some central government financing,
some municipal financing and some from the individual person who
benefited from the improvement. It could be described as a three-way
split with the individual providing 25 % of the costs associated.

Professor John SWAN then asked Professor DEWEES what problems might
prove to be totally unsolvable under the effluent charge system which
he had just proposed in his paper. Dr. DEWEES indicated that there were
no problems which he believed could not be solved, although some materials
might have to be prohibited outright for their toxic or persistent natures.
Certainly many of the offending substances such as SO_2 at present would
be suitable for effluent charges.

Professor SWAN further asked what would be the size of the administrative
system required for this proposal. Professor DEWEES indicated that the
administrative system would be smaller to handle effluent charges since
prohibition per se requires years and years of public negotiations.

Professor SWAN finally asked what might be the costs required to
collect the effluent charges involved. Dr. DEWEES indicated they would
certainly be no more expensive than to enforce effluent standards since
both required effectively monitoring and policing. If the effluent

standard system, of course, was designed not to be enforced, then this
would clearly be the cheapest, but also the least effective method.

Dr. GRIMA then asked Professor DEWEES if effluent charges are that
much more attractive, why are they not more popularly used ? Dr. DEWEES
indicated that in fact many of them have been adopted to some extent.
Sewer surcharges on industrial wastewater is an example of the effluent
charge principle. The problem of public acceptance is one related to
the fact that people do not believe that this would reduce pollution
and that in fact it's simply a question of collecting money and allowing
the environment to deteriorate. Dr. DEWEES indicated that he was quite
certain that this would not be the case but that the public at present
seemed to believe this. Another reason why it may not be used is indeed
because it would be effective. Prohibition of certain substances can
bring about an industrial response suggesting that there is no technology
which exists which would provide for this prohibition. Clearly, this is
a more difficult question to answer from an authority's point of view,
whereas if there was an effluent charge, there is no discussion, there
is simply a payment.

Mr. Mark HALLE suggested to Dr. DEWEES that the market system could
be used to conserve energy and indeed other resources. Dr. DEWEES
indicated that this certainly is the case. However, North America has
insulated their domestic consumers from world prices in oil, for example,
thus promoting consumption. The political implications are rather obvious.

Dr. Steve COHEN then raised once again the question of the short run
versus the long run in economic terms and asked Dr. DEWEES to clarify.
Dr. DEWEES indicated that in economic terms the short run meant that
period of time when the existing plant and the existing populations and
labour forces would be in position, whereas the long run would permit
time for changes both in the location of labour forces and for the
alteration of capital investment. In the short run, it was felt that
pollution control might indeed cost jobs, whereas the employment picture
would not really change; it may improve in the long run. Perhaps the
deployment of the labour force may be different but the number of job
opportunities may increase. Effluent charges produce real revenue which
may be used to offset some of the inconveniences associated with relocation

and retraining. There may be some transitional problems.

Dr. COHEN raised the question of pollution havens. Dr. DEWEES indicated that in Canada it was well known that Ontario had for a long time taken a more aggressive line in pollution control than had the neighbouring province of Quebec. However, he had not noticed any major migration of industry from Ontario to Quebec as a result of this.

Dr. Ed. WOLFF then asked Dr. DEWEES what was the basic difference between the DEWEES proposal in his paper and the existing arrangements in what Dr. WOLFF thought was the Rhine Valley. Dr. DEWEES indicated that his understanding was that some tributaries of the Rhine River, such as the Emscher, had an industrial wastewater treatment authority and the costs associated there dealt entirely with wastewater treatment costs. DEWEES' proposal indeed deals with social costs as well as pollution costs.

Mr. MAXWELL said that Dr.DEWEES had closed his remarks by saying that we would either end up with a clean environment or a large amount of funds. Mr. MAXWELL indicated this was entirely inappropriate and these suggestions appeared to threaten industry with a possibility of putting them out of business. Mr. MAXWELL cited some examples of important industries which might be entirely priced out of the market if such an approach were adopted. Dr. DEWEES responded that of course in his closing statement he had given the two polar positions, neither of which was either attractive or achievable. It would, however, be expected that a middle of the road would be accomplished with a partially polluted environment and a modest or even a substantial amount of revenue to deal with this pollution. He certainly did not believe that such an eventuality would be any kind of a threat to industry. However, if industry were so inefficient that the inevitability of destroying the environment was associated with that industry, then perhaps it would be appropriate that that industry went out of business.

Professor SWAN, in response to Mr. MAXWELL's remarks, further added some comments about the protection of business.

Dr. SWAN indicated that he believed that the idea of protecting business at the expense of society went out over a hundred years ago

and he hoped that it would never return. Certainly with the labour
laws and industrial injuries compensation, it was acknowledged that
industry was responsible for the costs which it incurred certainly
concerning individuals and private property. Mr. MAXWELL was suggesting
that that was as far/we should go and that the damages which industry
caused to common property should be ignored if it was "too much money".

Mr. FRADIER was then asked if UNESCO could not help the United Kingdom
to save the field where the Battle of Hastings had been fought from the
developers and the garbage dumpers. The short answer Mr. FRADIER indicated was no. This was a cultural fight and there are some attempts to
develop an international fund to preserve internationally interesting
sites but this was not yet fully developed. Mr. HALLE suggested that the
Battle of Hastings field might be protected under the convention on the
Protection of the World Cultural and Natural Heritage.

In response to M. BEUX's paper, Mr. BOURNE indicated that he was
utterly and thoroughly appalled to hear that once again the ocean was
being proposed as a giant dust bin for the wastes which seemed to be the
tenor of Mr. BEUX's paper. The speaker indicated that the atmospheric
pollutants, as well as the water pollutants, reduced the light penetration
into the oceans, thus reducing photosynthesis. The surface contamination
reduced evaporation and thus interrupted our hydrologic cycle and also
the gaseous exchange.There seemed to be some considerable support from
the audience on this particular point.

Dr. CHESTNUT addressed the following question to Mr. CANNETTA. "Many
cities and people do not identify with the city managers nowadays. How
can we develop some dialogue to ensure compatible aims between the people
and the bureaucrats and managers". Mr. CANNETTA indicated that an experiment
was being conducted in Milan where the city is being divided into 20 parts
to break down to the grass roots. There were problems of communications.
Meetings with citizen's representatives are currently underway to find
resolutions to these communication problems and indeed to identify the
problems of the citizens. Dr. CAPEL-BOUTE observed that during the same
period while Milano is experimenting with the sub-division of their city
into 20 pieces, the city of Brussels is doing precisely the opposite and
giving serious consideration to amalgamating the 19 municipalities which

presently constitute Brussels. Mr. CANNETTA said that it would be interesting
to attend the meeting of Mayors of major cities of the world which would be
held in Milan next week. The question was posed, which of the 19 mayors
of Brussel's municipalities had been invited; if all of them had been
invited then perhaps an exchange might take place. However, if only one
mayor of the city of Brussels was invited it's unlikely that any exchange
could take place.

Mr. FERAHIAN asked Mr. CANNETTA if the land was owned by the city
and leased back to the builders and developers in Milan ? Mr. CANNETTA
said that until quite recently such a thing would be totally unthinkable
but that perhaps in the near future this might be possible. Mr. FERAHIAN
suggested that some of the cities which have done precisely this have had
some of the least problems concerning planning because the land was indeed
under their control.

Mr. CANNETTA was then asked how Milan was divided into 20 administrative
districts and how were the representatives selected, when were these
districts established and how are they working now, and are there any
English references reporting on these experiences ? Mr. CANNETTA reported
that the representatives were elected by the municipalities with political
parties assistance. They tried to have popular election but failed due
to the fact that there was no national law which permitted this. It was
also required to change the council every four years. There is presently
a new law going to the Italian Senate to help this situation.

Dr. GRIMA made an observation to Dr. CHESTNUT concerning the methods
whereby a citizen identifies with decision-makers. Dr. GRIMA indicated
that there were three ingredients to this matter. One being opportunity,
the second, information, and the third recourse to real power. In the U.S.A.,
the public information act gives that country an advantage over many other
countries. In Canada, for example, without that act it becomes that much
more difficult to obtain the information which would automatically be
available in the United States. Dr. GRIMA cited three examples in the
city of Toronto where the Spadina Expressway, a major expressway going
right down the centre of the city, was stopped by a citizen's group while
it was under construction. The result is that Toronto now has an unpaved
ditch going nowhere and stands as a continuous reminder to the power of
the citizens group. A further example was a major international airport

which was proposed for Toronto at Pickering and this was defeated by a
group of people operating under the name of 'People or Planes'. All these
people managed to obtain some information and took the opportunity and
they had somerecourse to power by, in the case of the Pickering airport,
one member of the "People or Planes" group ran for election and was elected
basically on the issue of the airport. Whereas some of the other issues
have in fact been stopped on the eve of an election.

Summary of the Tuesday Sessions By P. H. Jones

Essentially the papers under discussion in this session made it quite
clear that the successful human settlements is achieved only when all the
forces at play are at balance. A city designed by planners with no consultation with the people will be just as unsuccessful as a city which
is generated by private entrepreneurs whose main motivation is profit.

It is recognized that the decisions made at the grass roots level, or
in consultation with the grass roots level, are more likely to produce a
successful human settlement than those which may be taken at a higher level
of government. Thus the higher level of government must be involved in
ensuring the compatibility of interactions between human settlements and
for developing successful communication links on a larger scale.

The law was described as a means of achieving an end but in no way is
it possible for the law to define or prescribe the desirable end. Once
society has established the ends which they wish to achieve, the law and
economic forces can then be used to achieve that end. However, the identification of the optimum plan for human settlements is not an easy thing
to establish. Proposals were made whereby a complex system might be
analyzed using real data. However, many felt that such an approach would
be unlikely to produce a real or desirable solution.

It might be observed that cities are not built, they indeed grow,
and the culture and nature of a city is a dynamic thing just as a forest
where parts die and parts grow until a climax situation is achieved. The
role of citizen's groups were identified as being quite significant but
yet it was realized that certain vocal sectors of society can introduce
a bias and produce misleading data.

It was suggested that the articulate middle class may develop too significant a voice in the planning of human activities, simply because they are articulate and have time to devote to such activities as citizen's groups. There must clearly be large numbers of people who are not aware of plans and have no access to the information of plans and, therefore, can in no way influence these plans. Thus, a large variety of mechanisms must be developed to establish the views of the people to influence the plans. This does not mean to say that all cities should then be planned for the majority point of view; indeed, this would breed mediocrity and "sameness" in cities. It is important that certain activity centres be developed to satisfy minority groups on the assumption that the sum total of the minorities represent indeed the majority.

It was concluded that the decision-making process is in fact the key to the development of a successful human settlement and that the decision-making process represented the single greatest challenge to ensure that the views of all citizens and groups of citizens are heard and understood.

Discussion and Summary of Session No. 3
Wednesday April 7, 1976

Urban and Land Use Planning and Citizen Participation

The reports of Mr. Hoppenfeld and Mr. Hughes, who were not in attendance, were summarized by the chair.

Mr. Gibson opened the session with a remark on the severe time limitations under which the authors would work and reminded the audience of the films which, as on previous evenings, would be shown at the close of the session.

He described the proposed "Declaration of Brussels," which, while it would be published in the name of the editors since it would be impossible for the participants to review the final draft, would attempt to achieve a "sense of the conference." He invited individuals and groups to prepare material for the review of the editors, with a view toward including such concepts in the proposed declaration.

The authors were then introduced and made their presentations. The following is a summary report, much foreshortened, of the discussion which closed the first morning session.

Mr Tom Martineau asked Mr. Epstein if he or anyone else had attempted to get feedback from the residents of planned communities as to whether or not they were satisfied. Mr. Epstein did not answer this question, but went straight on to read Mr. Mark Halle's question. Halle asked Mr. Epstein whether he thought that the planning techniques which Mr. Epstein advocated could be brought to bear on the huge and chaotic cities already in existence, and whether this approach could be applied in the third world.

Mr. Epstein's answer to this question was "yes." He said that these tech-

niques were developed in order to bear on these vast and chaotic cities because
the concentric growth of cities is the reason for which there are access difficulties now. Therefore Epstein proposed a corridor growing out of a city as opposed
to continued concentric development. This is an alternative and more acceptable
form for growth of existing cities, he remarked. Mr. Chestnut then asked Mr.
Epstein how he would handle the matter of sizing basic utilities such as water,
electricity, roads, and communications if there was no approximate estimate of the
size of the community involved. (Mr. Epstein said in his paper that the eventual
size of a city or extension could not be foreseen and therefore should not be
written into a programme.)

Mr. Epstein answered that he felt it would be childlike try and say in advance what size a town ultimately will be. The infrastructure should not be sized
in advance, but be installed "a short step ahead" of development. Only the peripheral roads would then need to be enlarged, as the access roads would remain the
same whatever the city size, for example. He explained that water was a regional
planning matter and that energy utilities would be developed in "sections of
length," following the line of the pedestrian circulation.

Mr. Damian then asked Mr. Fukushima whether he thought that the lack of
refereences to the real needs and wishes of man (on short and long term) and the
"laws of evolution" in "fig. 1,matrix of the environmental studies" was due to a
lack of interest, a lack of data on the subject, or another reason.

Mr. Fukushima answered that they have serious problems in Japan and that
possible policies for improvement were the fundamental base for discussion in the
conference (International Conference of Scientists on the Human Environment,
November 1975, Kyoto) and that many proposals were made of possible solutions.

Mr. Martineau asked Mr. Marans if he thought that optimum urban density is a
function of what one is born into, that is, do people who are born into crowded
conditions find less dense conditions undesirable, while people born in areas of

low density find crowding unacceptable? Therefore, does optimum density vary by

social class, income groups, type of society and other similar categories? Further,

is high social crowding generally more acceptable to people if there is an escape

valve to solitude?

Mr. Marans answered that one could not say with certainty what the optimum

density was for different social groups, but he had his suspicions that people

brought up in high density surroundings might well find low densities undesirable.

Mr. Bourne asked Mr. Epstein to comment on the following: He had been an

"inmate" of Lancaster University and found that many staff lived outside the

campus, there was a sense of being cut off from the outside world, and from the

City of Lancaster, in particular, and the students often used the town facilities

in preference to those available in the University. He asked whether the failures

of the project were a demonstration of how social and individual behaviour is

still too little understood to form guidelines for the planner and architect, and

whether it would not have been better to have developed Lancaster University as an

extension of the existing city.

Mr. Epstein answered that the cut-off feeling did exist and that it was quite

normal early in its growth to want to get out. He thought it would have been much

better if the University had been inside the town, but he had had no choice in the

siting of the development and further, the cost of such a proposal would be

prohibitive.

Mr. Van Dunnick commented to Mr. Marans that each reason for which he fore-

sees higher densities in the future might well be in favour of lower densities.

1)   Social costs are lower in smaller units (threshold analysis), so de-

creasing overall density may lower total costs.

2)   Transport is, for a very large part, a cultural and economic habit, and

this can change.

3)   The value of open space depends on its accessibility and its quality

(better on a small scale).

Mr. Ferahian then said that optimum densities of cities are a function of their performance and that one must differentiate between settlement densities and overcrowding. He said that there are upper bounds to densities and that these are set by social, psychological, and cultural factors. What is perceived as over-crowding by an Englishman or a Frenchman is very comfortable for a Hong Kong dweller. He then mentioned the reference on this subject in his paper.

Mr. Marans then added that density is a measure of crowding and that crowding is in the eye of the beholder. This is the nature of the research presently being done on density and the quality of life. There are cases of total satisfaction in very crowded conditions, but this depends on the life style, cultural background, etc., of the person and also on the availability and accessibility of open space. He added that one must not confuse high density with the space inside the dwelling alone.

Mr. Epstein asked Mr. Marans why he is so pessimistic as to say that cities could only be lived in by escaping from them. He suggested that we ought to reduce noise, dirt, and ugliness and reduce the number of cars in favour of pedestrians and public transport.

Mr. Marans replied that this would take some time and that in the meantime conditions should be made as livable for people as possible.

This concluded the first morning session.

Applications to N.W. Europe

The discussion following the paper presentations proceeded thusly. Mr. Tom Martineau asked Mr. Robert what policies and action were implemented to effect active control on urbanisation and retain open space in the area of Southwest Holland which he referred to. How did it effectively work?

Mr. Robert answered that this was land use control by municipalities. The

National Ministry of Physical Planning may now give direct land use planning guidelines to municipalities. The Ministry may say to municipalities that they can expand if they wish, but that if they do, the will get no more money.

Mr. Martineau added that it is thus apparent that one could actually control urbanisation, although it had been said previously by Mr. Epstein that this was not possible.

Mr. Feludi then commented to Mr. Robert that there has been very little research done on decision making in environmental planning, and he asked if there were plans in this direction. He said that problems of controlling urbanisation were due to absence of "instruments of control," not political negligence, and finally he asked whether there are any concrete plans to study decision making, organisation and procedures at the level of implementation.

Mr. Robert answered that his group is interested in this topic and that this is soft-ware type of implementation instruments to develop the relationship between the social and political environment and the application of the system. He supported Mr. Feludi's request.

Ms. Capel-Boute pointed out that there is much experience to be gained in Northwest Europe with regard to the effects of high density, pollution, etc., on health. She felt that it is very bad that this had not been taken into account in the conference. In developing countries, people have been living in natural conditions for many years, she said, but we have changed all this in so-called developed countries, and we should consider the effects this has on our health. She criticised the nonsense of the artificial environments which we create with air conditioning and artificial lighting.

Mr. Van Wunnick asked Professor Kormos how culture (language, religion, etc.) has influenced the growth of connurbations in Northwest Europe, or whether territorial development was only related to coal and minerals in the land. Mr. Kormoss replied that he could not deal with linguistic or religious factors at the present

time, but that statistical figures should be weighted to take political and some
cultural facts into accoutn.

Mr. Van Wunnick pointed out that there are maps showing linguistic changes
and other cultural factors and rephrased his question as to whether there is any
correlation between religion or language and the development of connurbations.
There was not time to discuss this any further.

Mr. Sliwa asked Mr. Epstein if he had considered whether developing countries
actually need cities at all. He further suggested that linear town development is
alien to Africa, South America, and the Middle East, as traditions there suggest
cluster settlements. He said that linear cities relied on public transport and
that one had already criticised the noise which this produced. He asked further
if Mr. Epstein had considered the micro-climate of the courtyards in his project
for Lancaster University.

Mr. Epstein answered that he thinks that developing countries do need cities
because there is such a large flow of people from agricultural to urban areas and
these people have to be accommodated. He said that cluster settlements are acceptable so long as they do not grow too much, and that transport is required in any
large group whether it is a network or a linear system. He said that his proposal
is adapted to noise control by the lack of through roads. Mr. Epstein said finally
that the courtyards of the University would be quite different in Scotland and in
Africa, but that he did not have time to go into this.

Mr. Sauramo asked Mr. Epstein if it would not be possible to put a
public transport system in the central axis on the pedestrian area of a linear
town. He suggested a combined tram and pedestrian axes.

Mr. Epstein replied that he thought trams are too slow and noisy and that he
preferred to keep humans only in the pedestrian area. He also pointed out that
the covered arcades would prevent the flow of trams through the centre.

Mr. Evyapan asked Mr. Epstein if there are any basic differences between his main proposals and the idea of the linear city of Sorne y Mata, and Ms. O'Brien asked Mr. Epstein if there is a relationship between his proposals and the United States phenomenon of strip development along the fringe of cities.

Mr. Epstein answered these questions by explaining that it is logical for any city development to run along the main transport axes or main axes of energy. He said that the city is efficient in terms of energy and in terms of land use.

Mr. Martineau asked Mr. Epstein if he has any feedback from residents of areas he had built, to which Mr. Epstein replied that he has had positive feedback.

Mr. Polunin asked Mr. Epstein if the urban form he advocates could be effective for large cities. Mr. Epstein said that the definition of a city is a place where people can communicate with each other, and they need access everywhere. He feels that, yes, this kind of development can harbour many people because communication is easy and simple.

Mr. Bourne commented to Mr. Epstein that large cities are not what is wanted in Africa because they rely on fossil fuels, which they cannot afford. He said that developing countries are better advised to keep urban clusters as small communities in close relationship with agriculture since this is most efficient (scattered applause). He added that we must get over imposing our Northwestern Europe and U.S.A. ideas, which are well adapted to our eco-system, but not to developing nations (applause).

Lastly Mr. Manheim asked Mr. Marans if his conclusions of higher densities still held true in the light of recent population projections which indicate a considerable slowdown in growth.

Mr. Marans said that he had been talking about towns in the Western World in particular and that he did think that density would still increase at the micro-level.

Mr. Epstein warned of the danger of developed nations' offering gratuitous advice to developing nations. Mr. Bourne then deplored the imposition of European standards on developing nations, and Mr. Epstein closed a lively discussion by remarking on the complexity of the issue of development in developing nations.

Following the presentation of scheduled papers, the discussion commenced.

Mr. Feludi asked Professor Werz for some contextual information concerning his paper. Professor Werz said that there was little direct research done on this topic.

Mr. Ferhian asked Mr. Apgar what kind of information do investors have to have in order to predict the return on their investment. If one can only plan three years in advance, how can a planner convince the investor of the worth of a long-term project?

Mr Apgar said that large private investors are willing to accept ranges of probability as criteria for investment. They have to be certain that the assumptions will be reviewed periodically. However, public investors are much less willing to accept that major capital investments can be staged and that assumptions can change because there are severe bureaucratic constraints. Mr. Apgar went on to say that planners have to be more rigorous in trying to define the difference between what they know people need and what they think they want.

Dr. Chestnut asked Mr. Apgar whether the notion of 3 or 4-year plans could be reconciled with 8 to 10-year projects. Mr. Apgar replied that in major projects, 90 to 95% of the total capital investment costs occur in buildings and services, any of which can be constructed within 3 to 4 years. Only 5 to 10% of the projects cannot be staged in this time period. He added that this method is not of optimal engineering efficiency, but that it is more important to respond to the social and economic criteria.

Mr. Bourne commented on Mr. Musa's introduction on remote sensing. He pointed out that these technics were very expensive for most countries, let alone developing countries, and gave a word of caution from his experience as to certain technical difficulties with these methods, particularly in interpreting "side-looking" radar images.

Mr. Musa replied that oil spills in the ocean can be detected by satellite, but that remote sensing has not primarily been used in the case of oil spills. He said its major use is in the area of global monitoring of agriculture, and he agreed that it was not cheap, but considered it nevertheless more economical than in situ sensing.

Ms. Capel Boute commented to Ms. O'Brien Marchand that there was very little scientific criteria for establishing the quality of air or water. She said that even a beautiful landscape could hide radioactive waves and other pollutants which destroy the quality of air and water and which could not be monitored.

Ms. O'Brien Marchand agreed that such waves are very difficult to measure, but that there are scientific ways of doing so.

She further said that what is significant in her study is that her studies indicate a high statistical correlation of water quality and air quality to what people think was aesthetically pleasing and unpleasing in their total environment.

At this point the chairman, Mr. Cohen, remarked at his surprise to see no further discussion. Since time had expired in any case, he adjourned his session to permit the scheduled films to be shown.

In addition to the papers shown in the final program, Dr. J. Hedegaard present his paper, originally scheduled for Monday afternoon, at the end of this session. It was entitled "The Conversion of Urban Waste into Single Cell Protein: Practical Possibilities and Limits Today."

Dr. Dan Haggan, co-author with Dr. Yacovy Haines and Dr. Paul Riley, presented the paper on "Trade-Off Analysis in Urban Water Resources Planning."

Dr. David Maidment presented the paper, "A New Approach to Urban Resources Systems Optimization," co-authored with Dr. Ven T. Chow, and recommended: Urban water resources developments must be considered from the viewpoint of the total urban system of which they represent one component; and systems analysis, which includes mathematical modelling and optimization, has a useful role to play in the formation of urban water systems policy. These techniques allow the quantification of the effects of alternative solutions to environmental problems in a manner which is otherwise not feasible.

Dr. A. P. Grima's paper, "Alternative Policies in Water Pollution Control," concluded the following: Non-structural policy options should to be considered in water resources management include regulation, subsidies, tax incentives, grants, effluent charges, and assimulative majority rights. There are no preferred options for general application, and each policy alternative should be considered on its own merit for the case under consideration. The criteria against which these policy options should be considered are:

1)   efficiency, i.e., maximizing social welfare.

2)   equity, i.e., the "fair" distribution of benefits and costs emanating
      from policy options.

Equity does not provide intuitively obvious guidelines, but the necessary condition for satisfying this criternion in a limited sense is the compensation of the losers by the beneficiaries. If the efficiency criterion is satisfied (net benefits are maximized), then this would facilitate meeting the limited criterion of fairness.

Mr. Leonard T. Crook presented a report on the U.S. ERC Water Resources Panel workshop held in Washington, D. C., November 12-14, 1975.

Summary of the Special Session on Water
Resources By L. T. Crook and Dr. Maidment

The economical and social stability of the habitat and the well-being of man in his habitat depend on numerous factors. A well-nourished popluation, living on a well-balanced diet, is one of these essential factors. By recycling wastes (hydrocarbon residues, solid waste, sewage) and converting them into single cell protein, one can now combine two essential aims:_ clean up the habitat and, simultaneously, produce vital growth factors (proteins, essential amino acids, etc.) for the population of the habitat.

Due to a severe time limitation, there was no general discussion from the floor in this special session.

Summary of the Wednesday Sessions By J. E. Gibson

In a cross disciplinary conference such as this, a number of tensions seem sure to develop. Among these are the differing meanings placed on jargon terms and, more importantly, differing styles of problem solution common to the engineer, the planner, the architect, and so forth. At an international conference as well, there are the pressures produced by differing national styles of procedure and the linguistic problem of differing languages. Thus it seems to me a remarkable tribute to the participants to say that in only a few days they formed for themselves a community. They worked together, voluntarily, on position papers, and they reached out to each other in informal and social matters as well as technical ones. The pressure cooker atmosphere of such conferences as these seems to heighten the excitement and the urge to suck dry the opportunities for communication and participation.

The organizers made every attempt to achieve representation of a wide spread of nationalities and professional fields, but they also attempted to attract a representation of the younger, perhaps more enthusiastic, scientists along with those more senior and well known. All this seems to have made for an exciting and enjoyable event. As the general chairman, Mr. La Conte, remarked in the final plenary session, discussion from the floor grew steadily more lively, and the number of participants at sessions grew larger as the week progressed; and these are the marks, it seems to me, of a successful conference.

Each of the papers delivered at Brussels were summaries of whole scientific fields, and indeed two of the papers during the Wednesday session were reports on entire conferences. Thus for me to attempt in a few paragraphs to further summarize these summaries would be useless. Rather I shall attempt to focus on one or two themes which appeared in today's papers and discussion from the floor. But before doing so, I should mention that a number of individuals and groups responded to my invitation to submit statements for incorporation in the Declaration of Brussels. (Several of these statements appear in an appendix to this volume.) [For Mr. La Conte to decide.]

Optimum urban size, form and density were considered in this day's sessions, but from a broader, more humane point of view than is common in specialist journals. Much rich content was developed on various aspects of experience in N.W. Europe, and a lively debate developed as to whether this experience is of value to developing nations. Detailed views differed, of course, but a broad consensus developed on all sides, of the need to avoid advice giving. A more acceptable stance viz a viz the developing nations to most participants is to outline the specific situation along with the usual western solution along with the apparent outcomes. Beyond this, it is for developing nations to do with this experience as they think best.

Another clear theme, expressed more often in informal discussion perhaps than in the formal papers is the primary causal nature of population pressure and the need for population regulation.

Still a third theme is the fundamental purpose of cities. While they indeed are places of work and industry and commerce as well as centers of transportation and communication, cities are fundamentally for human well-being. This sounds so simple, but of course it is not.

And finally there emerged an important understanding common to social scientists and technologists as well, that simply because an urban project is technically and economically feasible is not a sufficient reason for pursuing it. It has been true only in recent decades that technology's grasp has matched its reach. Previously we were prevented many excesses by technical and/or fiscal impossibility. Thus we rarely if ever needed to exercise voluntary restraint. But now the situation is clearly different. We must become an "adult society," as Mr. Didishine said in his opening remarks to the conference. Clearly one mark of an adult is self-restraint. The adult refrains from personal excesses because he knows they are detrimental. Similarly an adult society will refrain from technological excesses, even though they could be achieved, because they would do ultimate harm.

STATEMENTS SUBMITTED BY INDIVIDUAL PARTICIPANTS

<u>STATEMENT BY MR. W. OWEN</u>

<u>Global Information Exchange</u>.

A key to resolving many of the problems of urban settlements in a period of rapid growth and change is the establishment of an effective international system for the exchange of relevant and meaningful information and experience.

There is now no global network performing this function. Yet the analysis of experience and its continuing dissemination is not only the most basic first requirement but also the least costly means of accomplishing world-wide cooperation in the field of human settlements.

To avoid an information overkill, it will be necessary to emphasize selection and utility in the kinds of knowledge interchanged, focussing on the goal of helping to provide resouce conserving, practical and feasible approaches to providing shelter, jobs, and life-support community services.

Existing agencies operating on a global basis in various key sectors could be utilized to begin filling the gaps that now exist in the information network, with integration under United Nations sponsorship

<u>STATEMENT BY Ms. MAURA O'BRIEN-MARCHAND</u>

The W.E.R.C. Conference on Human Settlements held in Brussels identified many common problems across disciplines, regions and cultures.

Papers and discussions expressed many real concerns :

1) Need to decrease population.

2) Need for planning, developing and renovating cities to enhance the "quality of life" for all its inhabitants.

3) Need to plan, build and maintain settlements with awareness of the ecological and physical (geological) constraints and processes that make those environments dynamic and livable.

4) Efficient use of energy needs to be a fundamental concern in land-use planning and habitat design, in terms of design, materials, transport, and the dynamics of daily life.

5) Need to minimize health hazards to be an important criteria in plan development.

I request these concerns be addressed at the Vancouver Conference on Habitat and implementable courses of action be developed as conference mandates.

STATEMENT BY Mr. T. MARTINEAU

All professionals involved in the process of decision-making for the planned growth and change of existing human settlements as well as for the planning of new human settlements must strive to develop systematic tools with which to carry out their work.

Such tools should have the following characteristics :

1) They must have the capacity to take into account the perceptions, needs and desires urban dwellers have for their well-being in the community.

2) They must be practical in that they permit themselves to be applied to solutions for immediate, short-term decision-making about specific issues of urban growth and change.

3) They must be flexible to such an extent that they can improve and mature by "learning" from every experience in which they are applied.

4) They must show promise of coming to such an eventual degree of maturity that urban theory could evolve as a result.

Without belittling what man knows and is capable of in creating successful urban settlements, it is apparent that his capabilities in this regard resemble by analogy those of the ancient alchemist. In contrast, however, man has developed, and continues to develop, a nearly limitless capability to build on a vast and grand scale. Thus the challenge for the remainder of this century is no longer whether man can expand his technological capacity to build. Instead, man must develop tools for intelligent planning and decision-making which are of equal sophistication to his technological abilities.

STATEMENT BY Mr. St. P. COHEN

Harmony, is the essential element to the success of mankind at keeping Earth a livable habitat. Our success at urban living, both in existing communities and new cities yet to be built depends on our living in harmony with other people and with the rest of the earth (nature).

At Brussels we have been reminded of our capacity to develop systems for acquiring knowledge and developing data on everything from seismic characteristics to subjective assessments of air quality. We have been reminded that we threaten the harmony of our biosphere, as to its physical characteristics and its ecological balance. There are already more than enough people, yet in less than thirty years there will be twice as many of us.

We have learned at Brussels that the supply of skills and information is enormous, such that we have more information to exchange than time allows. And that is doubly true for our habitat. We have no more lead time.

We have learned that we share a sense of need for human scale, that for a community to succeed its inhabitants must not be overwhelmed by a feeling of irrelevance, that as individuals all of us have a stake in our own lives and in the quality of life of neighbors.

Therefore we say it is time to begin to apply the theories. It is time to put action ahead of words. No single answer applies on a global scale: large cities and hamlets, high technology and low, all have their place in our habitat.

Our goals are so complicated, so complex and far-reaching, that they lend themselves to a certain simplification: Mankind must devote our collective resources to our own defence. (As the American cartoon character Pogo once said, "We have met the enemy and he is us.") We must continue to gather knowledge and develop technology, but we must begin to use it now. We must reduce population growth, work for a more equitable distribution of resources, work to restore a human scale for human life, and live in harmony with our habitat.

STATEMENT BY Ms. D. van der DOES

A suggestion for the resolutions for Habitat Vancouver, 1976.

Our old and new residential areas are polluted by noise, fumes and wheels.

From a world health point of view, motorized traffic is killer number one of young children.

On account of research done in the field it is known that the best road safety education cannot adapt a young child to modern traffic.

The traffic environment has to be adapted to them.
In residential areas anywhere in the world priority shall go to the three high risk groups : the young child, the elderly, the handicapped (of any age).

The car then shall, by the shape of the street behave as a guest.

The citizens shall turn to their political leaders and make their demands on their living environment very clear.

It is a challenge to townplanners and all other disciplines in this field anywhere in the world to adapt the living environment to meet the needs of the most vulnerable on our roads, as one of the most necessary contributions to world health and well being.

STATEMENT BY Mr. Robert W. MARANS

Although there is considerable discussion about improving the quality of life in urban areas, little attention is being paid to ways in which these improvements can be measured.

It is of course possible to quantify over a period of time such things as the amount of parkland, the quality of the air, the number of schools, the rate of unemployment, etc.

There is little question that such measures should be taken in urban areas at several points in time in order to assess changes and compare conditions across different geographic settings (cities and metropolitan areas).

At the same time, however, efforts should be made at quantifying peoples' perceptions of and satisfactions with various conditions in the urban environment.

These two sets of indicators (objective and subjective) are essential as input to the process of planning and building and to the evaluation of the effectiveness of public policy decisions.

Without both, we will have no idea whether the quality of urban life which we all seek is being achieved.

OVERALL SUMMARY AND CONCLUSIONS

Human Well-being in Cities

1. Use and misuse of modern technology.

Modern building techniques make it possible to increase urban
density almost without limit. The ever increasing use of lifts
and air-conditioning help   to create superblocks which are
"cubical cities within cities". These achievements, however
remarkable from a technical point of view, result in an artificial
environment which affects physical and mental health of the users
(Adams and Conway, 1974).

High overall density in cities may be useful to allow easier
contacts between people. However, it does not mean high density
and high rise on some plots,with empty spaces around them. This
brings about the concept of "high density low rise" as opposed to
"low density high rise" (Marans, 1976). Cities, such as Washington
and more recently Toronto and Brussels, have put a ban on any
buildings above ten storeys. Moreover, built forms allowing
natural light and ventilation are less demanding in energy.

Telecommunication is also a major factor in today's urban
context. Not only telephone, radio and television extend the
word-of-mouth communication but also computerized information
storage and flow. It   needs no monumental physical structures

and reflects the new environment of the post industrial information society as much as the visible features of our cities (Kalba, 1976).

Furthermore,careful scrutiny of the personal communication patterns in cities suggest the irreplaceable value of personal contacts within cities for decision-making (Goddard, 1975).

Here again modern technology opens up a non technical question, as to how far human beings are capable of facing and digesting an ever increasing amount of information.

With regard to the effect of modern technology on the quality of air in our cities, it can be said that technology has become capable of seriously reducing pollution caused by industry and domestic heating. However, its application largely depends on the enforcement of the regulations set up by public authorities (possibly combined with incentives).

The management of water resources is another field where technology (purification techniques) can attain remarkable achievements, but does not substitute for the need for a policy towards the careful use of clean water resources. It is now clear that water resources are utterly limited. Urbanization entails supplying water from places further and further away. The challenge is to satisfy the needs of city-dwellers today and tomorrow. This requires a long term stewardship of water resources (Patoharju, 1976 ; Haimes and Hoggan, 1976).

Conversion of urban refuse has progressed remarkably, for

example, the conversion to energy, pyrolisis or bioconversion
(MacAdam , 1976). But here again the actual implementation of this
technical progress has to rely on policies encouraging the use of
these new techniques. Better still, policies encouraging re-use
of goods by selective collection may slow down the ever increasing
flow of urban waste (Luoto and Naveau, 1976).

2. <u>From solution-orientated technology to solution-orientated
   decision-making, the Government of cities as if people mattered.</u>

The urban evolution is confronted with political choices. These
choices can be taken with or without consideration for human beings,
families and small scale communities. It is up to the citizens
themselves, adequately grouped in associations, to balance the power
of politics and technocracy. Organizations such as "Interenvironnement"
in Belgium, which is a federation of some 200 local citizen groups,
provide the link between the people and the official decision-makers.
They are the means by which the small scale community (or ward or
tribe) can be involved in the planning process (Didisheim, 1976;
Schoonbroodt, 1976).

The organisers of the WERC conference (mostly engineers), have
noticed a shift of interest from the technological problems to the
political and social problems. The dialogue between decision-makers,
technicians and the ultimate users of the cities, i.e. the inhabitants,
has been the main topic of discussion.

Using the discussions as a basis, the board of editors have
produced a declaration which includes some guidelines for urban

forms. The aim of these guidelines is a better awareness of the

people concerned and their advisers, on some of the possibilities

for better, and therefore more human, urban settlements.

REFERENCES.

ADAMS, B. CONWAY, J., Social Effects of Living off the Ground,
Department of the Environment, London 1974.

GODDARD, J., Office Location in urban and regional Development,
Oxford University Press, 1975, p.51.

The other names refer to their contributions to the proceedings.

Clean Air Act 1968

CHAPTER 62

ARRANGEMENT OF SECTIONS

Dark smoke

Section
1. Prohibition of dark smoke from industrial or trade premises.

Grit, dust and fumes

2. Emission of grit and dust from furnaces.
3. Requirement to fit arrestment plant to new furnaces.
4. Exemptions from requirement to fit arrestment plant.
5. Measurement of grit, dust and fumes emitted from furnaces.
6. Height of chimneys.
7. Application to fumes of certain provisions as to grit and dust.

Smoke control areas

8. Power of appropriate Minister to require creation of smoke control areas.
9. Acquisition and sale of unauthorised fuel in a smoke control area.
10. Miscellaneous amendments of procedure for making orders with respect to smoke control areas.

Alkali, etc., works

11. Relation of Clean Air Acts to, and amendment of, Alkali Act.

Supplemental

12. Regulations.
13. Interpretation.
14. Adaptation and minor and consequential amendments of principal Act, and repeals.
15. Short title, citation, commencement and extent.

ELIZABETH II

1968 CHAPTER 62

An Act to make further provision for abating the pollution of the air. [25th October 1968]

BE IT ENACTED by the Queen's most Excellent Majesty, by and with the advice and consent of the Lords Spiritual and Temporal, and Commons, in this present Parliament assembled, and by the authority of the same, as follows:—

Dark smoke

1.—(1) Subject to the following provisions of this section, dark smoke shall not be emitted from any industrial or trade premises and if, on any day, dark smoke is so emitted the occupier of the premises shall be liable on summary conviction to a fine not exceeding £100.

[margin: Prohibition of dark smoke from industrial or trade premises.]

(2) Subsection (1) above shall not apply to the emission of dark smoke from a chimney of a building or from any other chimney to which section 1 of the principal Act (prohibition of dark smoke from chimneys) applies.

(3) The Minister may by regulations exempt from subsection (1) above, subject to compliance with such conditions if any as may be prescribed, the emission of dark smoke caused by the burning of any prescribed matter.

(4) In proceedings for an offence under this section it shall be a defence to prove that the contravention complained of was inadvertent and that all practicable steps had been taken to prevent or minimise the emission of dark smoke.

(5) In this section "industrial or trade premises" means premises used for any industrial or trade purposes or premises not so used on which matter is burnt in connection with any industrial or trade process...

Grit, dust and fumes

2.—(1) The Minister may by regulations prescribe limits on the rates of emission of grit and dust from the chimneys of furnaces to which this section applies, and different limits may be prescribed under this subsection for different cases and according to different circumstances.

[margin: Emission of grit and dust from furnaces.]

(2) If on any day grit or dust is emitted from a chimney serving a furnace to which this section applies at a rate exceeding the relevant limit prescribed under subsection (1) above, the occupier of any building in which the furnace is situated shall be liable on summary conviction to a fine not exceeding £100.

(3) In proceedings for an offence under subsection (2) above it shall be a defence to prove that the best practicable means had been used for minimising the alleged emission.

(4) If, in the case of a building containing a furnace to which this section applies and which is served by a chimney to which there is no limit applicable under subsection (1) above, the occupier fails to use any practicable means there may be for minimising the emission of grit or dust from the chimney, he shall be liable on summary conviction to a fine not exceeding £100.

(5) This section applies to any furnace in which solid, liquid or gaseous matter is burnt, not being a furnace designed solely or mainly for domestic purposes and used for heating a boiler with maximum heating capacity of less than 55,000 British thermal units per hour.

(6) Section 5 of the principal Act (grit and dust from solid fuel furnaces) shall cease to have effect.

3.—(1) Subject to the provisions of section 4 of this Act no furnace to which section 2 above applies shall be used in a building—

[margin: Requirement to fit arrestment plant to new furnaces.]

(a) to burn pulverised fuel; or

(b) to burn, at a rate of 100 pounds or more an hour, any other solid matter; or

(c) to burn, at a rate equivalent to $1\frac{1}{4}$ million or more British thermal units an hour, any liquid or gaseous matter;

unless the furnace is provided with plant for arresting grit and dust which has been approved by the local authority or which has been installed in accordance with plans and specifications submitted to and approved by the local authority, and that plant is properly maintained and used.

(2) The Minister may by regulations substitute for any rate mentioned in subsection (1)(b) or (c) above such other rate as he...

thinks fit, but no regulations shall be made under this subsection so as to reduce any such rate unless a draft of the regulations has been laid before Parliament and approved by each House of Parliament.

(3) If on any day a furnace is used in contravention of subsection (1) above, the occupier of the building shall be liable on summary conviction to a fine not exceeding £100.

(4) Subsection (1) above and regulations under subsection (2) above reducing any rate mentioned in subsection (1)(b) or (c) above shall not apply to a furnace which has been installed, the installation of which has been begun, or an agreement for the purchase or installation of which has been entered into, before the commencement of this section or the coming into operation of the regulations, as the case may be.

(5) Section 6(1) of the principal Act (new furnaces to be fitted with plant to arrest grit and dust) shall not apply to a furnace to which subsection (1) above applies; and subsections (3) to (5) of that section (power of the appropriate Minister with respect to approvals under that section) shall apply in relation to an approval under subsection (1) above as they apply in relation to an approval under that section.

(6) Where a local authority determine an application for approval under the said section 6(1) or subsection (1) above, they shall give the applicant a written notification of their decision and, in the case of a decision not to grant approval, shall state their reasons for not doing so.

(7) The right of a person to appeal under section 6(4) of the principal Act against a decision of a local authority under that section or this section shall not be exercisable more than twenty-eight days after he is notified of the decision.

Exemptions from requirement to fit arrestment plant.

4.—(1) The Minister may by regulations provide that furnaces of any prescribed class shall while used for a prescribed purpose be exempted from the operation of section 3(1) above.

(2) If on the application of the occupier of a building a local authority are satisfied that the emission of grit and dust from any chimney serving a furnace in the building will not be prejudicial to health or a nuisance if the furnace is used for a particular purpose without compliance with section 3(1) above, they may exempt the furnace from the operation of that subsection while used for that purpose.

(3) An application for exemption under subsection (2) above shall be made to the local authority in the prescribed form and shall be accompanied by the prescribed particulars, but the foregoing provision shall not preclude a local authority from granting an exemption under that subsection on an application in writing which does not comply with the foregoing provision if the information provided by the applicant is sufficient to enable the authority to determine the application.

(4) If a local authority to whom an application is duly made for an exemption under subsection (2) above fail to determine the application and to give a written notice of their decision to the applicant within eight weeks of receiving the application or such longer period as may be agreed in writing between the applicant and the authority, the furnace shall be treated as having been granted an exemption from the operation of section 3(1) above while used for the purpose specified in the application.

(5) If a local authority decide not to grant an exemption under subsection (2) above, they shall give the applicant a written notification of their decision stating their reasons, and the applicant may within twenty-eight days of receiving the notification appeal against the decision to the appropriate Minister.

(6) On an appeal under this section the appropriate Minister may confirm the decision appealed against, or may grant the exemption applied for or may vary the purpose for which the furnace to which the application relates may be used without compliance with section 3(1) above, and shall give the appellant a written notification of any decision of the Minister on an appeal under this section, stating his reasons for the decision.

(7) If on any day a furnace which is exempt from the operation of section 3(1) above is used for a purpose other than a prescribed purpose or, as the case may be, a purpose for which the furnace may be used by virtue of subsection (2), (4) or (6) above, the occupier of the building shall be liable on summary conviction to a fine not exceeding £100.

Measurement of grit, dust and fumes emitted from furnaces.

5.—(1) In section 7(1) of the principal Act (measurement of grit and dust emitted from furnaces) for paragraph (b) there shall be substituted the following paragraphs:—

" (b) to burn, at a rate of 100 pounds or more an hour, any other solid matter; or

(c) to burn, at a rate equivalent to 1¼ million or more British thermal units an hour, any liquid or gaseous matter."

(2) The Minister may by regulations substitute for any rate mentioned in the said section 7(1)(b) or (c) such other rate as he thinks fit, but no regulations shall be made under this subsection so as to reduce any such rate unless a draft of the regulations has been laid before Parliament and approved by each House of Parliament.

(3) In the case of a furnace to which section 7(2) of the principal Act is applied and which is used—

(a) to burn, at a rate less than one ton an hour, solid matter other than pulverised fuel; or

(b) to burn at a rate of less than 28 million British thermal units an hour, any liquid or gaseous matter;

the occupier of the building in which the furnace is situate may, by notice in writing given to the local authority, request the local authority to make and record measurements of the grit, dust and fumes emitted from the furnace.

(4) A notice given under subsection (3) above by the occupier of a building may be withdrawn by a subsequent notice in writing given to the local authority by him or any subsequent occupier of that building.

(5) While a notice is in force under subsection (3) above the local authority shall from time to time make and record measurements of the grit, dust and fumes emitted from the furnace to which the notice relates and the occupier shall not be under a duty to comply with any requirements of regulations under section 7(2) of the principal Act in relation to the furnace, except those imposed by virtue of paragraph (b) of that subsection.

(6) A direction under section 7(1) of the principal Act applying section 7(2) of that Act to a furnace which is used as mentioned in subsection (3)(a) or (b) above shall contain a statement of the effect of subsections (3) to (5) above.

(7) The occupier of a building who by virtue of the said section 7(2) is under a duty to make and record measurements of grit, dust and fumes emitted from a furnace in the building shall permit the local authority to be represented during the making and recording of those measurements.

Height of chimneys.

6.—(1) An occupier of a building shall not knowingly cause or permit a furnace therein to which this section applies to be used in the building as mentioned in section 3(1) above as originally enacted unless the height of the chimney serving the furnace has been approved under this section and any conditions subject to which the approval was granted are complied with, and if on any day he does so, he shall be liable on summary conviction to a fine not exceeding £100.

(2) A person having possession of a boiler or industrial plant attached to a building or for the time being fixed to or installed on any land, other than an exempted boiler or plant, shall not knowingly cause or permit a furnace thereof to which this section applies to be used as mentioned in section 3(1) above as originally enacted, unless the height of the chimney serving the furnace has been approved under this section and any conditions subject to which the approval was granted are complied with, and if on any day he does so, he shall be liable on summary conviction to a fine not exceeding £100.

(3) An application for approval under this section shall be made to the local authority on the prescribed form and shall be accompanied by the prescribed particulars, but the foregoing provision shall not preclude the local authority from granting their approval under this section on an application in writing which does not comply with the foregoing provision if the information provided by the applicant is sufficient to enable the authority to determine the application.

(4) A local authority shall not approve the height of a chimney under this section unless they are satisfied that its height will be sufficient to prevent, so far as practicable, the smoke, grit, dust, gases or fumes emitted from the chimney from becoming prejudicial to health or a nuisance having regard to—

(a) the purpose of the chimney;

(b) the position and descriptions of buildings near it;

(c) the levels of the neighbouring ground;

(d) any other matters requiring consideration in the circumstances.

(5) An approval of the height of a chimney by a local authority under this section may be granted without qualification or subject to conditions as to the rate or quality, or the rate and quality, of emissions from the chimney.

(6) If a local authority to whom an application is duly made for approval under this section fail to determine the application and to give a written notification of their decision to the applicant within four weeks of receiving the application or such longer period as may be agreed in writing between the applicant and the authority, the approval applied for shall be deemed to have been granted without qualification.

(7) If a local authority decide not to approve the height of a chimney under this section or to attach conditions to their approval, they shall give the applicant a written notification of their decision, stating their reasons and, in the case of a decision not to approve the height of the chimney, specifying the lowest height, if any, which they are prepared to approve unconditionally or the lowest height which they are prepared to approve if approval is granted subject to any specified conditions, or (if they think fit) both, and the applicant may within twenty-eight days of receiving the notification appeal against the decision to the appropriate Minister.

(8) On an appeal under this section the appropriate Minister may confirm the decision appealed against, or may approve the height of the chimney without qualification or subject to conditions as to the rate or quality, or the rate and quality, of emissions from the chimney, or may cancel any conditions imposed by the local authority or substitute for any conditions so imposed any other conditions which the authority had power to impose.

(9) The appropriate Minister shall give the appellant a written notification of any decision of the Minister on an appeal under this section, stating his reasons for the decision, and, in the case of a decision not to approve the height of a chimney, specifying the lowest height, if any, which he is prepared to approve unconditionally or the lowest height which he is prepared to approve if approval is granted subject to any specified conditions, or (if he thinks fit) both.

(10) This section applies to the following furnaces:—

(a) any furnace served by a chimney other than a chimney the construction of which was begun or the plans for which were passed before the commencement of this section;

(b) any furnace the combustion space of which has been increased since the commencement of this section; and

(c) any furnace the installation of which was begun after the commencement of this section and which replaces a furnace which had a smaller combustion space;

not being a furnace forming part of a generating station as defined in the Electricity (Supply) Act 1919, other than a private generating station as so defined.

1919 c. 100.

(11) In this section "exempted boiler or plant" means a boiler or plant which is used or to be used wholly for any prescribed purpose, and references to the applicant shall, in a case where the original applicant notifies the local authority that his interest in the application has been transferred to another person, be construed as references to that other person.

(12) Section 10 of the principal Act (requirement for approval of height of chimneys on submission of plans) shall cease to have effect as respects any chimney serving a furnace.

Application to fumes of certain provisions as to grit and dust.

7.—(1) The Minister may by regulations—

(a) apply all or any of the provisions of sections 2, 3 and 4 of this Act and of sections 18(2), 19(3), 20(4) and 22(1) of the principal Act (provisions relating to grit and dust) to fumes as they apply to grit and dust; and

(b) apply all or any of the provisions of section 3 of the principal Act (requirement that new furnaces shall be so far as practicable smokeless) to fumes as they apply to smoke;

subject, in either case, to such exceptions and modifications as the Minister thinks expedient.

(2) Regulations under this section may make different provision for different cases.

(3) No regulations shall be made under this section unless a draft of the regulations has been laid before Parliament and approved by each House of Parliament.

Smoke Control Areas

Power of appropriate Minister to require creation of smoke control areas.

8.—(1) If after consultation with a local authority the appropriate Minister is satisfied that it is expedient to abate the pollution of the air by smoke in the area or part of the area of the authority and that authority have not exercised, or have not sufficiently exercised, their powers under section 11 of the principal Act (smoke control areas) to abate the pollution, he may direct the authority to prepare and submit to him for his approval, within such period not being less than six months from the direction as may be specified in the direction, proposals for making and bringing into operation one or more orders under that section within such period or periods as the authority think fit.

(2) Any proposals made by a local authority in pursuance of a direction under subsection (1) above may be varied by further proposals made by the authority within the period specified for the making of the original proposals or such longer period as the appropriate Minister may allow.

(3) The appropriate Minister may reject any proposals submitted to him under this section or may approve them in whole or in part, with or without modifications.

(4) Where a local authority to whom a direction has been given under subsection (1) above fail to submit proposals to the appropriate Minister within the period specified in the direction, or where any proposals so submitted are rejected in whole or in part, the appropriate Minister may make an order declaring them to be in default and directing them for the purposes of removing the default to exercise their powers under section 11 of the principal Act in such manner and within such period as may be specified in the order.

(5) An order under subsection (4) above may be varied or revoked by a subsequent order made by the appropriate Minister.

(6) While proposals made by a local authority and approved by the appropriate Minister under this section are in force, it shall be the duty of the authority to make such order or orders under section 11 of the principal Act as are necessary to carry out the proposals as for the time being in force.

(7) Sections 321 and 322 of the Public Health Act 1936 and sections 193 and 194 of the Housing (Scotland) Act 1966 (default powers) shall not apply to a failure by a local authority to discharge their functions under section 11 of the principal Act or to submit proposals to the appropriate Minister in pursuance of a direction under subsection (1) above or to perform a duty imposed on them by or by virtue of subsection (4) or (6) above.

[margin: 1936 c. 49. 1966 c. 49.]

(8) Any increase attributable to the provisions of this section in the sums payable out of moneys provided by Parliament under section 13 of the principal Act (Exchequer contributions towards expenditure incurred for the purpose of avoiding emissions of smoke in smoke control areas) shall be defrayed out of moneys so provided.

[margin: Acquisition and sale of unauthorised fuel in a smoke control area.]

9.—(1) Any person who—

(a) acquires any solid fuel, other than an authorised fuel, for use in a building in a smoke control area otherwise than in a building or fireplace exempted from the operation of section 11 of the principal Act; or

(b) acquires any solid fuel, other than an authorised fuel, for use in a boiler or plant to which this paragraph applies in a smoke control area, not being a boiler or plant so exempted; or

(c) sells by retail any solid fuel, other than an authorised fuel, for delivery by him or on his behalf to a building in a smoke control area or to premises in such an area in which there is a boiler or plant to which paragraph (b) above applies;

shall be liable on summary conviction to a fine not exceeding £20.

(2) Subsection (1)(b) above applies to any boiler or industrial plant attached to a building or for the time being fixed to or installed on any land.

(3) Subsection (1) above shall, in its application to a smoke control area in which the operation of section 11 of the principal Act is limited by an order under that section to specified classes of buildings, boilers or plant, have effect as if references therein to a building, boiler or plant were references to a building, boiler or plant of a class specified in the order.

(4) The power of the appropriate Minister under section 11 of the principal Act to suspend or relax the operation of that

section in relation to the whole or any part of a smoke control area shall include power to suspend or relax the operation of subsections (1) and (2) above in relation to the whole or any part of such an area.

(5) A person shall not be convicted of an offence under this section consisting of the sale of fuel for delivery to a building or premises if he proves that he believed and had reasonable grounds for believing—

(a) that the building was exempted from the operation of section 11 of the principal Act or, in a case where the operation of that section is limited to specified classes of building, was not of a specified class; or

(b) that the fuel was acquired for use in a fireplace, boiler or plant so exempted or, in a case where the operation of that section is limited to specified classes of boilers or plant, in a boiler or plant not of a specified class.

[margin: Miscellaneous amendments of procedure for making orders with respect to smoke control areas.]

10.—(1) Notwithstanding anything in paragraph 6 of Schedule 1 to the principal Act (local authority orders under section 11 of that Act to come into operation not earlier than six months from confirmation thereof) an order made by a local authority under the said section 11 varying a previous order under that section so as to exempt specified buildings or classes of building or specified fireplaces or classes of fireplace from the operation of that section may come into operation on, or at any time after, the date of its confirmation.

(2) A local authority shall not without the consent of the appropriate Minister exercise their power under the proviso to the said paragraph 6 of postponing the coming into operation of an order under the said section 11 for a period of more than twelve months or for periods amounting in all to more than twelve months.

(3) An order made under the said section 11 before the commencement of this section which, apart from this subsection, would in pursuance of a resolution under the said proviso come into operation after the expiration of the year beginning with the commencement of this section shall, unless the appropriate Minister otherwise directs, come into operation on the expiration of that year, and, where he so directs, shall come into operation on a day specified in the direction (being not later than that specified in the resolution).

(4) In paragraph (4) of Schedule 1 to the principal Act (procedure for confirming orders under section 11 of the principal Act) for the words from "in any other case" to the end there shall be substituted the words "in any other case he shall, before confirming the order either cause a local inquiry to be held

Appendix 1

345

Clean Air Act 1968

Clean Air Act 1968

CH. 62

CH. 62

or afford to any person by whom an objection has been duly made as aforesaid and not withdrawn an opportunity of appearing before and being heard by a person appointed by him for the purpose, and, after considering the objection and the report of the person who held the inquiry or the person appointed as aforesaid, may confirm the order either with or without modifications".

(5) In section 95(2) of the Housing Act 1964 (power of local authority after making an order under section 11 of the principal Act to designate unsuitable heating appliances which are not to qualify for adaptation grants in smoke control areas) for the words " after an order has been made by a local authority" there shall be substituted the words " after a local authority has resolved to make an order".

Alkali, etc., works

11.—(1) Subject to the following provisions of this section, sections 1 to 16 of the principal Act and sections 1 to 10 above shall not apply to any work subject or potentially subject to the Alkali Act.

(2) Subject as aforesaid, the Alkali Act shall have effect in relation to smoke, grit and dust from any work subject or potentially subject to that Act as it has effect in relation to noxious or offensive gases, and references therein to noxious or offensive gases shall be construed accordingly.

(3) If, on the application of the local authority, the appropriate Minister is satisfied that in all the circumstances it is expedient so to do, he may by order exclude the application of subsections (1) and (2) above to the whole or any specified part of any work subject or potentially subject to the Alkali Act and, while those subsections are so excluded,—

(a) in any proceedings brought by virtue of section 1 or 11(2) of the principal Act (dark smoke, and smoke control orders) or section 1 of this Act in respect of the emission of smoke from the work or, as the case may be, the specified part thereof it shall be a defence to prove that the best practicable means had been employed to prevent or minimise the alleged emission; and

(b) in any proceedings brought by virtue of section 16(1) of the principal Act (smoke nuisances) in respect of smoke emitted from the work or, as the case may be, the specified part thereof, the defence provided for by the proviso to the said section 16(1) shall be available whether the smoke was emitted from a chimney or not

Margin note: 1964 c. 56.

Margin note: Relation of Clean Air Acts to, and amendment of, Alkali Act.

(4) Any order made under subsection (3) above may be revoked or varied by a subsequent order made by the appropriate Minister.

(5) Nothing in this section shall extend the operation of section 4(3) of the Public Health (Smoke Abatement) Act 1926 or section 2 of the Alkali, &c., Works Regulation (Scotland) Act 1951 (power of inspectors to enter and inspect works not subject to the Alkali Act).

Margin note: 1926 c. 43.
Margin note: 1951 c. 21.

(6) In this section—

" Alkali Act " means the Alkali, &c., Works Regulation Act 1906;

Margin note: 1906 c. 14.

"work subject or potentially subject to the Alkali Act" means—

(a) so much of any work registered under section 9 of that Act as is directly concerned in the processes which necessitate its registration under that section; and

(b) so much of any work in the course of erection or alteration as will on the completion of the erection or alteration be directly concerned in such processes.

(7) The Minister may from time to time determine how much of any work mentioned in subsection (6) above is or will be directly concerned as aforesaid and his determination shall, until revoked or varied by him, be conclusive.

(8) Subsections (1), (2), (5) and (6) of section 17 of the principal Act (which make provision corresponding to the foregoing provisions of this section) shall cease to have effect, but any order made before the commencement of this section under the said subsection (2) as respects any work or any part thereof shall be treated as an order under subsection (3) above excluding the application of subsections (1) and (2) above to that work or, as the case may be, that part thereof and any determination made before the commencement of this section under the said subsection (3) shall be treated as if made under subsection (7) above.

(9) In section 17(3) and (4) of the principal Act " Alkali Act " has the same meaning as in this section.

Supplemental

12.—(1) Any power of the Minister under this Act to make regulations and any power of the Minister under section 14 or 15 of this Act to make orders shall be exercisable by statutory instrument.

Margin note: Regulations.

(2) Any statutory instrument containing regulations made under this Act, except an instrument containing regulations a draft of which is required by section 3(2), 5(2) or 7(3) of this Act to be approved by a resolution of each House of Parliament, shall be subject to annulment in pursuance of a resolution of either House of Parliament.

Interpretation.

13.—(1) In this Act, except so far as the context otherwise requires—

"the appropriate Minister" means, except as respects Scotland or Wales and Monmouthshire, the Minister of Housing and Local Government and, as respects Scotland or Wales and Monmouthshire, the Secretary of State;

"fumes" means any airborne solid matter smaller than dust;

"the Minister" means as respects England and Wales the Minister of Housing and Local Government and as respects Scotland the Secretary of State;

"prescribed" means prescribed by regulations made by the Minister;

1956 c. 52.

"the principal Act" means the Clean Air Act 1956;

and other expressions used in this Act and the principal Act have the same meanings in this Act as they have in that Act.

(2) In this Act any reference to the rate of emission of any substance or any reference which is to be understood as such a reference shall, in relation to any regulations or conditions, be construed as a reference to the quantities of that substance which may be emitted during a period specified in the regulations or conditions.

(3) Any reference in this Act to any enactment is a reference thereto as amended, and includes a reference thereto as extended or applied, by or under any other enactment, including this Act.

Adaptation and minor and consequential amendments of principal Act, and repeals.

14.—(1) Schedule 1 to this Act shall have effect for adapting the principal Act and for making amendments of that Act which are minor or are consequential on the foregoing provisions of this Act.

(2) The provisions of the principal Act specified in Schedule 2 to this Act (which include provisions which were wholly or partially obsolete or unnecessary before the passing of this Act) are hereby repealed to the extent specified in that Schedule.

(3) The appropriate Minister may after consultation with any of the following authorities who appear to him to be concerned, that is to say a local authority, a county council and the

Greater London Council, by order repeal any provision of any local Act which appears to him to be unnecessary having regard to the provisions of this Act and may by that order make such amendments of that or any other local Act as appear to him to be necessary in consequence of the repeal and such transitional provision as appears to him to be necessary or expedient in connection with the matter.

Short title, citation, commencement and extent.

15.—(1) This Act may be cited as the Clean Air Act 1968.

(2) The principal Act and this Act may be cited together as the Clean Air Acts 1956 and 1968.

(3) This Act shall come into operation on a day appointed by an order made by the Minister, and different days may be appointed under this section for different purposes and, in particular, different days may be so appointed for the coming into operation of the same provision in different areas.

(4) Any order made under subsection (3) above by the Minister may be varied or revoked by a subsequent order made by him.

(5) Any reference in this Act to the commencement of any provision thereof shall be construed as a reference to the day appointed for the coming into operation of that provision or, in the case of a provision which comes into operation on different days in different areas, shall, in relation to any area, be construed as a reference to the day appointed for the coming into operation of that provision in that area.

(6) This Act shall not extend to Northern Ireland.

SCHEDULES

SCHEDULE 1

Section 14(1).

ADAPTATION AND MINOR AND CONSEQUENTIAL AMENDMENTS OF PRINCIPAL ACT

1. In sections 18, 19(3), 20(4), 22, 26, 27(5), 28, 29 and 31 references to the principal Act, other than references to a specified provision of that Act, shall be construed as including references to this Act.

2. In section 7(2)(a) for the words "grit and dust" there shall be substituted the words "grit, dust and fumes".

3. In section 8(1) the reference to sections 6 and 7 of the principal Act shall be construed as including references to sections 2 to 5 of this Act.

4. In section 9 for the reference to sections 5 to 8 of the principal Act there shall be substituted a reference to sections 6 to 8 of that Act and sections 2 to 4 of this Act, and the reference to section 6(2) of that Act shall be construed as including a reference to section 3(4) of this Act.

5. In section 16(1), after paragraph (b) there shall be inserted the following words "or

(c) dark smoke emitted otherwise than as aforesaid from industrial or trade premises within the meaning of section 1 of the Clean Air Act 1968".

6. In section 21 for the words "the provisions of this Act" there shall be substituted the words "the under-mentioned provisions of this Act or the Clean Air Act 1968", and for paragraphs (a) to (c) there shall be substituted the following paragraphs:—

"(a) any chimney from the operation of sections 1, 11, 16 and 19 of this Act and section 2 of the Clean Air Act 1968;

(b) any furnace, boiler or industrial plant from the operation of section 3(1) of this Act;

(c) any premises from the operation of section 1 of the said Act of 1968;

(d) any furnace from the operation of sections 6 and 7 of this Act and section 3 of that Act;

(e) the acquisition or sale of any fuel specified in the notice from the operation of section 5 of that Act".

7. In section 27(5), for the words "ten pounds" there shall be substituted the words "fifty pounds".

8. In section 29(2), at the end there shall be added the words "and may institute proceedings for an offence under section 1 of the Clean Air Act 1968 in the case of any smoke which affects any part of their district notwithstanding that the smoke is emitted from premises outside their district".

9. In section 30 references to section 1 of the principal Act shall be construed as including a reference to section 1 of this Act.

10. In section 34(1), in the definition of "chimney" for the words from "smoke" to "emitted" there shall be substituted the words "smoke, grit, dust or fumes may be emitted and, in particular, includes flues", and after the definition of "fireplace" there shall be inserted the following definition, that is to say, "'fumes' means any airborne solid matter smaller than dust".

11. In section 34(2) the reference to section 1 of the principal Act shall be construed as including a reference to section 1 of this Act.

12. In section 34(7) the reference to sections 6 to 8 of the principal Act shall be construed as including a reference to sections 2 to 6 of this Act.

SCHEDULE 2

Section 14(2).

PROVISIONS OF PRINCIPAL ACT REPEALED

Section 2.

Section 5.

In section 6, in subsection (1), the words from "and no oven" to "heat"; in subsections (1) and (2), the words "or oven" wherever occurring; and in subsections (1) and (4) the words "or land", wherever occurring.

In section 7, in subsection (1), the words from "or if an oven" to "heat"; in subsections (1), (2) and (3), the words "or oven" wherever occurring; and, in subsections (1) and (2), the words "or land", wherever occurring.

In section 8(1), the words "or land", wherever occurring, and the words "or ovens", "or on the land" and "or subjected to any process in those ovens".

Section 10 as respects any chimney serving a furnace.

In section 14(1)(c), the words "flue or".

Section 17(1), (2), (5) and (6).

In section 20(1), the words "and two".

In section 34(1) the definition of "oven".

AUTHOR INDEX

Abu-Lighod, J. I, 174
Allott, K. I, 175
Altman, I. I, 176
Alvord, D.S. I, 198, 203, 212
American Society of Civil
    Engineers II, 210
Athans, M. I, 254
Attali, J. II, 11
Aziz, S. II, 72

Badakhshan, A. II, 72
Baker, J. I, 198
Barker, R.M. I, 204
Barlowe, R. I, 21
Barth, N. I, 175
Bauer, M.E. I, 72
Bauvin, J.D. II, 198
Bayes, K. II, 288
Beck, B. I, 254
Becker, R. II, 27
Belanger, W. I, 72
Bennett, I.C. II, 72
Berindan, C. II, 192, 198
Bernatsky, A. II, 198
Berry, R.S. II, 289
Bibo, I. II, 131
Birks, T. I, 161
Blumenfeld, H. II, 289
Borodah, R. I, 176
Boulanger, J. II, 198
Boulding, K.E. II, 286, 289
Boullard, B. II, 198
Bower, B.T. II, 235
Braybrooke, D. I, 51
Break, G.F. I, 85
Bretz, R. II, 11
Brown, L.R. II, 50
Brubaker, S. I, 195
Burby, R. I, 176
Bush, R.D. I, 195

Caborn, J.M. II, 50
Calder, N. II, 27
Calhoun, J.B. I, 169, 174
Canadian Council of Resources and
    Environment Ministers II, 288
Cannon, R.H.,Jr. I, 71
Cantril, H. I, 174

Cappon, D. II, 288
Carlestam, G. II, 280, 288
Carr, E.H. II, 120
Carrier, G.F. I, 72
Carter, V.G. II, 50
Cass-Beggs, D. II, 231
Castells, M. II, 113
Catlow, J. II, 101
Chadwick, G.F. I, 225
Chandler, T.J. II, 198
Chang, C-W. II, 50
Chayanov, A.V. II, 131
Child, I.L. I, 195
Choay, F. I, 286
Christian, J. I, 169, 174
Clark, B.D. II, 101
Coase, R. I, 233
Cobb, S. I, 175
Coffman, D.M. I, 220
Cohen, D. I, 128
Coker, A.E. I, 71, 72
Coll, D.C. II, 12
Commission of the European
    Communities II, 100
Cooper, C. I, 174
Cordes, E.H. I, 72
Coroniti, S.C. I, 71
Corsi, T.M. I, 20
Cortes-Rivera, G. I, 255
Council on Environmental Quality
    II, 100
Craik, K.H. I, 195
Cullen, G. I, 299

Dale, T. II, 50
Dales, J. I, 84, 85; II, 235
Dasilva, E.J. II, 73
Davis, D. I, 169, 174
Davis, P. II, 72
Dearinger, J.A. I, 195
Deedy, J. II, 27
Delcarte, E. II, 198
Deutsch, M. I, 71, 72
Didisheim, M. I, 287
Donnelly, T. I, 176
Downing, R.H. I, 40
Driver, B.L. I, 175
Dubos, R. I, 171, 174; II, 280, 288

349

SUBJECT INDEX

LIST OF PARTICIPANTS

AUSTRIA

AUBÖCK, C.	President	ICSID	45, Avenue Legrand, 1050 Brussels
PURSCHKE		Österreichisches Institut für Raumplanung	1011 Wien, Franz Josefs – Kai 27

BELGIUM

BAEYENS, H.	Secretary General	Mens en Ruimte v.z.w.	Froissartstraat, 118, Brussels
BERNAERTS	Service Environnement	Crédit Communal de Belgique	Boulevard Pachéco, 44, 1000 Brussels
BLONDE, M.	Head Dept.–Urban Planning & Environment	Economic Council Province of Antwerp	Koningin Elisabethlei, 18, 2000 Antwerpen
BORMANS	Director	Ecochem	Maria Louisasquare, 49, 1040 Brussels
BOUILLON, J.	Secrétaire Général Adjoint	Institut National du Logement	10, Boulevard St-Lazare, 1030 Brussels
CAPEL–BOUTE, C.	Directeur Chef de Travaux	CIREFA Faculté des Sciences Appliquées Université Libre de Bruxelles	50, avenue F.D. Roosevelt, 1050 Brussels
CROCHET	Traffic Engineer	Université Catholique de Louvain	Avenue de l'Espinette, 28, 1348 Louvain-la-Neuve
DAMIEAN, G.	Directeur	"Eau & Relief"	4208 Boncelles-lez-Liège
DELCROIX, J.C.	Conseiller	Cabinet du Secrétaire d'Etat aux Affaires Economiques	47, avenue des Arts, 1040 Brussels
DENECKER	Directeur	Travaux Publics Commune de Woluwé-St-Lambert	Place du Tomberg, 1200, Brussels
DIDISHEIM, M.	Maître de Conférence	Université de Louvain	Drève du Sénéchal, 25, 1180 Brussels
DUESBERG, F.	Urban Sociologist	Service Environnement du Crédit Communal de Belgique Université de l'Etat	44, Boulevard Pachéco, 1000 Brussels 7000 Mons
DULAING, H.	Architect	City of Bruges	Stijn Streuvelsstraat, 56, 8000 Bruges
EXSTEYL, J.	Inspecteur Chimiste en Chef – Directeur	Laboratoire de Toxicologie Ministère de l'Emploi et du Travail	Rue Belliard, 53, 1040 Brussels
FEUILLAT, F.	Chargé de Recherche	Université Libre de Bruxelles Institut d'Etudes Européennes	39, av. F.D. Roosevelt, 1050 Brussels
HAMBYE, F.	Chef de Cabinet Adjoint du Ministre	Ministère des Affaires Wallonnes, de l'Aménagement du Territoire et du Logement	Rue Joseph II, 30, 1040 Brussels
HANSSENS, M.	Directeur–Adjoint	INTERCOM	Place du Trône, 1, 1000 Brussels
HAUMONT, F.	Juriste–Urbaniste	S.E.R.E.S.	26, Leopoldstraat, 3000 Leuven
HARROY, J.–P.	Head	Service Environnement Crédit Communal de Belgique	Boulevard Pachéco, 44, 1000 Brussels
IMPENS, R.	Professeur	Faculté des Sciences Agronomiques	5800 Gembloux
KORMOSS, I.B.F.	Professor Secretary General	College of Europe NWPPC	Dyver, 7, 8000 Brugge
LACONTE, P.	Directeur Président du WERC	Service Expansion Université Catholique de Louvain	Avenue de l'Espinette, 14, 1348 Louvain-la-Neuve
LAFONTAINE, A.	Directeur Général	Institut d'Hygiène et d'Epidémiologie Ministère de la Santé Publique	Rue Juliette Wijtsman, 1050 Brussels
LIEVENS, J.		ELECTROBEL S.A.	1, Place du Trône, 1000 Brussels
MERTENS, R.	Coordinateur–Gérant	Société de Recherche Appliquée pour l'Urbanisme et l'Aménagement S.U.R.B.R.A.	Chaussée de Bruxelles, 89, 1310 La Hulpe
NASSAUX, J.–P.	Urbaniste	Agglomération de Bruxelles	Rue de France, 69-71, 1060 Brussels
NAVEAU, H.	Chargé de Cours	Laboratoire des Polymères Naturels Université Catholique de Louvain	Pl. Croix du Sud, 1, 1348 Louvain-la-Neuve
NEUHUYS	Service Environnement	Crédit Communal de Belgique	Boulevard Pachéco, 44, 1000 Brussels
PAQUAY		Institut National du Logement	Boulevard St-Lazare, 1030 Brussels
PUTTEMANS, P.		URBAT	Rue J-B Colyns, 103, 1060 Brussels
REGINSTER, J.	Attaché	Société de Développement Régional pour la Wallonie (S.D.R.W.)	Rue Grafé, 5, 5000 Namur
REYNDERS, M.	Ingénieur Responsable	Service de l'Environnement et de la Qualité de la Vie, Ville de Liège, Cabinet du Bourgmestre Hôtel de Ville	4000 Liège
SCHOONBROODT, R.	Maître de Conférence	Université Catholique de Louvain	Rue Alexandre Markelbach, 36 1030 Bruxelles

SOUPART, G.   Directeur Général   Service Communal de Belgique   Rue d'Arlon, 53, Bte 13, 1040 Brussels
STENBOCK—FERMOR, K.   Chargé de Recherches   Faculté des Sciences Agronomiques   5800 Gembloux
STEPPE, J.   Agglomération de Bruxelles   Rue de France, 71, 1070 Brussels
TANGHE, J.   Architect & Town Planner   Groep Planning   Wijngaartplein, 13, 8000 Brugge
THIERS   Service de Biologie   Institut d'Epidémiologie   Quartier de l'Esplanade
                                                      Ministère de la Santé Publique   1010 Brussels
VAN BEVER, A.   Urbaniste   Ministère de la Culture Française   Avenue de Cortenbergh, 1040 Brussels
VANOVERSCHELDE   Chef du Service de   Institut d'Epidémiologie   Quartier de l'Esplanade, 1010 Brussels
                          Biologie   Ministère de la Santé Publique
van WUNNIK, P.   Ingénieur ppl.   Urbanisme—Architecture — U.C.L.   28, avenue de l'Espinette,
                                                                                          1348 Louvain-la-Neuve
VERHEYEN, R.E.   Kabinetschef   Staat Secretariaat voor Leefmilieu Avenue de Berlaimont, 12, 1000
                                                                                          Brussels

BRAZIL

BEUX, A.   President   Federaçao Nacional dos Engenheiros Rua Andrade Neves, 14-3A—Conj.301
                                                                                          Porto Alegre — RS
FONTELES—A., L.   Member, Agriculturist   Federaçao Nacional dos Engenheiros Rua Andrade Neves, 14-3A—Conj.301
                          Engineer   Porto Alegre — RS

CANADA

AGARWAL, B.P.   Senior Policy Advisor   Ministry of State — Urban Affairs   Ottawa, P.O., K1A 0P6
BREMNER   Commissioner   Public Works and City Engineer   City Hall, Toronto, Ontario
                                                      Department of Public Works
                                                      City of Toronto
DEWEES, D.N.   Associate Professor   Dept. of Political Economy and
                                                      Institute for Environmental Studies
                                                      University of Toronto   Toronto, P.O.
FERAHIAN, R.H.   Consulting Engineer   4998 de Maisonneuve ⌗ 1416
                                                                                          Westmount, P.Q. H3Z IN2
FUNK, H.F.   President   Silvichem Corp.   73 Simcoe St. Suite 205, Toronto, P.O.
GRIMA, A.P.   Department of Geography   100, St-George Street, Toronto M5S IAI
                                                      University of Toronto
HANCOCK, M.L.   Chairman of the Board   Project Planning Associates   111, Avenue Road, Toronto, P.O.
                          and Chief Executive
                          Officer
JONES, Ph.H.   Consulting Sanitary   Institute of Environment Sciences   Toronto
                          Engineer   & Eng.
                          Director   University of Toronto
  SCRIVENER, M. MPP.   Parliamentary Assistant   Ministry of Housing   Parliament Buildings, Queen Park
                                                                                          Toronto, Ontario
SWAN, J.   Professor   Faculty of Law
                                                      University of Toronto   Toronto P.O.

DENMARK

HEDEGAARD, J.   Professor   Department of Microbiology
                                                      The Polytechnical University   DK 2800 Lingby, Copenhagen

FINLAND

LAUKKANAN, A.   Engineer   Town Planning Office   Helsinki
  LUOTO, U.   Senior Consultant   EKONO Consulting Engineers   P.O. Box 27, SF-00131 Helsinki
PATOHARJU, O.   Secretary   Environment Protecting Commission   N. Esplanade 15-17
                                                      The City Office of the   SF-00170 Helsinki 17
                                                      Municipality of Helsinki
SAURAMO, V.   Dipl. Eng.   City Planning Office of Helsinki   Nilsjank 6, Helsinki
WESTERBERG, E.N.   Executive   EKONO Consulting Engineers   P.O. Box 27
                          Vice—President   SF-00131 Helsinki 13

FRANCE

BELOT, Th.   Student   Sorbonne   Paris
COUSIN, R.P.   Engineer   Louis Berger S.A.R.L.   Rue Fondary, 71, 75015 Paris
FRIEDMAN, Y.   Professor   S.C.A.   Boulevard Pasteur, 42, 75015 Paris
                          Consultant   M.I.T.
KOROSEC—SERFATY, P.   Professeur   Université Pasteur   12, rue Goethe, 67000 Strasbourg
                          Maître—Assist.   Institut de Psychologie Sociale
                                                      U.E.R. des Sciences du Comportement

GERMANY

MARKELIN, A.   Professor   Städtebauliches Institut der   7 Stuttgart—1, Keplerstr.11
                                                      Universität Stuttgart
RASSAERTS, Ch.P.   Architect—Urbanist   Heinle, Wischer und Partner   Rotenbergstrasse, 8, 7000 Stuttgart 1
                                                      Freie Architekten

SCHMIDT, A.			Keplerstrasse 10, 7 Stuttgart
TRIEB, M.	Dr. Ing.	Städtebauliches Institut der	7 Stuttgart, 1, Keplerstr. 10
		Universität Stuttgart	
WERTZ, E.	Professor	University of Stuttgart	Hoppenlaustrasse, 7, 7 Stuttgart 1

GREAT BRITAIN

APGAR, M., IV	Principal	McKinsey & C°, Inc.	75 St. James Street, London SWIA IPS
ATKINSON, Ch.R.	Director	Development Services	25, Eccleston Square, London SWIV INX
		City of Bradford	
		Metropolitan Council	
		Institution of Municipal Engineers	
BOURNE, A.G.	Consultant		17, Church Road, Flitwick,
			Bedfordshire
CHAMPNESS, C.P.	Associate Partner	Gerald Eve & C°	
COALES, J.F.	Professor		2, Little Smith Street, Westminster
	Past-President WERC		London SW.1P 3DL
	Chairman	Council of Engineering Institutions	
COOPER, K.C.	Architect		Rue des Sables, 8, Rhode-St.Genèse
EPSTEIN, G.	Architect	Shepheard Epstein & Hunter	60 Kingly street Regent st.
			London WIR 6EY
HISCOCK, D.	Principal Lecturer	North East London Polytechnio	Forest Road, London E17 4JB
HUGHES, J.T.	Professor	University of Glasgow	Adam Smith Bldg. GLASGOW G12 8RT
HUGHES-EVANS, D.	Senior Lecturer Life	Farnborough College of	Boundary Road, Farnborough, Hampshire
	Science	Technology	
KING, G.A.D.	County Planning Officer	County Planning Dept.	Orchard Street
		West Glamorgan County Council	SWANSEA, SAI 35G
		WestGlamorgan House	
LECHUGA G., L.E.			36 Warrender Park Terrace, 1st floor
			flat Edinburg, Scotland
LEE, N.	Senior Lecturer	Faculty of Economic & Social Studies	Oxford Road, Manchester M 139 TL
	in Economics	University of Manchester	
LEWIS, C.	Chairman	County Planning Committee	Orchard Street, SWANSEA, SAI 35G
		West Glamorgan County Council	
		West Glamorgan House	
MAXWELL R.M.C.	Chairman	Pergamon Press	Headington Hill Hall, Oxford OX3 OBW
REILLY, P.	Director	Design Council	28 Haymarket, London SW1Y 4SV
SLIWA, J.A.	Principal Lecturer	North East London Polytechnic	Forest Road, London EI7 4JB
STRANGE, R.E.	Director	Pergamon Press	Headington Hill Hall, Oxford OX3 OBW
WILLIAMS, S.		Building Design	30, Calderwood Street, London SE18 6QH
		Morgan Grampian Ltd.	
SZELENYI, I.	Professor, Dpt. Sociology	University of Canterbury at Kent	Canterbury (Kent)

INDIA

ARORA, C.R.	Assistant Professor	University of Wisconsin-Oshkosh	Oshkosh, Wisc. 54901 - U.S.A.
CORREA, C.M.	B. Arch.	Michigan	249 Dadabhai Naordji Road, Bombay 1
	M. Arch.	M.I.T.	
GRATIER, G.	Student-Economist		Avenue Maurice, 46, 1050 Brussels

IRAN

VADI'I, K.	Professor	Center for Coordination of	TEHERAN
	General Secretary	Environmental Studies	
		University of Teheran	

IRELAND

| MULLIN,M. | Assistant to the Chairman | Kilkenny Design Workshops | Kilkenny |

ITALY

CANNETTA, A.	Architect		Via C.B. Vico 4, Milano
CASTAGNOLI	Professor	Laboratorio Cosmo Geofisico	Torino Vaglia Risparmi
GUIDUCCI	Professor of Sociology	University of Milan	Milano
MALDONADO, T.	Professor	Environmental Design	Bologna
		University of Bologna	

JAPAN

FUKUSHIMA, Y.	Professor		Takaraike, Sakyo-ku, Kyoto 606
	Secretary General	HESC Organizing Committee	
		Kyoto International Conf. Hall	
MATSUZAKI, T.	Senior Researcher	Tokyo Scientific Center	Nagata-Cho I Chome II-32
		IBM Japan, Ltd.	Chiyoda-Ku, Tokyo 100
SHIINA, T.	President	IBM Japan C° Ltd.	2-12, Roppongi 3 - Chome
		Scientific Center	Minato-Ku, Tokyo 106

THE NETHERLANDS

BERENDS, J.H.D.	Urban Planner	Rijksplanologische Dienst	Willem Witsenplein, 6, Den Haag
BLOK	Deputy Secretary General	International Federation for Housing and Planning	Wassenaarseweg, 43, The Hague
BUISSINK, J.D.		Planologisch Studiecentrum TNO	P.O. Box 45, Delft
de RUITER, J.J.	Drs. - M.A.	Ministry of Public Health & Environmental Protection	Dokter Reijersstraat, 12 Leidschendam
EISMA, D.	Member of the Executive Committee	Landelijke Vereniging tot Behoud van de Waddenzee	"Het Waddenhuis" Harlingen Postbus 90 - Voorstraat, 18
FALUDI, A.	Hoogleraar	Technische Hogeschool Delft	Berlageweg, Delft
LOGTENBERG, M.A.	Gemeente Leiden	Afdeling der Bouwkunde	Stadhuisplein, 1, Leiden
OOSTERMAN, B.D.	Alderman	Gemeente Leiden	Stadhuisplein, 1, Leiden
ROBERT, J.		ERIPLAN	Molenstraat, 15, The Hague
SCHENK, D.C.P.	Ir./Urban Planner	Rijks Planologische Dienst	Willem Witsenplein, 6, Den Haag
TESSELAAR, D.J.	Alderman	Gemeente Leiden	Stadhuisplein, 1, Leiden
TOPPINGA, M.L.	Ir. - Director	Study & Information Centre TNO for Traffic & Transport Research	P.O. Box 535, Delft
van den DOES, V.I.	General Secretary	International Federation of Pedestrians	Buitenhof, 5, 's-Gravenhage

NORWAY

SKAGE, O.R.	Assistant Director	Norwegian Institute for Urban and Regional Research	

PORTUGAL

FERREIRA, C.M.A.	Engenheiro Agronomo	Gabinete do Plano da Regiao de Porto	Porto
FERREIRA DOS SANTOS A.A.	Arquitecto	Gabinete do Plano da Regiao de Porto	Porto
PACHECO, A. de F. MONTEIRO	Arquitecto	Gabinete do Plano da Regiao de Porto	Porto

SPAIN

CARRASCO-MUÑOZ DE VERA	Secrétaire Général	Associacion Espanola para la Ordenacion del Medio Ambiente (A.E.O.R.M.A.)	Apartado de Correos 6.170 Madrid
del GIORGIO, J.A.	Dir. Eng. in Communications	Standard Electrica	Av. de America-Km.7, 200, Madrid 27

SWITZERLAND

LEUSCHNER, R.M.	Dr. phil.II	Allergy Dept. - Allogic - Abteilung der Dermatolog Univ. Klinik Klentonsspital	CH-4004 BASEL
POLUNIN, N.	Professor, Chief Editor	"Environmental Conservation"	15 Chemin F.-Lehmann 1218 Grand-Saconnex, Geneva

TURKEY

EVYAPAN, A.	Instructor	Faculty of Architecture Middle East Technical University	ANKARA

U.S.A.

CHESTNUT, H.	Consultant	Systems Engineering General Electric C°	CRD-K-1 3C38 P.O. Box 8 Schenectady, N.Y. 12301
CHOW, V.T.	Professor President	University of Illinois International Water Resources Ass.	c/o Hydrosystems Laboratory Urbana Champaign, Ill. 61801
CHURCH III, A.M.	Associate Professor of Economics	University of New Mexico	Albuquerque, New Mexico 87131
COHEN, S.P.	Executive Director	Boston Air Pollution Control Commission	31 State Street Boston, Mass. 02109
CROOK, L.T.	Executive Director	Great Lakes Basin Commission	Box 999, Ann Arbor, Michigan 48106
DORNBUSCH, D.M.	President	David M.Dornbusch & Co.,Inc.	1736 Stockton Street San Francisco, California 94133
EYERLY, R.	Assistant Professor of Business Logistics Asst. to the Director	Land & Water Research The Pennsylvania State University Dept. College of Business Administration	University Park Penna. 16802
FUNK, Dr. H.F.	Consultant	Silvichem Corporation	73 Simcoe St. - Suite 205 Toronto, P.O.
GAMBLE, H.B.	Professor	Penn. State University	104 Land & Water Bldg. University Park, Pa. 16802
GIBSON, J.E.	Dean	School of Engineering & Applied Sciences University of Virginia	Charlottesville, VA.22901

HAYMES, Y.Y.Ph.D.	Associate Professor of Engineering	Case Western Reserve University	408 Wickenden Building University Circle Cleveland, Ohio 44106
HIDALGO, H.		Institute for Defense Analyses	Army and Navy Drive 400 Arlington, Va. 22202
HOGGAN, D.	Engineer	Case Western Reserve University	408 Wickenden Bldg. University Circle Cleveland, Ohio 44106
HOPPENFELD, M.	Director of Planning	Greater Hartford Process, Inc.	100 Constitution Place, Hartford, Conn.
KALBA, K.		Harvard University — Dpt. of City & Regional Planning Graduate School of Design	208 Gund Hall Cambridge, Mass. 02138
MANHEIM, U.	Economic Consultant		250 Park Avenue, New York, N.Y.
MARANS, R.W.	Director of Urban Environmental Research Programme	Institute of Social Research University of Michigan	Ann Arbor, Mich. 48106
MARTIN, R.		Stanford Research Institute	Menlo Park, Ca. 94025
MARTINEAU, T.	Research Architect	Battelle — Columbus Laboratories	505 King Ave. Columbus, Ohio 43201
MacADAM, W.K.	Sr. Engineering Consultant	Wheelabrator Frye Inc.	Liberty Lane, Hampton, N.H. 03842
MUSA, S.A.		The Institute for Defense Analyses	400 Army & Navy Drive Arlington, Va. 22202
O'BRIEN—MARCHAND, M.	Environmental Geologist	U.S. Geological Survey	345 Middlefield Road, Menlo Park, Ca. 94025
OWEN, W.	Senior Fellow	The Brookings Institute	1775 Massachusetts Avenue, N.W.
SAUERLANDER, O.H.		Penn. State University	104 Land & Water Building University Park, Pa. 16802
STANFORD, G.		Agro City Incorporated	Greenhills R.1.Box 861 Cedar Hills, Texas 75104
WOLFF, E.A.	Associate Chief Communications & Navigation Division	NASA Godard Space Fligth Center Code 950	Greenbelt, Md. 20771

INTERNATIONAL ORGANIZATIONS

UNITED NATIONS

GASTAUT, Th.	Chief	U.N. Information and Liaison Office	11 A, rue Van Eyck, 1050 Brussels, Belgium
HEREMANS, R.	Information Assistant	U.N. Information and Liaison Office	11 A, rue Van Eyck, 1050 Brussels, Belgium

W.H.O.

MAHLER	Director General		Avenue Appia, 1211 Geneva 27, Switzerland
NOVICK, R.E.	Sanitary Engineer		Avenue Appia, 1211 Geneva 27, Switzerland

U.N.E.S.C.O.

EVSTAFIEV, A.	Director	Division of Technological Research and Higher Education (TER)	7, place Fontenoy, 75007 Paris, France
FRADIER, G.	Coordinator	Division of Human Settlements	7, place Fontenoy, 75007 Paris, France

U.N.E.P.

HALLE, M.	Assistant Officer	U.N. Environment Programme Geneva Liaison Office	16, avenue Jean Trembley Petit—Saconnex, Geneva, Switzerland

EUROPEAN COMMUNITIES

McSWINEY, M.	Administrateur Principal	Service de l'Environnement et de la Protection des Consommateurs Commission des Communautés Européennes	200, rue de la Loi, 1040 Brussels, Belgium

N.A.T.O.

SAMPAS, J.G.	Project Officer	Committee on the Challenges of Modern Society	1110 Brussels, Belgium